Tafsīr al-Qurṭubī

Vol. 3

Juz' 3: Sūrat al-Baqarah 254 – 286 & Sūrah Āli 'Imrān 1 – 95

Tafsīr al-Qurṭubī

The General Judgments of the Qur'an and Clarification of what it contains of the Sunnah and *Āyah*s of Discrimination

Abū 'Abdullāh Muḥammad ibn Aḥmad ibn Abī Bakr ibn Farḥ al-Anṣārī al-Khazrajī al-Andalusī al-Qurṭubī

Vol. 3

Juz' 3: Sūrat al-Baqarah 254 – 286 & Sūrah Āli 'Imrān 1 – 95

translated by
Aisha Bewley

Diwan Press
Classical and Contemporary Books on Islam and Sufism

Published by: Diwan Press Ltd.

Website: www.diwanpress.com
E-mail: info@diwanpress.com

By: Abu 'Abdullah Muhammad ibn Ahmad al-Qurtubi
Translated by: Aisha Abdarrahman Bewley
Edited by: Abdalhaqq Bewley

A catalogue record of this book is available from the British Library.

ISBN13: 978-1-908892-79-9 (Paperback)
978-1-908892-80-5 (Casebound)
978-1-908892-82-9 (Hardback)
978-1-908892-81-2 (ePub & Kindle)

Contents

Table of Transliterations

ء	'
ا	a
ب	b
ت	t
ث	th
ج	j
ح	ḥ
خ	kh
د	d
ذ	dh
ر	r
ز	z
س	s
ش	sh
ص	ṣ
ض	ḍ
ط	ṭ
ظ	ẓ
ع	'
غ	gh
ف	f
ق	q
ك	k
ل	l
م	m
ن	n
ه	h
و	w
ي	y

Long vowel

ا	ā
و	ū
ي	ī
أَوْ	aw
أَيْ	ay

Short vowel

ـَ	a [*fatḥah*]
ـُ	u [*ḍammah*]
ـِ	i [*kasrah*]

Translator's note

The Arabic for the *āyat*s is from the Algerian State edition of the *riwāyah* of Imam Warsh from the *qirā'ah* of Imam Nāfi' of Madina, whose recitation is one of the ten *mutawātir* recitations that are mass-transmitted from the time of the Prophet ﷺ.

There are minor omissions in the text. Some poems have been omitted which the author quotes to illustrate a point of grammatical usage or as an example of orthography or the usage of a word, often a derivative of the root of the word used in the *āyah*, but not the actual word used. Often it is difficult to convey the sense in English. Occasionally the author explores a grammatical matter or a tangential issue, and some of these may have been shortened. English grammatical terms used to translate Arabic grammatical terms do not have exactly the same meaning, sometimes rendering a precise translation of them problematic and often obscure.

The end of a *juz'* may vary by an *āyah* or two in order to preserve relevant passages.

2. Sūrat al-Baqarah – The Cow 254 – 286

يَٰٓأَيُّهَا ٱلَّذِينَ ءَامَنُوٓا۟ أَنفِقُوا۟ مِمَّا رَزَقْنَٰكُم مِّن قَبْلِ أَن يَأْتِىَ يَوْمٌ لَّا بَيْعٌ
فِيهِ وَلَا خُلَّةٌ وَلَا شَفَٰعَةٌ وَٱلْكَٰفِرُونَ هُمُ ٱلظَّٰلِمُونَ ٢٥٤

254 You who believe! give away some of what We have provided for you before a Day arrives on which there is no trading, no close friendship and no intercession. It is the unbelievers who are the wrongdoers.

Al-Ḥasan said that this *āyah* refers to obligatory *zakāt.* Ibn Jurayj and Sa'īd ibn Jubayr said that it includes both obligatory *zakāt* and *ṣadaqah.* Ibn 'Aṭiyyah says that this is sound, but the previous *āyah*s, which mention fighting and tell us that Allah drives back the unbelievers by means of the believers, makes it probable that this is a recommendation rather than an explicit command. It is in the Way of Allah. That is reinforced by the words at the end: *'It is the unbelievers who are the wrongdoers,'* meaning: 'Fight with your lives and also by spending your wealth.'

According to this interpretation, spending wealth is sometimes mandatory and sometimes recommended according to whether *jihād* is obligatory individually or not. Allah commands His slaves to spend from what He has provided them with and blessed them by, and warns them against withholding from spending until a day comes on which it is not possible to buy or sell or obtain maintenance. It is as He says: *'He says, "My Lord, if only You would give me a little more time so that I can give* ṣadaqah.*"'* (63:10)

'Khullah' (close friendship) means sincere mutual love. It is derived from the word *takhallala*, which refers to the interpenetration of secrets between friends. *Khilālah*, *khulālah* and *khalālah* are all words for true friendship and love. A poet says:

How do you connect with someone
whose true friendship (*khalālah*) is like the welcoming shade?

Khullah can also mean sweet herbage. It is said that '*khullah*' is the bread of camels and salty herbage is their fruit. *Khallah* means need and poverty. It is also a male camel in its second year, as al-Aṣmā'ī said. An expression says, 'They brought them a round cake of bread as though it were the foot of a *khallah*.' One says of a dead person, 'May Allah put right the gap (*khallah*) he has left.' *Khallah* is also sour wine. *Khillah* is the scabbard of a sword. More will be said about the derivation of Khalīl (friend) in *Sūrat an-Nisā'*. Allah tells us that there will no friendship or intercession in the Next World except by the permission of Allah. Its reality is mercy from Him to honour the one who is permitted to intercede.

Ibn Kathīr and Abū 'Amr recited *'bay'a fīhi walā khullata walā shafā'ata'* in the accusative without *tanwīn*. The same is found in 14:31 and 42:23. The rest recite all of that in the nominative and with *tanwīn*. Having a *fatḥah* in the general negative embraces all the aspects of this category. It is as if it is an answer to the person who asks, 'Is there any trading on that day?' asking a general question which has a general negative response. '*Lā*' with a negative noun is in the position of one noun in the nominative case by the inceptive whose predicate is 'on it'. If you wish, you can make it an adjective of 'Day'. Those who make it nominative put '*lā*' in the position of '*laysa*' and give an answer which is not undefined. It is as if it is the answer to someone who asks, 'Is there trading on it?' omitting 'any'. So the answer is not changed from the nominative case. Makkī said, 'The nominative is preferred because most reciters have it, and it is permitted outside of the Qur'an. [SOME OMISSION]

It is the unbelievers who are the wrongdoers.

'Unbelievers' is the inceptive and 'who' is a second inceptive and 'wrongdoers' is the predicate of the second. If you wish, 'who' can be redundant for the distinction and 'wrongdoers' is the predicate of 'unbelievers'. 'Aṭā' ibn Dīnār said, 'Praise be to Allah who said this, and did not say that the wrongdoers are the unbelievers!'

ٱللَّهُ لَآ إِلَٰهَ إِلَّا هُوَ ٱلْحَىُّ ٱلْقَيُّومُ لَا تَأْخُذُهُۥ سِنَةٌ وَلَا نَوْمٌ لَّهُۥ مَا فِى
ٱلسَّمَٰوَٰتِ وَمَا فِى ٱلْأَرْضِ مَن ذَا ٱلَّذِى يَشْفَعُ عِندَهُۥٓ إِلَّا بِإِذْنِهِۦ يَعْلَمُ مَا بَيْنَ
أَيْدِيهِمْ وَمَا خَلْفَهُمْ وَلَا يُحِيطُونَ بِشَىْءٍ مِّنْ عِلْمِهِۦٓ إِلَّا بِمَا شَآءَ وَسِعَ كُرْسِيُّهُ
ٱلسَّمَٰوَٰتِ وَٱلْأَرْضَ وَلَا يَـُٔودُهُۥ حِفْظُهُمَا وَهُوَ ٱلْعَلِىُّ ٱلْعَظِيمُ ﴿٢٥٥﴾

255 Allah, there is no god but Him, the Living, the Self-Sustaining. He is not subject to drowsiness or sleep. Everything in the heavens and the earth belongs to Him. Who can intercede with Him except by His permission? He knows what is before

them and what is behind them but they cannot grasp any of His knowledge save what He wills. His Footstool encompasses the heavens and the earth and their preservation does not tire Him. He is the Most High, the Magnificent.

Allah, there is no god but Him,

This is the Throne Verse, the Master of the *āyah*s of the Qur'an and the greatest *āyah*. It was revealed at night and the Prophet ﷺ summoned Zayd and he wrote it down. It is related that Muḥammad ibn al-Ḥanafiyyah said, 'When the *Āyat al-Kursī* was revealed, every idol in this world prostrated, every king in this world prostrated and the crowns fell from their heads. The *shayṭān*s fled, hitting one another, and went to Iblīs and told him what was happening among them. He commanded them to investigate what had occurred and they went to Madīnah and heard that the Throne Verse had been revealed.'

The Imams report from Ubayy ibn Ka'b: 'The Messenger of Allah ﷺ said, "Abu-l-Mundhir! Do you know which verse of the Book of Allah is the greatest?" I said, "Allah and His Messenger know best." He repeated, "Abu-l-Mundhir! Do you know which verse of the Book of Allah is the greatest?" I said, *"Allah, there is no god but Him, the Living, the Self-Sustaining."* He struck my chest and said, "May you enjoy this knowledge, Abu-l-Mundhir!"' Abū 'Abdullāh at-Tirmidhī al-Ḥakīm added, 'By the One Who has my soul in His hand, this *āyah* has a tongue and two lips with which it proclaims the sanctity of the King at the foot of the Throne.' Abū 'Abdullāh said, 'Allah revealed this *āyah* and made the reward for its reciter both immediate and later. The immediate reward is that it protects the one who recites it from disasters.' It is related that Nawf al-Bikālī said, 'In the Torah the Throne Verse is called the friend of Allah.' He means that the one who recites it is called 'dearest' (*'azīz*) in the domains of the heaven and earth.' When 'Abd ar-Raḥmān ibn 'Awf entered his house, he would recite the *Āyat al-Kursī* in the four comers of his house, intending by that to guard the four sides and to expel Shayṭān from the House.

It is related that 'Umar wrestled a jinn and threw him to the ground. The jinn said to him, 'Let me go and I will teach that which will protect you from me.' He let him go and he said, 'You will be protected from me by the Throne Verse.' This is sound. We read in a tradition, 'If someone recites the *Āyat al-Kursī* after every prayer, the Master of Majesty and Nobility will take his spirit directly and he will be like one who fights alongside the Prophets of Allah until he is martyred.' 'Alī said, 'I heard your Prophet ﷺ say on the minbar, "If someone recites the *Āyat al-Kursī* after every prayer, only death keeps him from entering the Garden, and only someone who is true or a worshipper will persist in it. If someone recites it when he goes to bed, Allah will protect him, his neighbour, his neighbour's neighbour and the houses around him."'

We find in al-Bukhārī in the story of Abū Hurayrah regarding Shayṭān, when the Prophet ﷺ put him in charge of guarding the *zakāt* of Ramadan, that he said, 'Messenger of Allah, he claimed that he would teach me some words by which Allah would benefit me. So I let him go.' 'What were they?' he asked. He said, 'He told me, "When you go to bed, recite the Throne Verse from beginning to end." He told me, "A guardian will continue to watch over you and Shayṭān will not come near you until morning."' They were the most eager of people for good. The Prophet ﷺ said, 'He has told you the truth although he is a liar. Do you know to whom you were speaking the past three nights, Abū Hurayrah?' 'No,' he answered. He said, 'That was Shayṭān.'

We find in the *Musnad* of Abū Muḥammad ad-Dārimī that ash-Sha'bī said that 'Abdullāh ibn Mas'ūd said, 'One of the Companions of Muḥammad ﷺ met a man of the jinn and they wrestled and the human being threw him down. The human told him, 'I see that you are scrawny and thin, with forearms like those of a dog. Are all the jinn like this or just you?' He answered, 'No, by Allah! I am considered one of the strong ones among them! Let us wrestle again. If you throw me down, I will teach you something which will be of benefit to you!' 'Yes,' he replied. So he wrestled and he threw him down. The jinn said, 'Recite the Throne Verse.' 'Yes,' he agreed. He said, 'No one recites it in a house but that *shayṭān* leaves it, breaking wind like a donkey and then will not enter it again until morning.' Abū Nu'aym transmitted it from Abū 'Āṣim ath-Thaqafī from ash-Sha'bī. Abū 'Ubaydah mentioned it in the *gharīb* hadiths of 'Umar from Abū Mu'āwiyah from Abū 'Āṣim ath-Thaqafī from ash-Sha'bī from 'Abdullāh. 'Abdullāh was asked, 'Was it 'Umar?' He said, 'Who else could it have been but 'Umar?'

It is reported in at-Tirmidhī from Abū Hurayrah that the Messenger of Allah ﷺ said, 'Whoever recites the beginning of *Sūrah al-Mu'min* (40:1-3) and the Throne Verse in the morning will be protected until evening. Whoever recites them in the evening will be protected until morning.' He said that it is a *gharīb* hadith. Abū 'Abdullāh at-Tirmidhī al-Ḥakīm said that it is related that the believers are recommended to seek protection by reciting it after every prayer.

Anas has a *marfū'* hadith going back to the Prophet ﷺ in which he said, 'Allah revealed to Mūsā: "If someone continues to recite *Āyat al-Kursī* after every prayer he will be given what the thankful are given: the reward of the Prophets and the actions of the true. I will stretch out my hand to him with mercy, and all that keeps him from entering the Garden is the arrival of the Angel of Death." Mūsā said, "Lord, is there anyone who hears this who will not persevere in it?" He replied, "Among My slaves I will only give it to a Prophet, a true person, a man I love, or a man I want to be martyred in My Path."' It is reported from Ubayy ibn Ka'b that Allah Almighty said to Musa, 'Musa, anyone who recites the *Āyat al-Kursī* after every prayer will be given the reward of the Prophets.' Abū 'Abdullāh said, 'I think that it means that he will be given the reward of the action of the Prophets. None but the Prophets have the reward of Prophethood.' This *āyah* contains the truth of *tawḥīd* and the lofty attributes. It is fifty words long, and each word contains fifty blessings. It is equal to a third of the Qur'an, as a hadith reports. Ibn 'Aṭiyyah mentioned that. Within a long hadith, Abū Dharr said, 'I asked the Messenger of Allah ﷺ which is the greatest *āyah* revealed by Allah in the Qur'an. He answered, *'Allah, there is no god but Him, the Living, the Self-Sustaining.'* Ibn 'Abbās said, 'The noblest *āyah* in the Quran is the Throne Verse.' One scholar said, 'That is because the name of Allah is repeated it, either directly or indirectly, eighteen times.'

the Living, the Self-Sustaining.

These are combined attributes of Allah. *'Al-Ḥayy'* (The Living) is one of His Beautiful Names. It is said that it is the Greatest Name of Allah. It is said that when 'Īsā wanted to bring the dead to life, he made this supplication, 'O Living, O Self-Sustaining.' It is said that it was used by Āsaf ibn Barkhiyā when he wanted to bring the throne of Bilqīs to Sulaymān. He made the supplication: 'O Living, O Self-Sustaining.' It is said that the tribe of Israel asked Mūsā about the Greatest Name of Allah and he said to them, 'Ayā Hayā Sharā Hayā' which means: 'O Living, O Self-Sustaining.' It is said that it is the supplication people at sea should make when they fear drowning. Aṭ-Ṭabarī said that some people said that it is like a description of Himself and that should not be examined. It is said that He called Himself 'Living' since He disposes of matters exactly and determines things precisely. Qatādah says that it is the Living who does not die. As-Suddī says that it means the One who goes on forever. Labīd said:

If you see me sound today,
  I am not among the living from Kilāb and Ja'far.

'Al-Qayyūm' (The Self-Sustaining), means the One who undertakes to uphold everything He has created, as Qatādah said. Al-Ḥasan said that it means the One who attends to every self in respect of what it earns until He has repaid it for its

actions, as He knows them, and nothing is hidden from Him. Ibn 'Abbās said, 'It means: the One who does not change or vanish.' Umayyah ibn Abi-ṣ-Ṣalt said:

The heavens and the stars as well
as the sun and the moon only abide
As determined by the Self-Sustaining Guardian.
The gathering, the Garden and bliss
are only for a matter which is immense.

Al-Bayhaqī said that he saw in *'Uyūn at-tafsīr* that Ismā'il aḍ-Ḍarīr said, '*Qayyūm* means the One who does not sleep,' which is taken from the verse after it. Al-Kalbī said, '*Al-Qayyūm* is the One with no beginning.' Al-Anbārī mentioned that. A poet says:

The Master of the Throne is the One Who provides for people.
He is Living and the One Who sustains them.

He is not subject to drowsiness or sleep.

Then Allah denies that He is subject to drowsiness or sleep. Drowsiness, according to all, is what affects the eyes and sleep is what affects the heart. Al-Mufaḍḍal made a distinction between them: *sinah* is what is in the head, *nu'ās* is in the eye, and sleep (*nawm*) is in the heart. Ibn Zayd said that *wasnān* is when someone rises from sleep so confused that he might even unleash his sword against his family. Ibn 'Aṭiyyah said, 'What Ibn Zayd said is debatable. It is not understood from Arabic.' As-Suddī said, '*Sinah* is the wind of sleep which touches the face and makes a person drowsy.' Generally speaking, it is fatigue which affects a person. What is meant by the *āyah* is that Allah Almighty is not affected by lapses or weariness in any way. The root of *sinah* (drowsiness) is *wasnah*. Sleep is that which is heavy and removes a person's consciousness.

People mention what Abū Hurayrah reported about a story which the Messenger of Allah ﷺ recounted on the minbar: 'Once Mūsā wondered about whether Allah slept and so Allah sent an angel to him to keep him awake for three nights and then gave him two bottles, one in each hand, and commanded him to look after them. He began to fall asleep and his hands almost released them. Then he moved them apart. When he fell asleep, his hands banged together and the bottles broke. He said that Allah made an example by that illustrating the fact that if He were to sleep, the heavens and the earth would not be maintained.' This hadith is not sound. Others, including al-Bayhaqi, said that it is weak.

Everything in the heavens and the earth belongs to Him.

He owns them, so He is the Owner and Lord of all. *'Mā'* is used even though sentient beings are included in the whole. Aṭ-Ṭabarī said, 'This *āyah* was revealed when the unbelievers said, "We only worship idols so that they might bring us close to Allah."'

Who can intercede with Him except by His permission?

It is affirmed in this *āyah* that Allah gives permission to whomever He wishes to be an intercessor. They are the Prophets, the people of knowledge, those who strive, angels and others whom Allah has honoured and ennobled. Then they only intercede for those with whom Allah is pleased as we know from His words: *'They do not intercede except on behalf of those with whom He is pleased.'* (21:28)

Ibn 'Atiyyah said, 'It appears that the scholars and righteous intercede for those who have not reached the Fire and are between the two stages, or have arrived there, but have righteous deeds to their credit.' In *Ṣaḥīḥ al-Bukhārī* in 'One of the remaining chapters on the Vision' we find: 'The believers will say, "Our Lord, our brothers used to pray with us and fast with us."' This is intercession for those who are borderline cases. As for the intercession of miscarried children at the gate of the Garden, it is for their parents. This intercession is for relatives and acquaintances. The Prophets intercede for the rebels of their community who are in the Fire for their wrong actions. It is not on account of kinship or acquaintance, but on account of faith alone. There then remains the intercession of the Most Merciful of the Merciful for those who were immersed in errors and wrong actions for which the intercession of the Prophets does not prevail. As for the intercession of Muhammad ﷺ to hasten the reckoning, that is his alone.

In his *Ṣaḥīḥ*, Muslim adequately explains how intercession takes place. The intercessors will enter the Fire and bring people out who deserve to be punished. So it is not unlikely that the believers have two intercessions: intercession for those who have not reached the Fire and the intercession for those who have reached it and entered it. May Allah protect us from it! We find mentioned in the hadith of Abū Sa'īd al-Khudrī: 'Then the bridge will be set up over Hell and intercession will be allowed. They will say, "O Allah, safety! Safety!"' It was asked, 'Messenger of Allah, what is the bridge?' He answered, 'A very slippery place on which are snares, hooks, and hard thorns which are like that found in Najd known as *sa'dān*. Some of the believers will cross over it like the blink of an eye, some like lightning, some like the wind, some like a bird, and some like the faster steed and camel. Some will escape unhurt, some will be scratched but released, and some will be pushed into the Fire until the believers are delivered from the Fire. By the One

Who has my soul in His hand, on the Day of Rising there is none of you who will make more earnest entreaties of Allah for his rights than those the believers will make for their brothers in the Fire. They will say, "Our Lord, they used to fast with us, pray with us and go on ḥajj!" They will be told, "Go and bring out those you know." Their forms are forbidden to the Fire and they will bring out many people who were taken by the Fire up to middle of their thigh or up to their knees. Then they will say, "None of those about whom You commanded us remains in it." Then the Almighty will say, "Return and bring out whoever you find who has the weight of a dinar of good in his heart." They will bring out many people and then will say, "Our Lord, we have not left in any of those about whom You commanded us." Then He will say, "Return and bring out whoever you find who has the weight of half a dinar of good in his heart." They will bring out many people and then will say, "Our Lord, we have not left in any of those about whom You commanded us." Then He will say, "Return and bring out whoever you find who has an atom's weight of good in his heart." They will bring out many people and then say, "Our Lord, we have not left any good in it."' Abū Sa'īd said, 'If you do not believe me in respect of this hadith, then, if you wish, recite: *"Allah does not wrong anyone by so much as the smallest speck. And if there is a good deed Allah will multiply it and pay out an immense reward direct from Him."* (4:40) Then Allah Almighty will say, "The angels have interceded, the Prophets have interceded and the believers have interceded. None remains but the Most Merciful of the merciful." He will take a handful from the Fire, bringing out people who never did any good at all and have been turned into charcoal...'

It is mentioned from Anas that the Prophet ﷺ said, 'I will say, "O Allah, give me permission for those who said, 'There is no god but Allah.'" He said, "That is not for you. By My might, pride, immensity and omnipotence, I will bring out those who said, 'There is no god but Allah.'"' Abū Hurayrah mentioned that he ﷺ said, 'When Allah has finished judging between His slaves and wants to bring out those among the people of the Fire He wishes to, He will command the angels to bring out of the Fire anyone among those to whom Allah desires to show mercy who did not associate anything with Allah, those who said, "There is no god but Allah." They will recognise them in the Fire by the mark of prostration. The Fire will consume all of the son of Ādam except for the mark of prostration. Allah has forbidden the Fire to consume the mark of prostration.'

These hadiths indicate that the intercession of the believers and others is for those who have entered the Fire. May Allah protect us from it! Ibn 'Aṭiyyah said that it applies both to those who have reached it and those who have not reached it. It is possible that that is taken from other hadiths. Allah knows best. Ibn Mājah transmitted in the *Sunan* from Anas ibn Mālik that the Messenger of Allah ﷺ said, 'People will be lined up in rows on the Day or Rising (Ibn Numayr said 'the people of the Garden') and a man from the people of the Fire will pass by a man and say, "Do you not remember me? Do you not remember the day you asked me for water and I gave you a drink?" The man will intercede for him. A man will pass another man and say, "Do you not remember the day I brought you water for purification?" and he will intercede for him.' Ibn Numayr said: 'He will say, "Do you not remember the day when you sent me to get something you needed and I did it?" and he will intercede for him.'

As for the intercession of our Prophet Muhammad ﷺ, there is disagreement about it. It is said that it will occur three times, or two or five times. It will be dealt with elsewhere. We have also dealt with this in *Kitāb at-Tadhkirah*.

He knows what is before them and what is behind them

'Them' in this phrase refers to everyone who has sentience. They are all included in '*everything in the heavens and the earth*.' Mujāhid said that '*what is before them*' is this world and '*what is behind them*' is the Next World. Ibn 'Aṭiyyah said, 'All this is valid and there is nothing wrong with it because "what is before" means everything to which a person advances and "what is behind" is all that came before.' Something similar to this was stated by as-Suddī and others.

but they cannot grasp any of His knowledge save what He wills.

Knowledge here means what is known, meaning that people do not encompass any of what He knows. This is like the statement of al-Khiḍr to Mūsā when the sparrow dipped its beak in the sea, 'My knowledge and your knowledge does not diminish the knowledge of Allah except as this sparrow would diminish this sea.' This and examples like it refer to known things because the knowledge of Allah is an attribute of His Essence which cannot be separated from it. The meaning is that no one knows other than what Allah wishes him to know.

His Footstool encompasses the heavens and the earth

In his *History*, Ibn 'Asākir mentioned from 'Alī that the Messenger of Allah ﷺ said, 'The Footstool is made of pearl and the Pen is made of pearl and the length of the Pen is seven thousand years and the height of the Footstool is only known by Allah.' Ḥammād ibn Salamah related from 'Āṣim ibn Bahdalah, who is 'Āṣim ibn Abi-n-Nujūd, from Zirr ibn Ḥubaysh that Ibn Mas'ūd is reported as saying,

'There is a distance of five hundred years between every heaven and five hundred years between the seventh heaven and the Footstool, and between the Footstool and the Throne is a distance of five hundred years. The Throne is above the water and Allah is above the Throne. He knows what you are in and what you are on.'

Ibn 'Abbās said that His Footstool is His knowledge, and aṭ-Ṭabarī preferred that. Indicating that is the derived word *kurrāsah* (notebook) which contains knowledge. Scholars are also called '*karāsīy*' (thrones) because they are relied on. That is similar to the saying, 'the supporting pegs of the earth.' A poet said:

Noble people and a troop surround them,
those who know (*karāsīy*) events when they occur.

It is also said that the Footstool is Allah's Power by which He sustains the heavens and the earth, as the word *kursī* can be used for the underpinning of a thing. *Kursī* is the base of a wall which holds it up. This is close to what Ibn 'Abbās said about '*His Footstool encompasses*'. Al-Bayhaqī said, 'We related from Ibn Mas'ūd and Sa'īd ibn Jubayr that Ibn 'Abbās said that "*His Footstool encompasses*" means His knowledge.

Other transmissions from Ibn 'Abbās and others indicate that what is meant by the Footstool is something connected to the Throne. Isrā'īl related from as-Suddī reported that Abū Mālik said, 'It is the rock on which the seventh earth stands and is the whole extent of creation in all its vastness. Four angels are over it. Each of them has four faces: a human face, a lion's face, an ox's face and an eagle's face. They attend to it and encompass the earths and heavens. Their heads are under the Footstool, and the Footstool is under the Throne. Allah has placed His Footstool above the Throne.' Al-Bayhaqī said, 'This statement indicates that there are two Footstools. One is under the Throne and one is above the Throne.' It is related in what Asbāṭ related from as-Suddī from Abū Mālik, and from Abū Ṣāliḥ from Ibn 'Abbās, from Murrah al-Hamdānī from Ibn 'Abbās, and from Murrah al-Hamdānī from Ibn Mas'ūd from some of the Companions of the Messenger of Allah ﷺ about this that the heavens and earth are inside the Footstool and the Footstool is in front of the Throne.

The people of atheism apply it to the immensity of the kingdom and majesty of the sultan. They deny the existence of the Throne and Footstool and say that they are nothing. The people of the truth consider their existence conceivable since the power of Allah is vast and one must believe in it. Abū Mūsā al-Ash'arī said, 'The Footstool is the place where the feet are put. It creaks as a saddle creaks.' Al-Bayhaqī said, 'We also related this from Ibn 'Abbās and we mentioned that it means, as he thinks, that it is part of the Throne, where the feet of someone on a throne would be placed. There is, however, no affirmation of "place" in it.' Ibn Buraydah related that his father said, 'When Ja'far came from Abyssinia, the Messenger of Allah ﷺ asked him, "What was the most extraordinary thing you saw?" He answered, "A woman with a basket of food on her head. A horse passed and knocked it off. She sat down, collecting her food and then she turned to it and said, 'Woe to you for a Day when the King will sit on His Throne and hear a tale from the wrongdoer and give to the wronged!'" The Messenger of Allah ﷺ affirmed her words and said, "A nation is not pure (or 'how can a nation be pure?') when its weak do not take their due from the strong?"'

Ibn 'Aṭiyyah said, 'The statement, "The Footstool is the place of the feet" mean that it is part of the Throne of the All-Merciful, like the place for the feet on the thrones of kings. It is an immense created thing in front of the Throne. It is ascribed to it as the footstool is ascribed to a king's throne.' Al-Ḥasan ibn Abi-l-Ḥasan said that the Footstool is the Throne itself, but this is not acceptable. The hadiths clearly state that the Footstool is a creation which is in front of the Throne and the Throne is greater than it.

Abū Idrīs al-Khawlānī related that Abū Dharr said, 'I asked, "Messenger of Allah, what is the greatest *āyah* revealed to you?" He replied, "The *Āyat al-Kursī*." Then he said, "Abū Dharr, the heavens and the Footstool are only like a ring cast in the desert, and the size of the Throne compared to that of the Footstool is like the size of the desert compared to the ring."' Al-Ajurrī, Abū Ḥātim al-Bustī in his sound *Musnad* and al-Bayhaqī transmitted it and said that it is sound. Mujāhid said, 'The heavens and the earth in comparison to the Throne are like a ring cast into the desert.'

their preservation does not tire Him

This *āyah* informs us about the immensity of what Allah has created. It is deduced from that that Allah is greater still since the preservation of this immense matter does not tire Him at all.

The word 'tire' means to find something burdensome and hard. This is how Ibn 'Abbās, al-Ḥasan, Qatādah and others explained it. Az-Zajjāj says that the 'him' can refer to Allah or it can refer to the Throne. If it is the Footstool, that is part of the business of Allah.

He is the Most High, the Magnificent.

'Al-'Alī' (The Most High) refers to height of power and position, not place,

because Allah is free of being confined by space. Aṭ-Ṭabarī related that some people said that He is High above His creation as His place is above the places of creatures. Ibn 'Aṭiyyah said, 'This is the view of ignorant anthropomorphists! The aspect is not related.' 'Abd ar-Raḥmān ibn Qurṭ related that in the Night Journey the Messenger of Allah ﷺ heard glorification in the high heavens: 'Glory be to Allah, the High, the Most High! Glory be to Him and exalted is He!' *'Alī* and *'ālī* is the one who conquers and overcomes things. The Arabs use the verb *'alā* for overcoming and overpowering. A poet said:

When we overpowered (*'alawnā*) and firmly were over them,
We left them flat for the vultures and wild beasts.

'Al-'Aẓīm' (The Magnificent) describes His immense power, importance and nobility, not His physical size. Aṭ-Ṭabarī related that some people said *'aẓīm* means esteemed (*mu'aẓẓam*) as is said that *'atīq* (ancient) means *mu'attiq*. Other people rejected that and said, 'Had it meant "esteemed", that would imply that He is not magnificent before He created creation and after it is annihilated since there would be none to esteem Him then.

لَآ إِكْرَاهَ فِى ٱلدِّينِ قَد تَّبَيَّنَ ٱلرُّشْدُ مِنَ ٱلْغَىِّ فَمَن يَكْفُرْ بِٱلطَّٰغُوتِ وَيُؤْمِنۢ
بِٱللَّهِ فَقَدِ ٱسْتَمْسَكَ بِٱلْعُرْوَةِ ٱلْوُثْقَىٰ لَا ٱنفِصَامَ لَهَا وَٱللَّهُ سَمِيعٌ
عَلِيمٌ ٢٥٦

256 There is no compulsion where the *dīn* is concerned. Right guidance has become clearly distinct from error. Anyone who rejects false gods and believes in Allah has grasped the Firmest Handhold, which will never give way. Allah is All-Hearing, All-Knowing.

There is no compulsion where the *dīn* is concerned.

The word '*dīn*' in this *āyah* means what is believed and religion since it is followed by '*Right guidance has become clearly distinct from error*'. Compulsion can take place in judgments regarding oaths, sales, gifts and other things. This will be explained in *Sūrat al-Naḥl* (16:106), since this is not the place for it. Abū 'Abd ar-Raḥmān recited '*ar-rashad*'. That is also related from al-Ḥasan and ash-Sha'bī. The form *rashada, yarshudu, rushd* is used when something you love is attained but the form *rashida, yarshadu, rashad* is also possible. *Ghawā* is its opposite. An-Naḥḥās said that.

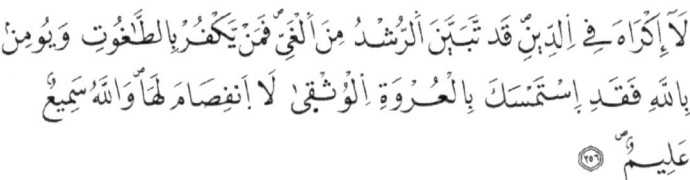

Ibn 'Aṭiyyah related that Abū 'Abd ar-Raḥmān as-Sulamī recited *rushād* rather than *rushd* and al-Ḥasan recited *rushud.* The root of '*ghayy*' (error) refers to when someone is misguided in what he believes or thinks. The word 'error' (*ghayy*) is not used to denote complete misguidance.

Scholars disagree and hold various positions regarding the legal status and meaning of this *āyah.*

– It is said that it is abrogated because the Prophet ﷺ forced the Arabs to adopt the *dīn* of Islam and fought them and was only pleased with Islam for them. Sulaymān ibn Mūsā took that view, saying, 'It is abrogated by *"O Prophet! Do jihād against the unbelievers and the hypocrites."* (9:73)' That is related from Ibn Mas'ūd and many commentators.

– It is not abrogated and was sent down about the people of the Book in particular and means that they are not forced to adopt Islam when they pay *jizyah.* Those who are forced are the idolaters. Only Islam is accepted from them, and they are the ones about whom the *āyah*: *'O Prophet! Do jihād against the unbelievers and the hypocrites'* (9:73) was revealed. This is the position of ash-Sha'bī, Qatādah, al-Ḥasan and aḍ-Ḍaḥḥāk. The evidence for this position is related by Zayd ibn Aslam from his father, 'I heard 'Umar ibn al-Khaṭṭāb say to an old Christian woman, "Become Muslim, old woman, you will be safe. Allah sent Muḥammad with the Truth." She replied, "I am an old woman and close to death." 'Umar said, "O Allah, bear witness!" and he recited, *"There is no compulsion where the* dīn *is concerned."*'

– Abū Dāwūd reported from Ibn 'Abbās that this was revealed about the Anṣār. There was a woman all of whose children had died. She made a vow that if she had a child who lived she would make it a Jew. When the Banu-n-Naḍīr were exiled, among them were many of the children of the Anṣār. They said, 'We will not abandon our children!' Then Allah revealed this. One variant has, 'We did what we did and we thought that their *dīn* is better than what we had.' When Allah brought Islam, they denied it and this was revealed. Whoever wished remained with them and whoever wished, entered Islam. This is the position of Sa'īd ibn Jubayr, ash-Sha'bī and Mujāhid, but he added that the reason that they were with the Banu-n-Naḍīr was through suckling. An-Naḥḥās said, 'The position of Ibn 'Abbās regarding this *āyah* is the best position since its *isnād* is sound.'

– As-Suddī said that the *āyah* was revealed about a man of the Anṣār called Abū Ḥuṣayn who had two sons. Some merchants came from Syria to Madīnah with oil and when they wanted to leave, his sons went to them. They invited the two sons to become Christians and they did so and went back with them to Syria.

Their father went to the Messenger of Allah ﷺ to complain about this and asked the Messenger of Allah to send someone to bring them back. Then the words: *'There is no compulsion where the dīn is concerned'* were revealed. He had not at that time been commanded to fight the People of the Book. He said, 'Allah has put them far away. They are the first to disbelieve.' Abu-l-Ḥuṣayn felt annoyed that the Prophet ﷺ did not send someone after them. Then Allah revealed: *'No, by your Lord, they are not believers until they make you their judge in the disputes that break out between them'* (4:65). Then *'No compulsion'* was abrogated and he was commanded to fight the People of the Book in *Sūrat at-Tawbah*. The sound view for the reason behind the words: *'No, by your Lord, they are not believers ...'* is the hadith of az-Zubayr with his Christian neighbour about water as will be dealt with in *Sūrat an-Nisā'*, Allah willing.

– It is said that it means 'do not call those who have submitted through the sword compelled and forced'.

– It is said that it was related about captives who were People of the Book. They are not compelled when they are adults. If they are Magians, young or old, or idolaters, they are compelled to adopt Islam because their captivity does not help them when they are idolaters. Do you not see that their slaughtered animals are not eaten nor their women married? That is what Ibn al-Qāsim reported from Mālik. Ashhab said that children are considered to have the *dīn* of those who have captured them. If they refuse that, they are compelled to become Muslim. Children have no *dīn* and that is why they are compelled to enter Islam so that they do not go to a false *dīn*. When other types of unbelievers pay the *jizyah*, they are not forced to become Muslim, whether they are Arabs or non-Arabs, Quraysh or otherwise. This will be dealt with in *Sūrat at-Tawbah*.

Anyone who rejects false gods and believes in Allah

The word for 'false gods' (*ṭāghūt*) comes from the root *ṭaghā* which means 'to exceed the bounds'. The word can indicate the plural or the singular. It is said that the root of *ṭāghūt* is *ṭughyān* which means 'overstepping the limits'. Al-Mubarrad said that it is a plural, but Ibn 'Aṭiyyah says that that is rejected. Al-Jawharī said that the word *ṭāghūt* refers to soothsayers, *shayṭān*s and every leader in misguidance. It can have a singular meaning as we see in 4:60 or a plural meaning as we see in 2:257. It does have an actual plural: *ṭawāghīth*.

has grasped the Firmest Handhold,

This phrase is a metaphor. Commentators disagree about metaphorical usage (*tashbīh*). Mujāhid says that 'the Firmest Handhold' is true belief and as-Suddī says that it means Islam. Ibn 'Abbās, Sa'īd ibn Jubayr and aḍ-Ḍaḥḥāk said, 'It is *'lā ilāha illa-llāh*.' All these understandings actually amount to the same thing.

which will never give way.

Mujāhid said, 'This should be understood alongside Allah's statement that *"He never changes a people's state unless they change what is in themselves."* (13:11)' In other words, He will not remove the designation of believer from them until they actually disbelieve. The word for 'give way' (*infiṣām*) means to break, but not completely. *Qaṣm* is completely breaking. Al-Jawharī said, '*Faṣm* is breaking, but not completely.' The verb is used of rain stopping and a fever ending. When rejection of falsehood and faith in Allah are part of what the tongue articulates and the heart believes, Allah hears what is said and knows what is believed.

اللَّهُ وَلِيُّ الَّذِينَ آمَنُوا يُخْرِجُهُم مِّنَ الظُّلُمَاتِ إِلَى النُّورِ
وَالَّذِينَ كَفَرُوا أَوْلِيَاؤُهُمُ الطَّاغُوتُ يُخْرِجُونَهُم مِّنَ النُّورِ إِلَى الظُّلُمَاتِ
أُولَٰئِكَ أَصْحَابُ النَّارِ هُمْ فِيهَا خَالِدُونَ ﴿٢٥٧﴾

257 Allah is the Protector of those who believe. He brings them out of the darkness into the light. But those who disbelieve have false gods as protectors. They take them from the light into the darkness. Those are the Companions of the Fire remaining in it timelessly, for ever.

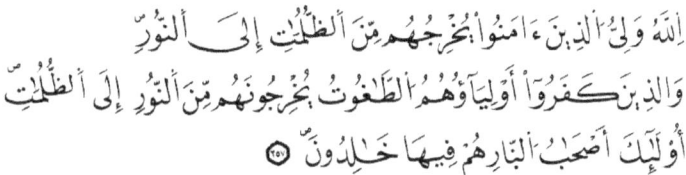

The word '*walī*' (Protector) signifies the One who helps His believing slaves as al-Khaṭṭābī said. Qatādah said that the darkness mentioned in the *āyah* refers to misguidance and light to guidance. Aḍ-Ḍaḥḥāk and ar-Rabī' said much the same thing. Mujāhid and 'Abdah ibn Abī Lubābah said that this was revealed about some people who believed in 'Isā ﷺ. When Muhammad ﷺ came, they rejected him. That was their being taken out of the light into the darkness. Ibn 'Aṭiyyah said, 'The one with this belief who had a stronger light in it left it for darkness. The wording of the *āyah* has no need of specification. It applies to every disbelieving community who had partial belief, like the Arabs had. That is because Allah is the Protector of those of them who believed and He brought them out of the darkness of disbelief into the light of belief. Those who disbelieved after the coming of the sent Prophet ﷺ were misguided by their *shayṭāns*. It is as if Shayṭān brought them out of faith when they were ready to enter it and so they will enter the Fire for their disbelief. That is justice and Allah is not asked about what He does.' Al-Ḥasan recited '*ṭawāghīt*' in the plural which means *shayṭāns*. Allah knows best.

أَلَمْ تَرَ إِلَى ٱلَّذِى حَآجَّ إِبْرَٰهِۦمَ فِى رَبِّهِۦٓ أَنْ ءَاتَىٰهُ ٱللَّهُ ٱلْمُلْكَ إِذْ قَالَ
إِبْرَٰهِۦمُ رَبِّىَ ٱلَّذِى يُحْىِۦ وَيُمِيتُ قَالَ أَنَا۠ أُحْىِۦ وَأُمِيتُ قَالَ
إِبْرَٰهِۦمُ فَإِنَّ ٱللَّهَ يَأْتِى بِٱلشَّمْسِ مِنَ ٱلْمَشْرِقِ فَأْتِ بِهَا مِنَ ٱلْمَغْرِبِ
فَبُهِتَ ٱلَّذِى كَفَرَ ۗ وَٱللَّهُ لَا يَهْدِى ٱلْقَوْمَ ٱلظَّٰلِمِينَ ﴿٢٥٨﴾

258 What about the one who argued with Ibrāhīm about his Lord, on the basis that Allah had given him sovereignty? Ibrāhīm said, 'My Lord is He who gives life and causes to die.' He said, 'I too give life and cause to die.' Ibrāhīm said, 'Allah makes the sun come from the East. Make it come from the West.' And the one who was an unbeliever was dumbfounded. Allah does not guide wrongdoing people.

The expression '*What about?*' (*a lam tara*) literally means 'Have you seen?' and is frequently used in Arabic to introduce something surprising or astonishing. The 'one' referred to in the *āyah* is generally taken to be Nimrod, Numrūdh ibn Kūsh ibn Kan'ān ibn Sām ibn Nuḥ, the king of his time and the one who built the fire into which Ibrāhīm was thrown and who was killed by a gnat. This is the position of Ibn 'Abbās, Mujāhid, Qatādah, ar-Rabī', as-Suddī, Ibn Isḥāq, Zayd ibn Aslam and others. He was destroyed when he tried to fight against Allah. Allah sent a great cloud of gnats against him and they covered the sun and consumed his army until only their bones were left. One entered his brain and ate it until it became the size of a mouse. The dearest of people to him after that was the one who hit his head with a hammer! He suffered for forty days.

Ibn Jurayj said that he was the first king in the earth. Ibn 'Aṭiyyah says that this is rejected. Qatādah said that he was the first to become a tyrant; he was the one who built the tower at Babel. It is said that he was king of the entire earth and was one of two unbelieving kings. The second king was Nebuchadnezzar. It is also said that the one who argued with Ibrāhīm was Numrūdh ibn Fālikh ibn 'Ābir ibn Shālikh ibn Arfakhshand ibn Sām. Ibn 'Aṭiyyah related all of that. As-Suhaylī related that he was Numrūdh ibn Kan'ān ibn Ḥām ibn Nūḥ. He was king over the black people. He was appointed by aḍ-Ḍaḥḥāk who was known as al-Azdahāq. His name was Bīwarāsb ibn Andarāst and he was the king of all regions. He is the one who was killed by Afīdūn ibn Athfiyān.

Aḍ-Ḍaḥḥāk was a tyrant whose kingdom lasted a thousand years. He was the first to crucify people and the first to cut off hands and feet. Nimrod had a son called Kush, or a similar name, and a son called Nimrod the younger. Nimrod the younger ruled for a year and Nimrod the elder ruled for four hundred years, as they say.

There are two versions of how the debate reported in this *āyah* occurred. One is that the people went out to a festival they used to observe and Ibrāhīm went to their idols and broke them. When they returned, he said to them, 'Do you worship something you have carved?' They asked, 'Who do you worship?' He said, 'I worship my Lord who gives life and causes to die.' It is also said that Nimrod had complete control of the food stores of his people and, when they wanted to eat, they had to buy food from him. When they went to him, they prostrated to him. Ibrāhīm entered and did not prostrate. He asked him, 'Why do you not prostrate to me?' He replied, 'I prostrate only to my Lord.' Nimrod demanded, 'Who is your Lord?' Ibrāhīm answered, 'My Lord is He Who gives life and causes to die.'

Zayd ibn Aslam said, 'This Nimrod had control of all the provisions of his people. When people came, he demanded, "Who is your Lord and God?" "You," they answered. "Give them provision," he said. Ibrāhīm came to seek provision and he asked him the same question. Ibrāhīm replied, "My Lord is He who gives life and causes to die." When he heard this, Nimrod said, "I give life and cause to die." Then Ibrāhīm asked him the question about the sun and he was dumbfounded. He said, "Do not give him provision." Ibrāhīm returned to his people with nothing. He passed by a heap of fine sand and said to himself. "If I fill my sacks with this, when I enter the children will be happy until I can see to them." He did that and when he reached his house, the children were happy and began to play on the sacks. He fell asleep from exhaustion and his wife said, "I will prepare some food for him and he will find it ready when he wakes up." She opened one of the sacks and found it to be the finest flour and baked it. When he rose, she put it before him. He asked, "Where is this from?" She said, "From the flour you brought." Ibrāhīm knew that Allah had done that.'

Abū Bakr ibn Abī Shaybah mentioned that Abū Ṣāliḥ said, 'The Prophet Ibrāhīm went to obtain food and was unable to obtain it. He passed by some red sand and took some of it and returned to his family. They asked, 'What is this?' He answered, 'Red wheat.' They opened it and found that it was red wheat. When any of it was planted, it produced ears that were full of grain from bottom to top.

Ar-Rabīʿ and others said about this story that, when Nimrod said, 'I give life and cause to die,' he summoned two men. He killed one and released the other. He said, 'I gave life to that one and made that one die.' Then Ibrāhīm countered that with the question about the sun which dumbfounded him. It is related in a hadith that Allah said, 'The Final Hour will not come until I bring the sun from the west so that it is known that I have the power to do that.' Then Nimrod commanded Ibrāhīm to be thrown into the fire. That is what tyrants do. When they are opposed in something and unable to offer proof of their position, they inflict punishment. Allah saved Ibrāhīm from the fire as we will see later.

As-Suddī said, 'When Ibrāhīm emerged from the fire, they brought him to the King. He had not been in his presence before that time. He spoke to him and asked, "Who is your Lord?" He replied, "My Lord is the One who gives life and causes to die." Nimrod said, "I give life and cause to die. I will take four people and put them in a room and will not give them food or water until they are starving. I will bring them out and feed two and they will live and not feed two who will die." Then Ibrāhīm countered with the question about the sun and he was dumbfounded.'

Legists have mentioned about this *āyah* that, when Ibrāhīm described his Lord with bringing to life and making die, it was a statement that could be taken literally or metaphorically. It should be pointed out that Ibrāhīm meant essential qualities in the first instance while Nimrod took what he said metaphorically and misrepresented it to his people. So Ibrāhīm left the argument and moved to an example which cannot be made metaphorical. *'And the one who was an unbeliever was dumbfounded.'* The king could not argue and refute the second example nor could he say, 'I am the one who brings it from the east' because intelligent people would reject that.

This *āyah* indicates the permissibility of giving an unbeliever the title of 'king' when he has kingdom, might and elevation in this world. It also is an affirmation of the use of evidential argument in establishing the proof of a matter and this is often found in the Sunnah and Qur'an. Allah says: *'Produce your evidence if you speak the truth,'* (2:111) and: *'Have you authority to say this?'* (10:68), meaning any evidence. Allah also described how Ibrāhīm argued with his people and refuted their worship of idols as we find in *Sūrat al-Anbiyā'* and elsewhere. He says in the story of Nūḥ: *'They said, "Nūḥ, you have argued with us and argued much...'* (11:32) until he said, *'I am innocent of the crimes which you commit.'* (11:36) Mūsā also argued with Pharaoh as seen in many *āyahs*.

All of this is instruction by Allah through question and answer and debate in the *dīn* because that shows the difference between truth and falsehood by the demonstration of the proof of the truth and the invalidity of false evidence. The Prophet ﷺ debated with the People of the Book and called on them to invoke Allah against themselves after the argument as will be dealt with in *Āli 'Imrān*. Ādam and Mūsā argued and Ādam won the argument. The Companions of the Messenger of Allah ﷺ argued with one another on the Day of the Verandah. They pushed one another, made affirmations and debated until the truth came from its people and allegiance was given to Abū Bakr. They also debated about the people of the Riddah. There are very many instances of that. The words of Allah: '*You are a people arguing about something of which you have knowledge*' (3:66) are evidence that arguing about something with knowledge is permitted for those who reflect. Al-Muzanī, the follower of ash-Shāfi'ī, said, 'Among the conditions of debate is that Allah should be intended by it and that what is clear should be accepted from it.' It is said that debating is not sound unless those who are debating are close or equal in respect of their level of knowledge of the *dīn*, intelligence, understanding and fairness. Otherness it is merely quarrelling and arrogance.

'Alī ibn Abī Ṭālib recited '*a lam tar*' with the jussive, but the majority vowel the *rā'* and the *yā'* is elided in the jussive. '*An ātāhu-llāhu-l-mulka*' is in the position of the accusative, meaning 'because Allah had given him' or 'for the sake of what Allah had given him.' Most recite '*ana uḥyī*,' discarding the *alif* after the *nūn* of '*anā*' (I) in the connection, while Nāfi' and Ibn Abī Uways keep it because of meeting with the *hamzah*, as is the case throughout the Qur'an except in 7:188 where it is discarded as is done by the other reciters since that is rare. It only occurs three times in the Qur'an. It acts like that which does not have *hamzah* after it because of its rareness and so the *alif* is elided in the connection.

Grammarians said that in the case when the pronoun of the speaker has a *hamzah* and a *nūn*, as when you say '*ana*' or '*anah*', the *alif* and the *hā'* are to make the vowelling clear in the stop. When the word is connected to something, they are dropped because the word to which it is connected takes the place of the *alif*. It is rare to say '*anā fa'altu*' except in poetry. An-Naḥḥās said that the fact that Nāfi' kept the *alif* and recited '*anā uḥyī*' has no logic. Makkī said that the Basrans consider the *alif* to be redundant and believe that the name is implied by the *hamzah* and *nūn* and the *alif* is added for strengthening. It is said that it is added by the stop to make the vowel of the *nūn* clear. According to the Kufans, the noun is '*anā*' in full. Nāfi' confirms the *alif* in the root according to their position, and those who elide it do so to lighten it, and because it is indicated by the *fatḥah* (a).

Al-Jawharī said, 'As for saying *ana* (I) it is a metonymic noun and is for the first person alone. It only has the *fatḥah* (a) invariably to distinguish it from *an* (that) which is a preposition that puts the verb in the subjunctive case, and the final *alif* is to make clear the vowelling when there is a stop. If it occurs in the middle of speech it is dropped except when there is poor usage of language.

The word 'dumbfounded' (*bahita* and *buhita*) is used when someone is stopped and falls silent out of confusion. An-Naḥḥās and others said that. Aṭ-Ṭabarī said that some of the Arabs said that it is *bahata.* Ibn Jinnī said that Abū Ḥaywah recited '*bahuta*' which is a dialectical form of *buhita.* Ibn as-Samayfa' recited '*bahata*' meaning, 'Ibrāhim stunned the one who disbelieved.' He said that it is permitted for *bahata* to be a dialectical variant of *bahuta.* Abu-l-Ḥasan al-Akhfash related '*bahita*' like *khariqa* and *dahisha* and said that most of them have *bahuta.* Ibn 'Aṭiyyah said that some people interpret the reading '*bahata*' to mean 'insulted and ejected' when he was stopped and had no further device to use.

أَوْ كَالَّذِي مَرَّ عَلَىٰ قَرْيَةٍ وَهِيَ خَاوِيَةٌ عَلَىٰ عُرُوشِهَا قَالَ أَنَّىٰ يُحْيِي
هَٰذِهِ اللَّهُ بَعْدَ مَوْتِهَا فَأَمَاتَهُ اللَّهُ مِائَةَ عَامٍ ثُمَّ بَعَثَهُ قَالَ كَمْ لَبِثْتَ
قَالَ لَبِثْتُ يَوْمًا أَوْ بَعْضَ يَوْمٍ قَالَ بَل لَّبِثْتَ مِائَةَ عَامٍ فَانظُرْ إِلَىٰ
طَعَامِكَ وَشَرَابِكَ لَمْ يَتَسَنَّهْ وَانظُرْ إِلَىٰ حِمَارِكَ وَلِنَجْعَلَكَ
آيَةً لِّلنَّاسِ وَانظُرْ إِلَى الْعِظَامِ كَيْفَ نُنشِرُهَا ثُمَّ نَكْسُوهَا لَحْمًا
فَلَمَّا تَبَيَّنَ لَهُ قَالَ أَعْلَمُ أَنَّ اللَّهَ عَلَىٰ كُلِّ شَيْءٍ قَدِيرٌ ﴿٢٥٩﴾

259 Or the one who passed by a town which had fallen into ruin? He asked, 'How can Allah restore this to life when it has died?' Allah caused him to die a hundred years, then brought him back to life. Then He asked, 'How long have you been here?' He replied, 'I have been here a day or part of a day.' He said, 'Not so! You have been here a hundred years. Look at your food and drink – it has not gone bad — and look at your donkey so We can make you a Sign for all mankind. Look at the bones – how We raise them up and clothe them in flesh.' When it had become clear to him, he said, 'Now I know that Allah has power over all things.'

Or the one who passed by a town which had fallen into ruin?

'*Aw*' (or) is a conjunction which has its normal meaning here. According to al-Kisā'ī and al-Farrā' it refers back to the '*What about...?*' in the previous *āyah.* Al-

Mubarrad said that it means: 'Have you not looked at the one who argued with Ibrāhīm about his Lord? Have you not seen who he is? Like the one who passed by a town…' The words imply that. Abū Sufyān ibn Ḥusayn recited 'or' as '*a wa*' with a *fatḥah* on the *wāw* as a conjunction to which the interrogative *alif* is added, and it indicates confirmation. A '*qaryah*' (town) is called that because people gather (*qarā*) in it. The verb is used for water collecting in a place.

Sulaymān ibn Buraydah, Nājiyyah ibn Ka'b, Qatādah, Ibn 'Abbās, ar-Rabī', 'Ikrimah and aḍ-Ḍaḥḥāk said, 'The one who passed by the town was 'Uzayr.' Wahb ibn Munabbih, 'Abdullāh ibn 'Ubayd ibn 'Umayr and 'Abdullāh ibn Bakr ibn Muḍar said that it was Irmiyā' (said by some to be Jeremiah), who was a Prophet. Ibn Isḥāq said that Irmiyā' is al-Khiḍr. An-Naqqāsh related that from Wahb ibn Munabbih. Ibn 'Aṭiyyah said, 'This is as you see, although one name is the same as the other because al-Khiḍr was a contemporary of Mūsā. The one who passed by the town was one of the clan of Hārūn some time later according to what Wahb ibn Munabbih related.'

If al-Khiḍr is Irmiyā', it is not improbable since al-Khiḍr has been alive from the time of Mūsā until now according to the sound position on that, which will be talked about in *Sūrat al-Kahf*. If he died before this story, then the position of Ibn 'Aṭiyyah is sound. Allah knows best.

An-Naḥḥās and Makkī related from Mujāhid that he was an unnamed man of the tribe of Israel. An-Naqqāsh said that it is said that he was the servant of Lūṭ. As-Suhaylī related that al-Qutaybī has one statement saying that it is Shu'ayb and the one who restored it to life after it was ruined was Kūshik al-Fārisī. The town is Jerusalem as stated by Wahb ibn Munabbih, Qatādah, ar-Rabī' ibn Anas and others. He said that he came from Egypt and that his food and drink – referred to in the *āyah* – consisted of green figs, grapes and a pot of wine. It is also said that it was juice and it is said that it was a small amount of water.

It was Nebuchadnezzar who destroyed the town. He was the governor of Iraq for Lohorasp and then Gushtasp, the son of Lohorasp, who was the father of Isfandiyar. An-Naqqāsh related that it is 'the Overturned Cities'. Abū Ṣāliḥ transmitted from Ibn 'Abbās that Nebuchadnezzar attacked the tribe of Israel and captured many of them and took them to Babylon. 'Uzayr ibn Sharkhiyā was one of them. He was one of the scholars of the Israelites. He went out one day for something he needed to Dayr Hizqal on the banks of the Tigris. He stopped under the shade of a tree. He tied his donkey up in the shade of the tree and then went around the town and did not see anyone living there. It was fallen down and deserted. He said, 'How can Allah restore this to life when it has died?'

It is said that it was the town from which thousands fled out of fear of death referred to earlier in 2:243. Ibn Zayd said that. Ibn Zayd said that it was those people who left their homes in thousands in fear of death and Allah told them, 'Die!' A man passed by their decayed bones and stopped to look and said. 'How can Allah restore this to life when it has died?' Allah caused him to die a hundred years. Ibn 'Aṭiyyah, however, says that this position of Ibn Zayd is contrary to the words of the *āyah* since the *āyah* mentions a town fallen into ruin with no one in it. So it indicates the town. Its being brought to life was by flourishing and the re-establishment of buildings and houses.

Wahb ibn Munabbih, Qatādah, aḍ-Ḍaḥḥāk, ar-Rabī' and 'Ikrimah said that the town was Jerusalem when Nebuchadnezzar of Babylon destroyed it. There is a long account about the history of the tribe of Israel and when Irmīyā' or 'Uzayr stopped at the town which was a great hill in the middle of Jerusalem brought about when Nebuchadnezzar had commanded his army to move the earth to it until he made it like a mountain. Irmīyā' saw that the walls of the houses were collapsed onto their roofs and said, 'How will Allah bring this to life after its death?'

In the expression 'fallen into ruin' (*khāwiyatun 'alā 'urūshihā*) the word *'urūsh* means roofs of houses and anything that is set up for the sake of shade or shelter. Part of the usage of *'arīsh* is a trellis as in 16:68. As-Suddī said that the roofs fell in and the walls fell on top of them. Aṭ-Ṭabarī prefers it. Others said that it simply means that the place was uninhabited with the houses still standing and the expression simply means 'empty'. The root of the verb is *khalw*. 'Empty' can also mean 'collapsed'. *Khawā'* also describes a stomach empty of food. The verb is used of a woman whose womb becomes empty after giving birth. *Khawī* describes easy ground. Form II of the verb describes a camel kneeling with its belly off the ground and it also describes a man in prostration.

He asked, 'How can Allah restore this to life when it has died?'

This means: 'by what means and method?' The literal meaning of the expression is about bringing the town back to life by restoring its inhabitants and prosperity, as one uses the expression today for empty cities which are unlikely to be re-inhabited. So it means: 'How will this flourish after it has fallen into ruin?' It is as if this was a question expressing regret when the man who was standing reflected on his city where his family had lived and which he loved. Allah made a greater response than the asker had intended by his question: actually bringing the dead to life. Aṭ-Ṭabarī related that one of them said, 'This statement implies doubt about Allah's power to bring things to life. This is an example he made to himself.' Ibn 'Aṭiyyah said that the question does not imply doubt about the power of Allah Almighty to bring the town to life and make it flourish. The doubt comes from being ignorant in another way. It is not correct to interpret the *āyah* as expressing doubt.

Allah caused him to die a hundred years then brought him back to life.

'Hundred' is in the accusative as an adverb. *'Ām* means a year, and one says *'sinwan 'uwwam'* for stress. We see this in poetry. It is implied that it is the plural of *'ā'im* although it alone is mentioned because it is not a noun, but rather stress, as al-Jawharī said. An-Naqqāsh said that *'ām* is a verbal noun like *'awm*, which means swimming. A year (*'ām*) is called that because it is the amount of time it takes for the sun to 'swim' (*'āma*) around the celestial sphere. So *'awm* is like *sabḥ*. Allah says: '*...each one is swimming (*yasbaḥūna*) in a sphere.*' (36:40) Ibn 'Aṭiyyah said, 'This is the idea behind what an-Naqqāsh said.' The literal meaning of this *āyah* is to make someone die by removing their *rūḥ* from their body.

In the story behind this *āyah*, it is related that Allah sent a king to refurbish it and renew it so that it was complete by the time the speaker was revived. It is said that seventy years after his death Allah sent a Persian king called Kushk [Cyrus] who refurbished it in thirty years. *Ba'atha* is to bring back to life.

Then He asked, 'How long have you been here?'

There is disagreement about the asker here. It is said that it was Allah Almighty. It is said that the man heard an unseen voice. It is said that it was Jibrīl or a Prophet or a believing man of the people who saw him. The most apparent position is that it was Allah because of the rest of the *āyah*. Allah knows best.

He replied, 'I have been here a day or part of a day.'

This is what he thought and so he was not lying when he said it. It is similar to the answer the People of the Cave gave in 18:19 when they said that they had been there for a day or part of a day when in fact they had been there for 309 years. They were not lying, but expressing what they thought to be the case. It is as if they were saying, 'What we think in our opinion is that we have been here for a day or part of a day.' That is similar to what the Prophet ﷺ said in the story about Dhu-l-Yadayn in respect of the prayer: 'I did not shorten and I did not forget.' Some people have said that it was an actual lie but he was not punished for it. A lie is to report something to be other than what it actually is. That is the same in both knowledge and ignorance. This is clear in respect of fundamental principles. On this basis it is permitted to say that the Prophets are not protected from reporting something to be other than what it actually is when that is not intentional, just as they are not protected from oversight and forgetfulness. This is connected to this *āyah*, but the first view is sounder.

Ibn Jurayj, Qatādah and ar-Rabī' said that Allah made him die in the morning and then raised him up before sunset so that he thought that it was the same day. When he saw the remaining sun, he was afraid that he had lied in saying, 'a day,' so he added 'or part of a day.' He was told that he had been there a hundred years and he saw how the town was flourishing and its trees and buildings as evidence of that.

Look at your food and drink — it has not gone bad —

It is said that his food and drink consisted of green figs which he had gathered from the trees of the town he passed by. Ibn Mas'ūd recited *'hādhā ṭa'āmuka wa sharābuka'* (this is your food and drink) Ṭalḥah ibn Muṣarrif and others recite *'unẓur li-ṭa'āmika wa-sh-sharābika li-mi'ati sannah* (Look at your food and drink for a hundred years.)' Most recite *'yatasannah'* with the '*hā*'' at the end while the two brothers [Ḥamzah and al-Kisā'ī] elide it. There is no disagreement that one stops at the '*hā*''. Ṭalḥah ibn Muṣarrif also recited '*lam yassanna*' and '*wa-nẓur*' (with *wāw* not *fā'*), assimilating the *tā'* into the *sīn*. According to the recitation of the majority, the *hā'* is part of the root and the *ḍammah* is elided for the jussive. It comes from '*sannah*' (year), meaning that it has not been altered by the years.

Al-Jawharī says that *sannah* is the singular of *sunūn* or *sinīn*. Two things are said about what it is missing. The first is that it is a *wāw* and the other is that it is *hā'* and that its root is *sanhah*, like *jabhah* because it is from the expression *sanahat* and *tasannahat* used for palm-trees which have lasted for years. A palm-tree that is *sannā'* bears fruit some years and not other years. It is also called *sanhā'*. One of the Anṣār said:

It is not a tree that is *sanhā'* or propped up,
but *'ārīyah* loans for years (*sanīn*) of drought.

Asnahtu means 'I stayed with' as does *tasannaytu*. You hire someone for a year (*musānāh* and *musānahah*). The diminutive is *sunayyah* and *sunayhah*. An-Naḥḥās said, 'If someone recites "*lam yatasanna*" he says *sunayyah* for the diminutive and the *alif* is elided for the jussive and stops on the *hā'* and says *'yatasannah'*, the *hā'* being for making the vowel clear.'

Al-Mahdawī said, 'It is possible that its root is from *sānaytuhu musānah*, i.e. "I hired him year by year' or from *sānahtu* with a *hā'*. If it is from *sānaytu*, its root is *yatasannā* and the *alif* has been omitted for the jussive. It has a *wāw* in the root as indicated by *sanawāt* and the *hā'* in it is for silence. If it is from *sānahtu*, then the *hā'* is the *lām* of the verb and according to this, the root of *sanah* is *sanhah*. According to the first, it is *sanawah*. It is also said that it is derived from *asina*, the verb for water becoming brackish, but this would oblige an extra *alif* in the word.'

Abū 'Amr ash-Shaybānī said that it came from Allah's words: '*fetid* (masnūn) *black mud*'. (15:26) What it means is that it has not changed. Az-Zajjāj said. 'That is not the case because "*masnūn*" does not mean "changed", but poured out on the surface of the earth.' Mujāhid said that it means 'it has not become foul'. An-Naḥḥās said that the soundest of what is said about this is that it is from *sannah*, and that it has not been changed by the years. It is possible that it comes from the meaning 'drought' as Allah says: '*We seized Pharaoh's people with years of drought* (sinīn)' (7:130) and the words of the Prophet ﷺ, 'O Allah, impose on them years of drought like those of Yūsuf.' So it means 'your food has not been changed by drying up' or 'it has not been changed by the passage of years,' and so has remained fresh.

– and look at your donkey

Wahb ibn Munabbih and others said, 'Look at how We re-connect its bones and bring it to life bit by bit.' It is related that Allah brought it to life by re-connecting its bones and then clothing them in flesh until the donkey was completely restored. Then an angel came and breathed the spirit into it and the donkey stood up and brayed. This is what most commentators say. Wahb and aḍ-Ḍaḥḥāk also said that it can mean: look at your donkey standing, untouched after a hundred years, and the bones that he looked at were the actual bones after Allah brought its eyes and head to life while the rest of the body was dead. They said that Allah made people's eyes blind to Irmīyā' and his donkey for this period of time.

so We can make you a Sign for all mankind.

Al-Farrā' said that putting the *wāw* before the word here indicates that it is a precondition for what is after it. It is a sign of resurrection after death. It can also indicate an interpolation. He was still the age he had been when he died and his sons and grandsons were old men. 'Ikrimah said that he was forty when he died. 'Alī related that 'Uzayr's wife was pregnant when he left and that he was fifty when Allah made him die for a hundred years. Then he was brought back to life and returned to his family after his resurrection still fifty years old. He had a son who was a hundred years old and his son's son was fifty years old. Ibn 'Abbās related, 'When Allah brought 'Uzayr to life and he mounted his donkey and rode to his home, he did not recognise people nor did they recognise him. He found an old blind woman in his house who was the mother of the household. This woman had been twenty years old when 'Uzayr left. He asked her, "Is this Uzayr's house?" She said, "Yes!" and wept and then said, "'Uzayr left us in such and such a year." He said, "I am 'Uzayr." She stated, "'Uzayr has been gone for a hundred years." He replied, "Allah made me die for a hundred years and then brought me to life again." She said, "'Uzayr was someone whose supplication for the sick and afflicted was answered. Ask Allah to restore my sight to me." He prayed to Allah and wiped her eyes with his hand and she was healed where she was, as if she had been released. She said, "I testify that you are 'Uzayr!" She went to the assembly of the tribe of Israel, which included a son of 'Uzayr's, who was one hundred and twenty-eight years old, and his grandsons who were old men. She said, "People! By Allah, this is 'Uzayr!" His son went to him with the people and said, "My father had a black mole like the crescent moon between his shoulders." He saw it and knew that it was 'Uzayr.'

It is said that when he came he found that everyone he had known had died. He was a sign for those of his people who were alive since they had heard about his state and were certain. Ibn 'Aṭiyyah said, 'The greatest sign is in him being made to die for this period and then brought to life after that. His entire business is a sign throughout time and there is no need to specify which of the details are correct.'

Look at the bones – how We raise them up and clothe them in flesh.'

'Raise them up' is read as *nunshizuhā* by the Kufans and Ibn 'Āmir and as *nunshiruhā* by everyone else although Abān related from 'Āṣim that it is *'nanshuruhā'* as did Ibn 'Abbās, al-Ḥasan and Abū Ḥaywah. In either case it means to bring to life. It is known linguistically that Allah brings the dead to life (*anshara*) and they are revived (*nasharū*). Allah says: *'When He wishes, He brings him to life.'* (80:22) It is like a garment being unfolded (*nashara*). The verb is used for being resurrected after death and the noun is *nushūr*. Al-A'shā said:

> Until, when people see it, they say,
> 'Wonder! The resurrected (*nāshir*) dead!"

It is as if death rolls up the bones and limbs, and revivification and joining the limbs together is like spreading them out and opening them up (*nashara*) again. If it is read *nashaza* it means an elevated place and the verb means to raise. A poet said:

You see the young fox in it.
As if a majestic fortress rose high (*nashz*).

Makkī says, 'It means: "Look at the bones and how We raise them up and put them together in order to bring them to life" because *nashz* means elevating. Part of that is describing a disobedient wife as *nushūz* because she puts herself above agreeing with her husband. It is also used in the words of the Almighty: *'When you are told: "Make room (*fa-nshuzū*) in the gathering," then make room.'"'* (58:11) This means: get up and press together. When it is read with *rā'*, then it means to bring to life. Bones do not come to life on their own until they are connected to one another. The *zāyy* is more appropriate in this context since it means to join together rather than bring to life. That which is described as being brought back to life is the man rather than the bones on their own. One does say, 'This bone is alive.' So it means: 'Look at the bones and how We raise them from their place on the ground to the body so that it can be brought to life.' An-Nakha'ī recited *'nanshuzuhā'* and that is related from Ibn 'Abbās and Qatādah. *Kuswah* is clothing that covers a person. The flesh is likened to it. An-Nābighah uses it as a metaphor for Islam:

'So that I was clothed in a shirt from Islam.'

When it had become clear to him, he said, 'Now I know that Allah has power over all things.'

It is related that Allah brought some of him back to life and then he saw how Allah brought the rest of his body to life. Qatādah said, 'He looked at how the bones are connected to one another because the first part of him Allah brought back to life was his head and then he was told to look. At that point he said, 'I know,' meaning 'I know this.' Aṭ-Ṭabarī said that it means: when it was clear to his own eyes what he denied of Allah's power before he saw that. Then he said, 'I know.' Ibn 'Aṭiyyah said that this is an error because it demands something not obliged by the words. His explanation is based on an aberrant view and weak probability. This is what I think because there is no confirmation that he denied before that as aṭ-Ṭabarī said. What he said was prompted by reflection, as a believing person might say when he sees something unusual of Allah's power, 'There is no god but Allah' and the like. Abū 'Alī said that it means: 'I know this sort of knowledge which I did not know previously.'

We already mentioned this idea from Qatādah. That is what Makkī said: 'He reported about himself when he witnessed the power of Allah to bring the dead to life and had certainty of that by actually witnessing its occurrence. He affirmed that he truly knew that Allah has power over all things. In other words he is saying, "I now know by eye-witnessing this sort of knowledge which I did not know before."' This is based on the reading of *'a'lamu'* with the *alif* disconnected which is the reading of most reciters. Ḥamzah and al-Kisā'ī connect the *alif* (*i'lam*) which has two possible meanings. One is that the angel told him, 'Know' and the other is that he put himself in the position of a separate speaker. So it means: 'When it was clear to him, he said to himself, "Soul, know with this definitive knowledge which you did not know by eye-witnessing."' Abū 'Alī composed something about this understanding:

Bid farewell to Hurayrah. The caravan is leaving.
Your bleary eyes have not closed in the night.

Makkī said, 'It is unlikely that it is a command from Allah to know because He had demonstrated His power to him and shown him something that is certainly sound and affirms His power. So there is no point in Allah commanding that. He is commanding himself to do that. That is an excellent possibility.' The mode (*ḥarf*) of 'Abdullāh indicates that it is a command from Allah to know, meaning that this knowledge is necessary because of what you have seen and are certain about. His mode has *'qīla i'lam'* (It was said, 'Know...'). That also agrees with the command before it: *'Look at your food,' 'Look at your donkey,'* and *'look at the bones.'* So the same is true in the case of 'Know that Allah...'. Ibn 'Abbās used to recite it in that way and said, 'Who is better: him or Ibrāhīm, since he was told, "*Know that Allah is Almighty, All-Wise*"?' This makes it clear that it is part of the words of Allah to him when he witnessed the bringing of everything back to life.

وَإِذْ قَالَ إِبْرَٰهِيمُ رَبِّ أَرِنِي كَيْفَ تُحْيِ ٱلْمَوْتَىٰ قَالَ أَوَلَمْ تُؤْمِن قَالَ بَلَىٰ وَلَٰكِن
لِّيَطْمَئِنَّ قَلْبِي قَالَ فَخُذْ أَرْبَعَةً مِّنَ ٱلطَّيْرِ فَصُرْهُنَّ إِلَيْكَ ثُمَّ ٱجْعَلْ عَلَىٰ كُلِّ جَبَلٍ
مِّنْهُنَّ جُزْءًا ثُمَّ ٱدْعُهُنَّ يَأْتِينَكَ سَعْيًا وَٱعْلَمْ أَنَّ ٱللَّهَ عَزِيزٌ حَكِيمٌ ﴿٢٦٠﴾

260 When Ibrāhīm said, 'My Lord, show me how You bring the dead to life.' He asked, 'Do you not then believe?' He replied, 'Indeed I do! But so that my heart may be at peace.' He said, 'Take four birds and train them to yourself. Then put a part of them on each mountain and call to them; they will come rushing to you. Know that Allah is Almighty, All-Wise.'

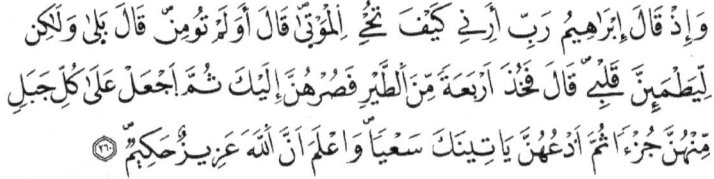

When Ibrāhīm said, 'My Lord, show me how You bring the dead to life.' He asked, 'Do you not then believe?'

People disagree about Ibrāhīm's request and whether it arose out of doubt or not. The majority say that Ibrāhīm did not doubt that Allah could bring the dead to life but simply wanted to see it happen with his own eyes. That is because people have a natural desire for direct proof of what they are told. That is why the Prophet ﷺ said, 'A report about something is not the same as actually seeing it.' Ibn 'Abbās related that and no one else related it. Abū 'Umar said that. Al-Akhfash said, 'He did not mean the seeing of the heart. He meant the seeing of the eye.' Al-Ḥasan, Qatādah, Sa'īd ibn Jubayr and ar-Rabī' said that Ibrāhīm was asking in order to add certainty to his certainty. Ibn 'Aṭiyyah said, 'Aṭ-Ṭabarī has a chapter in his *Tafsīr*: "Others said that he asked his Lord for that because he doubted the power of Allah." He included in this section from Ibn 'Abbās: "I consider this the most hopeful of *āyahs*."' It is mentioned that 'Aṭā' ibn Abī Rabāḥ said, 'Something that enters the hearts of ordinary people entered Ibrāhīm's heart and he said, "My Lord, show me how You bring the dead to life."' He mentioned the hadith of Abū Hurayrah in which the Messenger of Allah ﷺ said, 'We are more entitled to doubt than Ibrāhīm.' Then aṭ-Ṭabarī preferred this view.

The hadith from Abū Hurayrah was transmitted by al-Bukhārī and Muslim in which the Messenger of Allah ﷺ said, 'We are more entitled to doubt than Ibrāhīm. He said, "Lord, show me how You bring the dead to life," and He asked, "Do you not then believe?" He said, "Yes, but so that my heart will be at rest." Allah had mercy on Lūṭ. He took refuge in a strong pillar. If I had remained imprisoned for as long as Yūsuf, I would have answered the invitation.' This is mentioned by aṭ-Ṭabarī, but Ibn 'Aṭiyyah says that his interpretation [about the permissibility of doubt] is rejected.

As for what Ibn 'Abbās said, 'I consider this the most hopeful of *āyahs*,' that is because it contains boldness (*idlāl*) to Allah Almighty and asking for revivification in this world and there is no suspicion concerning it. It is permitted to say, 'I consider this the most hopeful of *āyahs* since Allah asked, "Do you not believe?" which shows that faith is enough and there is no need for delving and investigation.' 'Aṭā's statement can refer to direct witnessing of bringing the dead to life, and the meaning of the hadith is: 'If he had doubted, then we would have been more entitled to doubt. We do not doubt, and so it is more likely that Ibrāhīm did not doubt either.'

The hadith is, in fact, negating any doubt on the part of Ibrāhīm. It is related that the Prophet ﷺ said about it, 'That is pure faith.' It concerns passing thoughts which do not last. Doubt means to hesitate between two matters without preferring one to the other. The Khalīl was not subject to that. Bringing the dead to life was affirmed when he heard it. Ibrāhīm knew it, as he said, *'My Lord gives life and causes to die,'* earlier in this *sūrah*. Doubt is far from someone whose feet are firm in faith, so how much more must that be the case with someone whose rank is that of a Prophet and Friend. It is agreed that Prophets are protected from major wrong actions and minor vile ones by consensus.

If you reflect on the request he made and all the words of the *āyah*, you will find that they do not imply doubt. It is a question of 'how'. It is a matter of the manner of the occurrence of a phenomenon which exists and is affirmed by the asker. It is like the questions, 'How does Zayd know?', 'How is cloth woven?' and other such things. When you say, 'How is your garment?' and 'How is Zayd?' it is a question about a state. 'How' can apply to something which is understood as when you say, 'Be however you wish.' It is also like the words of al-Bukhārī, 'How the beginning of the revelation was'. The 'how' in this *āyah* is asking about the manner of bringing to life. Bringing to life is confirmed. However, we find some of those who deny the existence of something refer to that denial by asking about the state of that thing which the person knows not to be sound, indicating that they find that thing itself not to be sound. That is like when someone claims, 'I will lift up this mountain!' and the person who denies him says, 'How could you possibly lift it up?' Here the expression is used metaphorically with the aim of denial. It is a disputatious remark and is as if he were saying, 'Supposing that you can raise it, tell me how you are going to do that!' Since the words used by Ibrāhīm also involve this metaphorical usage, Allah absolved him of doing that and had Ibrāhīm make the reality clear by asking him, 'Do you not then believe?' He replied, 'Indeed I do.' So the business was complete and he was shown to be free of any doubt. Then he said that the reason for his question was to have his heart be at peace.

What Ibn 'Aṭiyyah mentioned is conclusive. Doubt of this sort is not permissible for the Prophets. It constitutes disbelief. The Prophets agree about Resurrection. Allah reported that Shayṭān has no way against His Prophets and *awliyā'*. He says: *'You have no authority over any of My slaves.'* (15:42) The accursed one said, *'only Your slaves among them who are sincere.'* If he has no power over them, how could he make them doubt? He was asking about how the parts of the dead are gathered together after they have been separated and how their sinews and skins are reconstituted after they have fallen apart. He wanted to move from the knowledge of certainty to the eye-witnessing of certainty. His words, *'show me how,'* are asking for direct witnessing of the manner in which it is achieved. Some of the people who deal in meanings say that Ibrāhīm wanted his Lord to show him how He brings the hearts to life, but this is false and rejected because of the following explanation. Al-Māwardī mentioned it. The *alif* in *'Do you not* (a wa lam) *believe'* is not the interrogative *alif*, but the *alif* of affirmation.

He replied, 'Indeed I do! But so that my heart may be at peace.'

'I make this request to You so that my heart will be tranquil through seeing the difference between what is known by intellectual proof and what is known by direct experience.' The tranquillity of the heart consists in balance and stillness. The tranquillity of the limbs is known, as in *rukū'* when they are still, as the Prophet ﷺ instructed: 'Then bow until you are still in bowing.' The tranquillity of the heart occurs when someone's thoughts have been stilled concerning the thing believed. Reflecting about the manner in which revivification occurs is not forbidden, just as we still reflect on it today when there are lessons to be learned from it. Ibrāhīm wanted to actually see it take place and witness the manner in which it occurs. Aṭ-Ṭabarī said that this means that he wanted to have certainty. The same was related from Sa'īd ibn Jubayr. It is also related from him that it was about increasing his certainty. Ibrāhīm and Qatādah said that.

Some of them said that it is to further increase faith. Ibn 'Aṭiyyah points out that this is nonsensical since certainty is indivisible. As-Suddī and Ibn Jubayr said that it means: 'Do you not believe that you are My Khalīl?' He replied, 'Yes, but so that my heart may be at peace about it.' It is said that he prayed to be shown how the dead are brought back to life so that he would know whether Allah would answer His prayer. So Allah said to him, 'Do you not believe that I answer your prayer?' He replied, 'Yes, but so that my heart may be at peace about Your answering my prayer.'

There is disagreement about what moved him to do this. It is said that Allah promised to make him His Khalīl and he wanted a sign of that. As-Sā'ib ibn Yazīd said that. It is said that it was the words of Nimrod, 'I give life and cause to die,' which made him ask. Al-Ḥasan said that he saw a riding animal which wild beasts and snakes had eaten and asked the question. It was half on the land and half in the sea. When he saw how it was split up, he wanted to know how it would be gathered back together so that his heart would be at peace by seeing how the parts would be rejoined when he saw how they were separated.

He said, 'Take four birds and train them to yourself. Then put a part of them on each mountain and call to them; they will come rushing to you.

It is said that they were a cock, a peacock, a dove and a crow. Ibn Isḥāq mentioned that from some scholars. Mujāhid, Ibn Jurayj, 'Aṭā' ibn Yasār and Ibn Zayd said that. Ibn 'Abbās said it was a crane instead of a crow, and elsewhere an eagle in place of the dove.

Ibrāhīm took these birds as he was commanded and then slaughtered them and then cut them into small pieces. He mixed their flesh together with the blood and feathers so that they were all jumbled together and then put parts of that mixture on each mountain. He stood where he could see those pieces while he kept the heads of the birds in his hand. Then he said, 'Come by Allah's permission,' and those parts flew and the blood flew to the blood and feathers to feathers until they were as they had been at first but headless. Then he repeated the call and they ran to him. The verb *sa'y* is not used when a bird flies except metaphorically. An-Naḥḥās said that. Ibrāhīm pointed at each of them which was without a head. When he pointed with its head, it came close until each bird joined its head and they flew away by Allah's permission. Az-Zajjāj said that it means: 'put a piece of each on each mountain.' Abū Bakr from 'Āṣim and Abū Ja'far recited '*juzu*''. Abū Ja'far recited "*juzz*" while the rest have '*juz*''. They are different dialects. It means a portion.

The words "*ṣurhunna ilayka*" (train them to yourself) may mean make them incline to you but are also said to mean 'cut them up'. Ibn 'Abbās, Mujāhid, Abū 'Abīdah and al-Anbārī said that. Ibn Isḥāq said that. Abu-l-Aswad ad-Du'alī said that its means 'cutting' in Syriac. Tawbah ibn al-Ḥumayyir said in a description:

When I tugged the rope, the thongs of the saddle-girth creaked
with the ends of sticks, its thongs being strong.
The ropes were close to me when I reached them
when I stood, and my rising almost cut them (*yaṣūruhā*).

Ṣawr is cutting. Aḍ-Ḍaḥḥāk, 'Ikrimah, and Ibn 'Abbās in another transmission, said that it means 'cut' in Nabatean. It is said that it means 'to make them incline to you', i.e. bring them to you and gather them to you. A man who is described as '*aṣwar*' has his neck bent. The word also means to incline to in the sense of yearning for. A woman is described as *ṣawrā'* and the plural is *ṣūr*, like *aswad* and *sūd*. A poet said:

Allah knows that in my turning
To my neighbours on the day of separation, I yearn (*ṣūr*).

If it means 'cut', '*to*' is connected to '*take*' and there is no need for implying something elided. If it means 'incline to', it is connected to '*ṣurhunna*' and there is something elided: 'make them incline to you and then cut them up.'

There are five readings here, two of which are from the seven readings: '*ṣurhunna*' and '*ṣirhunna*'. Some people recite '*ṣurrahunna*' as if He were saying, 'Bind them.' Connected to that meaning is the purse (*ṣurrah*) for dinars. Some people recite '*ṣirrahunna*', meaning 'make them call out' from the verb *ṣarra* for the creaking of a door and the noise of a pen. An-Naqqāsh related it. Ibn Jinnī said that it is a rare reading and that the form '*yaf'ilu*' in doubled transitive verbs is rare. Normally the middle letter has a *ḍammah*. Ibn Jinnī said, 'As for the reading of 'Ikrimah with a *ḍammah* on the *ṣād*, it is possible for the *rā'* to have a *ḍammah*, *fatḥah* or *kasrah*, but what is proper is to have a *ḍammah* because of the *ḍammah* on the *hā'* after it. The fifth reading is '*ṣarrihinna*' which al-Mahdawī and others related from 'Ikrimah. It means: 'restrain them' from *ṣarrā*, *yuṣarrī*. Connected to that meaning is a sheep which is *muṣarrāh*, whose milk is left to collect in the udder.

Here al-Māwardī interjects an objection. Why should Ibrāhīm be given a response when asking for the Signs of the Next World when that was denied to Mūsā when he asked, *'Lord, show yourself to me so that I may look at You!'* (7:143)? There are two answers to this. One is that what Mūsā asked for does not correspond with continuing responsibility while what Ibrāhīm asked for is particular and continued responsibility corresponds with it. The second is that the circumstances were different. It may be proper for something to be granted at certain times but denied at other times regarding that for which there is no permission. Ibn 'Abbās said, 'Allah commanded Ibrāhīm to do this before he had children and before the Scrolls were sent down to him.' Allah knows best.

مَّثَلُ ٱلَّذِينَ يُنفِقُونَ أَمْوَٰلَهُمْ فِى سَبِيلِ ٱللَّهِ كَمَثَلِ حَبَّةٍ أَنۢبَتَتْ سَبْعَ
سَنَابِلَ فِى كُلِّ سُنۢبُلَةٍ مِّا۟ئَةُ حَبَّةٍ ۗ وَٱللَّهُ يُضَٰعِفُ لِمَن يَشَآءُ ۗ وَٱللَّهُ وَٰسِعٌ
عَلِيمٌ ٢٦١

261 The metaphor of those who spend their wealth in the Way of Allah is that of a grain which produces seven ears; in every ear there are a hundred grains. Allah gives such multiplied increase to whoever He wills. Allah is All-Encompassing, All-Knowing.

After Allah has given evidence in support of fighting in the Way of Allah, He encourages *jihād* and confirms that those who do *jihād* after this evidence, which only a Prophet could have brought them, will have an immense reward for it. It is reported by al-Bustī in his sound *Musnad* from Ibn 'Umar, 'When this *āyah* was revealed, the Messenger of Allah ﷺ said, "Lord, give my community even more," and then Allah revealed: *"Is there anyone who will make Allah a generous loan so that He can multiply it for him many times over?"* (2:245) The Messenger of Allah ﷺ said, "Lord, give my community even more than that," and Allah revealed: "*The steadfast will be paid their wages in full without any reckoning*" (39:10)."

This *āyah* stresses the nobility of spending in the Way of Allah and its excellence and encourages people to do that. There is an elision in the Arabic, which implies, 'The metaphor of the "spending" of those who spend...' or 'The metaphor of those who spend their wealth is like a farmer who plants his crop of grain in the earth...' meaning that it produces seven ears in each of which there is a hundred grains. So He likens the one who gives *ṣadaqah* to a cultivator and likens the *ṣadaqah* to grain set aside for sowing, and so Allah gives him for every *ṣadaqah* of his seven hundred good deeds.

The metaphor makes it clear that a good action is worth seven hundred good deeds. *'Allah gives such multiplied increase to whomever He wills'* means that it can amount to even more than seven hundred. So the person who gives *ṣadaqah* is like a farmer. If he is intelligent in his work and the seed is good and the earth is fertile, the crop will be abundant. The same applies if the one who gives *ṣadaqah* is righteous and the wealth is good and he spends it in a place where the reward will be great. Some say that seven hundredfold is the maximum possible increase.

It is related that this *āyah* was revealed about 'Uthmān ibn 'Affān and 'Abd ar-Raḥmān ibn 'Awf on the occasion when the Messenger of Allah ﷺ encouraged people to give *ṣadaqah* when he was going on the Tabūk expedition. 'Abd ar-Raḥmān brought him four thousand and said, 'Messenger of Allah, I have eight thousand. I have kept four thousand for myself and my dependants and I am lending four thousand to my Lord.' The Messenger of Allah ﷺ said, 'May Allah bless you in what you have kept and what you have given.' 'Uthmān said, 'Messenger of Allah, I will kit out all those who have no equipment,' and this was revealed about them.

It is said that it was revealed about voluntary *ṣadaqah*. It is also said that it was revealed before the *Āyah* of Zakat and then abrogated by the *Āyah* of Zakat. There is no need to claim abrogation because spending in the Way of Allah is recommended at every time. The ways of spending are numerous, and the greatest of them is for *jihād* to raise high the word of Allah.

The type of grain referred to is not specified. The word used is *ḥabbah* and can designate all grains that are cultivated and stored as food. Wheat, however, is the most famous of them. Part of that is the words of al-Mutalammis [Jarīr ibn 'Abd al-Masīḥ]:

I wish that I could always eat the wheat (*ḥabb*) of Iraq.
The wheat which is eaten in the town is worms.

Ḥabbat al-qālib is one's beloved or its fruit. *Ḥibbah* are seeds of plants that are not foodstuffs. We find in the hadith of intercession: 'They will grow as a seed (*ḥibbah*) grows in what the flood has carried.' The plural is *ḥibab*. *Ḥubbah* is love as is *ḥibb*, which also means 'beloved'.

Sunbulah (ear) comes from the verb, *asbala*, to put forth ears [of grain], and they are released as a curtain is let down (*isbāl*). It is said that it means that covered grain appears in it as a thing is covered when a curtain is dropped over it. The plural of *sunbulah* is *sanābil*. It is said that what is meant are ears of millet which has that number in its ears. However, this is baseless because the ears of millet have many times more than this number as we can see.

Ibn 'Aṭiyyah said, 'The ears of wheat have a hundred grains. As for other grains, they have more than that. The example, however, merely uses this number.' Aṭ-Ṭabarī said about this *āyah* that it is a hundred grains if that exists. Otherwise, it is an estimation. Aḍ-Ḍaḥḥāk said that it means that every ear has a hundred grains. Ibn 'Aṭiyyah said, 'What aṭ-Ṭabarī said is more or less the same as aḍ-Ḍaḥḥāk said.' Abū 'Amr ad-Dānī said that some recite '*mi'ata*' in the accusative, implying, 'It produces a hundred grains.' Ya'qūb al-Ḥaḍramī said that some recite '*mi'ata*' in the accusative, implying, 'It produces a hundred grains,' just as some recite 'punishment' in the accusative in 67:6, meaning 'We have prepared for those who disbelieve the punishment of Hell.' Abū 'Amr, Ḥamzah and al-Kisā'ī recite '*anbatas-sab'*' with the *tā'* assimilated into the *sīn* because they are both letters with soft articulation and sometimes replace one another. The rest have them as distinct because they are two words.

The Qur'an reports that a good action of any type is worth ten like it. This *āyah* tells us that spending in *jihād* is worth seven hundred. Scholars disagree about the meanings of '*Allah gives such multiplied increase to whomever He wills.*' One group say that it is simply a reference to the seven hundred fold mentioned and does not indicate a greater increase than that. Another group of scholars says that it is to inform us that Allah can multiply it more than seven hundred times if He wishes. I consider this to be the soundest because of hadiths which mention that possibility.

Ibn Mājah related from Hārūn ibn 'Abdullāh al-Ḥammāl from Ibn Abī Fudayk from al-Khalīl ibn 'Abdullāh from al-Ḥasan from 'Alī ibn Abī Ṭālib, Abu-d-Dardā', 'Abdullāh ibn 'Amr, Abū Umāmah al-Bāhilī, 'Abdullāh ibn 'Amr, Jābir ibn 'Abdullāh and 'Imrān ibn Ḥuṣayn that the Messenger of Allah ﷺ said, 'If someone sends support for the Cause of Allah while he remains in his house, he will have seven hundred dirhams for every dirham. If someone goes on an expedition in the Cause of Allah and spends on it, he will have 700,000 dirhams for every dirham.' Then he recited this *āyah*: *'Allah gives multiplied increase to whomever He wills.'* It is related from Ibn 'Abbās that the multiplication reaches a million for whomever Allah wishes. Ibn 'Aṭiyyah said, 'This does not have a verified *isnād*.'

This *āyah* contains evidence that agriculture is one of the highest professions adopted by people and is a legitimate way of earning a living. This is why Allah uses it for metaphors. We read in *Ṣaḥīḥ Muslim* that the Prophet ﷺ said, 'There is no Muslim who plants a seedling or cultivates a crop from which birds, humans or animals eat without that being *ṣadaqah* for them.' Hishām ibn 'Urwah related from his father that 'Ā'ishah reported that the Messenger of Allah ﷺ said, 'Cling to cultivation in the hidden places of the earth.' At-Tirmidhī transmitted it. The Prophet ﷺ said about palm trees, 'They are firm in muddy conditions and give food in drought.' This is praise for them. Agriculture is one of the communal (*kifāyah*) obligations and so a ruler must compel people to do it. This includes planting trees. 'Abdullāh ibn 'Abd al-Malik met Ibn Shihāb az-Zuhrī and said, 'Direct me to property I can apply myself to.' Ibn Shihāb said:

I say to 'Abdullāh on the day I meet him,
when the camels are saddled for the east,
'Follow the plants of the earth and leave their owners.
Perhaps one day you will receive an answer and be provided for.
You will be given vast recurring wealth
when the waters of the earth gush forth.'

It is related that al-Mu'taḍid said, 'I saw 'Alī ibn Abī Ṭālib in a dream handing me a spade and he said, "Take it. It is the key to the treasures of the earth."'

ٱلَّذِينَ يُنفِقُونَ أَمْوَٰلَهُمْ فِى سَبِيلِ ٱللَّهِ ثُمَّ لَا يُتْبِعُونَ مَآ أَنفَقُوا۟ مَنًّا
وَلَآ أَذًى لَّهُمْ أَجْرُهُمْ عِندَ رَبِّهِمْ وَلَا خَوْفٌ عَلَيْهِمْ وَلَا هُمْ
يَحْزَنُونَ ٢٦٢

262 Those who spend their wealth in the Way of Allah, and then do not follow what they have spent by demands for gratitude or insulting words will have their reward with their Lord. They will feel no fear and will know no sorrow.

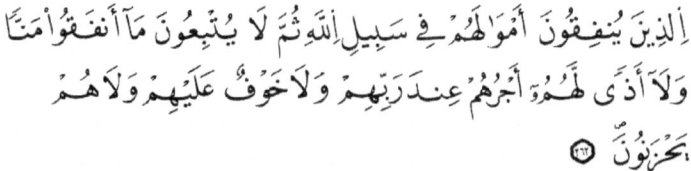

Those who spend their wealth in the Way of Allah,

This was revealed about 'Uthmān ibn 'Affān. 'Abd ar-Raḥmān ibn Samurah said, "Uthmān brought a thousand dinars for the Army of Hardship and put it in the lap of the Messenger of Allah ﷺ. I saw him put his hand in it and turn it about. He said, "It does matter what 'Uthmān does after today. O Allah, do not forget this day for 'Uthmān!"' Abū Sa'īd al-Khudrī said, 'I saw the Prophet ﷺ raise his hands to pray for 'Uthmān, saying, "My Lord, 'Uthmān! I am pleased with 'Uthmān, so be pleased with him." After dawn, this *āyah* was revealed.'

Spending in the Way of Allah in general was mentioned in the previous *āyah* and then it is made clear in this *āyah* that judgment about it and reward for it are for the one who does not follow up what he gives with demands for gratitude or insult of any kind. For such an action would invalidate the *ṣadaqah* as Allah tells us in the next *āyah*. You must desire the face of Allah and His reward by spending and not hope for any kind of return for it from the one to whom you give it. Allah Almighty says: *'We do not want any repayment from you or any thanks.'* (76:9) If you desire something in exchange for it from the person you give it to then it is not for the Face of Allah. This is the case when someone follows up his spending with demands and insult. The same is also true when someone has to spend to avert harm since the one on whom he spent will owe him a favour or some similar feeling of indebtedness. He does not desire to please Allah when he does this. Allah only accepts what is given for the sake of Allah and when most of the aim is to seek that which is with Allah. It is as it is related that a desert Arab came to 'Umar ibn al-Khaṭṭāb and said:

"Umar! Charity is rewarded with the Garden.
Clothe my little daughters and their mother!
Be a protection for us against time!
I ask you by Allah to do it!'

'Umar said, 'And if I do not do it, what then?' He replied: 'Then, Abū Ḥafṣ, I will go.' He said, 'And if you go, what then?' He said:

'You will be questioned about my state
on the day when there are gifts,
In a place of standing when one will be questioned about it,
and will either go to the Fire or to the Garden.'

'Umar wept until his beard was wet and then said, 'Lad, give him this shirt of mine because of that Day, not because of his poem! By Allah, I do not own any other shirt!'

Al-Māwardī said, 'When the gift is like this, free of seeking recompense or gratitude, and free of seeking indebtedness or publicity, that is more noble for the giver and more pleasant for the one who accepts it. As for someone who gives while seeking recompense for his gift and demanding gratitude and praise, he is someone showing off, seeking reputation. These cases entail censure which negates the generosity. If someone seeks something, he is a trader looking for a profit who does not deserve praise.' Ibn 'Abbās said that the *āyah*: *'Do not give out of a desire for gain'* (74:6) means: 'Do not give a gift whereby you seek one better than it.' Ibn Zayd believed that this *āyah* was about those who do not go out in *jihād*, but give while they remain at home. The *āyah* before it is about those who go out themselves. He said, 'That is why there is a precondition for these people, but not for the first ones.' Ibn 'Aṭiyyah said, 'This statement is debatable because its arbitrary nature is evident.'

and then do not follow what they have spent by demands for gratitude or insulting words

The expression 'demands for gratitude' (*mann*) means to mention the blessing by enumerating it and rebuking the person by it, as when you say 'I was good to you', 'I restored you', 'After all I have done for you' and other such things. Some say that *manna* means to speak about what you gave so that the recipient hears about it and to insult him. *Mann* is one of the great wrong actions. That is confirmed in *Ṣaḥīḥ Muslim* and elsewhere. Someone who does that is one of the three whom Allah will not look at and whom He will not purify on the Day of Rising, and they will have a painful punishment. An-Nasā'ī related from Ibn 'Umar that the Messenger of Allah ﷺ said, 'There are three who will not enter the Garden: the one who disobeys his parents, a habitual drinker, and someone who demands gratitude for his gift.' One of the paths of transmission in Muslim has: 'someone who only gives something in order to receive gratitude for it.'

The expression '*adhā*' (insulting words) means insulting and complaining and is more general than *mann* which is mentioned because it frequently occurs. Ibn Zayd said, 'If you think that your greeting will be onerous for someone on whom you have spent desiring the Face of Allah, then do not greet him.' A woman asked him, 'Abu Usāmah, show me a man who will truly go out in the Way of Allah. They only go out for what they can get. I have arrows and a quiver.' He said, 'May Allah not bless your arrows and quiver! You have harmed them even before giving to them!' Our scholars have said that if someone spends in the Way of Allah and does not follow it by demands for gratitude or insulting words such as

'How strongly you entreat!', 'May Allah deliver us from you!' and the like, Allah has guaranteed him the reward, which is the Garden, removed fear of what is to come from Him after his death, and sorrow for what he missed of this world because he delights in His Hereafter.

They will feel no fear and will know no sorrow.

They will feel no fear for the future after death and no sorrow for what has passed of this world because they will delight in the Next World. This *āyah* also contains evidence for the excellence of the rich over the poor as will come later, Allah willing.

قَوْلٌ مَّعْرُوفٌ وَمَغْفِرَةٌ خَيْرٌ مِّن صَدَقَةٍ يَتْبَعُهَآ أَذًى وَاللَّهُ غَنِيٌّ
حَلِيمٌ ﴿٢٦٣﴾

263 Correct and courteous words accompanied by forgiveness are better than *ṣadaqah* followed by insulting words. Allah is Rich Beyond Need, All-Forbearing.

Correct and courteous words

It means that correct words are more appropriate as an-Naḥḥās and al-Mahdawī said. An-Naḥḥās said, based on an elided inceptive, that it can mean: 'That which you are commanded is to use correct and courteous words.' Words which are described as '*ma'rūf*' include making supplication, putting people at their ease and giving them hope for what is with Allah. That is better than *ṣadaqah* which is merely outward with no inward dimension, because correct words will have a reward while outward *ṣadaqah* may have no reward. The Prophet ﷺ said, 'A good word is *ṣadaqah*, and an aspect of correct behaviour is to meet your brother with a cheerful face.' Muslim transmitted it. One should meet the beggar with a smile and welcome him so that he will be thankful if you give to him and excuse you if you do not. One of the sages said, 'Meet the one with a need with a smile. Even if you miss his gratitude you will not miss his pardon.' Ibn Lankak related that Abū Bakr ibn Durayd went to a government official for something he needed and his request was not granted. The official showed some vexation, so he said:

Do not be vexed by someone who makes a request.
    It is a good thing to be seen as someone to whom requests are made.
Do not show the face of rejection to a hopeful face.
    Your might continues when you are seen as a source of hope.

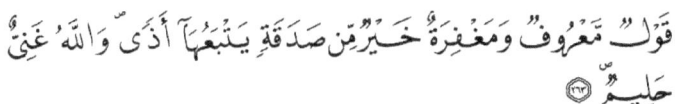

You meet the noble and show joy.
You meet the blameworthy and your frown is a guide.
Know that soon you will be reported,
So be a report that gives delight.

In the hadith of 'Umar we find that the Messenger of Allah ﷺ said, 'When a beggar asks of you, do not interrupt his request until he finishes. Then turn to him with gravity and leniency, or spend a little, or give a good reply. One who is neither human nor jinn will come to you to see what you do with what Allah has given you.'

Its proof is the hadith about the leper, the person with scabies and the blind man which Muslim and others transmitted. In that account an angel took the form of a leper, a bald man and a blind man to test the individual concerned. Bishr ibn al-Ḥārith said, 'I saw 'Alī in a dream and said, "Amīr al-Mu'minin! Tell me something by which Allah will benefit me!" he answered, "How excellent is the kindness of the Prophets to the poor out of desire for the reward of Allah Almighty, and better still is the poor escaping the rich by putting their trust in what Allah has promised." I said, "Amīr al-Mu'minin! Tell me more!" He recited:

"You were dead and then became alive,
and you soon will be dead again.
Ruin a house in the abode that is transient.
Build a house in the abode that will abide!"'

accompanied by forgiveness

This can refer to disregarding the defects and bad state of the needy. This is like the case of the desert Arab who begged from people with eloquent language. Someone asked him, 'Where are you from?' He answered, 'O Allah, forgiveness! It is an evil earning that it is denied because of lineage!' It is also said that its meaning is that to excuse a beggar when he is insistent, rude and harsh is better than giving him *ṣadaqah* with demands of gratitude and insults. An-Naqqāsh said something to that effect. An-Naḥḥās said, 'This is a problem explained by the desert Arab.'

The words '*better than ṣadaqah*' mean, and Allah knows best, that an action that leads to forgiveness is better than *ṣadaqah* followed by insulting words. It can be like your words, 'Allah's graciousness to you is greater than *ṣadaqah* by which gratitude is intended.' So Allah's forgiveness is better than this sort of *ṣadaqah*.

Allah is Rich Beyond Need, All-Forbearing.

Allah is Rich beyond need of the *ṣadaqah* of his slaves. He orders them to do it so that He can reward them for it. An aspect of His Forbearance is that He does not hasten the punishment to the one who insults when he gives *ṣadaqah*.

يَٰٓأَيُّهَا ٱلَّذِينَ ءَامَنُواْ لَا تُبْطِلُواْ صَدَقَٰتِكُم بِٱلْمَنِّ وَٱلْأَذَىٰ كَٱلَّذِى
يُنفِقُ مَالَهُۥ رِئَآءَ ٱلنَّاسِ وَلَا يُؤْمِنُ بِٱللَّهِ وَٱلْيَوْمِ ٱلْءَاخِرِ فَمَثَلُهُۥ
كَمَثَلِ صَفْوَانٍ عَلَيْهِ تُرَابٌ فَأَصَابَهُۥ وَابِلٌ فَتَرَكَهُۥ صَلْدًا لَّا
يَقْدِرُونَ عَلَىٰ شَىْءٍ مِّمَّا كَسَبُواْ وَٱللَّهُ لَا يَهْدِى ٱلْقَوْمَ ٱلْكَٰفِرِينَ ﴿٢٦٤﴾

264 You who believe! do not nullify your *ṣadaqah* by demands for gratitude or insulting words, like him who spends his wealth, showing off to people and not believing in Allah and the Last Day. His likeness is that of a smooth rock coated with soil, which, when heavy rain falls on it, is left stripped bare. They have no power over anything they have earned. Allah does not guide disbelieving people.

You who believe! do not nullify your *ṣadaqah* by demands for gratitude or insulting words,

This tells us that Allah does not accept *ṣadaqah* which is marred in this way and that the reward for it is made null and void. What is referred to is *ṣadaqah* by which gratitude and insults are meant. It is an article of faith that, in general, evil deeds do not invalidate good deeds or cancel them out. Demands for gratitude and insults do not invalidate other *ṣadaqah* which has been made without them. The majority of scholars say that it is only the *ṣadaqah* Allah knows has been used to impose gratitude or used as an insult that is not accepted. It is said that Allah appoints an angel over the giver who does not register that. This is good.

The Arabs say of someone who demands gratitude, that he has 'a black hand'. When he gives without being asked, he has 'a white hand'. If someone gives after being asked, he has 'a green hand'. One of the eloquent said, 'Whoever expects gratitude for charity has lost gratitude. If someone admires his deeds, his reward is lost.' A poet said:

I borrowed from a friend of mine.
	I was slow in repaying him and he was hostile to me.

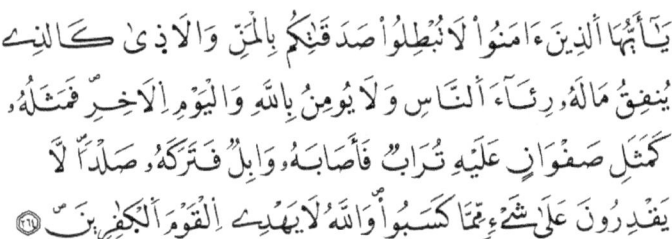

When he was certain that time was fighting me,
he showed regret in his dealing with me.

Someone else said:

You corrupted the good that you gave by seeking thanks.
When a generous person gives, he does not seek thanks.

Abū Bakr al-Warrāq spoke well when he said:

The very best of good at every time and moment
is a gift which is free of seeking gratitude.

Ibn Sīrīn heard one man say to another, 'I did this and that for you!' He told him, 'Be quiet! There is no good in charity which is counted.' The Prophet ﷺ said, 'Beware of demanding gratitude for charity. It invalidates thankfulness and erases the reward.' Then he recited this *āyah*.

Our scholars say that, on the basis of this *āyah*, Mālik disliked a man giving his obligatory *zakāt* to his relatives in case he might be praised in return for it or they might feel the need to show gratitude to him and recompense him for it. Then it would not be sincerely for the Face of Allah. He preferred it to be given to non-relatives and also preferred that someone other than the giver should undertake to distribute it, if there is no ruler to do so, to prevent the danger of demands for gratitude or insults, and that of praise, or recompense by service from the recipient. This is not the case with *ṣadaqah* because, even its if reward is nullified, he is safe from any threat and is just like someone who has not done anything. When the obligatory is nullified, he is threatened about something he has failed to do.

like him who spends his wealth, showing off to people and not believing in Allah and the Last Day.

Allah likens someone who demands gratitude and inflicts insults through his *ṣadaqah* to someone who spends to show off to people, not for the Face of Allah, and to an unbeliever who spends so that people will say that he is generous and praise him for it.

His likeness is that of a smooth rock coated with soil, which, when heavy rain falls on it, is left stripped bare.

Then this person is likened to a smooth rock covered with soil. One would think, to look at it, that it is fertile, good earth but then the rain comes and washes it away and all that is left is bare rock. That is a metaphor for someone who gives in order to show off. His intention of seeking gratitude, insult and showing off will be disclosed in the Next World and the act of *ṣadaqah* will be null and void, in the same way that the heavy rain exposes the smooth stone. *Ṣafwān* is a large smooth stone. It is said that what is meant is that any person who spends to show off is, like an unbeliever, not rewarded because he does not intend the Face of Allah by his act so as to merit the reward, even if he gives multiple times, and so the excellence of the action is voided. It is said that the reward is nullified from the moment he demands gratitude or behaves insultingly. What was before that is written for him and multiplied. Then the insult stops the multiplication because *ṣadaqah* grows and grows until it is as big as a mountain. When it leaves his hand sincerely in the prescribed manner, it is multiplied, but when gratitude it sought by it or an insult made, it stops there and the multiplication is cut off. The first position, however, is more evident, and Allah knows best.

Ṣafwān is the plural and *ṣafwānah* is the singular. Al-Akhfash said that. Some have said that *ṣafwān* is a singular. Al-Kisā'ī said that *ṣafwān* is a singular and its plural is *ṣifwān*, *ṣufiyy* or *ṣifiyy*. Al-Mubarrad, however, denied that and said that *ṣifiyy* is the plural of *ṣafā*. From this comes *ṣafwā'* and *ṣafā* (stones). Sa'īd ibn al-Musayyab and az-Zuhrī recited it as *ṣafawān*, which is a dialectical usage. Quṭrub recited *ṣifwān*. An-Naḥḥās said that *ṣafwān* and *ṣifwān* can be either plural or singular, although it is more likely to be singular since Allah uses the singular *hā'* in referring to it. It is still permitted to mention the plural, but a thing is only removed from its normal place by a definitive proof. As for what al-Kisā'ī related about the plural, it is not sound based on true investigation, but *ṣifwān* is the plural of *ṣafā* which means *ṣafwān*. This is like *waral* and *wirlān*, *akh* and *ikhwān*, and *karā* and *kirwān*.

Wābil is heavy rain. The verb *wabala* is used when it rains heavily. The earth which receives it is described as *mawbūlah*. Corroborating that meaning are Allah's words: '*We seized him with terrible severity* (wabīl).' (73:16) A blow or a punishment described as *wabīl* is severe. *Ṣald* is smooth stone. Al-Kisā'ī said that the verb is *ṣalida*. *Ṣald* is any part of the earth on which no plants grow. It describes the forehead where no hair grows. An-Naqqāsh said that *aṣlad* means 'stripped' in the dialect of Hudhayl.

They have no power

This refers to those who show off, unbelievers and those who demand gratitude.

over anything they have earned.

This means that they will not reap the reward of their spending. What they give is simply considered as something they spend for their own needs since it is for other than Allah. Spending is called 'earning' because they intend earning by it. It is said that this is a metaphor for the nullifying of the reward of those who show off in their giving and the voiding of the excellence of the giving of those who look for gratitude or who cause harm by it. Al-Māwardī mentioned that.

وَمَثَلُ ٱلَّذِينَ يُنفِقُونَ أَمْوَٰلَهُمُ ٱبْتِغَآءَ مَرْضَاتِ ٱللَّهِ وَتَثْبِيتًا مِّنْ أَنفُسِهِمْ
كَمَثَلِ جَنَّةٍۭ بِرَبْوَةٍ أَصَابَهَا وَابِلٌ فَـَٔاتَتْ أُكُلَهَا ضِعْفَيْنِ فَإِن لَّمْ
يُصِبْهَا وَابِلٌ فَطَلٌّ ۗ وَٱللَّهُ بِمَا تَعْمَلُونَ بَصِيرٌ ٢٦٥

265 The metaphor of those who spend their wealth, desiring the pleasure of Allah and firmness for themselves, is that of a garden on a hillside. When heavy rain falls on it, it doubles its produce; and if heavy rain does not fall, there is dew. Allah sees what you do.

The metaphor of those who spend their wealth, desiring the pleasure of Allah and firmness for themselves,

Ibtighā' (desiring) is a causative object and '*tathbīt*' (firmness) is conjoined to it. Makkī said that both '*tathbīt*' (firmness) and 'desiring' are causative objects. Ibn 'Aṭiyyah says that it is not, because spending does not 'make firm' and so *tathbīt* cannot be a causative object and, in fact, *ibtighā'* (desiring) is a verbal noun used adverbially. Allah mentions the *ṣadaqah* of those who gain nothing from their *ṣadaqah* and forbade the believers to vitiate their *ṣadaqah* like that in any way. He mentions the spending of the people whose *ṣadaqah* is pure since it is given in keeping with the commands of the *Sharī'ah.*

The word *ibtighā'* means 'seeking' and '*marḍāt'* (pleasure) is the verbal noun from the verb *raḍā*, to please. It is said that the word *tathbīt* means that they confirm where they should give their *ṣadaqah*. Mujāhid and al-Ḥasan said that. Al-Ḥasan said, 'When a man wants to give *ṣadaqah*, he "confirms" it by examining himself. If it is truly for Allah, he should give it. If it is mixed with doubt, he should refrain from doing so.' It is said that it means to confirm it and be certain about it, as Ibn 'Abbās said. Ibn 'Abbās and Qatādah also said that it means examining their own motives. Ash-Sha'bī, as-Suddī, Qatādah, Ibn Zayd, Abū Ṣāliḥ and others said that it means to make certain, in other words they should look into themselves and confirm that their spending is out of obedience to Allah. These three positions are more correct than that of al-Ḥasan and Mujāhid who both believed that '*tathbīt*' is a verbal noun not based on another verbal noun. Ibn 'Aṭiyyah said that this is only allowed when mentioning the verbal noun and it is made clear by a prior use of verb as we see elsewhere in the Qur'an as in 71:17 and 73:8. If there is no mention of the verb first, then you cannot use the verbal noun with other than its meaning. Ibn 'Aṭiyyah said, 'This is the pathway taken in Arabic as far as I know.' An-Naḥḥās said, 'If it had been as Mujāhid says, it would be *tathabbut* from *tathabbata*. The statement of Qatādah about it being examination is not known, although it can be meant that their selves are firm and examined. This is unlikely.' The position of ash-Sha'bī is good: it means making it firm in themselves that they are spending that to obey Allah. One uses the verb *thabbata* to refer to someone verifying his resolve and strengthening his opinion. So here they are certain of Allah's promise to make them firm in that. It is also said that it means to affirm that Allah makes them firm in themselves that they will have the reward for that, which is not the case with a hypocrite who does not expect a reward.

is that of a garden on a hillside.

A '*jannah*' (garden) is a piece of land with trees which shade it, taken from the linguistic root which means 'to cover and conceal'. The word '*rubwah*' (hillside) indicates a slightly elevated place which usually has a thick layer of good earth and is very fertile, which is why it is mentioned. Ibn 'Aṭiyyah said, '*Riyāḍ al-Ḥazan* is not being referred to here as aṭ-Ṭabarī claims. Rather those are the meadows ascribed to Najd because they are the best meadows of Tihāmah. The plants of Najd are fragrant and are called *abrad* and *araqq*. Najd is called *Ḥazan* (sorrow). Sometimes the air of Tihāmah is only good at night. That is why the desert Arabs say, 'My spouse is like the night of Tihāmah.' As-Suddī said that it is at a *rabāwah*, and that means the lower ground.' Ibn 'Aṭiyyah said, 'This is an undetermined expression because *rubwah* is derived from *rabā*, which is to grow.'

What as-Suddī said is of no consequence because the Arabic root *r-b-w* means 'increase' in Arabic. It is used for asthma (*rabw*), when the breath is short, and it is also used generally for being short of breath. Al-Farrā' mentions about '*He seized them in an ever-tightening grip* (rābiyah)' (69:9) that it means 'increasing'. *Arbā* is to give more. The verb is also used for growing up among a people.

Al-Khalīl also says that *rubwah* is an elevated place which Allah singled out because the water does not flood such a place as frequently happens with flash floods in Arab lands. So it is a situation that they like. Ibn 'Abbās said that it is an elevated place through which rivers do not flow because Allah mentioned heavy rain in a manner that indicates that there is no running water there. It does not mean there cannot be running water because elsewhere Allah mentions, *'a mountainside (*rabwah*) where there was a meadow and a flowing spring.'* (23:50) What is known in Arabic is that it is an elevated place, whether or not there is flowing water there.

'Rubwah' (hillside) has five dialectal forms. *'Rubwah'* is the *qirā'ah* of Ibn Kathīr, Ḥamzah, al-Kisā'ī, Nāfi' and Abū 'Amr. 'Āṣim, Ibn 'Āmir and al-Ḥasan have *'rabwah'*. *'Ribwah'* is the reading of Ibn 'Abbās and Abū Isḥāq as-Sabī'ī. *'Rabāwah'* is the reading of Abū Ja'far an Abū 'Abd ar-Raḥmān. This form is found in a poem. *'Ribāwah'* is the reading of al-Ashhab al-'Aqīlī. Al-Farrā' said that one says *rabāwah* and *ribāwah* and all are from *rābiyah* and the verb is *rabā', yarbū*.

When heavy rain falls on it, it doubles its produce; and if heavy rain does not fall, there is dew.

'It' is the hillside. *Wābil* is heavy rain. A poet said:

There are none of the meadows of Ḥazan with green grass
on which heavy rain (*wābil*) falls.

Ukul (produce) is the fruit which is eaten. The same word is used in 14:25. It is also used for anything that is eaten. *Uklah* is a morsel. The hadith in Muslim describes the reward for every morsel a husband puts in his wife's mouth using the word *'uklah'*. Here it is ascribed to the garden to make it specific, like the saddle of a horse or the door of a house.

Nāfi', Ibn Kathīr and Abū 'Amr recite *'uklahā'*. That is the case with all that is attributed to something feminine. 'Āṣim, Ibn 'Āmir, Ḥamzah and al-Kisā'ī distinguish it when it is ascribed to something masculine, as in 6:141 (*ukuluhu*), and when it is not ascribed as in 36:16 (*ukulin*). Abū 'Āṣim makes that heavy while the other two lighten it [of the middle vowel]. 'Āṣim, Ibn 'Āmir, Ḥamzah and al-Kisā'ī recite it with full pronunciation in all we mentioned. It is also said that *ukl* and *ukul* mean the same.

The verb 'double' means that it gives twice the amount of fruit produced by other land. One of the scholars said that means it bears fruit twice in a year. The first view is the more frequently cited one, meaning that it produces in one year what other lands produce in two years.

Mentioning dew continues the praise of the land because dew is enough moisture for it on account of its excellent soil and it still produces double. That is because of the fine nature and good quality of the soil. Al-Mubarrad and others said that it implies that dew is enough for it. Az-Zajjāj says that it is the dew that forms on it. The word for 'dew' (*ṭall*) can mean drizzle or light rain which is very fine. Ibn 'Abbās and others said that and it is a well-known meaning for the word. Others, including Mujāhid, said that it means dew here. Ibn 'Aṭiyyah says that it is metaphorical. An-Naḥḥās said that linguists say the verbs are *wabala* and *awbala*, and *ṭalla* and *aṭalla*. According to *aṣ-Ṣiḥāḥ*: '*Ṭall* is the weakest form of rain and the plural of *ṭilāl*.' Al-Māwardī said, 'Crops watered by dew are weaker than those watered by rain and are less plentiful, but even if they are less, they are more cohesive and beneficial.' Some of them said that there is a change in the normal order and it means: like a garden on a hillside watered by heavy rain, and if heavy rain does not fall on it, then there is dew and it produces its produce twice over, meaning that the leaves of the garden are green and it produces a bumper crop.

The first interpretation is more correct and there is no need for a change in order. So the Almighty likens the growth of the spending of those sincere people whose *ṣadaqah* Allah causes to grow, in the same way that a foal or young camel grows, like the plants in a garden on such a hillside grow. It is not like smooth stone whose earth is stripped from it so that it remains bare. Muslim and others transmitted from Abū Hurayrah that the Prophet ﷺ said, 'No one gives a rightfully earned date as *ṣadaqah* without Allah taking it in His right hand and making it grow as one of you would raise a foal or young camel, until it is like a mountain or larger still.' It is also transmitted in the *Muwaṭṭā'*.

Allah sees what you do.

This is both a promise and a threat. Az-Zuhrī recited this with a *yā'* (they do) as if it means all people or only the hypocrites. In that case, it is a pure threat.

أَيَوَدُّ أَحَدُكُمْ أَن تَكُونَ لَهُۥ جَنَّةٌ مِّن نَّخِيلٍ وَأَعْنَابٍ تَجْرِي مِن تَحْتِهَا ٱلْأَنْهَٰرُ لَهُۥ فِيهَا مِن كُلِّ ٱلثَّمَرَٰتِ وَأَصَابَهُ ٱلْكِبَرُ وَلَهُۥ ذُرِّيَّةٌ ضُعَفَآءُ فَأَصَابَهَآ إِعْصَارٌ فِيهِ نَارٌ فَٱحْتَرَقَتْ ۗ كَذَٰلِكَ يُبَيِّنُ ٱللَّهُ لَكُمُ ٱلْءَايَٰتِ لَعَلَّكُمْ تَتَفَكَّرُونَ ۝

266 Would any of you like to have a garden of dates and grapes, with rivers flowing underneath and containing all kinds of fruits, then to be stricken with old age and have children who are weak, and then for a fierce whirlwind containing fire to come and strike it so that it goes up in flames? In this way Allah makes His Signs clear to you, so that hopefully you will reflect.

Would any of you like to have a garden of dates and grapes, with rivers flowing underneath

Aṭ-Ṭabarī related from as-Suddī that this *āyah* is a metaphor of spending for the sake of showing off to others. It is related from Ibn 'Abbās: 'This is an example Allah made of those who show off by their actions which will then be nullified on the Day of Rising when they will be most in need of them. They are like a man who has a garden and children who cannot help him. He becomes old and then a firestorm strikes his garden and burns it up, leaving him absolutely destitute.' It is related that Ibn Zayd recited: *'You who believe! do not nullify your* ṣadaqah *by demands for gratitude or insulting words'* (2:264) and then said, 'Then Allah made an example of that and said: *'Would any of you like…'*

Ibn 'Aṭiyyah said, 'This is clearer than what aṭ-Ṭabarī preferred. This *āyah* is not another example of spending to show off because of the context in which it occurs. As for the meaning in this context, it is a metaphor of the state of every hypocrite or unbeliever who does an action which he supposes to be good. Then comes the moment of need and he finds it was nothing.'

It is related from Ibn 'Abbās that it is a metaphor for those who act for the sake of other than Allah, and the hypocrites and unbelievers, as will come, even though we find something else stated in *Ṣaḥīḥ al-Bukhārī.* Al-Bukhārī transmitted from 'Ubayd ibn 'Umayr that one day 'Umar ibn al-Khaṭṭāb asked the Companions of the Prophet, quoting this *āyah*, 'About what was this *āyah* related?' They replied, 'Allah and His Messenger know best.' 'Umar became angry and said. 'Say: "We know" or "We do not know!"' Ibn 'Abbās said, 'I know something about it, Amīr al-Mu'minīn.' He said, 'Nephew, speak and do not undervalue yourself.' Ibn 'Abbās said, 'It is a metaphor about action.' 'Umar asked, 'What action?' Ibn 'Abbās replied, 'The action of a rich man who works in obedience to Allah and then Allah sends a *shayṭān* to him and he does acts of disobedience until his good actions are burned up.' One variant has, 'When his life is over and term is near, he seals it with the actions of the wretched.' 'Umar was pleased with that interpretation.

Ibn Abī Mulaykah related this *āyah* and said, 'This is a metaphor of a human being who does righteous actions until the end of his life when he needs his actions and then does bad actions.' Ibn 'Aṭiyyah said, 'This is speculative. The *āyah* can be taken to mean all that its words convey.' Mujāhid, Qatādah, ar-Rabī' and others said the like of that. Palm trees and grapes are mentioned because of their honour and excellence over other trees. Al-Ḥasan recited '*jannāt*' in the plural.

containing all kinds of fruits

This means that it does not lack any kind of fruit.

and then for a fierce whirlwind containing fire to come and strike it

Al-Ḥasan says that this means a wind which is intensely cold. Az-Zajjāj said that it is the strong wind which throws the soil into the sky like pillars, which is called a whirlwind. Al-Jawharī said that a 'whirlwind' (Zawba'ah) is one of the leaders of the jinn which is why that is the name for a whirlwind. It is also said that it is a wind that raises a cloud containing thunder and lightning. Al-Mahdawī said that it is called (*i'ṣār*) because it wraps around like a garment is wrung (*'uṣira*). Ibn 'Aṭiyyah said that this is weak.

I say that it is sound because it is physically witnessed. It rises like a twisting pillar. It is said that the wind is called *i'ṣār* because it presses the clouds, and the clouds are pressed (*mu'ṣirāt*) either because they carry [rain], like a young girl who is ready to menstruate but has not yet done so, or because they are pressed by the winds. Ibn Sīdah said that some people say that *mu'ṣirāt* are the winds rather than the clouds. Ibn Zayd said that *i'ṣār* is a fierce wind and strong simoom. Ibn 'Aṭiyyah said, 'That is either in intense heat or intense cold. All of that is from the exhaling of and breathing of Hell as we find in the words of the Prophet ﷺ: "When it is very hot, wait for the prayer until it cools. Intense heat is from the exhaling of Hell," and "The Fire complained to its Lord…"'

It is related from Ibn 'Abbās and others that this is a metaphor made by Allah of unbelievers and hypocrites, like a man who plants a garden which has an abundance of fruits and then becomes old and has weak children, boys and girls, and his livelihood and that of his children comes from that garden. Then Allah sends a wind containing fire on the garden which burns it up. He lacks the strength to rework the garden and his sons have no wealth with which to help their father. That is also the case with unbelievers and hypocrites when they come to Allah Almighty on the Day of Rising. They will not have another chance to be revived and go back a second time, just as the man with the garden cannot replant his garden a second time. Nothing can help him at that time of his old age and the weakness of his children.

In this way Allah makes His Signs clear to you, so that hopefully you will reflect.

It means: 'so that you will refer to My immensity and lordship and not take other than Me as protectors.' Ibn 'Abbās said: '…so that you might reflect on the vanishing and annihilation of this world and the coming and everlasting nature of the Next World.'

يَٰٓأَيُّهَا ٱلَّذِينَ ءَامَنُوٓا۟ أَنفِقُوا۟ مِن طَيِّبَٰتِ مَا كَسَبْتُمْ وَمِمَّآ أَخْرَجْنَا لَكُم مِّنَ
ٱلْأَرْضِ ۖ وَلَا تَيَمَّمُوا۟ ٱلْخَبِيثَ مِنْهُ تُنفِقُونَ وَلَسْتُم بِـَٔاخِذِيهِ إِلَّآ
أَن تُغْمِضُوا۟ فِيهِ ۚ وَٱعْلَمُوٓا۟ أَنَّ ٱللَّهَ غَنِىٌّ حَمِيدٌ ﴿٢٦٧﴾

267 You who believe! give away some of the good things you have earned and some of what the earth produces for you. Do not have recourse to bad things when you give, things you would only take with your eyes tight shut! Know that Allah is Rich Beyond Need, Praiseworthy.

You who believe! give away some of the good things you have earned

This is addressed to the entire Community of Muhammad ﷺ. Scholars disagree about what is meant by giving here. ʿAlī ibn Abī Ṭālib, ʿAbīdah as-Salmānī and Ibn Sīrīn said that it refers to the obligatory *zakāt*. In the *āyah* Allah forbids people to use bad things to pay it rather than good. Ibn ʿAṭiyyah stated that the position of al-Barāʾ ibn ʿĀzib, al-Ḥasan and Qatādah is that the *āyah* is about voluntary *ṣadaqah*. They recommended that people should only give good property. The *āyah* is general to both ideas but, in the case of *zakāt*, it is connected to an actual command, and, as the command is mandatory, it means that it is, therefore, forbidden to pay *zakāt* with bad property. That command is particular to the obligatory duty.

As for voluntary giving, a person can give a little, and so give what is less in value. A dirham is better than a date. The people who believe that it is a recommendation say that the imperative is as suitable for the recommendation as it is for the command. It is as forbidden to give bad quality in voluntary charity as it is in what is obligatory. Allah is more entitled to receive the best. Al-Barāʾ related that a man hung up a bunch of poor quality dates and the Messenger of Allah ﷺ saw it and said, 'An evil hanging,' and the *āyah* was revealed. At-Tirmidhī transmitted the full report. The command, according to this, is a recommendation to only give what is good. Most commentators state that 'good things' means things of high quality and which are favoured by people. Ibn Zayd said that it means from what is lawful earning.

Earning can be by physical toil, which is working for a wage, the rulings governing which will be dealt with later, or by trade, which is buying and selling. Inheritance is included in this because, although the heir did not earn it, someone else did. Sahl ibn ʿAbdullāh mentioned that Ibn al-Mubārak was asked about a man who wants to earn and intends by his earning to maintain his ties of kinship, do *jihād*, do good deeds and to engage in the pitfalls of earning for this reason. He said, 'If he has enough livelihood to spare himself from asking people, then leaving this is better because when he seeks the lawful and spends it in a lawful way, he will be asked about it and his earning and his spending. Leaving that is *zuhd*, for *zuhd* consists in leaving what is *ḥalāl*.'

Ibn Khuwayzimandād said, 'According to this *āyah*, it is permitted for a parent to consume some of their child's earnings. That is because the Prophet ﷺ said, "Your children are part of your good earning. Eat from the property of your children with good cheer."'

and some of what the earth produces for you.

This includes plants, mineral wealth and treasure. These three categories are included in this phrase. As for plants, ad-Dāraquṭnī related that 'Ā'ishah said, 'The Sunnah of the Messenger of Allah ﷺ is that there is no *zakāt* on less than five *wasqs*.' A *wasq* is sixty *ṣā'*s, so that makes three hundred *ṣā'*s of wheat, barley, dates and raisins. There is no *zakāt* on vegetables produced by the earth. Some of the Ḥanafīs argue by the words here that the ruling is general to both a little and a lot of all varieties of what the earth produces and believe, by the literal understanding, that *zakāt* on vegetables is, therefore, mandatory. This will be fully dealt with in *Sūrat al-An'ām* (6).

As for minerals, the Imams related from Abū Hurayrah that the Messenger of Allah ﷺ said, 'There is no penalty for a wound inflicted by a dumb beast. There is no penalty for an injury due to a well and no penalty for an injury due to a mine. There is a fifth due on treasure.' Our scholars say that since the Prophet ﷺ said, 'A fifth due on treasure,' that indicates that the ruling for minerals is not the same as that for treasure because the Prophet ﷺ distinguished between minerals and treasure. Allah knows best.

The linguistic root of '*rikāz*' (buried treasure) is something that is 'placed' (*irtakaza*) in the earth: like gold, silver and gems. That is what most of the *fuqahā'* say because they maintain that what is rare of minerals found embedded in the earth obtained without work, effort or toil, that there is a fifth due on it because it is *rikāz*. It is related from Mālik that the ruling of the rare case when minerals are extracted without work is the same as that when work is required to extract minerals in the form of buried treasure. The first view mentioned is his final position, and the majority of *fuqahā'* give that ruling.

'Abdullāh ibn Sa'īd ibn Abī Sa'īd al-Maqburī related from his father from his grandfather that Abū Hurayrah said, 'The Messenger of Allah ﷺ was asked about *rikāz* and said, "It is the gold which Allah created in the earth on the day when He created the heavens and the earth."' 'Abdullāh ibn Sa'īd said that the hadith is *matrūk* (not acted upon). Ibn Abī Ḥātim mentioned that. It is related by another path from Abū Hurayrah which is not sound and which was mentioned by ad-Dāraquṭnī. There is no disagreement that things buried in the time of Jāhiliyyah are considered as treasure. If it was buried during the time of Islam, it is classified as a find.

There is disagreement about the discovery of buried treasure. Mālik says, 'Buried treasure that was buried during the Jāhiliyyah and is found in the land of the Arabs or the wilderness in territory owned by the Muslims without fighting belongs to the one who finds it and he owes a fifth on it. What is found in Muslim territory is like a find. What is found in land taken by conquest belongs to the group who conquered it rather than just the one who found it. What is found in lands obtained by treaty belongs to the people of that land rather than people in general. The finder has nothing of it unless he is one of the people of that abode. In that case, it belongs to him rather than them.' It is also said that it belongs to the people with the treaty. Ismā'īl said that the ruling of buried treasure is the same as that of booty which is that it is property belonging to an unbeliever that a Muslim has found. Therefore he is in the position of someone who fights and seizes property: so he has four-fifths of it.

Ibn al-Qāsim said, 'Mālik used to say that there is a fifth due on goods, gems, iron, lead and the like that are found as buried treasure. Then he retracted that and said, "I do not think that there is anything due on it." His final position expressed to us was that there was a fifth due on it.' That is sound based on the general meaning of the hadith and it is also the position of most *fuqahā'*.

Abū Ḥanīfah and Muḥammad said that buried treasure found in a house belongs to the owner of the house rather than the finder and there is a fifth due on it. Abū Yūsuf disagreed with him and said that it belongs to the finder rather than the owner of the house. The position of ath-Thawrī is that when it is found in the wilderness, it all belongs to the finder and there is a fifth due on it. They do not distinguish between land taken by fighting and land obtained by treaty. They also think that the ruling is the same in Arab or other lands. They believe that it is permitted for its finder to keep the fifth for himself if he is needy, and he can also give it to the poor. Some of the people of Madīnah and followers of Mālik do not make a distinction regarding any of that. They said that it is the same whether the buried treasure is found in land taken by fighting or land obtained by treaty, Arab land or abode of war, when no one has ownership and no one claims it: it goes to the finder and a fifth is due on it, based on the general wording of the hadith. That is the view of al-Layth, 'Abdullāh ibn Nāfi', ash-Shāfi'ī and most scholars.

There is disagreement about ores that are found and then mined. Mālik and his people say that there is nothing due on gold or silver that is mined until it reaches twenty *mithqāl*s of gold or five *ūqiyyah*s of silver. When it reaches that amount, then *zakāt* is owed on it. Anything that exceeds that is accounted according to that as long as the mine is producing. When it stops and then there is another lode that produces, *zakāt* then begins there anew.

They consider buried treasure to be like a crop from which *zakāt* is taken immediately and is not delayed for a year. Saḥnūn said about a man who has mines that what is found in one mine is not added to another and *zakāt* is only taken from two hundred dirhams or twenty dinars on each mine. Muḥammad ibn Maslamah said that they are added together and *zakāt* is paid on the total as is the case with crops. Abū Ḥanīfah and his people said that a mine is like buried treasure. Any gold or silver after the fifth has been paid is considered according to each of them. If someone obtains the amount on which *zakāt* is obliged, he pays *zakāt* on it when he still possesses the *niṣāb* after a full year. This is when he does not already have gold or silver on which *zakāt* is owed. If he already has that on which *zakāt* is obliged, then the new gold or silver is added to that and he pays *zakāt* on it. They believe that that is the case with every profit which is added to the *niṣāb* in the year in the same category: *zakāt* is paid based on the year of the principal. That is the view of ath-Thawrī.

Al-Muzanī mentioned that ash-Shāfi'ī said, 'My position regarding it is that it is what is produced from mines.' Al-Muzanī said, 'What is most appropriate is that the principle is that what mines produce is profit on which *zakāt* is paid a year after it is produced.' Al-Layth ibn Sa'd said, 'Any gold and silver which mines produce is in the position of profit on which a new year begins.' That is the view of ash-Shāfi'ī in what al-Muzanī deduced from his school. That is the position of Dāwūd and his people when a year has passed over it in the sound possession of its owner based on the words of the Prophet ﷺ: 'If someone obtains property, there is no *zakāt* on it until he has had it for a year.' At-Tirmidhī and ad-Dāraquṭnī transmitted it.

They also argue by what 'Abd ar-Raḥmān ibn An'am related from Abū Sa'īd al-Khudrī when the Prophet ﷺ gave some of those whose hearts were to be reconciled some good ore which 'Alī had sent from Yemen. Ash-Shāfi'ī said, 'Those whose hearts are to be reconciled have a right to *zakāt*. By that it is clear that the custom on mines is the custom of *zakāt*.' The argument of Mālik is based on the hadith of Rabī'ah ibn 'Abd ar-Raḥmān which states that the Prophet ﷺ granted to Bilāl ibn al-Ḥārith the mines of al-Qabaliyyah which were in a region of al-Fur'. Up until today those mines only have *zakāt* taken from them. The *isnād* of this hadith is broken and the people of hadith do not take something like that as being authoritative, but it was the normative practice which was followed in Madīnah. Ad-Darāwardī related it from Rabī'ah ibn al-Ḥārith ibn Bilāl al-Muzanī from his father. Al-Bazzar mentioned it. Kathīr ibn 'Abdullāh ibn 'Amr ibn 'Awf related from his father from his grandfather from the Prophet ﷺ that he gave a grant of the mines of al-Qabaliyyah, above and below ground, to Bilāl ibn al-Ḥārith. This is the ruling on what the earth produces. In *an-Naḥl* we will deal with what the sea produces since it is the partner of the earth. In *al-Anbiyā'* we will discuss the meaning of the hadith which says: 'There is no penalty for a wound inflicted by a dumb beast.'

Do not have recourse to bad things when you give,

'*Tayammamū*' means to aim for something. The *āyah* indicates that earnings can be good or bad. In an-Nasā'ī it is related from Abū Umāmah ibn Sahl ibn Ḥunayf that these words refer to bad quality dates. The Messenger of Allah ﷺ forbade this type of dates being taken in payment of *zakāt*. Ad-Dāraquṭnī related Abū Umāmah ibn Sahl ibn Ḥunayf that his father said, 'The Messenger of Allah ﷺ commanded that *ṣadaqah* be given, and a man brought bunches of bad quality dates. The Messenger of Allah ﷺ said, 'Who has brought this?' Normally no one brought anything without it being attributed to him. Then it was revealed: *'Do not have recourse to bad things when you give.'* He said, 'The Prophet ﷺ forbade that *ju'rūr* and *ḥubayq* (inferior quality dates) be taken in payment of *zakāt*.' Az-Zuhrī said that they are two types of dates in Madīnah. At-Tirmidhī transmitted it from al-Barā' and said that it is sound.

Aṭ-Ṭabarī and an-Naḥḥās related that 'Abdullāh recited '*ta'ammamū*'. It is a dialectical form. Muslim ibn Jundub recited '*tuyammimū*'. Ibn Kathīr recited '*ittayammamū*' with a double *tā'*. There are various dialectical forms of the word: '*amamtu*' and '*ammamtu*', '*yammamtu*' and '*tayammamtu*'. Abū Amr related that Ibn Mas'ūd recited '*walā tu'ammimū*' with a *hamzah*.

Al-Jurjānī said in *Naẓm al-Qur'ān* that a group of people said that the words end at 'bad things' and then a new sentence begins which describes them: 'you give things you would only take with your eyes tight shut.' It is as if the meaning is to blame and censure people. The pronoun in '*minhu*' refers to the bad things. He said that another group say the speech is connected to '*minhu*' and so the pronoun refers to '*you have earned*'.

things you would only take with your eyes tight shut!

This refers to things you would only take in payment from people if you were making things easy for them and forgoing your rights: they are things you dislike and are not pleased with. So when a debt to Allah is involved, do not give what you would not be pleased to take for yourselves. Al-Barā', Ibn 'Abbās and aḍ-Ḍaḥḥāk stated that. Al-Ḥasan said that the meaning is things you would not take, if you found them being sold in the market, unless their price was reduced. Something similar is also related from 'Alī. Ibn 'Aṭiyyah said, 'These two statements are similar inasmuch as they are both about *zakāt*.'

Ibn al-'Arabī said, 'If the *āyah* had been about obligatory *zakāt*, Allah would not say, "*you would only take*", because bad or defective things are not permitted to be taken in *zakāt* in any case, not with the eyes shut or by overlooking them. Such things can be taken while lowering the eyes in supererogatory *ṣadaqah*.' Al-Barā' ibn 'Āzib also said that it means: 'You would not take it if you had been given it except with your eyes shut,' meaning that you would be embarrassed before the giver and would accept it from him although you have no need of it and consider it to be of no value.' Ibn 'Aṭiyyah said, 'This is consonant with the *āyah* being about voluntary charity.' Ibn Zayd said, 'You would not take the unlawful unless you shut your eyes to its disliked nature.'

The majority recitation is '*tughmiḍū*' from the verb *aghmaḍa* which is used for when a man affects to be easy about something and overlooks in it and is satisfied to take only part of his due. Part of that is what aṭ-Ṭirimmāḥ said:

People did not wake us for the *witr* and humility.
They are content with closing their eyes to it.

It is possible that it comes from shutting the eyes (*taghmīḍ*) because someone who wants to be patient with something disliked closes his eyes. He said:

How many things will you show me
which I disregard (*ughanniḍu*) even though I am not blind to them!

This is ignoring what is disliked. An-Naqqāsh mentioned this meaning for the *āyah* and Makkī indicated it. The Arabs say, '*aghmaḍa-r-rajulu*' when a man ignores something. This sort of derivation is frequent. Az-Zuhrī recited '*taghmiḍū*' and also '*tughammiḍū*'. The first means: 'you ignore the offer from the seller so that he lowers it for you.' The second, which is the reading of Qatādah according to what an-Naḥḥās mentioned, means: 'you take it for less'. Abū 'Amr ad-Dānī said that the meaning of both readings of az-Zuhrī is that 'you take it for less.' Makkī related from al-Ḥasan '*tughammaḍū*' and Qatādah also recited '*tughmaḍū*'.

Abū 'Amr ad-Dānī said that it means 'unless it is reduced for you.' An-Naḥḥās related it from Qatādah himself.

Ibn Jinnī said, 'It means that you find that you have been unclear about the interpretation of the business or your tolerance, and you have proceeded in a manner that is not normally anticipated. This is as you say, "I praised the man," meaning that you found him to be praised.'

Ibn 'Aṭiyyah said, 'The majority reading is based on overlooking and lowering the eye because *aghmaḍa* is in the position of *ghammaḍa*. So it means that you overlook the interpretation in taking it, either because it is unlawful, as Ibn Zayd says, or because it is a gift or taken for a debt, according to another.' Al-Mahdawī says that it means: you close your eyes to taking it. Al-Jawharī says that the verb refers to acting in an easy way in buying and selling. It is as if you wanted more than it because of its poor quality or a reduction in its price.

Know that Allah is Rich Beyond Need, Praiseworthy.

Allah tells us about His attribute of absolute wealth, meaning that He has no need of our *ṣadaqah*. So whoever tries to draw near and seeks a reward should do that with something that has a value and importance. He is advancing something for himself. Allah is Praiseworthy in every state. Az-Zajjāj points out that He does not command people to give *ṣadaqah* when they are poor, but He tests them. So He is Praiseworthy in that as in all His blessings.

ٱلشَّيْطَٰنُ يَعِدُكُمُ ٱلْفَقْرَ وَيَأْمُرُكُم بِٱلْفَحْشَآءِ ۖ وَٱللَّهُ يَعِدُكُم مَّغْفِرَةً مِّنْهُ
وَفَضْلًا ۗ وَٱللَّهُ وَٰسِعٌ عَلِيمٌ ﴿٢٦٨﴾

268 Shayṭān promises you poverty and commands you to avarice. Allah promises you forgiveness from Him and abundance. Allah is All-Encompassing, All-Knowing.

Shayṭān promises you poverty and commands you to avarice.

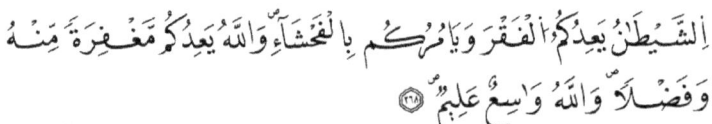

The derivation of the word Shayṭān has already been mentioned in the commentary on 2:14. The expression *'promises you poverty'* here means 'threatens you with poverty', making you afraid of it so that you do not spend. This *āyah* is connected to the one before it. Shayṭān has a way of hindering someone from spending in the Way of Allah. He also commands 'avarice' (*faḥshā'*), which refers to acts of self-gratification and spending on them. It is said that it means: 'Do not give *ṣadaqah*; rather disobey and cut people off.' '*Faqr*' (poverty) is also recited as '*fuqr*' in one dialect. Al-Jawharī said that *fuqr* is a dialectical usage.

Allah promises you forgiveness from Him and abundance.

In Arabic when the word *wa'ada* is used undefined, then it is about good. When it is limited by something, then it can mean to promise good or to threaten evil, as is also the case with *bishārah.* This *āyah* contains both meanings. Ibn 'Abbās said, 'This *āyah* contains two things from Allah and two things from Shayṭān. At-Tirmidhī reports from Ibn Mas'ūd that the Messenger of Allah ﷺ said, 'Shayṭān has a touch he uses on the son of Ādam and the angel has a touch. The touch of Shayṭān has the effect of threatening evil and denying the truth. The touch of the angel has the effect of promising good and confirming the truth. Anyone who experiences that should know that it is from Allah. Anyone who experiences other than that should seek refuge with Allah from Shayṭān.' Then he recited this *āyah.* He said that it is a sound *ḥasan* hadith. Outside of the Qur'an, it is permitted to have 'commands avarice' without a *bā'*.

The word 'forgiveness' (*maghfirah*) indicates Allah's veiling of the wrong actions of His slaves in this world and the Next. '*Faḍl*' (abundance) here means provision in this world and expansion and blessing in the Next. Both are promised by Allah.

An-Naqqāsh mentioned that some people use this *āyah* to claim that poverty is better than wealth because Shayṭān distances the human being from what is good and does that by alarming them about poverty. Ibn 'Aṭiyyah said, 'There is no definitive evidence in the *āyah.* In fact, this idea is strongly contradicted.' It is related in the Torah: 'My servant spends from My provision and I grant him My bounty. My hand is stretched out over every outstretched hand.' It is confirmed in the Qur'an where He says: '*Anything you expend will be replaced by Him. He is the best of Providers.*' (34:39) Ibn 'Abbās mentioned it.

Allah gives from His vast wealth and knows where to bestow it. He knows the Unseen and the visible. They are two of His names which we mentioned in *Kitāb al-Asnā.*

يُؤْتِي ٱلْحِكْمَةَ مَن يَشَآءُ ۚ وَمَن يُؤْتَ ٱلْحِكْمَةَ فَقَدْ أُوتِيَ خَيْرًا
كَثِيرًا ۗ وَمَا يَذَّكَّرُ إِلَّآ أُو۟لُوا۟ ٱلْأَلْبَٰبِ ﴿٢٦٩﴾

269 He gives wisdom to whomever He wills and he who has been given wisdom has been given great good. But no one pays heed but people of intelligence.

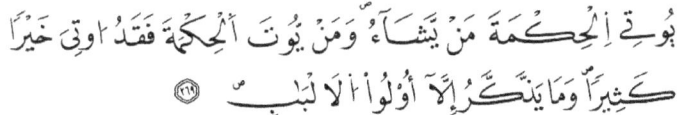

He gives wisdom to whomever He wills.

Allah gives it to whomever He wishes of His slaves. Scholars disagree about the meaning of the word '*ḥikmah*' (wisdom) here. As-Suddī said that it refers to Prophethood. Ibn 'Abbās said that it means understanding of the Qur'an: its *fiqh*, abrogations, *āyahs* of judgment, ambiguous *āyahs*, unusual expressions, and changes in the normal order of words. Qatādah and Mujāhid also said that it means understanding of the Qur'an. Mujāhid said that it means being correct in word and deed. Ibn Zayd said, 'Wisdom is understanding the *dīn*.' Mālik ibn Anas said, 'Wisdom is recognition of the *dīn* of Allah, understanding it, and putting it into practice.' Ibn al-Qāsim related that he said, 'Wisdom is reflecting on the commands of Allah and following them.' He also said, 'Wisdom is obeying Allah and understanding the *dīn* and acting on it.' Ar-Rabī' ibn Anas said, 'Wisdom is humility.' Ibrāhīm an-Nakha'ī said, 'Wisdom is understanding the Qur'an.' Zayd ibn Aslam also said that. Al-Ḥasan said, 'Wisdom is scrupulousness.'

Most of these ideas are close in meaning as *ḥikmah* (wisdom) is a verbal noun which comes from *iḥkām*, which means perfection in word or deed. All the things mentioned above are wisdom. The Book of Allah is wisdom. The Sunnah of His Prophet ﷺ is wisdom. All that is mentioned of excellence is wisdom. The basic meaning of *ḥikmah* is something which prevents foolishness. It is said that it is knowledge because it prevents foolishness and, by it, one knows how to prevent foolishness, which is every ugly action. The same is true for the Qur'an, intelligence and understanding. Al-Bukharī has the hadith: 'When Allah desires good for a person, He gives him understanding in the *dīn*.' Here He says: *'He who has been given wisdom has been given much good.'*

The fact that Allah repeats the word 'wisdom' here rather than using a pronoun the second time is to show concern for it to indicate its honour and excellence as was already explained in 2:59. Abū Muḥammad ad-Dārimī mentioned in his *Musnad* from Marwān ibn Muḥammad from Rifdah al-Ghassānī that Thābit ibn 'Ajlān al-Anṣārī said, 'It was said that Allah desired to punish the people of the earth, but when he heard a teacher teaching wisdom to children, He averted that from them.' Marwān said that the wisdom was the Qur'an.

Anyone who is given wisdom and the Qur'an has been given the best of what can be given of all the knowledge of the books of the early people and others because He said about those: *'You have only been given a little knowledge.'* (17:85) This is called '*great good*' because the Qur'an is the all-inclusive Book. One of the sages said, 'Whoever is given knowledge and the Qur'an should value himself properly and not humble himself to the people of this world for the sake of worldly things. What he has been given is better than what the people of this world have been given because Allah called this world "a little good" and called knowledge and the Qur'an "great good".'

Most recite '*he who is given*' as '*man yu'ta*' in the passive form of the verb. Az-Zuhrī and Ya'qūb recite '*man yu'ti*' meaning 'he to whom Allah gives'. *Albāb* means intelligence. The singular is *lubb.*

وَمَآ أَنفَقْتُم مِّن نَّفَقَةٍ أَوْ نَذَرْتُم مِّن نَّذْرٍ فَإِنَّ ٱللَّهَ يَعْلَمُهُۥ ۗ وَمَا
لِلظَّٰلِمِينَ مِنْ أَنصَارٍ ﴿٢٧٠﴾

270 Whatever amount you spend or vow you make, Allah knows it. The wrongdoers have no helpers.

Vows were part of the culture of the Arabs and they used to make them a lot. Allah mentions two types of vows: those a man makes voluntarily, and those he makes after obliging himself to do so. This *āyah* is both a promise and threat, telling us that those with sincere intention will be rewarded. Anyone who spends to show off or for any other reason like inducing gratitude or as an insult is a wrongdoer. His action is worthless and he gains no benefit from it.

The phrase '*knows it*' means that Allah takes account of it, according to Mujāhid. The pronoun is singular although it mentions two things. An-Naḥḥās says that it implies: 'Whatever amount you spend, Allah knows it. Whatever vow you make, Allah knows it.' So there is elision. It is possible that what is implied is: 'whatever you spend, Allah knows it' and the *hā'* (it) refers to *mā* (what), and '*vow you make*' is added to it. Ibn 'Aṭiyyah said, 'The pronoun is singular in "*knows it*" when two things have been mentioned since He means what was mentioned or stated.'

This is good. All that was mentioned is implied, even if it is a lot. The reality of a vow is that you say that it is whatever acts of worship a responsible person has made mandatory for himself which were not mandatory or necessary for him. You say, 'The man took a vow to do such-and-such' when he obliges himself to do it. The present tense can be *yandhuru* or *yandhiru*. Its rulings will be explained elsewhere, Allah willing.

إِن تُبْدُوا۟ ٱلصَّدَقَٰتِ فَنِعِمَّا هِىَ ۖ وَإِن تُخْفُوهَا وَتُؤْتُوهَا ٱلْفُقَرَآءَ فَهُوَ خَيْرٌ لَّكُمْ ۚ وَنُكَفِّرُ عَنكُم مِّن سَيِّـَٔاتِكُمْ ۗ وَٱللَّهُ بِمَا تَعْمَلُونَ خَبِيرٌ ﴿٢٧١﴾

271 If you make your *ṣadaqah* public, that is good. But if you conceal it and give it to the poor, that is better for you, and We will erase some of your bad actions from you. Allah is aware of what you do.

Commentators believe that this *āyah* is about voluntary *ṣadaqah* because concealment of it is better than making it public. This is the case with all acts of worship: concealment is better in respect of voluntary acts because it precludes showing off. That does not, however, apply to obligatory *zakāt*. Al-Ḥasan said that making *zakāt* public is better but that concealing voluntary acts of giving is better because it is closer to what Allah desires with respect to that. Ibn 'Abbās said, 'Secret giving when it is voluntary is seventy times better than public giving. In the case of obligatory *zakāt*, its public payment is better than paying it secretly by up to twenty-five times according to some. It is the same with all obligations and supererogatory actions.' He said that that is the case in all obligatory and voluntary actions in all matters.

Such a position is not taken on the basis of mere opinion. In *Ṣaḥīḥ Muslim*, the Prophet ﷺ said. 'The best prayer a man can perform is the one he does in his house except for the obligatory prayer.' That is because there is no showing off in the obligatory, while supererogatory prayers are subject to that. An-Nasā'ī reported from 'Uqbah ibn Āmir that the Messenger of Allah ﷺ said, 'Someone who recites the Qur'an aloud is like the one who gives *ṣadaqah* publicly. Someone who recites the Qur'an silently is like someone who gives *ṣadaqah* secretly.' We find in a hadith: 'Secret *ṣadaqah* extinguishes the wrath of the Lord.'

Ibn al-'Arabī said, 'There is no preference in sound hadith for public *zakāt* over that given secretly nor for secret *zakāt* over that given publicly, but there is a firm consensus regarding that. As for voluntary *ṣadaqah*, the Qur'an clearly states that it is better given secretly than publicly. Our scholars say that this is generally the case. The truth about this matter is that the state of giving *ṣadaqah* varies according to the circumstances of the giver, the recipient and those who witness it. The public giver has the benefit of demonstrating the Sunnah and the reward for acting as a model for others.'

This refers to someone whose state is strong and intention good and who is safe from showing off. As for someone whose state falls below this, doing it secretly is better for him. As for the recipient, when giving is done secretly, he is kept safe from people's disdain or from the claim that he took what he did not need and failed to be abstinent. Generally speaking, keeping *ṣadaqah* secret from people is better than making it known to them since they might attack the giver for showing off and the taker for being able to do without it. On the positive side, doing it publicly encourages people to give *ṣadaqah*. But this is rare today.

Yazīd ibn Abī Ḥabīb said, 'This *āyah* was revealed about the giving of *ṣadaqah* to the Jews and Christians. It was as if Allah was commanding that a portion of *zakāt* should be secret.' Ibn 'Aṭiyyah said that this position is rejected, especially by the righteous Salaf. Aṭ-Ṭabarī said that the consensus is that doing what is obligatory is better.

Aṭ-Ṭabarī mentioned that this *āyah* indicates that it is generally better to conceal *zakāt*. It is the right of the poor and it is better for the owner of property to distribute it himself. This is one of the two positions of ash-Shāfi'ī. In his other position, he stated that what is meant by *ṣadaqah* here is the voluntary *ṣadaqah* rather than obligatory *zakāt*. It is more appropriate to perform the obligatory publicly so that there will be no suspicion. That is why it is said, 'It is better to do the *nāfilah* prayers alone, but praying in the group removes suspicion about whether someone is fulfilling the obligatory prayer or not.'

Al-Mahdawī said, 'What is meant by the *āyah* is both the obligation of *zakāt* and what is voluntary. Concealment was better in the time of the Prophet ﷺ. Then people's suspicions arose after that and so scholars recommended making what is obligatory public so that no suspicion would remain.' Ibn 'Aṭiyyah remarked, 'This position is contrary to the traditions (*āthār*). In our time it seems that it is recommended to conceal obligatory *zakāt*. Those who refuse to do it are numerous and paying it publicly opens a person to the accusation of showing off.' Ibn Khuwayzimandād said, 'It is permitted for the *āyah* to mean both obligatory and voluntary *ṣadaqah* because He mentioned the hidden and praises it, and the public and praises it, and so it can be directed to both of them.' An-Naqqāsh said that this *āyah* was abrogated by Allah's words: '*Those who give away their wealth, night and day, secretly and openly.*' (2:274) So, in the *āyah* public *ṣadaqah* is praised and then the ruling is given that when it is given secretly it is better. That is why one of the sages said, 'When you give charity, conceal it. When you are given it, then make it known.' Di'bil al-Khuzā'ī said:

When they take revenge, they make it public.
  When they bestow, they conceal that.

Sahl ibn Hārūn said:

When one day you go to a friend to ask of him,
he gives you what he owns and apologises.
He conceals his action while Allah makes it known.
When you give what is beautiful, it shows.

Al-'Abbās ibn 'Abd al-Muṭṭalib said, 'A charitable act is only complete when it has three characteristics: hastening it, thinking it small, and concealing it. When you hasten it, you make it more welcome. When you consider it small, you make it great. When you conceal it, you perfect it.' A poet said:

I consider your charity to be greater
when it is concealed and small in your sight.
You forget it as if you had not given it,
while it is famous among people.

There are different readings of the phrase '*that is good*'. Abū 'Amr, Nāfi' in the transmission of Warsh, 'Āṣim in the transmission of Ḥafṣ and Ibn Kathīr recite '*ni'immā*', and Abū 'Amr (again), Nāfi' in other than the transmission of Warsh, 'Āṣim in the transmission of Abū Bakr and al-Mufaḍḍal recite '*ni'mā*'. Al-A'mash, Ibn 'Āmir, Ḥamzah, and al-Kisā'ī recite '*na'immā*'. Outside of the Qur'an we find: '*ni'ma mā*'. An-Naḥḥās said that it is connected in the script and so assimilation is necessary.

There are four dialectical forms of *ni'ma*. The root is *na'ima*, but there is also *ni'ima* where the *nūn* has a *kasrah* because the *'ayn* does, *na'ma* (where the root is *na'ima* and the *kasrah* has been elided because of being heavy), and *ni'ma*, which is the most eloquent. The root of them is *na'ima*. It is used for every praise, and lightened and the *kasrah* of the *'ayn* changed and the *'ayn* becomes silent. Two things are implied by '*fa-ni'immā hiya*'. One is that it is based on the dialectical form *ni'ima*, and the other is that is based on the good dialect and the root is *ni'ma* and *the 'ayn* has a *kasrah* because of two silent letters meeting. What Abū 'Amr and Nāfi' relate about the *'ayn* being silent is impossible. It is related that Muḥammad ibn Yazīd said, 'As for a *sukūn* on the *'ayn* and double *mīm*, no one is able to pronounce it. It tries to combine two silent letters and vowel them which does not happen.' Abū 'Alī said, 'The statements of those who give the *'ayn* a *sukūn* are not proper because it is combining two silent letters, the first of them is not a letter of extension and softness. That is permitted by grammarians when the first letter has extension since the extension replaces the vowel, as in *dābbah* and *ḍawāl*.'

Perhaps Abū 'Amr concealed the vowel and sneaks it in as he does in '*bāri'ikum*' and '*ya'murukum*' and someone listening thought that it was a *sukūn* because of the subtleness of that to the ear. Abū 'Alī said, 'As for the one who recites '*ni'immā*', he brings the word according to its root.' He also said that the *mā* is in the accusative and '*hiya*' explains the implied subject before it is mentioned. It implies: 'Making it public is good,' and 'making public' is singled out for praise even though the *muḍāf* is elided and replaced by the *muḍāf ilayh*.

The following words: '*That is better for you*', lead you to the fact that concealing is better. The pronoun in 'that' refers to concealing, not to *ṣadaqah*. 'If you conceal it' is a precondition which is why the *nūn* of the verb is omitted. 'Give it' is added to it. Its apodosis is: '*That is better for you*'.

The word '*erase*' is subject to various readings. Abū 'Āmir, Ibn Kathīr, 'Āṣim in the transmission of Abū Bakr, Qatādah and Ibn Abī Isḥāq have *nukaffiru (*We will erase). Nāfi', Ḥamzah, and al-Kisā'ī have *nukaffir* (We will erase) with a *sukūn* on the *rā'*. The same is related from 'Āṣim. Al-Ḥusayn ibn 'Alī al-Ju'fī from al-A'mash has *yukaffira* (it will erase). Ibn 'Āmir has *yukaffiru* (it will erase) and Ḥafs related that from 'Āṣim. It is also related from al-Ḥasan as it is related from him as '*yukaffir*'. Ibn 'Abbās recited '*tukaffir*'. 'Ikrimah recited '*tukaffar*'. Al-Mahdawī related that Ibn Hurmuz recited '*tukaffir*,' and it is related that 'Ikrimah and Sahr ibn Ḥawshab recited '*tukaffira*'. The clearest reading is '*yukaffiru*', and this is what al-Khalīl and Sībawayh said. An-Naḥḥās said that Sībawayh said, 'It is proper with the *ḍammah* and good because the words after the *fā'* act normally without the apodosis. The jussive is permitted when it is applied to the meaning because it means: if you conceal it and give it to the poor, that is better for you and Allah will erase bad actions from you. Abū Ḥātim said that al-A'mash recited '*yukaffir*' without the preceding *wāw*. An-Naḥḥās said, 'What Abū Ḥātim related from al-A'mash without the preceding *wāw* is jussive based on the appositive. It is as if it were in place of the *fā'*. What is related from 'Āṣim, "*yukaffiru*" means "Allah will erase".' This is the position of Abū 'Ubayd. Abū Ḥātim says that it means, 'the giving will erase'. The reading of Ibn 'Abbās with a *tā'* means '*ṣadaqah* will erase'.

Generally speaking, the readings with *nūn* in the first person plural, is the Divine 'We', and those with a *tā'* in the third person feminine refer to *ṣadaqah*, except for what is related from 'Ikrimah with a *fatḥah* on the *fā'* where it refers to bad actions. If it is with the *yā'* of the third person masculine, then it is Allah Who does the erasing and the concealed giving is also that which erases as we mentioned. Makkī mentioned that.

There are two reasons for the verb having a *ḍammah* at the end. One is that it is the predicate of an implied inceptive and so implies: 'We will erase' or 'it (*ṣadaqah*) will erase' or 'Allah will erase'. The second is that there is a stop and a new sentence and the conjunctive *wāw* is not for sharing, but conjoins one sentence to another. We have already mentioned the meaning of the recitation with the *sukūn*. As for the *naṣb* (with *fatḥah*) 'and *nukaffira* (We shall erase)', that is weak, and is based on the ellipsis of *an* (that), which is possible but unlikely. Al-Mahdawī said, 'It resembles the *naṣb* in the apodosis of the interrogative since the apodosis which the thing necessitates is is based on the existence of something else, which is also the case with the interrogative.' The *sukūn* on the *rā'* is the purest of these recitations, linguistically speaking, because it notifies us that the erasure is comprised in the recompense, and the fact that it is stipulated if concealment occurs. As for with the *ḍammah*, this sense is not in it.

This is contrary to what al-Khalīl and Sībawayh chose. In the words 'some of your bad actions' (*min sayyi'ātikum*) the '*min*' (some) is partitive. Aṭ-Ṭabarī reports that some have said that it is redundant, but Ibn 'Aṭiyyah says that is a mistake on their part. *'Allah is aware of what you do'* is both a threat and a promise.

لَّيْسَ عَلَيْكَ هُدَىٰهُمْ وَلَٰكِنَّ ٱللَّهَ يَهْدِى مَن يَشَآءُ ۗ وَمَا تُنفِقُوا۟ مِنْ خَيْرٍ فَلِأَنفُسِكُمْ ۚ وَمَا تُنفِقُونَ إِلَّا ٱبْتِغَآءَ وَجْهِ ٱللَّهِ ۚ وَمَا تُنفِقُوا۟ مِنْ خَيْرٍ يُوَفَّ إِلَيْكُمْ وَأَنتُمْ لَا تُظْلَمُونَ ﴿٢٧٢﴾

272 You are not responsible for their guidance, but Allah guides whomever He wills. Whatever good you give away is to your own benefit, when you give desiring only the Face of Allah. Whatever good you give away will be repaid to you in full. You will not be wronged.

You are not responsible for their guidance but Allah guides whomever He wills.

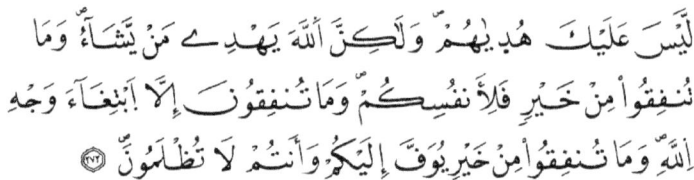

These words are connected to the mention of *ṣadaqah*. It is as if Allah were making it clear that it is permitted to give *ṣadaqah* to the idolaters. There is a *mursal* hadith related by Sa'īd ibn Jubayr where the Prophet ﷺ said that the reason for the revelation of this *āyah* was that the Muslims used to give *ṣadaqah* to the poor among the *dhimmīs*. When there were a lot of poor Muslims, the Messenger of Allah ﷺ said, 'Only give *ṣadaqah* to the people of your own *dīn*.' Then this *āyah* was revealed to make it clear that it is permitted to give *ṣadaqah* to those who are not part of the *dīn* of Islam. An-Naqqāsh mentioned that the Prophet ﷺ was given *zakāt* and a Jew came and said, 'Give to me.' The Prophet ﷺ answered, 'There is no share in the *zakāt* of the Muslims for you.' The Jew went away and this *āyah* was revealed. The Messenger of Allah ﷺ called for him and gave some to him. Then that was abrogated by the *āyah* of *zakāt*.

Ibn 'Abbās said, 'Some of the Anṣār had relatives in the Jewish tribes of the Banū Qurayẓah and the Banu-n-Naḍīr. They used to not give *ṣadaqah* to them out of the desire that they would become Muslim if they were needy and the *āyah* was revealed because of them.'

One of the commentators related that Asmā' bint Abī Bakr wanted to give *ṣadaqah* to her grandfather, Abū Quḥāfah, and then did not do so because he was an unbeliever, and the *āyah* was revealed about that. Aṭ-Ṭabarī related that the aim of the Prophet ﷺ in not giving *ṣadaqah* was so that they would become Muslims and enter into the *dīn* and for that reason Allah said: '*You are not responsible for their guidance.*' It is also said that this is not connected to the *āyah* before it but is totally a new statement and so it is apparently about *ṣadaqah* and giving it to the unbelievers.

Our scholars say that the *ṣadaqah* which non-Muslims are permitted according to these traditions is voluntary *ṣadaqah*. As for *zakāt*, it is not permitted to give it to an unbeliever since the Prophet ﷺ said, 'I was commanded to take *ṣadaqah* (meaning here *zakāt*) from your rich and give it to your poor.' Ibn al-Mundhir said, 'The consensus among all the scholars I learned from is that a *dhimmī* is not given any of the *zakāt*.' Then he mentioned a group who said something different to that. Al-Mahdawī said that this *āyah* is an allowance for the Muslims to give some of the *zakāt* to their relatives who are unbelievers. Ibn 'Aṭiyyah said, 'This is rejected by consensus, and Allah knows best.' Abū Ḥanīfah said that *zakāt al-fiṭr* can be given to them, but Ibn al-'Arabī says that this is baseless and weak. Our evidence is that *zakāt* on livestock and money is an obligatory purification and may not be given to unbelievers. The Prophet ﷺ said, 'Spare them from having to beg on this day,' meaning *'Īd al-Fiṭr*.

We reply that this is the case because the Muslims are busy with the *'Īd* and the *'Īd* prayer, while this is not the case with the idolaters. It is permitted to give it to non-Muslims if one holds the position that it is a sunnah to do so. It is one of our positions, and it is also the position of Abū Ḥanīfah, as we mentioned. It is adopting the general meaning of the *āyah* about kindness, feeding people and general *ṣadaqah*. Ibn 'Aṭiyyah said, 'This ruling is conceivable for the Muslims when dealing with the *dhimmī*s and enslaved *ḥarbī*s.'

In the Qur'an we read: *'They give food, despite their love for it, to the poor and orphans and captives.'* (76:8) A captive in the Abode of Islam can only be an idolater. The Almighty says: *'Allah does not forbid you from being good to those who have not fought you in the dīn or driven you from your homes, or from being just to them.'* (60:8). So the literal meaning of these *āyah*s allows *ṣadaqah* to be given to non-Muslims. The Prophet ﷺ, however, excepted *zakāt* from that, saying, 'Take *ṣadaqah* from their rich and give it to their poor,' and scholars agree on that. So non-Muslims can be given voluntary *ṣadaqah* if they are needy, and Allah knows best.

Ibn al-'Arabī said, 'There is no disagreement that *zakāt al-fiṭr* can be given to disobedient Muslims, unless they have abandoned the pillars of Islam: prayer and fasting. Then it may not be given to them until they repent. Zakat is given to other disobedient Muslims because they are included under the general category of "Muslims".' We find in *Ṣaḥīḥ Muslim* that a man gave *ṣadaqah* to a wealthy man, a thief and a prostitute, and his *ṣadaqah* was accepted.

but Allah guides whoever He wills.

This refutes the Qadariyyah and groups of the Mu'tazilites as we have already explained (2:5).

Whatever good you give away is to your own benefit

The word 'good' in this *āyah* refers to wealth because it is accompanied by the words 'give away'. The context indicates that it is wealth. In other contexts, the word 'good' can have other meanings as in 99:7. This negates the statement of 'Ikrimah that every 'good' in the Book of Allah is wealth. It is related that one of the scholars used to give away a lot in charity and he swore that he had not done good to anyone. He was asked about that and said, 'I did that for myself and he recited, *"Whatever good you give away is to your own benefit."*'

when you give desiring only the Face of Allah.

Then Allah made it clear that the only spending which is accepted is that by which the Face of Allah is sought. It is also said that it is testimony by Allah for the Companions that they sought the Face of Allah when they spent. This is preference and praise of them. According to the first view, it is a precondition for them, and the precondition applies to others in the community. The Messenger of Allah ﷺ said to Sa'd ibn Abī Waqqāṣ, 'You do not spend anything by which you desire the Face of Allah without being rewarded for it, even a morsel you place in your wife's mouth.' So the reward for spending is given in full to those who spend and none of it is stinted as that stinting would be an injustice to them.

لِلْفُقَرَآءِ ٱلَّذِينَ أُحْصِرُوا۟ فِى سَبِيلِ ٱللَّهِ لَا يَسْتَطِيعُونَ ضَرْبًا فِى
ٱلْأَرْضِ يَحْسَبُهُمُ ٱلْجَاهِلُ أَغْنِيَآءَ مِنَ ٱلتَّعَفُّفِ تَعْرِفُهُم بِسِيمَٰهُمْ
لَا يَسْـَٔلُونَ ٱلنَّاسَ إِلْحَافًا ۗ وَمَا تُنفِقُوا۟ مِنْ خَيْرٍ فَإِنَّ ٱللَّهَ بِهِۦ
عَلِيمٌ ﴿٢٧٣﴾

273 It is for the poor who are held back in the Way of Allah, unable to travel in the land. The ignorant consider them rich because of their reticence. You will know them by their mark. They do not ask from people insistently. Whatever good you give away, Allah knows it.

It is for the poor

The words '*for the poor*' are connected to '*whatever good you give away*' in the previous *āyah*. It is said that it implies that spending or *ṣadaqah* is for the poor alone. As-Suddī, Mujāhid and others said that what is meant by poor in this instance are the poor Muhājirūn of Quraysh and others. Then the *āyah* is extended so that it is applied to all who are considered poor throughout time. The poor Muhājirūn are singled out because they were those who were poor at that time. They were the People of the Ṣuffah, who numbered about four hundred men. That was because the poor used to come to the Messenger of Allah ﷺ. They had neither family nor property and so a verandah (*ṣuffah*) was built for them in the mosque of the Messenger of Allah ﷺ which is why they were called the People of the Ṣuffah.

Abū Dharr said, 'I was one of the people of the Ṣuffah. In the evening, we presented ourselves at the door of the Messenger of Allah ﷺ and he would order each of us to go with a man [as his guest for supper] until there remained ten or less of the people of the Ṣuffah and the Prophet ﷺ would bring us his supper and we would eat with him. When we finished, the Messenger of Allah ﷺ said. "Sleep in the mosque."' At-Tirmidhī transmitted that al-Barā' ibn 'Āzib quoted the *āyah*: '*Do not have recourse to bad things when you give*' (2:267) and said, 'It was revealed about us, the Anṣār. We owned some palm trees. A man would bring dates from his trees according to whether its fruits were a lot or a little. A man would bring a branch or two of dates and hang them in the mosque. The people of the Ṣuffah did not have any food, so when one of them was hungry, he would go to the bunch and hit it with his stick and some dates would fall and he would eat. People who did not truly desire to do good would bring branches of poor dates or broken ones and hang them in the mosque. Then Allah Almighty revealed: *"O you who believe, spend of the good things..."* (2:267). This means: "If one of you had been given the like of what he gave, you would only take it with your eyes closed due to embarrassment." After that a man would only bring good things.' This is a sound *gharīb ḥasan* hadith.

According to our scholars the people in the mosque were impoverished and they were in the mosque out of necessity and ate from *ṣadaqah* due to their compelling need. When Allah gave victory to the Muslims, they were relieved from that and went out and then had property of their own.

who are held back in the Way of Allah, unable to travel in the land.

Allah then described the states of those poor Muhājirūn in a manner which obliges compassion for them. These words indicate the fact that they were restricted in their ability to move. Qatādah and Ibn Zayd said that this means they were kept from going about to earn a living due to fear of the enemy. This is why Allah says that they are unable to travel because every direction was full of unbelievers. This was at the beginning of Islam. So their excuse kept them from earning and *jihād*, and the unbelievers' dislike of them kept them from going out in trade, so they remained poor. It is also said that it means they held themselves back from *jihād*, but the first interpretation is more likely, and Allah knows best.

The ignorant consider them rich because of their reticence.

This means that they have withdrawn and do not ask, and rely on Allah, so that someone who did not know would suppose them to be rich. This shows that the ascription of poverty can be applied to someone who has clothes of some value and that does not prevent *zakāt* being given to him. In fact Allah commands it to be given to these people. They were among the Muhājirūn who fought with the Messenger of Allah ﷺ and were not ill or blind. 'Reticence' (*ta'affuf*) in this context means to refrain from begging and put oneself above it. This is how it is explained by Qatādah and others. There are two readings of 'consider them': *'yaḥsabuhum'* and *'yaḥsibuhum'*. Abū 'Alī considers *'yaḥsabuhum'* to be better fitting but the other reading is also good.

You will know them by their mark.

This is evidence that the distinguishing marks of Islam have a legal bearing in respect of those on whom they appear, so that if we find a corpse in the Abode of Islam who is wearing a Christian belt and is not circumcised, it is not buried in the graveyard of the Muslims. Connected to that are His words: '*...you would know them* *by their mark and know them by their ambivalent speech.'* (47:30) That takes precedence over the normal ruling of most scholars that a dead person is deemed to belong to the *dīn* of the place where he is found. It also indicates the permissibility of giving *zakāt* to someone who has fine clothes and adornment. Scholars agree on that. Then they disagree about the amount he may take. Abū Ḥanīfah says that it is the same amount on which *zakāt* is obliged to be paid, ash-Shāfi'ī says that it is food for a year, and Mālik says it is forty dirhams. Ash-Shāfi'ī also said that *zakāt* should not be given to someone who is earning.

Scholars disagree about what the '*sīmā*' (mark) referred to is. Mujāhid says that it is humility and humbleness. As-Suddī said that it is the sign of poverty and need which can be seen in their faces. Ibn Zayd said that it is their tattered clothes. Some people, including Makkī, said that it is the mark of prostration, and Ibn 'Aṭiyyah says that this is better. That is because they were unoccupied and trusted in Allah and had no work except the prayer and so they had the mark of prostration on them.

This mark, which is the mark of prostration, was shared by all the Companions as Allah says at the end of *Sūrat al-Fatḥ*: *'Their mark is on their faces, the traces of prostration.'* (48:29) So in this respect there can have been no difference between them and others. So the only thing that the 'mark' can be is the effect of poverty and need, or an extra large mark of prostration. They were recognised by the sallowness of their faces from praying at night and fasting in the day, and Allah knows best. As for humility, its place is the heart, and rich and poor share in it. All that remains is what we preferred. Allah is the One Who gives success.

They do not ask from people insistently.

The word '*ilḥāf*' (insistently) is a verbal noun derived from *liḥāf* (blanket). It is called that because it covers all manner of asking in the same way that a blanket covers everything; an insistent beggar is one who begs from everyone and pesters them with his asking. Part of that is what Ibn Aḥmar said:

> It continued to surround them with its shivering,
> and cover them (*yalḥafuhunna*) with a thick thin blanket.

He describes a male ostrich protecting the eggs with its wings which become like a blanket which is thin in spite of its thickness.

An-Nasā'ī and Muslim reported from Abū Hurayrah that the Messenger of Allah ﷺ said, 'The very poor man is not the one who is turned away by a date or two, or a bite or two; the very poor man is the one who does not ask. Recite if you like: "*They do not ask from people insistently.*"'

Scholars disagree about the meaning of this and take two positions. Some people, including aṭ-Ṭabarī and az-Zajjāj, say that the meaning is: 'They do not beg at all.' This would mean that they completely refrain from asking. This is the position of the majority of commentators, and refraining from asking is their firm quality. They do not ask people either insistently or not insistently. Other people say that what is meant is the lack of asking insistently, meaning that they ask, but not insistently. This is easy to understand.

In any case the *āyah* calls attention to the bad state of those who do ask people insistently. The Imams related from Mu'āwiyah ibn Abī Sufyān that the Messenger of Allah ﷺ said, 'Do not be insistent in asking. By Allah, if any of you may ask me for something and get what he wants from me even though I dislike him doing it, he will not be blessed in what I give him.'

In the *Muwaṭṭā'* we read from Zayd ibn Aslam from 'Aṭā' ibn Yasār that a man of the Banū Asad said, 'My family and I dismounted to rest at Baqī' al-Gharqad. My family said to me, "Go to the Messenger of Allah ﷺ and ask him for something to eat," and they began to mention what they needed. I went to the Messenger of Allah ﷺ and found that a man was asking for something, and the Messenger of Allah ﷺ was saying, "I do not have anything to give you." The man turned away from him in anger, saying, "By my life! You give to those you wish to give to!" The Messenger of Allah ﷺ remarked, "He is angry with me because I do not have anything to give him. Whoever asks you for something while he has an *ūqiyyah* or its equivalent has asked insistently."' The man continued, 'I told myself that a camel we had was worth more than an *ūqiyyah*. (Mālik explained that an *ūqiyyah* was forty dirhams.) So I returned without having asked him for anything, and the Messenger of Allah ﷺ sent me barley and raisins later on. He gave us from his share until Allah, the Mighty, the Majestic, gave us relief.'

Ibn 'Abd al-Barr said, 'That is how Mālik related it and it is corroborated by Hishām ibn Sa'd and others. It is a sound hadith. The ruling on a Companion who is not named is not the same as the ruling on others who are not named. Scholars say that is because there is no impairment of them as a rule and integrity is established for them.' This hadith indicates that it is disliked for anyone who has an *ūqiyyah* of silver to beg. Anyone who begs when he has that amount of silver, or what is equivalent to it, is considered to be insistent. I do not know of anyone who possesses knowledge of the *dīn* who does not dislike someone begging when they have this amount of silver or its equivalent in gold according to the literal meaning of this hadith. They are permitted to take what comes to them without asking, provided it is not *zakāt*. There is disagreement if it is *zakāt* as will be explained later.

Ibn 'Abd al-Barr said, 'One of the best things related from the *fuqahā'* regarding begging and dislike of it, and the position of those who possess scrupulousness regarding it, is what al-Athram related from Aḥmad ibn Ḥanbal when he was asked about when begging becomes lawful. He said, "When a person does not have enough for lunch and supper. This is based on the hadith of Sahl ibn al-Ḥanẓaliyyah." Ibn Ḥanbal was then asked, "And if he is compelled to ask?" He replied, "It is permitted if he is in pressing need." He was asked, "And if he refrains?" He replied, "That is better for him." Then he added, "I do not think that anyone will die of hunger. Allah will bring him his provision." Then he mentioned the hadith of Abū Sa'īd al-Khudrī: "Whoever abstains, Allah will make him abstinent."'

In the hadith of Abū Dharr, the Messenger of Allah ﷺ said, 'Be abstinent.' Abū Bakr said, 'I heard him being asked about a man who does not have anything: should he beg or eat carrion? He replied, "Would he eat carrion when there is someone he can ask? This is abhorrent."' He said that he heard him being asked whether a man should beg on behalf of another man. He said that he should not, but can make an allusion. It is like what the Prophet ﷺ said when people came barefooted, naked, wearing stripped cloaks. He said, 'Give *ṣadaqah*.' He did not say, 'Give to them.' Abū 'Umar said, 'The Prophet ﷺ said, "Intercede and you will be rewarded." That has the general meaning of asking on behalf of someone else.' Allah knows best.

Abū Bakr said, 'It was said that a man was mentioned to Aḥmad ibn Ḥanbal and he asked, "Is he in need?" He said, "This is an allusion and there is nothing wrong with it. Asking is to say, 'Give to him.'" Then he added, "I do not like a person asking for himself, so what then is the case with him asking for another? I prefer making an allusion here."'

It is reported by Abū Dāwūd, an-Nasā'ī and others that a Persian asked the Messenger of Allah ﷺ, 'Should I beg, Messenger of Allah?' He said, 'No, but if you must, then ask of the righteous.' So he permitted asking the people of excellence and righteousness when that is necessary. Ibrāhīm ibn Adham said, 'Asking for your needs from people is a veil between you and Allah Almighty. Place your need with the One who controls harm and benefit. Take refuge in Allah Almighty and Allah will spare you from others and you will live in happiness.'

If something comes to someone without their asking for it, they should accept it and not reject it. It is provision which Allah has brought. Mālik reported from Zayd ibn Aslam from 'Aṭā' ibn Yasār that the Messenger of Allah ﷺ sent a gift to 'Umar ibn al-Khaṭṭāb and 'Umar returned it. The Messenger of Allah ﷺ asked, 'Why did you return it?' He replied, 'Messenger of Allah, did you not tell us that it is better for us not to take anything from anyone?' The Messenger of Allah ﷺ said, 'That is by asking. Provision which Allah gives you is not the same as asking.' 'Umar ibn al-Khaṭṭāb said, 'By the One in whose hand my self is, I will not ask anything from anyone, and anything that comes to me without my asking for it, I will accept.' This is a definitive text.

Muslim transmitted in his *Ṣaḥīḥ*, an-Nasā'ī in the *Sunan*, as well as others that Ibn 'Umar said that he heard 'Umar say, 'The Prophet ﷺ gave me a gift and I said, "Give it to someone who is more in need of it than I am." Once he gave me something and I said, "Give it to someone who is more in need of it than I am." The Messenger of Allah ﷺ said, "Take any wealth that comes to you without your looking for it or asking it for it. Take it as long as you yourself do not pursue it."' An-Nasā'ī added, 'Take it and either enrich yourself with it or give it away as *ṣadaqah*.' Muslim related from 'Abdullāh ibn as-Sa'dī al-Mālikī that 'Umar said, 'The Messenger of Allah ﷺ said to me, "When you are given something without asking, then eat and give *ṣadaqah*."' This is sound and *mursal* from Mālik.

Al-Athram said that he heard Abū 'Abdullāh Aḥmad ibn Ḥanbal being asked about the words of the Prophet ﷺ, 'what comes to you without you asking or looking for it' and what 'looking for it' mean. He said, 'It is that you look towards the thing and think in your heart, "Perhaps it will be sent to me."' He was asked, 'Even if one makes no allusion to it?' 'Yes,' he answered, 'because it is in the heart.' He was told, 'This is harsh!' He answered, 'Even if it is harsh, it is like that' He was asked, 'And if a man does not normally send me anything but it occurs to my heart, "Perhaps he will send something to me"?' He answered, 'This is looking for something. If it comes to you without you thinking about it and without it occurring to your heart, then it is something in which there is no looking for it.'

Abū 'Umar said, '*Ishrāf* (looking for) linguistically is raising one's head towards something that one desires and alluding to obtaining it. What Aḥmad said about the interpretation of *ishrāf* is a restriction which I find unreasonable because Allah has overlooked for the people of this community things that their selves say to them as long as it is not articulated on the tongue and acted on by a limb. As for thoughts in the heart that involve disobedience to Allah, except for outright unbelief, they are of no consequence, provided, of course, that they are not acted upon. The consensus is that the thoughts of the self are overlooked.'

Insistence in asking and being importunate in it when a person is wealthy is forbidden and not lawful. The Messenger of Allah ﷺ said, 'Anyone who asks people for an increase over what he has is asking for a hot ember. He can either seek to be independent or he is seeking increase.' Abū Hurayrah related it and Muslim transmitted it. Ibn 'Umar reported that the Prophet ﷺ said, 'One of you will continue to beg until he meets Allah without a single piece of flesh on his face.' Muslim also related it.

If the asker is needy, there is no harm in him asking three times, informing people of his state and apologising. But it is best to leave it. If the one asked knows of his need and is able to give him what he asks, he is obliged to give. If he does not know it, he gives to him out of fear that he is speaking the truth and that rejecting him will not be profitable.

Regarding someone who needs something to keep up appearances, such as having a good garment to wear on the *'Īd* and *Jumu'ah*, Ibn al-'Arabī said, 'While I was in the mosque of the Caliph in Baghdad, I heard a man say, "This is your brother who attends *Jumu'ah* and he has no other garment with which to support the sunnah of *Jumu'ah*." The following *Jumu'ah* I saw him in another garment and was told, "Abu-ṭ-Ṭāhir al-Burnusī gave it to him."'

الَّذِينَ يُنفِقُونَ أَمْوَالَهُم بِاللَّيْلِ وَالنَّهَارِ سِرًّا وَعَلَانِيَةً فَلَهُمْ
أَجْرُهُمْ عِندَ رَبِّهِمْ وَلَا خَوْفٌ عَلَيْهِمْ وَلَا هُمْ يَحْزَنُونَ ﴿٢٧٤﴾

274 Those who give away their wealth by night and day, secretly and openly, will have their reward with their Lord. They will feel no fear and will know no sorrow.

It is related from Ibn 'Abbās, Abū Dharr, Abū Umāmah, Abu-d-Dardā', 'Abdullāh ibn Bishr al-Ghāfiqī and al-Awzā'ī that this *āyah* was revealed about the fodder of horses which are used for *jihād* in the Way of Allah. In the *Ṭabaqāt*, Ibn Sa'd mentioned from Muḥammad ibn Shu'ayb ibn Shābūr from Sa'īd ibn Sinān from Yazīd ibn 'Abdullāh from his father that his grandfather 'Arīb reported that the Messenger of Allah ﷺ was asked about: '*Those who give away their wealth by night and day, secretly and openly, will have their reward with their Lord. They will feel no fear and will know no sorrow.*' He said, 'They are the owners of horses.' By means of the same *isnād*, the Messenger of Allah ﷺ is reported as saying, 'The one who spends on horses is like someone who stretches out his hand with *ṣadaqah* without closing it again. Their urine and droppings will be like fragrant musk on the Day of Rising.'

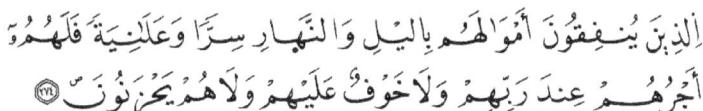

Ibn 'Abbās also reported that this *āyah* was revealed about 'Alī ibn Abī Ṭālib who had four dirhams and gave away one at night, one in the day, and one secretly and one openly. 'Abd ar-Razzāq mentioned it from 'Abd al-Wahhāb ibn Mujāhid from his father from Ibn 'Abbās. Ibn Jurayj said that it was revealed about a man who did that but he did not name 'Alī or anyone else. Qatādah said that this *āyah* was revealed about those who spend without being either extravagant or tightfisted. The *fā'* is added in '*lahum*' because the words have the meaning of an apodosis.

ٱلَّذِينَ يَأْكُلُونَ ٱلرِّبَوٰا۟ لَا يَقُومُونَ إِلَّا كَمَا يَقُومُ ٱلَّذِى يَتَخَبَّطُهُ
ٱلشَّيْطَٰنُ مِنَ ٱلْمَسِّ ذَٰلِكَ بِأَنَّهُمْ قَالُوٓا۟ إِنَّمَا ٱلْبَيْعُ مِثْلُ ٱلرِّبَوٰا۟
وَأَحَلَّ ٱللَّهُ ٱلْبَيْعَ وَحَرَّمَ ٱلرِّبَوٰا۟ فَمَن جَآءَهُۥ مَوْعِظَةٌ مِّن رَّبِّهِۦ فَٱنتَهَىٰ
فَلَهُۥ مَا سَلَفَ وَأَمْرُهُۥٓ إِلَى ٱللَّهِ وَمَنْ عَادَ فَأُو۟لَٰٓئِكَ أَصْحَٰبُ ٱلنَّارِ هُمْ فِيهَا
خَٰلِدُونَ ﴿٢٧٥﴾ يَمْحَقُ ٱللَّهُ ٱلرِّبَوٰا۟ وَيُرْبِى ٱلصَّدَقَٰتِ وَٱللَّهُ لَا يُحِبُّ كُلَّ
كَفَّارٍ أَثِيمٍ ﴿٢٧٦﴾ إِنَّ ٱلَّذِينَ ءَامَنُوا۟ وَعَمِلُوا۟ ٱلصَّٰلِحَٰتِ وَأَقَامُوا۟ ٱلصَّلَوٰةَ
وَءَاتَوُا۟ ٱلزَّكَوٰةَ لَهُمْ أَجْرُهُمْ عِندَ رَبِّهِمْ وَلَا خَوْفٌ عَلَيْهِمْ وَلَا هُمْ
يَحْزَنُونَ ﴿٢٧٧﴾ يَٰٓأَيُّهَا ٱلَّذِينَ ءَامَنُوا۟ ٱتَّقُوا۟ ٱللَّهَ وَذَرُوا۟ مَا بَقِىَ مِنَ ٱلرِّبَوٰٓا۟
إِن كُنتُم مُّؤْمِنِينَ ﴿٢٧٨﴾ فَإِن لَّمْ تَفْعَلُوا۟ فَأْذَنُوا۟ بِحَرْبٍ مِّنَ ٱللَّهِ وَرَسُولِهِۦ
وَإِن تُبْتُمْ فَلَكُمْ رُءُوسُ أَمْوَٰلِكُمْ لَا تَظْلِمُونَ وَلَا تُظْلَمُونَ ﴿٢٧٩﴾

275 Those who practise usury will not rise from the grave except as someone driven mad by Shayṭān's touch. That is because they say, 'Trade is the same as usury.' But Allah has permitted trade and He has forbidden usury. Whoever is given a warning by his Lord and then desists, can keep what he received in the past and his affair is Allah's concern. But all who return to it will be the Companions of the Fire, remaining in it timelessly, for ever.
276 Allah obliterates usury but makes *ṣadaqah* grow in value! Allah does not love any persistently ungrateful wrongdoer.
277 Those who believe and do right actions and establish the prayer and pay *zakāt*, will have their reward with their Lord. They will feel no fear and will know no sorrow.
278 You who believe! be fearful of Allah and forgo any remaining usury if you are believers.
279 If you do not, know that it means war from Allah and His Messenger.

But if you sincerely repent you may have your capital, without wronging and without being wronged.

These *āyahs* contain the ruling on usury and the permissibility of contracts in trade and a threat to those who consider usury lawful and persist in it. Many points emerge from them.

Those who practise usury

The word 'practise' (literally 'eat') means here 'take'. That is because they take it with the intention of consuming it. Linguistically '*ribā*' (usury) means 'increase' in general. Part of the usage of the verb is found in the hadith: 'By Allah, we did not take a morsel but that it grew (*rabā*) in size.' This refers to food for whose blessing the Prophet ﷺ prayed. Muslim transmitted it. Then the *Sharī'ah* limited this general usage to certain specific practices. Sometimes the word is applied to unlawful earning, as when Allah Almighty says about the Jews: '*…because of their practising usury when they were forbidden to do it.*' (4:160) What is meant by usury here is not the kind which is unlawful for us. What is meant is unlawful property, as when Allah says: '*They are people who listen to lies and consume ill-gotten gains*' (5:42), meaning unlawful wealth in the form of bribes and what they consider lawful of the property of non-jews when they say: '*We are under no obligation where the gentiles are concerned.*' (3:75) So according to this, the prohibition against usury includes all unlawful wealth whatever way it is earned.

The usury known in the *Sharī'ah* takes two forms: the usury entailed by delay and the usury entailed by disparity in contracts and foodstuffs as will be explained. The Arabs had a practice whereby they would say to a debtor, 'Will you settle now or pay more later?' The debtor could then increase the amount of money he owed, and the creditor would wait for it. This is forbidden by the consensus of the Community. Most prohibited sales are forbidden because of the idea of increase either in money or in benefit to one of the parties incurred by delay and the like. Some forbidden sales do not have increase in them, like selling fruit before it is ripe or selling after the *adhān* has been called for *Jumu'ah*, and the one who does it is said metaphorically to be practising usury.

The Imams relate from Abū Sa'īd al-Khudrī that the Messenger of Allah ﷺ said, 'Gold for gold, silver for silver, wheat for wheat, barley for barley, dates for dates and salt for salt, like for like, hand to hand. Anyone who increases or asks for increase practises usury. The taker and the giver are the same in respect of that.' In the hadith of 'Ubādah ibn aṣ-Ṣāmit we find, 'When the categories are different, sell however you wish when it is hand to hand.'

Abū Dāwūd related from 'Ubādah ibn aṣ-Ṣāmit that the Messenger of Allah ﷺ said, 'Gold for gold – ore and coins – silver for silver – ore and coins – wheat for wheat – *mudd* for *mudd* – barley for barley – *mudd* for *mudd* – dates for dates – *mudd* for *mudd* – and salt for salt – *mudd* for *mudd*. Anyone who increases or asks for increase practises usury. There is no harm in selling gold for silver when the amount of silver is more, provided it is hand to hand, and no delay is involved. There is no harm in selling wheat for barley when the amount of barley is more, provided it is hand to hand, and no delay is involved.'

Scholars agree that taking this position is following the Sunnah and that is the position of the majority of the Muslim *fuqahā'* except in the case of wheat and barley. Mālik considers them one category and does not permit two of them for one. That is also the position of al-Layth, al-Awzā'ī, and a large number of the scholars of Madīnah and Syria. Mālik adds sult-barley to them. Al-Layth considers them as one category and Ibn Wahb also holds that view.

The Sunnah is confirmed and there is no position other than it. The Prophet ﷺ said, 'When these categories are different, sell however you wish when it is hand to hand,' and he said, 'Wheat for wheat and barley for barley' which indicates that they are two different categories, just as wheat differs from dates, and because their attributes differ and they have different names. One does not consider plants which the *Sharī'ah* does not consider. They are different. This is the position of ash-Shāfi'ī, Abū Ḥanīfah, ath-Thawrī and the people who base their position on the hadith.

Mu'āwiyah ibn Abī Sufyān believed that the prohibition related from the Prophet ﷺ was about minted dirhams and dinars, not gold and silver ore for coins nor about things made from gold and silver. It is said that this was his position until an incident occurred to him with 'Ubādah which is transmitted by Muslim and others: 'We went on a sortie when Mu'āwiyah was in command of the people and took a lot of booty. Part of our booty consisted of a silver vessel. Mu'āwiyah ordered a man to sell it against the people's stipends. People argued about that. 'Ubādah ibn aṣ-Ṣāmit heard about it, went along and said, "I heard the Messenger of Allah ﷺ forbid selling gold for gold, silver for silver, wheat for wheat, barley for barley, dates for dates, and salt for salt except like for like, item for item. Anyone who increases or asks for increase practises usury." The people returned what they had been given. Mu'āwiyah heard about that and stood up and said, "What is the matter with men who relate hadiths from the Messenger of Allah ﷺ when we saw him and were his Companions and did not hear it from him!" 'Ubādah ibn aṣ-Ṣāmit stood up and repeated the story. He said, "We will relate what we heard from the Messenger of Allah ﷺ even if Mu'āwiyah dislikes it! – or 'in spite of him'. I do not care. I accompanied him in his army on a dark night."' Ḥammād said this or something similar to it.

Ibn 'Abd al-Barr said, 'It is related that the story concerned Abu-d-Dardā' with Mu'āwiyah. It is possible that that occurred to both of them together but the hadith on the custom is recorded from 'Ubādah. It is what scholars rely on regarding the subject of usury. There is no disagreement that what Mu'āwiyah did is not permitted and it is not denied that Abu-d-Dardā' and 'Ubādah knew something that was unknown to Mu'āwiyah. They were respected men among the *fuqahā'* of the Companions and two of their great men. Certain things were unknown to Abū Bakr and 'Umar while they were known to lesser men and the same holds true for Mu'āwiyah. It is also possible that his position was that of Ibn 'Abbās who was an ocean of knowledge but did not see anything wrong in two dirhams for one until Abū Sa'īd dissuaded him from it. The incident of Mu'āwiyah and 'Ubādah took place while he was governor for 'Umar. Qabīṣah ibn Dhu'ayb said, "Ubadah objected to something Mu'āwiyah did and said, "I will not live in the same land as you!" and went back to Madīnah. 'Umar asked him, "What has brought you here?" and he told him. He said, "Go back to your place. May Allah make ugly a land which does not contain you and those like you." He wrote to Mu'āwiyah, "You have no authority over him."'

The Imams (and the wording is that of ad-Dāraquṭnī) related from 'Alī that the Messenger of Allah ﷺ said, 'Dinar for dinar and dirham for dirham with no disparity between them. Anyone who needs silver should buy it with gold. If he needs gold, he should buy it with silver, thus and thus.' Scholars say that this indicates the genus of the coins. Silver is both white and black and gold is red and yellow. None of that can be exchanged except like for like, same for same, in every case. This is the position of the majority of the people of knowledge. The transmission from Mālik about minor coins of base metal (*fulūs*) varies. He at times compared them to dirhams since they are used to pay for things, while at other times he forbade doing that since they are not currency in every land and vary from one land to another.

There is no consideration given to one view which is related from several Mālikīs which some relate from Mālik, that when a merchant is preparing to leave and requires minted dirhams or dinars, he can take his silver or gold bullion to the mint and tell the minter, 'Take this silver or gold of mine and take out the fee for your work and give me minted dinars for my gold or minted dirhams for my silver because I am preparing to leave and I fear I will miss the people I am travelling with,' and that that is permitted due to necessity, and it is something which some people have to do. Ibn al-'Arabī related it in what he took from Mālik about someone other than a merchant and said that Mālik lightened the usual ruling in that case. The form of this transaction is that he sells his silver which weighs a hundred dirhams, adding five extra as the fee for minting, for a hundred. This is pure usury. A transaction which would be permissible would be if he told him, 'Mint this for me,' and then separately gives him the wage for it. When he mints it, he takes the whole amount from him and pays him the wage for doing it.

What Mālik did first is what he did last. Mālik looked at the outcome and on that basis made the judgement for the present circumstances. The rest of the *fuqahā'* reject it. Ibn al-'Arabī said, 'Mālik's argument concerning it is clear.' Abū 'Umar said, 'This is the same usury which the Messenger of Allah ﷺ forbade when he said, "Anyone who increases or asks for increase practises usury."' Ibn Wahb denied that this was Mālik's position and denied it himself. Al-Abharī claimed that it was out of compassion in seeking trade and so that the market was not missed, and the ruling of usury is only applicable against someone who desires an increase and intends that. Al-Abharī forgets Mālik's basic principle of cutting off the means to wrong (*sadd adh-dharā'ī*), including his position about someone who sells a garment, which he has no intention of rebuying, on credit and then finds it being sold in the market: he is not permitted to buy it for less than the amount he sold it for, even if he did not intend or desire that originally. Such examples are numerous. If usury only existed in a transaction when someone actually intended it, it would only be made unlawful for the *fuqahā'* [who would possess the necessary perspicacity to recognize it in the transaction]. 'Umar said, 'No one should trade in our market except someone with *fiqh*. Otherwise he will practise usury.' This is clear to anyone who is fair and inspired to right guidance.

Mālik went to great lengths to prevent forbidden increase, and so he considered something merely suspect to be the same as actual usury. He forbade exchanging a dinar and dirham for a dinar and dirham in order to block the means and to cut off suspicion, since they would not be exchanged except with some increase in mind. The reason for prohibiting that is the impossibility of making an equal distribution. It is exchanging gold and silver for gold, and it is evident that the intrinsic disparity in such an exchange is forbidden. Furthermore, he forbade exchanging a dinar of fine gold and a dinar of base gold [for two dinars of medium quality, because it is as if he considered the medium quality dinar] to correspond to the good quality one and considered the poor quality one negligible. This demonstrates the acuteness of his investigation into the matter and indicates that

that transmission about paying extra for minting should be rejected and is not sound, and Allah knows best.

Al-Khaṭṭābī said, 'Bullion is pieces of gold and silver before they are minted.' *'Ayn* (specie) are minted dirhams and dinars. The Messenger of Allah ﷺ forbade selling a *mithqāl* of gold coins for slightly over a *mithqāl* of unminted gold bullion, and he forbade a disparity between minted silver and unminted silver. He said, 'Bullion and coins have the same ruling.'

Scholars agree that dates for dates can only be like for like. They disagree about selling one date for two dates and one grain of wheat for two. Ash-Shāfi'ī, Aḥmad, Isḥāq, and ath-Thawrī forbid it. That is analogous to the position of Mālik. It is sound because if there is usury in a lot of something, then a little of it is included in the ruling by analogy. Those who permit that argue that when only one or two dates are consumed, they have no price because they cannot be weighed or measured and therefore disparity is permitted.

Know that the issues concerning this subject are numerous and its secondary rulings widespread. A measure of that can be gained by looking at what each of the scholars consider to be the legal reason (*'illah*) behind the prohibition of usury. Abū Ḥanīfah said that the reason is because it is a weighed or measured category. So in his view all that is subject to measurement or weight consists of one category. It is not permitted to sell some of it for the same category with disparity or with delay. So he forbids selling dirt for dirt with disparity because it can be measured, but permits one loaf of bread for two loaves because he does not think it falls under measurement which is its basis and so he removes it from a genus in which usury can exist.

Ash-Shāfi'ī says that the reason is that it is a category of food. This is his position in his new school. So he does not permit selling flour for bread or bread for bread with disparity or delay, whether the bread is leavened or unleavened. He thinks that it is not permitted to sell one egg for two, one pomegranate for two, or one melon for two melons, either hand to hand or with delay because all of those are consumable foods. In his old school, he said that the reason was that the prohibition was based on its being weighed or measured.

What the Mālikīs say about this matter varies. The best of what is said about it is that foodstuffs which can be stored form a general category, like wheat, barley, dates, and salt for which there is a text, as well as similar items like rice, millet, sorghum, sesame, and legumes like broad beans, lentils, cowpeas, and chickpeas. The same holds for conserved meats, milks, vinegars, oils and fruits like grapes, raisins, and olives. There is disagreement about figs. Honey and sugar are added to them. Usury can occur with all of those things with delay, but disparity is permitted in them by the words of the Prophet ﷺ, 'When these categories are different, sell however you wish if it is hand to hand.' There is no usury in respect of fresh fruits which are perishable, like apples, melons, pomegranates, pears, cucumbers, aubergines and other vegetables. Mālik said, 'It is not permitted to sell eggs for eggs with disparity because they can be stored.' He permits like for like. Muḥammad ibn 'Abdullāh ibn 'Abd al-Ḥakam said, 'It is permitted to sell one egg for two or more because they are not stored.' That is the position of al-Awzā'ī.

Grammarians disagree about the word *'ribā'* (usury). The Basrans say that its root has a *wāw* because the dual is *ribawān.* Sībawayh said that. The Kufans say that it is written with a *yā'* and the dual has a *yā'* because of the *kasrah* at the beginning of the word. Az-Zajjāj said, 'I have not seen an error worse than this or uglier than this! They are not satisfied with just an error in script; they even err in the dual!' in spite of the fact that they recite: "*What you give with usurious intent, aiming to get back a greater amount from people's wealth, does not become greater (*yarbū with *wāw) with Allah.*" (30:39) Muḥammad ibn Yazīd said that *'ribā'* is written with a *wāw* in the *muṣḥaf* to distinguish it from *zinā.* It is more appropriate for *ribā* to have a *wāw* because it is from the verb *rabā, yarbū.*

will not rise (from the grave) except as someone driven mad by Shayṭān's touch.

'Lā yaqūmūna' (they will not rise) here refers to rising from the grave according to Ibn 'Abbās, Mujāhid, Ibn Jubayr, Qatādah, ar-Rabī', aḍ-Ḍaḥḥāk, as-Suddī, and Ibn Zayd. One of them said, 'Allah appoints a *shayṭān* to choke him.' They all said, 'He will be raised like a madman to punish him and make him hated by all the people in the Gathering.' This agreed-upon interpretation is strengthened by the reading of Ibn Mas'ūd which is: 'They will not rise on the Day of Rising except as someone rises...'

Ibn 'Aṭiyyah said, 'The words of the *āyah* contain a simile for the state of someone who engages in trade in this world with avarice and greed, comparing him to a madman, because greed and desire affect him to the extent that his limbs become disordered. This is like when you say, "He's mad!" about someone walking quickly whose movements are addled, either by anxiety or something else.' The poet al-A'shā likened the movements of a camel to madness. However, the reading of Ibn Mas'ūd and the mutually supporting positions of commentators make this interpretation weak.

'Driven mad' (*yatakhabbaṭuhu*) is Form V of the verb *khabaṭa.* Allah will make this disorder a sign of practising usury. That is because He enlarges the usury in their bellies and it makes them heavy, so when they rise from their graves they will stand and then fall over. It is said that they will be raised on the Day of Rising with their bellies inflated like pregnant women and whenever they stand, they will fall down and people will walk over them. Some scholars say that that is the sign by which they will be known on the Day of Rising and then punishment comes after that. The image of 'eating' is used here for the practice of usury because consumption is the greatest goal of a person in property, and it also indicates greed, which is the severest form of avarice. So one of the consequences of earning takes the place of all earning, and clothing, dwelling, storing and spending on dependants is all included in 'eating' (*akl*), which is here translated as 'practise'.

This *āyah* contains evidence against those who deny that epilepsy is from the jinn and claim that it is natural and that Shayṭān does not move inside a person nor touch him. The refutation of this has already been discussed earlier. An-Nasā'ī related that Abu-l-Yasār said, 'The Messenger of Allah ﷺ used to make the following supplication: "O Allah, I seek refuge with You from falling from a high place, being crushed by a falling building, drowning, and burning. I seek refuge with You from being touched by Shayṭān at the time of death. I seek refuge with you from being killed in Your cause while retreating. I seek refuge with You from dying from a sting."' It is related from Muḥammad ibn al-Muthannā from Abū Dāwūd from Hammām from Qatādah from Anas that the Prophet ﷺ used to say, 'O Allah, I seek refuge with You from madness, leprosy, white leprosy, and evil diseases.' *Mass* means madness. One says that a man is 'touched' (*mussa*, *alisa*, *mamsūs* and *mal'ūs*).

That is the form usury will take in the Next World. It is related in the hadith of the Night Journey: 'I was taken by Jibrīl and passed by some men each of whom had a belly like a great house. They were in the path of the people of Pharaoh. The people of Pharaoh are exposed to the Fire morning and evening. They advance like camels maddened by thirst, trampling on stones and trees, not hearing or understanding. When the people with those bellies are aware of them, they stand up, but their bellies make them fall. When any of them stands up, his belly pulls him over and he falls. They cannot leave and then the people of Pharaoh envelop them, trampling them front and back. That is their punishment in the Interspace between this world and the Next. The people of Pharaoh are saying, "O Allah, let the Final Hour never come!" Allah Almighty says: *"On the Day the Hour takes place: 'Admit Pharaoh's people to the harshest punishment!'"* (40:46) I said, "Jibrīl, who are they?" He answered, "They are those who consumed usury who will only rise as someone driven mad by Shayṭān's touch."' *Mass* is insanity.

That is because they say, 'Trade is the same as usury.'

With all commentators this refers to the unbelievers and they are told to keep that which they received in the past. This is not what is said to a disobedient believer. He should cancel his sale and cancel what he did when he was ignorant of the prohibition. That is why the Prophet ﷺ said, 'If anyone does an action which is not part of our business, it is rejected.' The threat implicit in this *āyah* includes those who are disobedient.

They say that the increase at the end of the term is based on the price at the beginning of the contract. This is because of the way that the Arabs understood usury. When a debt was due, they would tell the debtor, 'Either you pay it or you increase it,' i.e. the amount of the debt. Allah says that that is unlawful and refutes them by saying: *'But Allah has permitted trade and He has forbidden usury.'* It is clear that when the terms ends and someone cannot pay it, he is given a deferral. This usury is what the Prophet ﷺ cancelled when he stated on the Day of 'Arafah, 'All usury is cancelled, and the first usury I cancel is our usury, that of 'Abbās ibn 'Abd al-Muṭṭalib. It is all cancelled.' He began with his uncle and singled him out. This is one of the customs which demonstrates justice in a ruler: to impose justice on himself and those close to him, and then on people in general.

But Allah has permitted trade and He has forbidden usury.

This is one of the generally applicable (*'āmm*) *āyah*s in the Qur'an. The definite article before the word 'trade' (*al-bay'*) is to indicate the genus, not to make it definite, since there is no prior mentioned trade to which it can refer. So trade is general, and then the usurious transactions we have mentioned and other things which are mentioned as being forbidden are specified. Such things include wine, carrion, a transaction known as *ḥabal al-ḥabalah* and other things confirmed in the Sunnah and by the consensus of the Community. This is similar to *'kill the idolaters'* (10:5) and other literal statements which are necessarily generally applicable but which are then made specific. This is the position of most of the *fuqahā'*. Some say that this *āyah* is included in the undefined (*mujmal*) parts of the Qur'an which, in turn, is further described by what is lawful and unlawful in sales, and so it is not possible to use it to make a sale lawful or unlawful unless that is accompanied by some clarification from the Sunnah of the Prophet ﷺ. It indicates the permissibility of sales in general, not particular transactions. This is the difference between *'āmm* and *mujmal*. The *'āmm* indicates the permissibility of sales in general when there is no evidence of a specific factor making them prohibited. The *mujmal* does not indicate the permissibility of the specific unless there is definite evidence of permissibility. The first is sounder, and Allah knows best.

Linguistically '*bay*'' (trade) is a verbal noun of the verb '*bā'a*' (to sell), meaning to give goods and take something in return. It stipulates a seller, who is the owner or one who acts on his behalf, and a buyer, who is the one who pays the price, and the goods which are paid for. So the pillars of the sale are four: seller, buyer, price, and thing paid for. Then among the Arabs the reciprocal transaction varies according to those it is connected to. If it is in exchange for ownership, it is called a sale. If it is in exchange for the use of allowing sex, it is called marriage (*nikāḥ*). If it is in exchange for another use, it is called hire. If it is coin for coin, it is money-changing. If it is a deferred debt, it is an advance (*salam*). This will be explained in the *Āyah* of Debt. The ruling on hire will be dealt with in *al-Qaṣaṣ*. The ruling on dower in marriage will be dealt with in *an-Nisā'*.

The sale involves a verbal offer and verbal acceptance, however it is expressed. In Arabic, this involves the expression using the past tense, which is actual, and the future tense, which is an allusion. The sale can also be made binding by a commonly understood allusion by which ownership is transferred. This is as when someone says, 'I have sold you these goods for ten dirhams,' and the buyer says, 'I have bought them.' Or the buyer says, 'I have bought it' and the buyer says, 'I have sold it to you.' Or the seller says, 'I will sell them to you for ten dirhams,' and the buyer says, 'I will buy them' or 'I have bought them.' The same is true if he says, 'Take this for ten,' or 'You will be blessed with them for ten,' or 'I have handed them over' when both parties intend a sale. All of this is a binding sale. If the seller says, 'I have sold them to you for ten,' and then retracts that before the buyer accepts, he cannot retract until he hears the buyer either accept or reject that because he has obliged that on himself and said it and because the contract is not complete.

If the seller then says, 'I was joking,' what is transmitted about that varies. Sometimes it is said that the sale is binding and one does not pay attention to his statement, and sometimes it is said that one looks at the value of the goods. If the price is similar to its value, then the sale is binding. If there is a great disparity, like selling a slave for a dirham or a house for a dinar, it is known that he did not intend a sale by that and was joking. So it is not binding.

A usurious contract is void and is never permitted since the Imams related from Abū Sa'īd al-Khudrī: 'Bilāl brought some Barni dates and the Messenger of Allah ﷺ asked him, "Where are these from?" Bilāl said, "From dates which we consider low quality. I exchanged two *ṣā*'s of them for a *ṣā'* to feed the Prophet ﷺ." The Messenger of Allah ﷺ said, "Oh! usury itself! Do not do it, but if you want to buy dates, sell them in another sale and then buy them."' In one variant, 'This is usury. Return them. Then sell our dates and buy for us from the price.' The words 'return them' indicate that a usurious contract is void and not valid in any way. That is the position of the majority, except for Abū Ḥanīfah who said, 'A usurious sale is permitted in as far as it is a sale, but forbidden since it entails usury. If the usury is removed, then the sale is permitted.' If this had been the case, then the Messenger of Allah ﷺ would not have voided the sale and would have merely commanded that the extra amount be returned and validated the transaction of the *ṣā'*.

Any sale which is clearly *ḥarām* is null and void and so the buyer must return the goods themselves. If they have been lost while in his possession, he must return the price paid. This is the case with real estate, goods and animals. Mālik said that what is unclearly unlawful is returned, whether or not it has gone.

Whoever is given a warning by his Lord

Ja'far aṣ-Ṣādiq said, 'Allah forbade usury so that people would lend to one another.' Ibn Mas'ūd reported that the Prophet ﷺ said, 'A loan is worth twice what *ṣadaqah* is worth.' Some people said that Allah forbade it because it destroys wealth and thereby destroys people.

'Ā'ishah recited this *āyah* when she was told about what Zayd ibn Arqam had done. Ad-Dāraquṭnī reported from al-'Āliyyah bint Anfa': 'Umm Muḥibbah and I went to Makkah and we visited 'A'ishah and greeted her. She asked, "Who are you?" We said, "We are from the people of Kufa." It was as if she turned away from us and Umm Muḥibbah said to her, "Umm al-Mu'minīn, I had a slave-girl and I sold her to Zayd ibn Arqam al-Anṣārī for eight hundred dirhams against his stipend. He wanted to sell her and then I bought her for six hundred dirhams cash." She turned to us and said, "Evil is what you sold and what you bought! Tell Zayd that he has nullified his *jihād* with the Messenger of Allah ﷺ unless he repents!" She asked her, "What do you think of the transaction if I only take the capital from him?" She recited: "*Whoever is given a warning by his Lord and then desists, may keep what he received in the past.*"' Al-'Ālīyah was the wife of Abū Isḥāq al-Ḥamdānī al-Kūfī as-Sabī'ī, Umm Yūnus ibn Abī Isḥāq.

Mālik relates this hadith in the transmission of Ibn Wahb regarding credit sales. If something leads to falling into the forbidden, then it is forbidden, even if it is outwardly a permissible sale. In this principle, Mālik differed from other *fuqahā'* who said, 'Rulings are based on the outward, not a supposition.' Our evidence is the position of 'blocking the means' (*sadd adh-dharā'i'*). If the transaction is safe, we deduce its soundness, as already stated. This hadith is a definitive text. What

'Ā'ishah said for Zayd was only to deter him, since such things are not a matter of opinion. Nullification of actions can only be known by revelation.

We read in *Ṣaḥīḥ Muslim* from an-Nu'mān ibn Bashīr that the Messenger of Allah ﷺ stated, 'The *ḥalāl* is clear and the *ḥarām* is clear. But between the two there are doubtful things about which most people have no knowledge. Whoever exercises caution with regard to what is doubtful, shows prudence in respect of his *dīn* and his honour. Whoever gets involved in the doubtful things is like a herdsman who grazes his animals near a private preserve (*ḥimā*). He is bound to enter it. Every king has a private preserve and the private preserve of Allah on His earth are the things that He has made forbidden.'

The legal sense of this, in terms of evidence, is that he forbade doing doubtful things out of the fear of falling into the forbidden and it is that which constitutes the legal principle of 'blocking the means' (*sadd adh-dharā'i'*). The Prophet ﷺ said, 'One of the major wrong actions is for a man to abuse his parents.' They said, 'O Messenger of Allah, is it possible for a man to abuse his parents?' He replied, 'He may curse another man's father who in turn curses his father, and curse his mother and he in turn curses his mother.' So he made all allusion to cursing parents in general like cursing one's own parents. The Prophet ﷺ, however, did curse the Jews when they consumed the price they obtained for selling what they were forbidden to eat.

In a letter, Abū Bakr said, 'There must be no joining together of animals that are kept separately nor separation of animals that are kept together out of the fear of having to pay *zakāt* on them.' Ibn 'Abbās forbade dirhams for dirhams when combining them would lead to an offence. Scholars agree that it is forbidden to combine a sale and a loan, that a little wine is *ḥarām*, even if it does not intoxicate, that being alone with an unrelated woman is forbidden, even if a man is impotent, that it is forbidden to look at the face of a young woman, and several other things which are known to be definite. It is confirmed that the *Sharī'ah* has forbidden them because they constitute the means to forbidden things. So it is more fitting that the potential causes of usury be defended against and the means to it blocked. If someone allows those means, he should allow digging wells and setting up ropes in situations where they might lead to the death of Muslim men and women. No one allows that.

There is also agreement that the *'īnah* sale is forbidden, and Allah is the One who grants success. Abū 'Ubayd al-Ḥarawī explained an *'īnah* sale as being 'a transaction in which someone sells goods to a man for a known price for a known term and then buys them back from him for less than the price for which he sold them.' He said, 'If he buys goods from someone else in the presence of the one who seeks the *'īnah* for a known price and then takes possession of them and then sells them to the one who seeks the *'īnah* for a higher price for a set term, and then the buyer buys them from the first seller for cash for a lower price, this is also *'īnah*, but less disliked than the first, and some permit it.' It is called *'īnah* because of the presence of cash for the one with the *'īnah*, *'ayn* meaning 'ready money'.

Abū Dāwūd reports that Ibn 'Umar said, 'I heard the Messenger of Allah ﷺ say, "When you sell by *'īnah*, follow the tails of cattle, are content to be farmers and abandon *jihād*, then Allah will impose abasement on you which will not be removed from you until you return to your *dīn*."' Abū 'Abd ar-Raḥmān al-Khurāsānī says that the *isnād* of this hadith contains someone who is not well-known. Abū 'Ubayd al-Harawī explained the *'īnah* sale and said, 'It is that you sell some goods to a man for a known price due at a specified term and then you buy them from him for a lesser price than the price for which you sold them.' He said, 'If, in the presence of someone who desires an *'īnah*, someone buys goods from someone else for a known price and takes possession of them and then sells them to the one who desires an *'īnah* for a greater price than that for which he purchased them with a known period of credit, and then the buyer sells them to the first seller for cash less than the price, that too is an *'īnah*, but it is less disliked than the first kind. Some people permit it. It is called an *'īnah* because of the presence of cash. That is because of the presence of ready money and the buyer. He bought it in order to sell it for ready money which he receives immediately.'

Our scholars say that if someone sells goods for a price on credit and then buys them for the same sort of payment for which he sold them, he must buy them for cash or with a term less than the term for which he sold to them or for a longer term for the same price, or greater or less. These are three possible situations. In the first and second cases, the transaction is permitted if the price paid is the same or greater, but it is not permitted if the price is less, according to 'Ā'ishah's hadith. As for the third case, which is to sell them for a longer term, if he buys the goods themselves or more, it is permitted to do that for the same price or less, but not for more. If he buys some of it, it is only permitted for the same price, not more or less. Our scholars have specified seventy-seven points on this topic, but the nub of them is what we have mentioned.

He can keep what he received in the past

This refers to past usury and makes clear that there will be no consequences in this world or the Next. As-Suddī and others said that. This is the judgment of

Allah for the unbelievers of Quraysh and Thaqīf and others who became Muslim who used to deal in usurious transactions before they were Muslim.

and his affair is Allah's concern.

There are four interpretations of the pronoun 'his' here. One is that it is really 'its' and refers to usury, meaning the business of usury is subject to Allah's command in making it unlawful or not. The second is that the pronoun refers to 'what was in the past' i.e. it is up to Allah to pardon that and remove its consequences. The third is that the pronoun refers to the usurer, meaning that his affair is up to Allah in making him firm in giving up usury or returning him to indulging in it. An-Naḥḥās preferred this position, saying that it is clear and good, i.e. his business is up to Allah in the future. If He wishes, He makes him firm in standing by the prohibition, and if He wishes, returning him to usurious transactions. The fourth is that the pronoun refers to what is forbidden (i.e. 'its' affair), but means to allow him to hope for the best.

But all who return to it

This means that they revert to usury before they die. Sufyān said that. Another said, 'Whoever reverts and says that trade is like usury has disbelieved.' Ibn 'Aṭiyyah said, 'We believe that the *āyah* is about the unbelievers, so being forever in the Fire is literal. In respect of the disobedient Muslim, it is metaphorical.'

Allah obliterates usury

In this world: meaning that He removes blessing (*barakah*) from usury, even if it is a lot. Ibn Mas'ūd related that the Prophet ﷺ said, 'Even if usury is a lot, its end is little.' It is said that it means in the Next World. Regarding these words, Ibn 'Abbās said, 'Neither *ṣadaqah*, ḥajj, *jihād* nor gifts to relatives are accepted from a usurer.' *Maḥaqa* (obliterating) has the meaning of 'to decrease and vanish.' The waning (*maḥāq*) of the moon is derived from the same root.

but makes *ṣadaqah* grow in value!

This means that He increases it in blessing in this world and makes its reward many times more in the Next World. In *Ṣaḥīḥ Muslim:* 'When someone gives *ṣadaqah*, Allah makes it grow, even if it is only a morsel of food, like one of you would raise his colt or foal until it comes on the Day of Rising the size of Uḥud.'

Allah does not love any persistently ungrateful wrongdoer.

An ungrateful person is also called a wrongdoer for emphasis. It is said that it is to remove any confusion about the word 'ungrateful' (*kaffār*) since the word can be used for a farmer who covers up the grain in the earth. Ibn Fūrak said that.

Those who believe and do right actions and establish the prayer and pay *zakāt*, will have their reward with their Lord. They will feel no fear and will know no sorrow.

Here Allah singles out the prayer and *zakāt*, even though they are no more than a component part of righteous deeds, to honour them and highlight their value since they are the best of actions: the prayer with respect to the body and the *zakāt* with respect to property.

You who believe! be fearful of Allah and forgo any remaining usury

Its outward meaning is that any uncollected usury is void, even if it was contracted before the revelation of the *āyah* of prohibition. It is said that this *āyah* was revealed because of Thaqīf. They made a treaty with the Prophet ﷺ that they would claim the usury which people owed them while the usury they owed others would be cancelled. When the terms of their usury were due, they sent to Makkah to settle them. The debts were against the Banū 'Abdah, who are the Banū 'Amr ibn 'Umayr of Thaqīf, and the Banū al-Mughīrah of Makhzūm. The Banū Mughīrah said, 'We will not give you anything. Usury has been abolished.' They went to 'Attāb ibn Usayd and he wrote about it to the Messenger of Allah ﷺ and the *āyah* was revealed. The Messenger of Allah then wrote it to 'Attāb, and Thaqīf learned of it and refrained. This is the reason for the revelation of the *āyah* as was reported by Ibn Isḥāq, Ibn Jurayj, as-Suddī and others. It means: place a screen between you and the punishment of Allah by abandoning any outstanding usury.

if you are believers.

This is a condition applying to Thaqīf because it was when they first became Muslim. We can suppose that, if the *āyah* is about those who affirm belief, it is a metaphorical condition, as you might say to someone who wants to establish himself, 'If you are a man, then do such-and-such.' An-Naqqāsh related Muqātil ibn Sulaymān said that the word 'if' here means 'when'. Ibn 'Aṭiyyah said that this is not known linguistically. Ibn Fūrak said that it is impossible that it means the Prophets before Muḥammad ﷺ. *'Forgo any remaining* ribā *if you believe'* in Muḥammad ﷺ since the first command is only of use if you believe. This is rejected by what is reported about the reason for the revelation of the *āyah*.

If you do not, know that it means war from Allah and His Messenger.

This is a threat to anyone who does not abandon usury. War calls for killing. Ibn 'Abbās said that on the Day of Rising it will be said to the practiser of usury, 'Take up your weapons for war.' Ibn 'Abbās also said, 'If someone insists on usury and does not desist, it is a duty for the leader of the Muslims to ask him to repent. If he does not desist, he strikes off his head.' Qatādah said, 'Allah threatened the people of usury with killing and made them lawful for killing wherever they are found.' It is said that the meaning is: 'If you do not desist, you are at war with Allah and His Messenger,' meaning you are their enemies. Ibn Khuwayzimandād said, 'If the people of a land think usury to be lawful, they are apostates and the ruling regarding them is the same as that of the people of apostasy, and it is permitted for the ruler to fight them. Do you not see that Allah Almighty has announced that when He says: "*...know that it means war from Allah and His Messenger*"?' Abū Bakr recited it from 'Āṣim as '*ādhinū*', meaning 'inform others'.

Ibn Bukayr narrated, 'A man came to Mālik ibn Anas and said, "Abū 'Abdullāh, I saw a drunkard, who was a chronic drinker, who was trying to catch the moon. I said, 'My wife is divorced if there is anything worse than wine which enters a man's belly.'" He said, "Go away while I investigate your problem." He came back to him the following day and he said the same thing. He came back the day after that and Mālik told him, 'Your wife is divorced. I have examined the Book of Allah and the Sunnah of His Prophet ﷺ and I did not see anything worse than usury because Allah has proclaimed war on account of it."'

This *āyah* indicates that practising usury and making use of it is one of the major wrong actions. There is no disagreement about that as we will make clear. It is related that the Prophet ﷺ said, 'A time will come upon people when there will not be anyone left who does not consume usury, and even one who does not consume it will be touched by its dust."' Ad-Dāraquṭnī related that 'Abdullāh ibn al-Ḥanẓalah reported that the Prophet ﷺ said, 'A dirham of usury is worse in the sight of Allah than thirty-six wrongful acts of fornication.' It is related that he said ﷺ, 'Usury has ninety-nine gates, the least of which is like a man having sex with his mother.'

Ibn Mas'ūd said, 'Those who take usury, pay it, its witnesses and scribes if they know of it, are cursed on the tongue of Muḥammad ﷺ.' Al-Bukhārī related that Abū Juḥayfah said, 'The Messenger of Allah ﷺ forbade the price of blood, the price of dogs, and the earnings of prostitutes, and cursed those who consume usury and those who pay it, the tattooer and women who are tattooed.' In *Ṣaḥīḥ Muslim*, Abū Hurayrah reported, 'Avoid the seven deadly wrong actions.' Usury was one of them. In Abū Dāwūd from Ibn Mas'ūd we find: 'The Messenger of Allah ﷺ

cursed those who take usury, those who pay it, its scribes and its witnesses.'

But if you sincerely repent, you may have your capital, without wronging and without being wronged.

Abū Dāwūd related that the father of Sulaymān ibn 'Amr said, 'I heard the Messenger of Allah ﷺ say in the Farewell Hajj, "Every usurious transaction of the Jāhiliyyah is cancelled. You have your capital, not wronging or being wronged."' So when there is repentance, Allah returns to usurers their capital and tells them not to wrong others by taking any more usury and that they will not 'be wronged' by their capital being retained causing them to lose it. It is possible that 'not being wronged' refers to procrastination because the procrastination of the wealthy is wrongdoing. The meaning is that the capital debt is settled straight away while any usury is removed. This is the sunnah of righteousness, and is the closest thing to righteousness. Do you not see that when the Prophet ﷺ indicated to Ka'b ibn Mālik to reduce the debt of Ibn Abī Ḥadrad by half, to which Ka'b agreed, the Messenger of Allah ﷺ told the other, 'Get up and pay it.' Scholars agree that the command referred to settling the debt. Reconciliation will be dealt with in *an-Nisā'*, Allah willing.

But if you sincerely repent you may have your capital,

This is to stress the invalidation of any usurious increase that is still outstanding, but permits receiving the capital in which there is no usury. Some scholars use this as evidence that anything that happens to the sale goods before they are received, which would oblige the prohibition of the contract, invalidates the contract, as when a Muslim buys game and then the buyer or seller assumes *iḥrām* before it is collected: the sale is forbidden because something has occurred which forbids the sale. Allah has invalidated what has not been collected because something has occurred which makes it forbidden before it has been collected. If it has already been collected before that happens, the sale is not affected. This is the school of Abū Ḥanīfah and the position of the Shāfi'īs. It is used as evidence that the destruction of the goods before they are collected, and while they are still in the possession of the seller, obliges the cancellation of the contract, although, according to Aḥmad ibn Ḥanbal, some early scholars disagreed with this position.

This is in keeping with the position of those who say that a basic contract in which there is usury is permitted but then becomes invalidated by the ruling of Islam before it can be collected. As for those who forbid the usurious contract at its source, these words are not sound. That is because usury is forbidden in all religions, and what was done in the Jāhiliyyah was the custom of the idolaters, and the usury they took is the same as what they had gained by usurpation and looting, and so what they did is not considered.

According to this, it is not correct to call witnesses to any contract involving usury. The laws of the Prophets before us forbid usury, and this is well known and mentioned in the Book of Allah, as He relates about the Jews: *'because of their practising usury when they were forbidden to do it.'* (4:161) Allah mentions in the story of Shu'ayb that his people rejected that and said: *'Do your prayers instruct you that we should abandon what our fathers worshipped or stop doing what we want to with our wealth?'* (11:87) So it is not valid to use testimony as evidence (i.e. for the validity of such contracts).

Some of the scrupulous who go to excess believe that when lawful property is mixed with the unlawful in such a way that it cannot really be separated, and then someone removes the unlawful amount mixed with it, what remains is not lawful or good, because the lawful might have been removed and the unlawful left. Ibn al-'Arabī said, 'This is excess in the *dīn*. With respect to things that cannot be easily differentiated, what is desired is the value, not the thing itself. If it is destroyed, then its equivalent replaces it. Mixing is tantamount to destruction as the individual item cannot be differentiated.' Allah knows best.

Our scholars say that the way to repent of unlawful property in one's possession, if it is usury, is to return it to the person from whom it was taken and to seek him out if he is not present. If you despair of finding him, then you should give that amount away as *ṣadaqah*. If you took something through injustice, you should follow the same procedure in dealing with the one you wronged. If the matter is unclear to you, and you do not know how much is lawful and how much is unlawful, you should examine the amount and return an amount sufficient to preclude any doubt that any of the unlawful remains in your possession. You should return that to those you know you wronged and from whom you took usury. If you despair of finding them, you must give *ṣadaqah* on their behalf. If your wrongs take up all you have and you know that you are obliged to pay what you can never do because it is so great, then your repentance is to give all of your possessions either to the poor or for the best interests of the Muslims so that there only remains in your possession the minimum clothing necessary for the prayer and covering your private parts and food for the day.

In the eyes of most scholars there is a difference between this and someone who is bankrupt, because the one who is bankrupt did not take people's property through transgression. They are the ones who go to him and so he is left with what will cover him in his normal dress. Abū 'Ubayd and others, however, think that the ruling is the same and a bankrupt is only left with what will be enough for the prayer and to cover his private parts. Whenever he obtains anything, it is taken from him and he only keeps what we mentioned until he and those who know his state know that he has settled what he owes.

This *āyah* is a threat from Allah about usury, and a similar threat about sharecropping (*mukhābarah*) is reported from the Prophet ﷺ. Abū Dāwūd reported from Yaḥyā ibn Ma'īn from Abū Rajā' from Ibn Khaytham from Abu-z-Zubayr that Jarīr ibn 'Abdullah said, 'Allah and His Messenger announce war against someone who does not abandon *mukhābarah*.' This is evidence for the prohibition of sharecropping, which is working land for a half, third or quarter of its produce. It is also called *muzāra'ah*. All the Mālikīs, ash-Shāfi'ī, Abū Ḥanīfah and their followers and Dāwūd agree that it is not permitted to rent land for a third, a fourth, or part of its produce because that is unknown, although ash-Shāfi'ī and his people and Abū Ḥanīfah say that it is permitted to rent land for food when what it produces is known, as it is known that the Prophet ﷺ said, 'As for something known and guaranteed, there is no harm in it.' Muslim transmitted it. That is the position of Muḥammad ibn 'Abd al-Ḥakam, while Mālik and his adherents forbid it.

That is also based on what Muslim related that Rāfi' ibn Khadīj said: 'In the time of the Messenger of Allah ﷺ we used to let out the land for cultivation and we would rent it in return for a third, a fourth and a specified amount of food. One day one of my uncles came to us and said, "The Messenger of Allah ﷺ has forbidden us something which used to contain benefit for us, but obeying Allah and His Messenger is more beneficial for us. He forbade us to rent out the land for cultivation in return for a third, a fourth and a specified amount of food. He commanded the owner of the land to cultivate it or give it for cultivation."' He disliked renting it and the like of that.

It is agreed that it is not permitted to rent land in exchange for any type of food or drink because that would be tantamount to selling food for food on credit. Therefore renting land for any of what it produces is forbidden, even if that is not normally eaten or drunk, except in the case of wood, reeds and firewood, as they fall under the category of *muzābanah* in their view. This is recorded from Mālik and his adherents. Ibn Saḥnūn mentioned from al-Mughīrah ibn 'Abd ar-Raḥmān al-Makhzūmī al-Madanī that 'There is no harm in renting land for food which is not produced from it.' It is also related from al-Mughīrah that it is not permitted, as the rest of the Mālikīs say.

Ibn Ḥabīb mentioned that Ibn Kinānah used to say, 'Land may not be rented for anything connected to any plants that it produces. There is nothing wrong in renting it for something else, whether it is something that it is eaten or not, and whether or not it is produced from it.' Yaḥyā ibn Yaḥyā stated that. He said that it is one of the positions of Mālik. He said that Ibn Nāfi' said, 'There is nothing wrong in renting land for anything, food or anything else, whether or not it is produced from it, except for wheat and similar grains. That is the *muḥāqalah* that is forbidden.'

Mālik said in the *Muwaṭṭā'*: 'As for a man who gives his uncultivated land for a third or a fourth of what comes out of it, that is an uncertain transaction because crops may be scant on one occasion and plentiful at another time. The crops may perish completely and the owner of the land will have abandoned a set rent which it would have been good for him to rent the land for. He takes an uncertain amount and does not know whether or not it will be satisfactory. It is like a man having someone travel for him for a set amount and then saying, "Shall I give you a tenth of the profit of the journey as your wage?" This is not lawful and must not be done.' Mālik said, 'A man must not hire out himself or his land or his ship or his animal unless it is for a known set amount.' That is also the position of ash-Shāfi'ī and Abū Ḥanīfah and his people.

Aḥmad ibn Ḥanbal, al-Layth, ath-Thawrī, al-Awzā'ī, al-Ḥasan ibn Ḥayy, Abū Yūsuf and Muḥammad said that there is nothing wrong in giving a man land in exchange for a part of what it produces, like a third or a fourth. That is the position of Ibn 'Umar and Ṭāwus. In their argument, they cited the story of Khaybar and the fact that the Messenger of Allah ﷺ employed its people for half of what the land produced and [half] of the fruit. Aḥmad said, 'The hadith of Rāfi' ibn Khadīj about forbidding renting fields has confused wording and is not sound. It is more fitting to take the story of Khaybar which is a sound hadith.'

One group of the Tābi'ūn and those after them allow giving a man a ship or a mount, as land is given, in exchange for a share of what Allah gives the person when working with it. They consider that the basis in that is the *qirāḍ* which is agreed about. It will be dealt with later in *al-Muzzammil* (73:20), Allah willing. Ash-Shāfi'ī said about the position of Ibn 'Umar, 'We used to practise sharecropping (*mukhābarah*) and did not see any harm in that until Rāfi' ibn Khadīj informed us that the Messenger of Allah ﷺ had forbidden it.' It means that they used to rent land in exchange for part of what is produced. He said that that was abrogated by the sunnah of Khaybar.

Part of what verifies the position of ash-Shāfi'ī that it was abrogated is what the imams related from Jābir. Ad-Dāraquṭnī reports it as: 'The Prophet ﷺ forbade *muḥāqalah*, *muzābanah*, *mukhābarah* and selling fruits before their condition is known.' Abū Dāwūd related that Zayd ibn Thābit said, 'The Messenger of Allah ﷺ forbade the *mukhābarah* and I asked, "What is the *mukhābarah*?" He answered, "That you take land in exchange for a half, third or fourth [of what is produces]."'

Most recite '*mā baqiya*' with the *yā'* vowelled. Al-Ḥasan gives it a *sukūn*. This is frequently seen in poetry. [OMITTED] The reason is that the *yā'* is like the *alif* and just as the vowel does not reach the *alif*, that is also the case with the *yā'*. Al-Ḥasan recite '*mā baqā* with *alif* which is the dialect of Ṭayy' who use *jarāh* for *jārīyah* and *nāṣāh* for *nāṣīyah*.

Abu-s-Sammāl among the reciters recites '*min ar-ribū*'. Abu-l-Fatḥ 'Uthmān ibn Jinnī said, 'This variant is aberrant for two reasons. One is leaving the *kasrah* for the *ḍammah*, and the other is having the *wāw* after *ḍammah* at the end of the word.' Al-Mahdawī said that the reason is that it intensifies the *alif* and takes it towards the *wāw* which the *alif* replaces. It should not be taken in other than this way since there is no noun with a silent *wāw* at the end preceded by a *ḍammah*. Al-Kisā'ī and Ḥamzah use *imālah* in *ribā* because of the place of the *kasrah* on the *rā'*. The rest make it emphatic by the *fatḥah* on the *bā'*.

Abū Bakr from 'Āṣim and Ḥamzah recite '*fādhinū*', meaning 'announce to others' and the object is elided. The rest recite '*fadhānū*,' meaning 'have notice'. It is like 'I have a knowledge (*innī 'alā 'ilm*). Abū 'Ubayd related it from al-Aṣma'ī. Linguists related that it is said, '*adhintu bihi idhnan*,' 'I know it.' Ibn 'Abbās and other commentators say that it means: 'be certain of war from Allah Almighty,' and it has the meaning of authorisation. Abū 'Alī and others preferred the reading with *maddah*. He said, 'because when they are commanded to inform others who do not cease doing that, they have to know it themselves.' He said that their informing them contains their own knowledge while their knowledge does not entail informing others. Aṭ-Ṭabarī preferred the reading without *maddah* because it is specific to them. According to the reading with *maddah*, they were commanded to inform others.

All the reciters recite '*lā taẓlimūna*' and '*walā tuẓlamūna*'. Al-Mufaḍḍal related from 'Āṣim '*lā tuẓlamūna walā taẓlimūna*' which is a reversal. Abū 'Alī said, 'The majority reading is preferred because it is in harmony with '*if you repent*' in the two verbs depending on the subject.

وَإِن كَانَ ذُو عُسْرَةٍ فَنَظِرَةٌ إِلَىٰ مَيْسَرَةٍ وَأَن تَصَدَّقُوا خَيْرٌ لَّكُمْ إِن كُنتُمْ تَعْلَمُونَ ﴿٢٨٠﴾

280 If someone is in difficult circumstances, there should be a deferral until things are easier. But making a free gift of it would be better for you if you only knew.

If someone is in difficult circumstances,

After Allah has decreed that usurers should receive their capital back from those to whom they lent it, He decrees that the one experiencing hardship should be granted a delay until a time when things are easier for him. The reason for the revelation of this *āyah* is that when Thaqif asked for the property which was owed to them, the Banu-l-Mughīrah complained of hardship and said, 'We have nothing,' and asked for a delay until the time when their fruits would be ready for harvesting. Then this *āyah* was revealed.

The words of this *āyah* as well as Allah's words: *'If you repent you may have your capital'* (2:279) indicate that it is affirmed that someone owed a debt can ask for it from the debtor and is permitted to take property without his consent. This indicates that when a debtor refuses to settle the debt when he is able to do so, he is a wrongdoer. Allah Almighty says: *'you may have your capital'* and so enabled people to seek their capital when it is not impossible for their debtor to pay it.

Al-Mahdawī and some scholars said. 'This *āyah* abrogates what was done in the Jāhiliyyah by way of selling people as slaves who were unable to pay their debts.' Makkī related that the Prophet ﷺ also instructed people to follow that practice at the beginning of Islam. Ibn 'Aṭiyyah said, 'If it is really confirmed that the Prophet ﷺ did that, then it was abrogated.' Aṭ-Ṭaḥāwī said, 'A free man would be sold for a debt at the beginning of Islam, if he did not have enough property to settle his debts, until Allah abrogated that practice by His words: *"If someone is in difficult circumstances, there should be a deferral until things are easier."*' Their evidence is a hadith related by ad-Dāraquṭnī from Muslim ibn Khālid az-Zanjī from Zayd ibn Aslam from Ibn al-Baylamānī that Surrāq said, 'I owed a man some money – or a debt – and he took me to the Messenger of Allah ﷺ and I did not have any money and so he bought me from him – or I was bought for him.' Al-Bazzār transmitted it with this *isnād*. Muslim ibn Khālid az-Zanjī and 'Abd ar-Raḥmān ibn al-Baylamānī are not used as authoritative.

there should be a deferral until things are easier.

These words are general to all people. Anyone who is in difficulty is given a deferral. This is the position of Abu Hurayrah, al-Ḥasan and most of the *fuqahā'*. An-Naḥḥās said, 'The best of what is said on this *āyah* is the position of 'Aṭā', aḍ-Ḍaḥḥāk and ar-Rabī' ibn Khaytham. They said that the deferral applies to everyone who is in difficulty both in respect of usury and in respect of all other debts. This combines all the positions because it can be an abrogation revealed about usury and then become another more general ruling.' Ibn 'Abbās and Shurayḥ said that it is specific to usury and there is no deferral in other debts and dealings. A debtor must pay people what he owes or be imprisoned until he pays it. That is the position of Ibrāhīm [an-Nakha'ī]. Their evidence is: *'Allah commands you to return to their owners the things you hold on trust.'* (4:58) Ibn 'Aṭiyyah said, 'This position applies when is there is no pressing poverty. If there is poverty, the ruling is that a deferral should be imposed.'

If someone has a lot of debts and his creditors ask for their money, the judge can divest him of all his property and leave him with just his bare needs. Ibn Nāfi' related from Mālik that he is only left with what will conceal his private parts. The well-known position is that a debtor is left his normal clothing without excess and his cloak is not removed if he normally wears it, and the clothing of his wife is left. There is disagreement about selling his books if he is a scholar. He is not left a house or servant or Friday clothes unless they are inexpensive and, in such a case, it is forbidden to imprison him. The basis for that is: *'If someone is in difficult circumstances, there should be a deferral until things are easier.'*

The Imams related that Abū Sa'īd al-Khudrī said, 'A man experienced loss in the time of the Messenger of Allah ﷺ in respect of the produce which he sold and his debts mounted up. The Messenger of Allah ﷺ said, "Give *ṣadaqah* to him." The people gave him *ṣadaqah* but that did not amount to enough to settle his debt. So the Messenger of Allah ﷺ told his creditors, "Take what you find and you may only have that."' In Abū Dāwūd we find: 'The Messenger of Allah ﷺ did not allow creditors more than the seizure of a debtor's property.' This is a definitive text. The Messenger of Allah ﷺ did not order debtors to be imprisoned or kept in confinement. According to Shurayḥ, the man concerned was Mu'ādh ibn Jabal. This differs from the position of Abū Ḥanīfah who said that he is kept in close confinement if there is a possibility that he might have money. He is not forced to work as we mentioned. Success is by Allah.

A bankrupt person should be imprisoned, according to Malik, ash-Shāfi'ī, Abū Ḥanīfah and others, until it becomes clear that he has no property. Mālik says that he should not be imprisoned if it is not suspected that he has hidden property and it is clear that he does not have anything. He should not be imprisoned if his difficulties are evident as we mentioned. If the property of a bankrupt man is collected, and then destroyed before it reaches its owner and can be sold, the bankrupt man is liable and the debt remains. If the qāḍī sells the property and keeps the price, and then the money is lost before the creditors get possession of it, they are responsible and the bankrupt man is free of further liability. Muḥammad ibn 'Abd al-Ḥakam, however, says that the debtor is always liable until the money reaches the creditors.

'Difficulties' (*'usrah*) refer to constricted circumstances due to lack of money. The name of the Army of Hardship (*Jaysh al-'Usrah*) is taken from it. *Naẓirah* means a deferral. *Maysarah* is a verbal noun meaning 'ease'. The copy of the Qur'an of Ubayy ibn Ka'b has '*dhā 'usratin*' which would mean: 'If the person who is the object of the demand is in hardship'. Al-A'mash recited '*mu'siran*'. Abū 'Amr ad-Dānī said that Aḥmad ibn Mūsā said that that is how it is in the copy of the Qur'an of Ubayy ibn Ka'b. An-Naḥḥās, Makkī and an-Naqqāsh said, 'According to this, the words of the *āyah* apply especially to the people who practice usury. If it is recited with "*dhū*", it is general to all of those who owe a debt.' Al-Mahdawī said that 'Uthmān's copy of the Qur'an had '*fa-in*', but al-Mu'tamir related that 'Uthmān's copy had '*wa-in*' with '*dhā*', which an-Naḥḥās mentioned.

Most recite 'deferral' as '*naẓirah*' while Mujāhid, Abū Rajā' and al-Ḥasan recited '*naẓrah*', which is a dialect of Tamīm. They say '*karm*' for '*karam*' and '*kabd*' for '*kabid*'. Nāfi' alone reads 'until things are easier' as *maysurah* while the others read it as *maysarah*. An-Naḥḥās related from Mujāhid and 'Aṭā' '*nāẓirhu*' as a command and '*maysurihī*'. Abū Ḥātim said that the reading of *nāẓiratun* is not permitted. Rather it is in *an-Naml* (27:35) because the woman said it about herself, from the verb *naẓara*, meaning she is waiting. Here in *al-Baqarah*, it is about deferral in respect of a debt, as we also see in 15:36. Abū Isḥāq az-Zajjāj permits that and says that it is a verbal noun as seen with other verbs throughout the Qur'an.

But making a free gift of it would be better for you if you only knew.

Here Allah recommends that *ṣadaqah* be given to a person faced with difficulties and makes that better than granting a deferral. As-Suddī, Ibn Zayd and aḍ-Ḍaḥḥāk said that. Aṭ-Ṭabarī and others said that the meaning of the *āyah* is, 'That you make it a free gift to both rich and poor is better for you.' The sound position is the first one. There is nothing about the rich in the *āyah*.

Aṭ-Ṭaḥāwī mentioned that Buraydah ibn al-Khaṣīb reported that the Messenger of Allah ﷺ said, 'If someone grants time to a person in difficulties, he is considered to have given *ṣadaqah* on every day [of the deferral].' He said, 'It is *ṣadaqah* for every day until the debt is due. When he defers it after it is due, he is considered to have given the same amount in *ṣadaqah* for every day.' Muslim reported that Abū Mas'ūd narrated that the Messenger of Allah ﷺ said, 'A man among those before you underwent the reckoning and no good at all was found for him except that, being a wealthy man, he used to do business with people and used to order his employees to make allowances for anyone in difficulties. So Allah, the Mighty and Exalted, said, "We have more right to do that than you," and he was pardoned.'

It is related from Abū Qatādah that he looked for a debtor of his who was trying to hide and found him. The man said, 'I am in difficulties.' 'By Allah?' Abu Qatadah asked. 'By Allah.' he said. Abū Qatādah said, 'I heard the Messenger of Allah ﷺ say, "Whoever wants Allah to save him from the calamity of the Day of Rising should give more time to someone in financial difficulties or absolve him."' We find in a long hadith that Abu-l-Yasār Ka'b ibn 'Amr heard the Messenger of Allah ﷺ say, 'If someone gives more time to someone in difficulties or reduces the amount he owes, Allah will shade him in His shade.' There are many hadiths which encourage doing that. The hadith reported by Abū Qatādah indicates that if the creditor knows that the debtor is in difficulty, or even suspects it, it is forbidden for him to demand payment from him, even if that has not been proven before a judge. A delay is granted to the one in difficulty until a time when he is in better circumstances. Reducing it is to cancel responsibility for the debt. Both ideas are included in the example of Abu-l-Yasār with his debtor when he said, 'Pay it if you find the means to do so. Otherwise you are free.'

وَاتَّقُوا يَوْمًا تُرْجَعُونَ فِيهِ إِلَى اللَّهِ ثُمَّ تُوَفَّىٰ كُلُّ نَفْسٍ مَا كَسَبَتْ
وَهُمْ لَا يُظْلَمُونَ ﴿٢٨١﴾

281 Be fearful of a Day when you will be returned to Allah. Then every self will be paid in full for what it earned. They will not be wronged.

It is said that this *āyah* was revealed nine days before the death of the Prophet ﷺ and that nothing else was revealed after it. Ibn Jurayj said that. Ibn Jubayr and Muqātil said it was seven days before his death. Three days is also mentioned. It is related that it was three hours before his death, and the Prophet ﷺ ordered, 'Put it between the *āyahs* of usury and the *āyah* of the debt.' Makkī reported that the Prophet ﷺ said, 'Jibrīl came to me and said put it after *āyah* 280.'

It is related from Ubayy ibn Ka'b, Ibn 'Abbās and Qatādah that the last *āyah* to be revealed was: *'A Messenger has come to you from yourselves.'* (9:128). The first position is more commonly reported, sounder and better known. It is related that Ibn 'Abbās said, 'The last *āyah* to be revealed was: *"Be fearful of a Day when you will be returned to Allah. Then every self will be paid in full for what it earned. They will not be wronged."* Jibrīl told the Prophet. "Muḥammad! Put it at the end of *āyah*: 280 of *al-Baqarah*."' Abū Bakr al-Anbārī mentioned in *Kitāb ar-Radd* that the position of Ibn 'Umar was that this was the last *āyah* to be revealed and the Prophet ﷺ lived twenty-one days after it. This will be dealt with in 110:1.

The *āyah* is a warning to all people and a command encouraging every human being. *'Day'* is in the accusative as the object, not as an adverb, and *'when you will be returned to Allah'* describes it. Abū 'Amr recited *'returned'* as *'tarji'ūna'* 'you will return', also see in 88:25, which reflects the reading of Ubayy (*taṣīrūna*) instead of *'turja'ūna'* as in 8:62 and 18:36 which the rest have and which reflects the meaning of 'Abdullāh (*turaddūna*). Al-Ḥasan recited *'yurja'ūna'* which means 'all people will be returned'. Ibn Jinnī said, 'It is as if Allah is showing kindness to the believers by directly addressing them when He mentions the return, since that is what awakens the hearts. He makes a grammatical change to the third person, which is also out of kindness to them.'

The majority of scholars say that the day referred to is the Day of Rising and Reckoning, while some people say that it is the day a person dies. Ibn 'Aṭiyyah said that the first is sounder because of the context.

There is an implied elision: 'you will be returned to the judgment and decision of Allah.' *'They'* here means 'all people'. This *āyah* conveys to us that reward or punishment is connected to actions and so it refutes the Jabriyyah, as we already mentioned.

يَٰٓأَيُّهَا ٱلَّذِينَ ءَامَنُوٓاْ إِذَا تَدَايَنتُم بِدَيۡنٍ إِلَىٰٓ أَجَلٖ مُّسَمّٗى
فَٱكۡتُبُوهُۚ وَلۡيَكۡتُب بَّيۡنَكُمۡ كَاتِبُۢ بِٱلۡعَدۡلِۚ وَلَا يَأۡبَ كَاتِبٌ أَن يَكۡتُبَ
كَمَا عَلَّمَهُ ٱللَّهُۚ فَلۡيَكۡتُبۡ وَلۡيُمۡلِلِ ٱلَّذِي عَلَيۡهِ ٱلۡحَقُّ وَلۡيَتَّقِ ٱللَّهَ رَبَّهُۥ وَلَا
يَبۡخَسۡ مِنۡهُ شَيۡـٔٗاۚ فَإِن كَانَ ٱلَّذِي عَلَيۡهِ ٱلۡحَقُّ سَفِيهًا أَوۡ ضَعِيفًا أَوۡ لَا
يَسۡتَطِيعُ أَن يُمِلَّ هُوَ فَلۡيُمۡلِلۡ وَلِيُّهُۥ بِٱلۡعَدۡلِۚ وَٱسۡتَشۡهِدُواْ شَهِيدَيۡنِ
مِن رِّجَالِكُمۡۖ فَإِن لَّمۡ يَكُونَا رَجُلَيۡنِ فَرَجُلٞ وَٱمۡرَأَتَانِ مِمَّن تَرۡضَوۡنَ مِنَ ٱلشُّهَدَآءِ
أَن تَضِلَّ إِحۡدَىٰهُمَا فَتُذَكِّرَ إِحۡدَىٰهُمَا ٱلۡأُخۡرَىٰۚ وَلَا يَأۡبَ ٱلشُّهَدَآءُ إِذَا مَا
دُعُواْۚ وَلَا تَسۡـَٔمُوٓاْ أَن تَكۡتُبُوهُ صَغِيرًا أَوۡ كَبِيرًا إِلَىٰٓ أَجَلِهِۦۚ
ذَٰلِكُمۡ أَقۡسَطُ عِندَ ٱللَّهِ وَأَقۡوَمُ لِلشَّهَٰدَةِ وَأَدۡنَىٰٓ أَلَّا تَرۡتَابُوٓاْ إِلَّآ
أَن تَكُونَ تِجَٰرَةً حَاضِرَةٗ تُدِيرُونَهَا بَيۡنَكُمۡ فَلَيۡسَ عَلَيۡكُمۡ جُنَاحٌ
أَلَّا تَكۡتُبُوهَاۗ وَأَشۡهِدُوٓاْ إِذَا تَبَايَعۡتُمۡۚ وَلَا يُضَآرَّ كَاتِبٞ
وَلَا شَهِيدٞۚ وَإِن تَفۡعَلُواْ فَإِنَّهُۥ فُسُوقُۢ بِكُمۡۗ وَٱتَّقُواْ ٱللَّهَۖ وَيُعَلِّمُكُمُ ٱللَّهُۗ
وَٱللَّهُ بِكُلِّ شَيۡءٍ عَلِيمٞ ٢٨٢

282 You who believe! when you take on a debt for a specified period, write it down. A writer should write it down between you justly. No writer should refuse to write; as Allah has taught him, so he should write. The one incurring the debt should dictate and should be fearful of Allah his Lord and not reduce it in any way. If the person incurring the debt is incompetent or weak or unable to dictate, then his guardian should dictate for him justly. Two men among you should act as witnesses. But if there are not two men, then a man and two women with whom you are satisfied as witnesses; then if one of them is confused, the other can remind her. Witnesses should not refuse when they are called upon. Do not think it too trivial to write down, whether small or large, with the date that it falls due. Doing that is more just in Allah's sight and more helpful when bearing witness and more likely to eliminate any doubt – unless it is an immediate transaction hand to hand, taken and given without delay. There is nothing wrong in your not writing that down. Call witnesses

when you trade. Neither writer nor witness should be put under pressure. If you do that, it is deviancy on your part. Be fearful of Allah and Allah will give you knowledge. Allah has knowledge of all things.

You who believe! when you take on a debt

Sa'īd ibn al-Musayyab said, 'I heard that the closest *āyah* in time in relation to the *Āyat al-Kursī* was the *āyah* of the Debt.' Ibn 'Abbās said, 'This *āyah* was revealed specifically about the *salam* sale,' meaning the fact that the people of Madīnah used the *salam* sale was the reason for the revelation of the *āyah*. Then it applied to all those with mutual debt obligations. Ibn Khuwayzimandād said that the *āyah* contains thirty rulings. Some of our scholars use it as evidence for the permission to put a term on loans according to what Mālik said, since there is no difference between a loan and any other contract which involves debts. The Shāfi'īs disagree with that and say that the *āyah* does contain permission for delay on all debts. The command is for there to be witnesses if the debt has a set term. Then there is other evidence for the permissibility or prohibition of deferment with respect to debts.

The word '*dayn*' (debt) is stress, and it is the correct term for any transaction in which one person is owed cash and the other is granted a delay. The word *'ayn* in Arabic refers to what is immediate and *dayn* refers to what is absent. A poet says:

She promised us *nabīdh* for two dirhams.
Immediate wine is not a debt.

Another said:

The fates take me wherever they wish,
wherever they desire to put me in the grave,
Or they kindle wood and fire.
That death is then cash and not a debt.

Allah made this clear by saying 'for a specified period'.

for a specified period

Ibn al-Mundhir said that this indicates that a *salam* sale without a known term is not permitted. The Sunnah of the Messenger of Allah ﷺ indicates something similar to the Book of Allah. It is confirmed that when the Messenger of Allah ﷺ came to Madīnah they used to give advances against fruit for two or three years ahead. The Messenger of Allah ﷺ said, 'Whoever gives an advance on dates, should give an advance for a known measure and known weight for a known term.' Ibn 'Abbas related it and al-Bukhārī, Muslim and others transmitted it.

Ibn 'Umar said, 'The people of the Jāhiliyyah used to sell meat to one another for the *ḥabal al-ḥabalah* (the offspring of a pregnant camel).' The Messenger of Allah ﷺ forbade them to do that. All scholars agree that the permitted *salam* sale is when a man gives an advance to his companion of known defined food with a known measure for a known term in known dinars or dirhams and the transaction is made before they leave the place. Our scholars say that the date set for when a *salam* becomes due can be the harvest, cutting of the fruit, or the festivals of Nayrūz or Mihrajān [New Year or the autumn equinox] since that is a particular time.

Our scholars define the *salam* sale as being a known sale on credit for goods which are defined for ready money or what has the same ruling for a known term. It must be known and anything unknown must be avoided. For instance, in Madīnah at the time the Prophet ﷺ came to them they used to give credit and make a loan on the basis of the expected fruits of the date-palms, and the Prophet ﷺ forbade them to do that because of the uncertainty inherent in it, since the trees might not produce anything.

'Defined' means in general, not in detail, as the sale can be for dates, garments or fish while their category or specific description is not mentioned. 'Ready money' is specified to avoid a debt in exchange for a debt. 'What has the same ruling' is to exclude two or three days in which it is permitted to delay the capital of the *salam*. We believe that it is permitted to delay it for that amount with or without the precondition of its proximity, but it is not permitted to stipulate that. Ash-Shāfi'ī and al-Kūfī do not permit a delay in the capital of the *salam* after the time of the contract and separation. They thought that that was like money-changing. Our evidence is that the two areas are different because of their particular description. Money-changing has a narrow remit but many preconditions which differs from the *salam*. There are more doubtful elements in transactions. Allah knows best. 'A known term' avoids the immediate *salam* which is not permitted according to the well-known position. Making the term known avoids having an unknown term which is what they used to do in the Jāhiliyyah.

Salaf and *salam* have the same meaning and they are both found in hadiths, however the term *salaf* can be used for a loan (*qarḍ*). It is agreed that the *salam* is one of the permissible business transactions, except for the Prophet's prohibition of selling what you do not have. There is an allowance in the *salam*, because when the *salam* is a known sale which is a debt, it is the sale of something absent which is required by necessity on the part of each of those involved in the transaction.

If the owner of the capital needs to buy fruit and the one with the fruit needs the price before they are clear in order to spend it on them, it becomes evident that the *salam* sale is a necessary benefit. *Fuqahā'* call it 'the sale of the needy'. If it was permitted immediately, this wisdom would be invalidated and the benefit removed and the exception about selling what is not in your possession would be pointless. Allah knows best.

There are nine preconditions of the *salam* which are both agreed upon and disputed. Six concern the object of the *salam* and three concern the capital. The object of the *salam* is that it is a debt which is owed, it is described, it is a specific amount, it is due in the future, the time when it is due is known and that it will exist when that time arrives. The three which concern the capital which are agreed upon is that it is known category, amount and cash. These are agreed upon with the exception of cash.

Ibn al-'Arabī said, 'As for the first condition, that it is a debt which is owed, there is no lack of clarity that what is meant is that it is something for which one is liable because it is a debt transaction. If it had not been for that, the person concerned would not have entered a debt and people would not have been directed to it in profit and kindness.' People agree on this position although Mālik said that a person is only permitted a *salam* on something specific with two conditions: one is that it is in a secure town and the other that it has begun to be taken, like milk from a sheep and fresh dates from a palm tree. He is the only one who stated that.

These two questions are sound in evidence because a specific article is forbidden in a *salam* out of fear of *muzābanah* and uncertainty so that it will not be difficult in the place. When that place is safe, and it is usually not difficult for it to exist in that place, then it is permitted, since there is no certainty of the guarantee of ends in legal questions. There must be the possibility of a small risk. That is frequently seen in secondary issues in the books of legal issues.

As for a *salam* in respect of milk and fresh dates which have started to be taken, it is a Madinan question about which the people of Madīnah agreed. It is based on the principle of public welfare because a person needs to take milk and dates on a daily basis and it is hard to take them every day anew because the cash may not be present and the prices fluctuate. Those who own palm trees and milk need cash because they have goods that are not exchanged. Then when both parties share in the need, there is an allowance for them to engage in this transaction, based on it being analogous with *'ārīyahs* and other basic needs and benefits.

The second condition is that it is described, and that is agreed upon as is the third condition. How it is measured can be in one of three ways: volume, weight or number. That is based on custom, either what is known by the people or what is known in the *Sharī'ah*.

There is disagreement about the fourth condition, which is that it is due in the future. Ash-Shāfi'ī said that an immediate *salam* is permitted. Most scholars forbid it. Ibn al-'Arabī said, 'The Mālikīs are unsettled about the length of the term, even referring it to a day, so that some of our scholars actually say that an immediate *salam* is permitted. What is sound is that there must be a term because sales are one of two sorts: immediate, which is the basis, or deferred. If it is immediate and there is no *salam* in it, then it is selling what is not in your possession. There must be a term so every contract has its description and preconditions and so that the rulings of the *Sharī'ah* are in their proper places and definitions. According to our scholars, its definition varies according to its market. Allah says: *'a specified period'* and the Prophet ﷺ said, 'a known term.' That requires no discussion.

That which our scholars permit in respect of the immediate *salam* is about things that have different prices in different towns. So a *salam* between them is permitted in one, two or three days. If it is in the same town, then that is not the case because the price will be the same. Allah knows best.

The fifth condition is that it be a known term and there is disagreement in the community about that. Since Allah and His Prophet ﷺ have described that. Only Mālik among all the *fuqahā'* of the cities permits selling until harvest and cutting because he saw that it was known. This was already discussed in 2:189.

The sixth condition is that it exists in the place. There is no disagreement in the community about that either. If the object of the sale ceases to exist in the place where the term is by something coming from Allah, then all scholars say that the sale is void.

It is not a precondition of the *salam* that the one who takes is the owner of the goods. There was some disagreement about this among the Salaf based on what al-Bukhārī related that Muḥammad ibn al-Mujālid said, "Abdullāh ibn Shaddād and Abū Burdah sent me to 'Abdullāh ibn Abī Awfā and told me, "Ask him whether in the time of the Prophet ﷺ, the Companions of the Prophet used to make advance payment for wheat." 'Abdullāh said, "We used to make advance payments to the peasants of the people of Syria for wheat, barley, and oil for a specified measure and for a specified time." I asked, "To the person who possessed the crop?" He answered, "We did not ask about that." Then they sent me to 'Abd ar-Raḥmān ibn Abzā and I asked him. He answered, "The Companions of the Prophet ﷺ used to make advance payments in the time of the Prophet ﷺ and we did not ask them whether they had the crops or not.""

Abū Ḥanīfah stipulated the existence of the object of the *salam* from the time of the contract to the time of the end of the term set, fearing that it would be demanded and not be present and that would amount to risk. The other *fuqahā'* differed from him and said that what one considers is its existence at the end of the term. The Kufans and ath-Thawrī stipulated that the place of taking possession be mentioned in respect of things that have to be transported with effort. They said that the *salam* is unsound if the place of taking possession is not mentioned. Al-Awzā'ī said that it is disliked. We believe that if it is not mentioned, then the contract is not unsound, and the place of taking possession is specified. Aḥmad, Isḥāq and a group of the people of hadith said that, based on the hadith of Ibn 'Abbās in which he did not mention the place where the *salam* was taken. If that had been one of the preconditions, then the Prophet ﷺ would have made it clear as he made the measure, weight and term clear. That is like what Ibn Abī Awfā said.

Abū Dāwūd related from Sa'd (aṭ-Ṭā'ī) from 'Aṭiyyah ibn Sa'd from Abū Sa'īd al-Khudrī that the Messenger of Allah ﷺ said, 'If someone pays in advance, he must not transfer what he has paid for to someone else before he receives it.' Abū Muḥammad 'Abd al-Ḥaqq ibn 'Aṭiyyah said, 'He is al-'Awfī, and no one considers his hadiths as authoritative, even if esteemed people related from him.' Mālik said, 'The business with us is that if someone buys food for a known price to be delivered at a stated date, and, when the date comes, the buyer does not find that the seller has what will satisfy what he paid for, then it is revoked. He should only take from him gold or silver or the exact price that he paid him. He should not buy anything from him for that price until he has taken that from him. That is because if he were to take other than the price which he paid or exchanged it for goods other than the food that he purchased from him, then it is selling food before it is received in full.' Mālik said, 'The Prophet ﷺ forbade selling food before it was received in full.'

write it down.

'Write down the amount and the term.' It is said that Allah commands writing, but what is meant is writing and witnessing, because writing without witnesses does not constitute proper evidence. It is said that He commands us to write so that we will not forget. Abū Dāwūd aṭ-Ṭayālisī reports in his *Sunan* that Ibn 'Abbās said that the Messenger of Allah ﷺ said about the words of Allah: *'when you take on a debt...'*: 'The first disavowal of Ādam occurred in this manner. When Allah showed him his descendants, he saw a radiant man, shining with light, and asked,

"O Lord, who is this?" The answer was, "This is your descendant, Dāwūd." He asked, "O Lord, how long will he live?" "Sixty years," was the reply. He said, "O Lord, increase his life!" "No," He replied, "unless you give him some of your life span." He asked, "What is my life span?" "A thousand years," He replied He said, "I have given him forty years." So Allah wrote it for him and the angels testified to it. When the angels came to him as he was dying, he said, "I still have forty years!" They replied, "You gave them to your descendant Dāwūd." "I did not give anyone anything!" he said. So Allah produced the document and the angels testified to it.' One version has: 'Dāwūd lived a hundred years and Ādam's life was a thousand years.' At-Tirmidhī transmitted it. Allah's words: *'write it down'* are a clear indication that its entire description is recorded in a manner that will remove any dispute between those involved for the judge who gives a ruling when the case is presented to him. Allah knows best.

Some people believe that writing accounts is obligatory for owners and obliged by this *āyah*, be it a sale or a loan, so that there will be no forgetfulness or disavowal. Aṭ-Ṭabarī prefers that. Ibn Jurayj said, 'The one who borrows should write it down and the one who lends should act as witness.' Ash-Sha'bī said, 'They used to think that Allah's words: *"If you leave things on trust with one another"* (2:283) were abrogated by the command to write.' Something similar is related by Ibn Jurayj. Ibn Zayd also said that and he reported it from Abū Sa'īd al-Khudrī. Ar-Rabī' believed that this was obligatory by these words and then the ruling was lightened by His words: *'If you leave things on trust with one another.'* Most say that the command to write is a recommendation to preserve property and remove uncertainty. If the debtor is trustworthy, writing the debt down does not harm him. If he is other than that, writing will put his debt in order and satisfy the need of the one with the right. One of them said, 'If you testify, it is decisive. If you trust, there is free disposal.' Ibn 'Aṭiyyah said, 'This is a sound view and there is no abrogation with respect to this because Allah recommended writing in what a man gives and leaves. His recommendation is to promote people's caution.

A writer should write it down between you justly.

'Aṭā' and others said that it is obligatory for a scribe to write, when he is the only available scribe. Ash-Sha'bī said that. So when he is the only available scribe, he is obliged to write it down. As-Suddī said that it is obligatory when he is unoccupied. The *lām* is elided from the first and kept in the second because the second is absent and the first is addressed to the person, and so it is kept.

The word *'justly'* means 'with trust and fairness'. He should not write more or less than the amount. The words '*between you*' are used because both sides are involved. That is because the one owed the debt is likely to be suspected in writing down the debt he is owed and the same suspicion exists in the case of the debtor. Therefore, Allah prescribed a scribe from other than those involved who should write justly and should not be moved by favouritism for either party. It is said that when people transact with one another, so that one is not isolated from another, and some write down debts and some do not, Allah commanded that the writer should write it down justly.

The *bā'* connected to 'justly' is connected to 'write', not to 'writer' because what is obliged is that he write the document justly, not that he is just in himself. A child, a slave and someone in care can write it down when they understand it. In the case of those appointed as scribes, it is not permitted for guardians to abandon them except for reputable witnesses with whom they are pleased. Mālik said that, based on this *āyah*, documents should only be written down by people who are known for being fair and trustworthy. According to this view, the *bā'* is connected to 'writer'.

No writer should refuse to write.

The scribe is forbidden to refuse when called upon to fulfil his function. People disagree about a scribe's obligation to write or witness's to bear witness. Aṭ-Ṭabarī and ar-Rabī' said that it is obligatory for a scribe to write when he is ordered to do so. Al-Ḥasan said, 'It is obligatory for him in a situation in which it is not possible to obtain another scribe. In that case the person with the debt would be harmed if the scribe refused. When that is the case, it is obligatory for him. If it is possible to obtain another scribe who is able to do it, then he does not have to. As-Suddī said, 'It is obligatory for him when he is free to do it.'

Al-Mahdawī said that ar-Rabī' and aḍ-Ḍaḥḥāk that '*refuse*' is abrogated by Allah's words: '*Neither writer nor witness should be put under pressure.*' This position is based on the opinion of those who think that writing was obligatory for anyone chosen by the two people involved in the transaction. A scribe was not permitted to refuse until that understanding was abrogated by the words: '*Neither writer nor witness should be put under pressure.*' This is unlikely. It is not confirmed that it was ever obligatory on anyone whom the people in the transaction wanted, whoever that was. If the writing had been an obligation, it would not be valid to be paid for it, because being paid for performing obligatory actions is invalid, and there is no disagreement among scholars that it is permitted to receive a wage for writing out documents.

as Allah has taught him, he should write.

The *kāf* in *'kamā'* is connected to 'write' meaning 'write as Allah has taught him.' It is possible that it is connected to idea in 'refuse', meaning 'As Allah has blessed with knowing how to write, he should not refuse and should be gracious in the same way that Allah has been gracious to him.'

The one incurring the debt should dictate

The one taking on the debt acknowledges his liability verbally so that it is known what he owes. The verb in Arabic for 'dictate' is *amalla* and *amlā*. These are two dialectical forms. *Amalla* is the dialect of the people of the Hijaz and the Banū Asad while Tamīm have *amlā*. Both are found in the Qur'an. The witnessing of the debt is because of the affirmation made by the one incurring it. Allah commanded the scribe to have fear of Allah and not reduce the amount owed. *Bakhs* is reduction. This is also found in His words: *'It is not lawful for them to conceal what Allah has created in their wombs.'* (2:228)

If the person incurring the debt is incompetent or weak

Some people say that this means young, but that is an error. An adult can also be an incompetent. The word 'weak' here implies an adult without intelligence.

or unable to dictate,

Allah puts people who incur debts into four categories: an independent person who can dictate for himself and three others who cannot dictate. They are always in existence. Their rights are also taken care of in matters other than business dealings, such as inheritance when it is divided up, as well as other things. They are the incompetent, the weak and those unable to dictate. An incompetent (*safīh*) is someone with deficient sense regarding property, and it is not proper for him to give or take for himself. He is like the *safīh* garment, which is one that is lightly woven. Someone with a vile tongue is called a fool (*safīh*) because foul language almost only occurs in ignorant people and people of defective intellect. Arabs sometimes use the word *safīh* for feebleness of the intellect and sometimes for weakness of the body. A poet says:

We fear that our understanding will be deficient (*tasfaha*)
and the time will be unknown for the sensible.

Dhu-r-Rummah said:

They walk as they are shaken (*tasaffahat*) by winds,

Their tops shaken by the movement of the winds.

It is said that *ḍuʿf* is physical weakness and *ḍaʿf* is mental weakness. It is also said that they are two dialectical forms with the same meaning. The first view is sounder. It is based on what Abū Dāwūd related from Anas ibn Mālik that a man in the time of the Prophet ﷺ used to trade and he had some weakness (*ḍaʿf*) in his intellect. His family went to the Prophet of Allah ﷺ and said, 'Prophet of Allah, stop so-and-so from trading. He trades and there is some weakness in his mind.' So the Prophet ﷺ summoned him and forbade him to sell. He said, 'Messenger of Allah, I cannot bear going for any time without trading.' The Messenger of Allah ﷺ said. 'If you will not stop trading, then say, "This for that, and no cheating."' Abū ʿĪsā Muḥammad ibn ʿĪsā as-Sulamī at-Tirmidhī transmitted it from Anas and said it is *ṣaḥīḥ*. He mentioned weakness in his intellect. Al-Bukhārī transmitted it with the words: 'When you buy something, say, "No cheating" and you have the option to return any goods you buy for three days."'

This man was Ḥabbān ibn Munqidh al-Anṣārī, the father of Yaḥyā and Wāsiʿ. It is also said that it was Munqidh, the grandfather of Yaḥyā and Wāsiʿ, the Shaykh of Mālik and father of Ḥabbān. He reached the age of 130. In one of his expeditions with the Prophet ﷺ, he received a head wound which muddled his intellect and speech. Ad-Dāraquṭnī related that Ḥabbān ibn Munqidh was a weak man and also blind. He suffered a head wound and the Messenger of Allah ﷺ gave him an option of three days in respect of his purchases. He found it hard to speak and the Messenger of Allah ﷺ said to him, 'Buy and say, "No cheating."' He could be heard saying, 'No cheating. No cheating.' He transmitted it from Ibn ʿAmr.

Scholars disagree about someone who is cheated in their dealings due to lack of experience and lack of intelligence and whether they should be debarred from trading based on this *āyah* and on the hadith. Aḥmad and Isḥāq said that they should be debarred, while others said that they should not be. Both positions are found in the School. What is sound is the first position based on this *āyah* and the words in the hadith, 'Prophet of Allah, stop so-and-so from trading' when he did not debar because he said, 'Messenger of Allah, I cannot bear going for any time without trading.' So he allowed him to buy and made it specific to him because someone who is cheated in sales should be debarred, especially if his mind is disordered.

Part of what indicates that it is a particular ruling is what Muḥammad ibn Isḥāq related from Muḥammad ibn Yaḥyā ibn Ḥabbān who said, 'He was my grandfather, Munqidh ibn ʿAmr. He suffered a head wound and his language was broken and his mind disordered. He would not stop trading and continued to be cheated. He went to the Messenger of Allah ﷺ and mentioned that to him and he said, "When you buy, say, 'No cheating.' Then you have the option of retraction for three days for the goods you buy. If you are pleased, keep them. If you are angry, return them to their owner.'" He lived a very long life to the age of 130. He was alive in the time of 'Uthmān ibn 'Affān when the people spread out and were numerous. He would buy goods in the market and return them when he was badly cheated. They would criticise him, saying, "You bought them!" He would reply, "I have the option. If I am satisfied, I keep them and if I am angry, I return them. The Messenger of Allah ﷺ granted me an option of three days." He would return the goods to their owner on the following day or the day after and would be told, "By Allah, I do not accept them. You took my goods and gave me dirhams." His answer was, "The Messenger of Allah ﷺ gave me an option of three days." One of the Companions of the Messenger of Allah ﷺ would pass by and say to the merchant, "Bother you! He spoke the truth! The Messenger of Allah ﷺ gave him an option for three days!'" Ad-Dāraquṭnī transmitted it and Abū 'Umar mentioned it in *al-Istī'āb*. He said that al-Bukhārī mentioned it in his *History* from 'Ayyāsh ibn al-Walīd from 'Abd al-A'lā from Ibn Isḥāq.

The 'weak' are those who have some defect in their mind and so cannot dictate, either because of a stammer, muteness or ignorance of the language. Their guardian is their father or a trustee. Those who cannot dictate are children and their guardian is their trustee or father. If someone is ill, he has an agent. As for the dumb, they can be one of the weak or, more appropriately, one who cannot dictate. These are distinct categories that will be dealt with in *an-Nisā'*.

then his guardian should dictate for him justly.

At-Ṭabarī believed that the pronoun 'him' refers to the 'right', (meaning the guardian entitled to the right) and has an *isnād* to that effect from ar-Rabī' and Ibn 'Abbās. It is also said that it refers to the one who owes the debt, which is correct, and what is reported from Ibn 'Abbās is not sound. How could it be considered evidence if the one responsible for dictating the debt owed by an incompetent is the one owed the money! This is something which is not part of the *Sharī'ah* unless the reason that the person is unable to dictate is that illness or great age make his words incomprehensible or he is mute. In such a case the one owed the debt can dictate while the one who is unable to do so listens and when it is finished, affirms it. But this is not what the *āyah* is about. This is only valid for someone who cannot dictate due to illness.

When Allah says: *'the one incurring the debt should dictate,'* that indicates that he is trusted in what he says. That demands accepting the statement of the one who left a pledge along with his oath when there is a disagreement between him and the broker about the amount of the debt when the pledge exists. This is when the pledger says, 'I pledged fifty' and the broker claims that it is a hundred. One takes the statement of the pledger when the pledge exists. That is the school of most of the *fuqahā'*: Sufyān ath-Thawrī, ash-Shāfi'ī, Aḥmad, Isḥāq and the People of Opinion. Ibn al-Mundhir preferred it because the broker claims the extra. The Prophet ﷺ said, 'The claimant provides evidence and the one against whom the claim is made takes an oath.' Mālik said, 'One takes the word of the broker about the value of the pledge and he is not believed about more than that.' It is as if he thought that pledge and his oath is a witness on behalf of the broker, but Allah's words: *'the one incurring the debt should dictate,'* refute him. The one incurring the debt is the pledger. This question will be dealt with.

If someone says that Allah Almighty has put the pledge in place of witnesses and writing when testimony indicates the truthfulness of what is testified to between him and the value of the pledge and, when it reaches its value, there is no document about the increase, then the answer to him is that it does not indicate that its value must be that of the debt. The pledge for a thing can be more or less than its value. The broker is believed when he swears an oath to the value of the debt up to the point where it is equal to the value of the pledge. The custom is not like that. It may be that the debt is less than the pledge. That is common, and so there is no point to this position.

If it is confirmed that what is meant by the 'guardian' here is a *faqīh*, then the text indicates that the affirmation of the *faqīh* regarding the matter is accepted when he takes an oath because when he dictated it, he carried out the instruction.

The dealings of a debarred incompetent without the permission of his guardian are null and void by consensus and do not ever effect anything. There is disagreement about the dealings of an incompetent who is not debarred. That will be dealt with in *Sūrat an-Nisā'*.

Two men among you should act as witnesses.

They are called upon to act as witnesses. People disagree about whether this is obligatory or merely recommended. The sound position is that it is recommended as will be explained. Allah regulates testimony by His wisdom in financial and physical matters and other *ḥudūd* and makes two witnesses necessary in each case except where fornication is concerned as will be explained in *Sūrat an-Nisā'*. The linguistic form of 'witness' or '*shahīd*' is an intensive form and that indicates that he may be called on to testify several times. This is also an indication of integrity. Allah knows best.

The word 'men' (*rijāl*) excludes unbelievers, children and women. The expression could include slaves but Mujāhid said that it means free men, which Qāḍī Abū Isḥāq prefers. Scholars disagree about the testimony of slaves. Shurayḥ, 'Uthmān al-Battī, Aḥmad, Isḥāq and Abū Thawr said that a slave's testimony is allowed when he possesses integrity. They rely on the meaning of the *āyah*. Mālik, Abū Ḥanīfah, ash-Shāfi'ī and most scholars say that a slave's testimony is not permitted and they rely in that on the defect inherent in slavery. Ash-Sha'bī and an-Nakha'ī allow it in minor matters. The sound position is that of the majority because Allah says: *'You who believe! when you take on a debt…'* and the address continues to '*two men among you*'. So the apparent meaning of the address is that it is dealing with those who contract debts and slaves do not have that capacity without their masters' permission.

If they say that the specificity of the beginning of the *āyah* does not prevent it from being general at the end, they are told that it is specific by His words: *'Witnesses should not refuse when they are called upon…'* as will be explained. The words '*your men*' also indicate that people who are blind can act as witnesses when they have definite knowledge about what they are testifying to, as is related from Ibn 'Abbās: 'The Messenger of Allah ﷺ was asked about testimony and said, "You can see this sun. So testify when you have the equivalent certainty about the matter or do not testify."' This indicates that a witness should actually see what he testifies to, and that testimony on the basis of logical deduction, which might be wrong, is not permitted. For instance, a blind man is permitted to have intercourse with his wife when he recognises her voice because it is permitted to engage in intercourse on the basis of the probability that it is lawful. If a woman is brought to him and he is told, 'This is your wife,' and he does not recognise her, he is permitted to have intercourse with her. He can accept a gift which comes to him by the statement of a messenger and he can testify to what he has been told.

If, however, someone informs him from Zayd about a confirmation, sale, slander or usurpation, he is not permitted to testify to what he was told because testimony requires certainty. It is permitted in other things to accept probability. That is why ash-Shāfi'ī, Ibn Abī Laylā and Abū Yūsuf said that if he knew of that before he went blind, them he is permitted to testify after he has become blind. The blindness may intervene between that to which he witnessed, as is the case with absence or death. This is the position of all of those scholars. That which prevents the testimony of a blind person in what he could have seen is of no consequence. His testimony is valid in respect of what is confirmed by extensive reports as when he reports about a ruling of the Messenger ﷺ which has multiple transmissions. Some scholars accept the testimony of a blind person on the basis of hearing the voice because he thought that deduction by that rises to the level of certainty. The similarity in voices is like the similarity of forms and colours. This is weak since it would require a sighted person to rely on the voice.

The position of Malik regarding the testimony of the blind on the basis of hearing a voice is that it is permitted in divorce and other things when he recognises the voice. Ibn al-Qāsim said, 'I asked Mālik, "A man hears his neighbour through a wall without seeing him and hears him divorce his wife. Can he testify to it if he recognises his voice?" Mālik answered, "His testimony is allowed."' That position was also related from 'Alī ibn Abī Ṭālib, al-Qāsim ibn Muḥammad, Shurayḥ al-Kindī, ash-Sha'bī, 'Aṭā' ibn Abī Rabāḥ, Yaḥyā ibn Sa'īd, Rabī'ah, Ibrāhīm an-Nakha'ī, Mālik and al-Layth.

But if there are not two men, then a man and two women

This means that if the claimant does not bring two men, then a man and two women suffice. This is the position of the majority. There is some elision and it means: 'then a man and two women should take their place.' Outside of the Qur'an, it might be in the accusative, namely 'call on a man and two women to testify.' Some say that the testimony of women is only permissible when there are no other men at all. Ibn 'Aṭiyyah said that this is weak and does not accord with the words of the *āyah*. The clear position is that of the majority, which is that if the person with the debt neglects to call two men, or does that intentionally for some reason, he calls a man and two women instead. In this *āyah* Allah has permitted the testimony of two women with a man when there are other men available. Allah does not mention this anywhere else. According to the majority, this is particular to property matters and on condition that there is a man with them. It is for property rather than other matters because Allah gives many means for confirming the ownership of property since there are many means of obtaining it and property is frequently subject to dispute. Sometimes confirmation is by writing, sometimes by witnessing, sometimes by pledges and sometimes by guarantee, and the testimony of women with men is part of that.

No intelligent person should suppose that Allah's words *'when you take on a debt'* include the debt of the dower with severance or the settlement of blood money owed for deliberate killing. Those cases are not about testimony to a debt, but testimony to other things. Scholars do permit the testimony of women alone regarding things which only they can know, as is also the case with the testimony of children, when it is necessary, about injuries. However, scholars also disagree about the testimony of children in such cases. Mālik allowed it as long as the children have not separated and do not disagree. The testimony of less than two of them is not permitted in the case of a child for an adult or an adult for a child. 'Abdullāh ibn az-Zubayr gave judgment regarding injuries in such cases, and Mālik said, 'It is the agreed practice here.' Ash-Shāfi'ī, Abū Ḥanīfah and the Ḥanafīs did not permit it because they are not 'men' nor *'those with whom you are satisfied'* nor *'two upright men from among yourselves'.* (65:2) These qualities are not found in a child.

Since Allah made the testimony of two women equal to that of one man, their ruling must be the same as his ruling. As we and ash-Shāfi'ī require that oaths are witnessed, it is obligatory for an oath to be witnessed by two men because this equivalence is undefined. Abū Ḥanīfah and his people disagree about this, and do not think that an oath needs a witness. They said, 'Allah Almighty places oaths in various categories and numbers them. He does not mention the need for a witness in any of them. Therefore it is not permitted to make a judgment contingent on that because it is a category additional to those Allah has specified. This is an addition to the text and it is abrogation.' Among those who take this position are ath-Thawrī, al-Awzā'ī, 'Aṭā', al-Ḥakam ibn 'Uyaynah and a group.

Some of them said that judging by an oath with a witness is abrogated by the Qur'an. 'Aṭā' claimed that the first to give judgment based on it was 'Abd al-Malik ibn Marwān. Al-Ḥakam said, 'Judging by an oath and a witness is an innovation, and the first to judge in this way was Mu'āwiyah.' All of this is an error and supposition and does not help in the face of the truth. Those who deny and are ignorant are not like those who affirm and know. Allah's words: *'Two men among you should act as witnesses…'* do not refute the Messenger of Allah ﷺ giving judgment with an oath and a witness, nor that it is not used to obtain rights, nor that it is only obliged by what Allah mentions and nothing else. If that were the case, it would be nullified by the refusal of the defendant to swear if the plaintiff swears. If that is the case, then the consensus is that he would be entitled to the money, and that is not what the Book of Allah says. This definitively refutes them.

Mālik said, 'Part of the argument of those who say that is that he is told, "Do you think that if a man claimed that another man owed him money, the defendant would not swear that he did not owe it?" If he swears that, then the right will be nullified for him. If he refuses to swear and the one who demanded the debt swears that his right is true and confirms that his companion owes him that, this is something in which no one disagrees about in any land. So on what basis does he claim this and where does he find it in the Book of Allah? Whoever affirms, affirms by an oath with a witness.'

Our scholars said that, in view of the fame and soundness of the hadiths, the wonder is that they have said that those who act on it are innovating and revoke their ruling and disparage their opinion. This is also in spite of the fact that it was the practice of the four Caliphs, Ubayy ibn Ka'b, Mu'āwiyah, Shurayḥ, and 'Umar ibn 'Abd al-'Azīz. He wrote to his governors to do that: Iyās ibn Mu'āwiyah, Abū Salamah ibn 'Abd ar-Raḥmān, Abu-z-Zinād and Rabī'ah. That is why Mālik said, 'The past practice of the Sunnah is enough for that. Do you see that these men cancelled their rulings and judged them to be innovators? This is indeed grave negligence and an incorrect reflection. The imams related from Ibn 'Abbās that the Prophet ﷺ gave judgment based on an oath with a witness.' 'Amr ibn Dīnār said it is particular to property.

Sayf ibn Sulaymān related it from Qays ibn Sa'd ibn Dīnar from Ibn 'Abbās. Abū 'Umar said that this is the soundest *isnād* of this hadith. No one attacks its *isnād* and there is no disagreement among the people who know the hadith that its men are trustworthy. Yaḥyā al-Qaṭṭān said, 'Sayf ibn Sulaymān is confirmed. I do not know of anyone with a better memory than him.' An-Nasā'ī said, 'This is an excellent *isnād*. Sayf is trustworthy and Qays is trustworthy.' Muslim transmitted this hadith of Ibn 'Abbās. Abū Bakr al-Bazzār said, 'Sayf ibn Sulaymān and Qays ibn Sa'd are trustworthy. Those after have no need of mentioning them because of their fame for trustworthiness and integrity.'

None of the Companions objected to an oath with a witness. Rather it is transmitted from them that it was their position. That was also the position of most of the people of knowledge in Madīnah. There is disagreement about it reported from 'Urwah ibn az-Zubayr and Ibn Shihāb. Ma'mar said, 'I asked az-Zuhrī about an oath with a witness and he said, "This is something which people have innovated. There must be two witnesses."' It is related from him that he was the first to give judgment based on a witness and oath. That is what was stated by Mālik and his people, ash-Shāfi'ī and his followers, Aḥmad, Isḥāq, Abū 'Ubayd, Abū Thawr, Dāwūd ibn 'Alī, and a group of the people of tradition. I believe that it is not permitted to oppose it because of the multiple reports about it from the Prophet ﷺ and the normative practice of the people of Madīnah generation after generation.

Mālik said, 'Judgment is given on the basis of an oath with a witness in all lands.' In his *Muwaṭṭā'* he does not justify a question by other than it. There is no disagreement reported from him about giving a ruling based on an oath with a witness. The same is true about all of his companions in Madīnah, Egypt and elsewhere. The Mālikīs in all lands know of only this in their School with the exception of those of us in Andalusia. Yaḥyā ibn Yaḥyā claimed that he did not see al-Layth giving a fatwa by it nor believing in it. Yaḥyā differed from Mālik in that as well as differing from the Sunnah and the normative practice in the Abode of Hijrah.

The oath with a witness is an additional ruling articulated on the tongue of the Messenger of Allah ﷺ, in the same way that he forbade being married to a woman while also being married to her paternal or maternal aunt, even though Allah says: *'Apart from that He has made all other women lawful for you'* (4:24) and like his forbidding eating the flesh of domestic donkeys and all beasts of prey with fangs although Allah says: *'Say: "I do not find..."'* (6:145). It is also like wiping over leather socks when the Qur'an states that one washes or wipes feet. There are many examples of this. If it were permitted to say that the Qur'an abrogates the ruling of the Messenger of Allah ﷺ about an oath with a witness, it would be permitted to say that the words of the Qur'an: *'Allah has permitted trade and He has forbidden usury'* (2:274) and *'only by means of mutually agreed trade'* (4:29) abrogate the *muzābanah*, a sale involving risk, selling what has not yet been created, and other forbidden sales. No one is allowed to do this because the Sunnah clarifies the Book.

If it is said that what comes in the hadith is a judgment about something specific and is not universal, we say that those are words that undermine this principle. So it is as if one is saying that the Messenger of Allah ﷺ made it obligatory to rule by an oath with a witness. What supports this interpretation is what Abū Dāwūd related from Ibn 'Abbās: 'The Messenger of Allah ﷺ gave judgment based on a witness and an oath in respect of rights.' Through analogy and investigation, we find that an oath is stronger than two women because they have no way to be part of the *li'ān* process while the oath is a part of it. When the Sunnah is sound, it is mandatory to take it and the Sunnah does not require corroboration because whoever opposes it is overcome by it. Success is by Allah.

When it is confirmed that a ruling is given on the basis of an oath with a witness, Qāḍī Abū Muḥammad 'Abd al-Wahhāb said, 'That is about property rather than physical rights based on the consensus about that among all who say that a ruling is given on the basis of an oath with a witness,' He added, 'That is because property rights are less important than physical rights. This is indicated by the fact that women's testimony is accepted in them.' The position of Mālik varies about deliberate wounding and whether retaliation for it can be obliged by a witness and an oath. There are two transmissions from him. One is that it obliges choosing between retaliation and blood money, and the other is that it does not oblige anything because that is a physical right. He said that that is what is sound. Mālik stated in the *Muwaṭṭā'*, 'This procedure pertains to property cases in particular.' 'Amr ibn Dīnār said that. Al-Māzirī said, 'There is no dispute that it is accepted in matters which purely concern property. There is no disagreement that it does not occur in what is simple marriage and divorce.'

If the testimony is about something which is not property, but which will lead to property, like testifying to a will and marriage after death, so that by its affirmation one only seeks property, there is disagreement about accepting it. Those who consider the property accept it and those who consider the circumstances do not accept it. Al-Mahdawi says that the testimony of women in cases involving *ḥudūd* is not permitted according to the position of most of the *fuqahā'* and most preclude it in marriage and divorce as well. That is the position of Mālik, ash-Shāfi'ī and others. They may testify about property but not about other things and so they do not testify against the testimony of others, even if there is a man with them. Judgment is, however, given on the basis of the testimony of two of them in all matters in which only women are present, like childbirth, the first cry of a newborn and the like. All of this is the school of Mālik, although there is some disagreement within it.

with whom you are satisfied as witnesses

This describes both the man and the two women. Ibn Bukayr and others said that this is addressed to judges. Ibn 'Aṭiyyah said, 'This is not a good interpretation. The *āyah* is addressed to all people, but someone confused by the context might think it referred to judges alone. This usage is frequent in the Book of Allah. Although the address is directed to some in particular, it is in fact universal.'

These words indicate that there are witnesses who are not considered to be satisfactory. Those are people who are not considered to be of sufficient integrity. That is, of course, in addition to being Muslim. This is the position of the majority. Abū Ḥanīfah said, 'Every Muslim who displays Islam and is free of impiety is considered to have integrity, even if his state is unknown.' Shurayḥ, 'Uthmān al-Battī and Abū Thawr said that they are the Muslims of integrity, even if they are slaves.

So they make the ruling universal and that obliges accepting the testimony of a bedouin against a townsperson when he is someone with whom they are satisfied and who possesses integrity. Ash-Shāfi'ī and those with him accept that, since he is one of our men and the people of our *dīn*. The fact that he is from the desert is like him being from another country. Undefined terms in the Qur'an indicate the acceptance of the testimony of men of integrity and that Bedouin and townspeople are the same in that respect. Allah says: '*...with whom you are satisfied as witnesses*' and '*...call two upright men from among yourselves as witnesses.*' (65:2) Therefore '*from among yourselves*' is addressed to the Muslims as a whole.

This demands absolutely that the meaning of integrity is necessarily additional to Islam because the attribute is additional to what is primarily described. The same is true of '*with whom you are satisfied*.' This differs from what Abū Ḥanīfah said. It is not known whether one is satisfied with someone unless his state is reported. Therefore it necessarily follows that outward Islam is not, by itself, sufficient. Aḥmad ibn Ḥanbal and Mālik, as transmitted by Ibn Wahb from him, believed that Bedouin should not testify against townspeople based on the hadith of Abū Hurayrah in which the Prophet ﷺ said: 'It is not permitted for a Bedouin to testify against a townsperson.' What is sound is that his testimony is permitted when he has integrity and people are satisfied with him, as will be dealt with in *an-Nisā'* and *at-Tawbah*. The hadith of Abū Hurayrah does not distinguish between a townsperson who is resident or one who is travelling. When he is travelling, then there is no disagreement that his testimony is accepted.

Our scholars say that integrity entails uprightness in religious matters, which includes avoiding major wrong actions and maintaining noble character and abandoning minor wrong actions, and being clearly trustworthy and not gullible. It is said that it is having a clear conscience and upright behaviour in the judgment of the one who assesses him. These ideas are similar.

Since giving testimony is a really important matter and has a lofty rank, entailing, as it does, the acceptance of the statement of one person over that of another, Allah Almighty stipulated for it the need for integrity and being considered satisfactory. Whoever judges that a witness possesses singular qualities and virtues, making him superior to others, stipulates that that prerogative accords him being singled out for giving testimony and the validity of judgment made on the evidence entailed by his testimony. This is the clearest proof of the permissibility of *ijtihād* and deduction based on indications and signs which our scholars believe contain hidden meanings and rulings. This will be further discussed in *Sūrat Yūsuf*, Allah willing. It indicates entrusting the matter to the *ijtihād* of judges. Sometimes a judge might discern lack of attention or doubt in the witness and therefore reject his testimony.

Abū Ḥanīfah says that outward affirmation of Islam is sufficient for someone to qualify as a witness in matters involving property but not in cases involving the *ḥudūd*. This is wrong and misses the point because property is one of people's rights. So, as Ibn al-'Arabī said, someone's outward Islam is not sufficient. Since Allah stipulated being satisfactory and possessing integrity in incurring debts as we have explained, it is more proper that He also stipulated that with respect to marriage, differing from Abū Ḥanīfah who says that a marriage may be contracted even if the witnesses are impious. So he denies to marriage the safeguards demanded in the case of property when they are even more necessary in the case of marriage because of its connection to lawfulness, sanctity, the *ḥadd* and lineage.

The position of Abū Ḥanīfah with regard to this matter is very weak indeed since Allah stipulated being satisfactory and possessing integrity and that cannot be known merely from the fact that someone is Muslim. It is known by investigating his circumstances so that one is not deceived by him merely saying, 'I am a Muslim.' It may well be the case that he has inside him that which would cause his testimony to be rejected. It like Allah's words: *'Among the people there is someone whose words about the life of this world excite your admiration and he calls Allah to witness what is in his heart … Allah does not love corruption.'* (2:204-205) He also says: '*When you see them, their outward form appeals to you.*' (63:4)

then if one of them is confused, the other can remind her.

Abū 'Ubayd says that the expression '*is confused*' (*ḍalla* lit. strays) here means 'forgets'. Straying from testimony happens by forgetting part of it and remembering another part so that a person is confused about it. That is not the case when someone forgets it all. They are not called 'confused'. Ḥamzah recites '*in*' whose apodosis is in '*fā'*' connected to '*tudhakkiru*'. If it is read as '*an*', it is the object and the regent in it is elided. The reading of the community of '*tudhakkira*' is added to the verb with a *fatḥah*. Ibn Kathīr and Abū 'Amr have '*tudhkira*' which means: one woman can make another equivalent to a male in witnessing since the testimony of a woman is half that of man. When both of them testify, as a whole they become like the testimony of a male. Sufyān ibn 'Uyaynah and Abū 'Amr ibn al-'Alā' said that. That is unlikely because the only thing opposite to *ḍalāl* when it means 'forgetfulness' is 'reminding' and that is found in the majority reading which is Form II, meaning to call attention when she forgets.

Witnesses should not refuse when they are called upon.

Al-Ḥasan says that this phrase deals with two issues. You should not refuse when you are asked to be a witness and you should not refuse to attest to the thing you are asked to bear witness to. Ibn 'Abbās said that. Qatādah, ar-Rabī' and Ibn 'Abbās said it means that people should not refuse to convey what they witnessed and confirm it in writing. Mujāhid said, 'This means when you are called to give testimony and are in possession of the evidence.' An-Naqqāsh reports that this is how the Prophet ﷺ explained the *āyah*. Mujāhid said, 'When you are first called to testify, if you wish, then go, and if you do not wish, do not.' Abū Miljaz, 'Aṭā', Ibrāhīm, Ibn Jubayr, as-Suddī, Ibn Zayd and others all said that.

According to this, it is not obliged for witnesses to attend when summoned to witness two people who made a contract, but they must attend in the case of two people who contracted a debt if they were present at the transaction. When they were witnesses to the original contract and are asked to affirm their testimony to the document, they must do so. This is the situation which is referred to in this *āyah*. What is involved is the confirmation of testimony already given. If the testimony is confirmed, then they are called upon to reconfirm it in the presence of the judge. So the being 'called upon' refers to attending the court.

Ibn 'Aṭiyyah said, 'The *āyah*, as al-Ḥasan said, combines two recommended matters. The Muslims are encouraged to help their brothers. When there are many witnesses and there is confidence that the person will not be deprived of his right, then it is merely recommended for the one summoned, and he can fail to attend for any excuse whatsoever. If he fails to attend without any excuse, there is no wrong action or reward for him. If it is necessary and there is the slightest risk that someone will be deprived of his right, the recommendation is strengthened to the point that is close to an obligation. If a witness knows that someone will be completely deprived of his right by his failing to testify, then it is obligatory for him to testify, especially if he is summoned to do so. This is even more emphatic because it is a yoke on his neck and a trust which he must fulfil.

This *āyah* provides evidence that it is permitted for a ruler to provide witnesses for people and to pay them from the treasury and for them to have no other work except attending to the preservation of people's rights. Otherwise those rights might be lost and rendered null and void. Then the meaning would imply: 'Witnesses should not refuse to testify when people demand what they are entitled to.' Allah knows best. If it is said that this refers to testifying in exchange for a wage, we reply that it is simple testimony from people who have their needs fulfilled by the treasury. That is like paying judges and guardians and for all the acts of public welfare which help the Muslims. This is part of it, and Allah knows best. The Almighty says: *'Those who collect it'* (9:60), giving a share of the *zakāt* to those who collect it.

This also indicates that a witness is someone who comes before a judge. This is the basis of the *Sharīʿah* and is acted on in every age and is understood by every nation. When this is confirmed, then a slave is outside of the bulk of witnesses, which is made specific by the words, '*your men*', because a slave cannot necessarily respond and it may not be possible for him to come, because he is not independent and only acts with the permission of someone else. Therefore, he falls below the level of giving testimony just as he also cannot reach the degree of being a guardian. He similarly is not required to attend *Jumuʿah*, go on *jihād* and perform ḥajj as will be explained.

Our scholars say that this applies when one is summoned to give testimony. As for the case when he acts as a witness for a man who does not know about him and who will benefit from it, some people say that it is recommended because Allah says: *'Witnesses should not refuse when they are called upon.'* So Allah obliges the duty to be carried out when one is called upon, and if he is not called upon, it is still recommended since the Prophet ﷺ said, 'The best witness is the one who brings his testimony before he is asked for it.' The imams related it. What is sound is that doing it is an obligation, even if he is not asked, as long as there is fear that someone's right will be lost or ignored, or it is about a divorce or an emancipation against someone who continues to enjoy his wife or employ that slave, and other such things. A person who is a witness to any of that must confirm that testimony, and his testimony is not dependent on him being asked so that the right is lost. That is why the Almighty says: '*...they should carry out the witnessing for Allah*' (65:2) and '*...only those who bore witness to the truth and have full knowledge.*' (43:86) We also have the sound hadith in which the Prophet ﷺ said, 'Help your brother, wronging or wronged.' It is incumbent to help him by giving testimony to make him ashamed to deny what he owes.

There is no ambiguity about the fact that if someone is obliged to give testimony regarding one of the matters we have mentioned and then does not testify, it impairs the witness and testimony. There is no distinction between the rights of Allah and the rights of human beings. This is the position of Ibn al-Qāsim and others. Some of them believe that if that testimony is about a human right, it only invalidates that particular testimony and it is not valid for him to give it afterwards. The first is the sound position because that which obliges its invalidation is his impiety in not performing what he was obliged to do without having any excuse for not doing it. Impiety (*fisq*) removes the qualification to be a witness in general. This is clearer.

There is no contradiction between the words of the Prophet ﷺ, 'The best witness is the one who brings his testimony before being asked for it' and his words in the hadith of 'Imrān ibn Ḥuṣayn, 'The best of you is my generation, then the one after them, and then the one after them.' 'Imrān ibn Ḥuṣayn said, 'I do not know whether he said "then the one after them" two or three times.' The hadith continues: 'Then after them there will come a people who give testimony when they are not asked to, who are treacherous and not trustworthy, who make vows but do not fulfil them, and plumpness will appear among them.' They transmitted both hadiths as sound.

This hadith can be taken in three ways. One is that it means a false witness who testifies to what he was not asked to testify to, meaning that he was not bound to do it. Abū Bakr ibn Abī Shaybah mentioned that 'Umar ibn al-Khaṭṭāb gave an address at al-Jabiya and said, 'The Messenger of Allah ﷺ stood among you as I am standing among you and said, "People! Have fear of Allah in respect of my Companions, then those who follow them, and then those who follow them. Then lies and false testimony will spread."' The second is that it means that greed impels him to perform his testimony, which is why he hastens to testify before he is asked. This is a rejected testimony. It indicates that the witness is overcome by passion. The third is what Ibrāhīm an-Nakha'ī said. He related various paths of transmission of this hadith: 'When we were boys, they used to forbid us to make contracts and act as witnesses.'

Do not think it too trivial to write down, whether small or large, with the date that it falls due.

The verb *sa'ama* means to become weary of doing something. Al-Akhfash said that and that it is as a poet said:

I was weary of the burdens of life.
    Whoever lives for eighty years is weary, and I do not care!

This is in order to avert the danger of tedium which may come about through the constant repetition of contracting debts as it is feared that people may become bored with writing them down. One of them may say, 'This is so little that it does not need to be written down', so it is stressed for both small and large amounts. Our scholars said that it excludes what is about a *qīrāṭ* or the like since it is insignificant and a person does not affirm or deny it.

Doing that is more just in Allah's sight

This means writing down both small and large transactions with witnesses.

'*Aqwam*' (more just) here means 'more correct and more likely to protect the rights of those concerned'. It is also more likely to remove doubts and uncertainty.

and more helpful when bearing witness

This is evidence that if a witness sees the contractual document but does not remember giving the testimony, he should not confirm it since there is some doubt about it. He should only testify to what he is sure about and may say, for instance, 'This is my handwriting, but I do not remember writing it.' Ibn al-Mundhir said, 'Most trustworthy scholars forbid a witness to testify to his writing when he does not remember giving the testimony.' Malik found evidence for the permissibility of doing that in Allah's words: *'We can do no more than to testify to what we know.'* (12:81). Some scholars say that since Allah ascribed writing to justice, he can testify to his handwriting, even if he does not remember writing it. Ibn al-Mubārak mentioned from Ma'mar from Ibn Ṭāwus from his father about a man who testified to a testimony that he had forgotten. He said, 'There is nothing wrong in him testifying if he finds his mark or his handwriting on the document.' Ibn al-Mubārak said, 'I find this very good.' There are also reports from the Messenger of Allah ﷺ that he gave judgment about more than one matter by evidence and testimony. What is reported from the Messengers before him indicate the soundness of this position. Allah knows best. This will be further explained in *al-Aḥqāf*, Allah willing.

unless it is an immediate transaction hand to hand,

This means that it takes place on the spot. 'Āṣim alone recites '*tijāratan*' in the accusative as the predicate of *kāna*. The noun is elided and so it implies: 'Unless the transaction is a cash transaction'. That is how Makkī and Abū 'Alī al-Fārisī assessed it. That is because Allah knew that it would be difficult for them. Therefore, He stated that it can be left and removed anything wrong in doing that in respect of every cash transaction. That is in respect of small things like food and the like, not when it is something great like property. As-Suddī and aḍ-Ḍaḥḥāk said, 'This is what is done hand to hand.'

taken and given without delay.

The transaction is achieved by each party taking their goods or cash and separating. When it is a question of land or buildings or a lot of animals, so that the conclusion of the contract is not subject to the two parties separating, then it is recommended that it be written down because a change in circumstances might occur in that instance. When the exchange is clearly made and they part, each with his goods, it is very unusual for there to be a dispute unless it is for concealed reasons. The *Sharī'ah* recommends this procedure as being in people's best interests in the case of credit sales whether the goods are absent or not, by means of writing, testimony and pledge. Ash-Shāfi'ī says: 'There are three forms of sale: selling with a document and witnesses, selling with a pledge, and selling on trust.' When Ibn 'Umar sold for cash, he called for witnesses and when he sold on credit, he wrote it down.

Call witnesses when you trade.

At-Ṭabarī says that this means that you should call witnesses to both small and large transactions. People disagree about whether that is obligatory or recommended. Abū Mūsā al-Ash'arī, Ibn 'Umar, aḍ-Ḍaḥḥāk, Sa'īd ibn al-Musayyab, Jābir ibn Zayd, Mujāhid, Dāwūd ibn 'Alī and his son Abū Bakr say that it is obligatory. One of the strongest in respect of that position was 'Aṭā'. He said, 'I call witnesses when I sell and buy for a dirham, or half a dirham, or a third or less. Allah says: *"Call witnesses when you trade."*' Ibrāhīm said, 'I call witnesses when I sell and buy, even for a bunch of onions.' One of those who believed it to be obligatory and preferred that was aṭ-Ṭabarī. He said, 'It is not lawful for a Muslim to buy and sell without calling witnesses. Otherwise he opposes the Book of Allah. If it is on credit, he must write it down and have witnesses if a scribe is at hand.'

Ash-Sha'bī and al-Ḥasan believe that the *āyah* is just recommendation and guidance and not a definite injunction. That is reported to be the position of Mālik, ash-Shāfi'ī, and the People of Opinion. Ibn al-'Arabī claimed that this is the position of all and he said that it is sound. No one related that it is mandatory except aḍ-Ḍaḥḥāk. He said, 'The Prophet ﷺ bought a slave and wrote: "In the Name of Allah. The All-Merciful, Most Merciful. This is what Muḥammad, Messenger of Allah, has purchased from al-'Addā' ibn Khālid, a sale from one Muslim to another, with no hidden defect, no taint and no wickedness (*ghā'ilah*) [i.e. in the slave sold.]."' He also bought without witnesses and left his armour in pawn to a Jew without witnesses being present. If having witnesses had been mandatory, it would have been obligatory when leaving a pledge out of fear of dispute.

We mentioned the view of it being obligatory from other than aḍ-Ḍaḥḥāk, namely the hadith of al-'Addā' in ad-Dāraquṭnī and Abū Dāwūd. He became Muslim after the Conquest of Makkah and Ḥunayn. He is the one who said, 'In the battle of Ḥunayn, we fought the Messenger of Allah ﷺ and Allah did not give us victory or help us.' Then he became Muslim and was a good Muslim.

Abū 'Umar mentioned him and mentioned this hadith. He said at the end of it, 'Al-Aṣmā'ī said, "I asked Sa'īd ibn Abī 'Arūbah about wickedness (*ghā'ilah*) and he said, 'Running away, stealing and fornication.' I asked him about badness (*khibthah*) and he said, 'Selling those who have a treaty with the Muslims.'"'

Imam Abū Muḥammad ibn 'Aṭiyyah said, 'The obligation in respect of that is undecided and the details are very difficult indeed. When it is something frequent, it may be that the merchant wants to seek friendship by not having witnesses or it may be the custom in some lands. He may be shy about a scholar or important esteemed man and so does not ask him to ask as a witness. All of that is part of trust, so the command to have witnesses remains a recommendation since it contains benefit in most cases as long as there is no excuse to prevent it.'

Al-Mahdawī, an-Naḥḥās and Makkī report that some people say that Allah's words: *'Call witnesses when you trade'* were abrogated by: *'If you leave things on trust with one another.'* (2:283) An-Naḥḥās reported from Abū Sa'īd al-Khudrī that the second *āyah* abrogated the one before it. An-Naḥḥās said that this is the position of al-Ḥasan, al-Ḥakam, and 'Abd ar-Raḥmān ibn Zayd. Aṭ-Ṭabarī disagrees, saying that is illogical, and says that the second *āyah* refers to someone who cannot find a scribe. Allah says: *'If you are on a journey and cannot find a writer, something can be left as a security. If you leave things on trust with one another...'* It means if he does not ask him for a deposit. He said that if were possible for this to abrogate the first, then Allah's words: *'If you are ill or on a journey, or any of you have come from the lavatory'* (4:43) could abrogate His words: *'You who believe, when you get up for the prayer.'* (5:6) Similarly, it would be possible for Allah's words: *'Anyone who cannot find the means should fast two consecutive months'* (4:92) to abrogate His words: *'free a believing slave.'* (4:92)

One scholar said that it is not clear that the phrase: *'If you leave things on trust with one another'* (2:293) was revealed later than the beginning of the *āyah* which contains the command to have witnesses. Rather it was revealed at the same time. It is not permitted for the abrogating and abrogated to come together at the same time. He said that it is related that when it was said to Ibn 'Abbās, 'The *Āyah* of Debt was abrogated,' he said, 'No, by Allah, the *Āyah* of Debt is one of judgment and there is no abrogation in it.' He said, 'Witnessing was instituted to bring about peace of mind. That is as Allah made different methods to secure debts. They include writing, pledges and witnesses. There is no disagreement among the people of the cities that the pledge is prescribed as a recommendation, not an obligation. It is known from that that the same must be true of witnesses. People continue to trade, resident and on journeys, on land and sea, on the flat and on mountains, without witnesses while people know that and do not object to it. If witnesses had been obligatory, they would have objected to the one who abandoned it.'

All of this is good deduction. Better than it is what comes from the clear Sunnah about not having witnesses. It is in what ad-Dāraquṭnī transmitted, namely that Ṭāriq ibn 'Abdullāh al-Muḥāribī said, 'We came in a group from Rabadhah and south of Rabadhah and camped near Madīnah. We had a woman in a sedan with us. While we were sitting down, a man wearing two white garments came to us and greeted us. We returned the greeting. He asked, "From where have you people come?" We answered, "From Rabadhah and south of Rabadhah." We had a red camel with us and he asked, "Will you sell me this camel of yours?" "Yes," we answered. "For how much?" he asked. We told him for a certain number of *ṣā*'s of dates. He did not ask us to reduce it at all, but said, "I have taken it." Then he took the camel's head and entered Madīnah and was hidden from us. We criticised one another and said, "You gave your camel to someone you do not know!" The woman said, "Do not blame one another. I saw the face of a man who would not deceive you. I have not seen a man with a face more like the full moon than his." In the evening, a man came to us and said, "Peace be upon you. I am the messenger of the Messenger of Allah ﷺ to you. He commands you to eat from this until you are full and to measure until you have full measure." We ate until we were full and took full measure.' Az-Zuhrī mentioned the hadith from 'Umārah ibn Khuzaymah from his uncle, who was one of the Companions of the Prophet, that the Prophet ﷺ bought a horse from a Bedouin. We find in it: 'The bedouin began to say, "Bring a witness who will testify that I sold it to you!" Khuzaymah ibn Thābit said, "I testify that you sold it." The Prophet ﷺ turned to Khuzaymah and said, "On what basis do you bear witness?" He answered, "By affirming that you speak the truth, Messenger of Allah!" The Messenger of Allah ﷺ made Khuzaymah's testimony equal to the testimony of two men.' An-Nasā'ī and other transmitted it.

Neither writer nor witness should be put under pressure.

One meaning of this is that a scribe should not write anything other than what has been dictated to him nor should the witness add to his testimony nor decrease it. Al-Ḥasan, Qatādah, Ṭāwus, Ibn Zayd and others said that. It is related from Ibn 'Abbās, Mujāhid and 'Aṭā' that the *āyah* means that the scribe should not be prevented from writing nor the witness from testifying.

Mujāhid, aḍ-Ḍaḥḥāk, Ṭāwus, and as-Suddī said – and the same thing is also related from Ibn 'Abbās – that the *āyah* means that the witness should not be summoned to testify or the scribe to write when they are busy and they should not be made to come when they have an excuse nor should they be abused. They should not be told, 'You have disobeyed Allah's command!' or similar things so as to put them under pressure. Allah forbade this because, if it was applied, it would distract them from their *dīn* and livelihood. The form of the verb *'yuḍārru'* which involves two people demands these ideas.

If you do that, it is deviancy on your part,

If someone testifies to what is not the truth or changes things when writing it down, he is called a deviant. This is even more appropriate in the case of someone who asks a witness to testify when is busy.

If you do put them under pressure it is disobedience to Allah, as Sufyān ath-Thawrī said. The scribe and witness disobey by adding or decreasing. That is a type of prevarication which harms property and people and invalidates their rights. Forcing the witness or scribe when they are busy is also disobedience and incorrect behaviour since it is disobeying Allah's command. *'Your part'* implies that deviancy will occur from you.

Be fearful of Allah and Allah will give you knowledge.

This is a promise from Allah that He will teach those who fear Him, meaning that He will put a light in their hearts by which they will understand what comes to them. He may put discrimination in their hearts, so that they will be able to distinguish between truth and falsehood. Allah says, *'O you who believe, if you fear Allah, he will give you discrimination.'* (8:29) Allah knows best.

وَإِن كُنتُمْ عَلَىٰ سَفَرٍ وَلَمْ تَجِدُوا كَاتِبًا فَرِهَٰنٌ مَّقْبُوضَةٌ فَإِنْ أَمِنَ
بَعْضُكُم بَعْضًا فَلْيُؤَدِّ الَّذِي اؤْتُمِنَ أَمَٰنَتَهُ وَلْيَتَّقِ اللَّهَ رَبَّهُ وَلَا
تَكْتُمُوا الشَّهَٰدَةَ وَمَن يَكْتُمْهَا فَإِنَّهُ ءَاثِمٌ قَلْبُهُ وَاللَّهُ بِمَا تَعْمَلُونَ
عَلِيمٌ ٢٨٣

283 If you are on a journey and cannot find a writer, something can be left as a security. If you leave things on trust with one another the one who is trusted must deliver up his trust and be fearful of Allah his Lord. Do not conceal testimony. If someone does conceal it, his heart commits a crime. Allah knows what you do.

If you are on a journey and cannot find a writer,

After Allah has mentioned the recommendation to testify and write for the benefit of preserving property and the *dīn*, He follows that by mentioning the excuses which may prevent people from writing and enjoins them to leave a pledge in such cases. He clarifies what constitutes a valid excuse by mentioning a journey, which is the usual reason, especially since there were a lot of expeditions at that time. But included in that are all valid excuses. There are often times when a person is resident and cannot make use of a scribe, as occurs when people are at work or during the night. Another instance is when there is fear for the loss of what the debtor owes and the lender seeks a pledge from him for that reason. The Prophet ﷺ left his armour in pledge with a Jew whom he asked for an advance of barley. He said, 'Muhammad wants to take away my property.' The Prophet ﷺ said, 'He lies. I am the one who is trustworthy on earth and trustworthy in heaven. If you trust me, I will pay. Take my armour to him.' He died with his armour still in pledge.

Most scholars say that a pledge should be left when travelling, going by the text of the Revelation. It is confirmed while a person is resident by the *sunnah* of the Messenger ﷺ. This is sound. We already explained its permissibility when resident from the idea in the *āyah* since excuses arise when someone is a resident. Excuses arise when one is resident and its prohibition while a person is a resident is only related by Mujāhid, aḍ-Ḍaḥḥāk and Dāwūd who hold to the *āyah*. There is no argument in that because even though the wording is that of a precondition, what is meant is most circumstances. The fact that in the *āyah* the pledge is on a journey does not prevent it being used in other cases. As we stated, we find in the two *Ṣaḥīḥ* collections and elsewhere from 'Ā'ishah that the Prophet ﷺ purchased food from a Jew on credit and left his iron armour as a pledge. An-Nasā'ī transmitted that Ibn 'Abbās said, 'The Messenger of Allah ﷺ died while his armour was in pledge with a Jew for thirty *ṣā*'s of barley for his family.'

Most recite 'writer (*kātib*)', meaning a man who can write, while Ibn 'Abbās, Mujāhid, aḍ-Ḍaḥḥāk, 'Ikrimah, and Abu-l-'Ālīyah recited '*kitāb*' (writing). Abū Bakr al-Anbārī said, 'Mujāhid explained it as meaning, 'If you do not find ink,' meaning with the scribes. Ibn 'Abbās related '*kuttāb* (scribes)'. An-Naḥḥās said that it is an aberrant reading, and the common people do not have it. Rarely is something outside of the common recitation other than attacked. The context of the words indicates 'writer'. Before this Allah said: *'A writer should write it down between you justly.'* *Kuttāb* demands a plural, but Ibn 'Aṭiyyah said that '*kuttāb*' is good because every occurrence has a writer and so the plural is used, even if there are not 'writers' present. An-Naḥḥās and Makkī said that it is the plural of *kātib*.

Al-Mahdawī related that Abū' 'l-'Āliyah recited '*kutub*', the plural of '*kitāb*' (book) since there are different occurrences. Makkī said that it means 'when inkwell, pen and paper are not available.' The lack of a writer is also the lack of the implement. It also demands the lack of writing. So both readings are good except from the aspect of the written word.

something can be left as a security.

Instead of *rihān* (security), Abū 'Amr and Ibn Kathīr recite '*ruhun*', and '*ruhn*' is also related from him. Aṭ-Ṭabarī said that some people take *ruhun* to be the plural of *rihān*. Az-Zajjāj related that from al-Farrā'. Al-Mahdawī said that 'security' is an inceptive whose predicate is elided. It means: 'something left as security is sufficient for that.' An-Naḥḥās said that 'Āṣim ibn Abi-n-Nujūd recited '*ruhn*' and that is related from the people of Makkah. *Rihān* is like *baghl* and *bighlān* and *kabsh* and *kibāsh*. *Ruhun* is the plural of *rihān* like *kutub* and *kitāb*. It is also said that it is the plural of '*rahn*' like *saqf* and *suquf*, *ḥalq* and *ḥuluq*, and the like. The second *ḍammah* in *ruhn* has been elided because it is heavy. [BIT MORE OMITTED]

The meaning of 'leaving a security' is that an item be kept by the lender as a guarantee against what is owed so that the amount can be paid in full from selling the security or renting it out, if the debt cannot be collected from the debtor. That is how scholars define it. The root of the verb (*rahana*) means 'to remain or last'. Ibn Sayyidah says that *rahana* means to make something last. It is as a poet says:

Bread and meat make them last.
    The pot of coffee is poured.

Al-Jawharī said that *rahana* means to make to make last. *Arhana* is used to make food and drink last. That which is *rāhin* continues and is fixed. *Rāhin* also describes a thin camel and thin people. He said:

Do you see my body is lean and has become emaciated (*rahan*)?
    The glory of men is not in plumpness.

Ibn 'Aṭiyyah said that *rahn* is the security which is deposited. One of them said that the verb *arhana* is used for that. Abū 'Alī said that *arhana* means to pay an excessive price either in a loan or a sale. Abū Zayd also said that it is to buy for an excessive price. He says about a she-camel:

An 'Īdiyyah camel for excessive (*urhinat*) dinars.

'Īd is a sub-tribe of Mahrah and their camels are described as noble.

Az-Zajjāj said that one says about a security (*rahn*), *rahanat* and *arhanat.* Ibn al-A'rābī and al-Akhfash said that. 'Abdullāh ibn Himā as-Salūlī said:

When I feared their talons,
I was saved and gave them your property as security (*arhantuhum*).

Tha'lab said that all transmitters say that it can be *rahantu*, except for al-Aṣma'ī who related *arhantu* as adding a future verb to a past verb. He said that it is like their words, 'I stood and slapped his face.' It is a good position because it is the *wāw* of the *ḥāl* in the sentence and so 'slap' is a *ḥāl* modifying the first verb and it means 'I stood, slapping his face.' [OMISSION]

Ibn as-Sikkīt said that the verb means to make an advance. A *murtahin* is someone who takes a pledge (*rahn*). The thing is called *marhūn.* The dual is *rahīnah. Rāhana* is to make a wager (*murāhanah*) with someone, and *'arhantu bihi waladī'* means 'I made my children a stake for it.' *Rahīnah* is the single of *rahā'in.* All of that comes from al-Jawharī.

Ibn 'Aṭiyyah said that there is no disagreement about its use in loans and sales, and then the verbal noun is used for the object.

Abū 'Alī said that since the word means to be fixed and constant, the pledge is void according to the *fuqahā'* the moment it goes from the possession of the one who takes it to the one who pledged it. This is what we believe. If the pledge is taken from the possession of the one who accepted it and returned to the pledger by the choice of the one who has taken it on pledge, the pledge then becomes invalid. Abū Ḥanīfah says that, although he adds that if it is returned to his keeping, it is not invalid. Ash-Shāfi'ī also says that it is not invalidated. Our proof is that He says, 'taken'. When it leaves the possession of the one who took it, then that term cannot be applied to it and it is not sound to base a ruling on it. This is clear.

If the pledge is verbal and not actually taken, no ruling applies since the *āyah* says 'taken'. Ash-Shāfi'ī says that Allah only gives a ruling to a pledge which is 'taken'. Without that, there is no ruling. This is very literal. The Mālikīs say that the pledge is binding by the contract and the pledger must hand over the pledge to the keeping of the person who takes it by the words of the Almighty: *'Fulfil your contracts.'* (5:1, 17:34). This is a contract. The Prophet ﷺ said, 'The believers abide by their conditions,' and this is a condition. We believe that taking possession of the pledge is a precondition for its being operative.

The word 'taken' (*maqbūḍah*) implies that the person accepting the pledge or his agent must clearly take it. They disagree about a third party with integrity taking it and whether that effects it or not. Mālik and all his people and most other scholars say that the taking by any just person constitutes 'taking', while Ibn Abī Laylā, Qatādah, al-Ḥakam, and 'Aṭā' said that it does not, and that it is only 'taken' when it is actually in the possession of the person accepting the pledge. They see it as an act of worship. The position of the majority is sounder because, if a just person takes it, it is still taken. If the pledge is in the possession of a just person who took it and he loses it, the pledgee is not liable since there is nothing in his possession for which he is liable.

Our scholars have said that the literal and non-specific nature of the word 'taken' demands that it is permitted to have a pledge for shared property. This differs from Abū Ḥanīfah and his people who do not permit a pledge for a third of a house, or half of a slave or a sword. Then they said that if a man owes something to two men, in which they are partners, it is permitted to give them land as a pledge for that when they both take it. Ibn al-Mundhir said, 'This permits a pledge for shared property because each of them is pledged half of a house.' Ibn al-Mundhir further says, 'A pledge of something jointly owned is permitted, just as it is permitted to sell it.'

Our scholars have said that it is permitted to leave a pledge of liability because it is 'taken'. Others forbid this. An example of that is two men who do business together and one owes a debt to the other and his pledge is his debt which he owes. Ibn Khuwayzimandād said, 'It is permitted to use as a pledge any goods which can be sold. This is why we permitted a pledge of liability because it is permitted to sell it and because it is property for which there is a receipt. It is analogous to available merchandise.' Those who forbid that say that it is forbidden because it cannot be properly taken and being taken is a precondition for the pledge to be binding because the right must be received in full at the place, and it must be able to be paid in full financially and that that is not conceivable with a debt.

Al-Bukhārī related from Abū Hurayrah that the Messenger of Allah ﷺ said, 'A mount may be ridden when it is a pledge because of its upkeep. Its milk may be drunk when it is a pledge because of its upkeep. Someone who rides it or milks it must pay for its upkeep.' Abū Dāwūd transmitted it with a different word for 'drink'. Al-Khaṭṭābī said, 'These are unclear words and it is not clear who is the one riding and milking and whether it is the pledger or the pledgee or the just purpose who has the pledge in his possession.'

The explanation of that is found in two hadiths, and it is because of them that scholars disagree about it. Ad-Dāraquṭnī related from Abū Hurayrah that the Prophet ﷺ said, 'When a riding animal is a pledge, then the pledgee must fodder it and may drink the milk. The one who drinks it is responsible for its upkeep.'

This is transmitted from Aḥmad ibn 'Alī ibn al-'Alā' from Ziyād ibn Ayyūb from Hushaym from Zakariyyā from ash-Sha'bī from Abū Hurayrah. It is the position of Aḥmad and Isḥāq that the pledgee can use the pledge for milk and riding according to the cost of its upkeep. Abū Thawr said, 'If it is the pledger that pays for its upkeep, then the pledgee cannot use it. If the pledger does not pay its upkeep and it remains in the possession of the pledgee and he pays for its upkeep, then he can ride it and he may also make use of a [pledged] slave.' Al-Awzā'ī and al-Layth said that.

The second hadith was also transmitted by ad-Dāraquṭnī, but there are things said about its *isnād*. It is related from Ismā'īl ibn 'Ayyāsh from Ibn Abī Dhi'b from az-Zuhrī from al-Maqburī from Abū Hurayrah that the Messenger of Allah ﷺ said, 'The pledge does not become forfeit. He has its gain and bears its loss.' That is the position of ash-Shāfi'ī, ash-Sha'bī and Ibn Sīrīn, and it is the position of Mālik and his people. Ash-Shāfi'ī said, 'The pledger makes use of the pledge and must pay for its upkeep. The pledgee does not use any of the pledge except for preserving the security.' Al-Khaṭṭābī said, 'That is the soundest and most fitting position as evidenced by the words of the Prophet ﷺ.'

Aṭ-Ṭaḥāwī said, 'That was at a time when *ribā* was still permitted, when it was not forbidden to have an interest-bearing loan or an unequal exchange of goods. *Ribā* was forbidden after that.' The community agree that it is not permitted for the pledger to have sex with his slave-girl who has been given as a pledge nor may he use her as a servant. Ash-Sha'bī said that he may not use any of the pledge. Ash-Sha'bī transmitted this hadith but gave a fatwa which differed from it! That is not permitted for him until it is abrogated. Ibn 'Abd al-Barr said that there is a consensus that the pledger can milk and ride the pledge. If the pledgee milks the pledge, it is either with or without the permission of the pledger. If it is without his permission, we find in a hadith that Ibn 'Umar related from the Prophet ﷺ: 'No one should milk an animal without permission.' This refutes him and demands that it be abrogated. If it is with permission, then it is one of the fundamental principles agreed upon about forbidding what is unknown and risky, selling what is not in your possession and selling what has not yet be created. That also refutes him. That was before the revelation of the prohibition of *ribā*'. Allah knows best.

Ibn Khuwayzimandād said, 'There are two situations that can arise when a pledgee stipulates the use of the pledge. If it is part of a loan, then it is not permitted. If it is part of a sale or hire, then it is permitted because he becomes someone who sells the merchandise for the price that was mentioned as well as the use of the pledge for a known period. So it is like a sale and hire. In the case of a loan, it would turn it into an interest-bearing loan. That is because the loan is a good action. If there is a benefit from it, then it becomes an increase and that is *ribā*.'

It is not permitted to take a pledge as forfeit. That is when the pledgee stipulates that he has a right to it if there is no payment at the end of the term. This was part of the action of the Jāhiliyyah. The Prophet ﷺ declared it void when he said, 'The pledge does not become forfeit.' 'A pledge being forfeit' is when it is in the possession of the pledgee when it is not redeemed.

Zuhayr said:

She separated herself with a pledge which was not redeemed
On the day of farewell, and so the pledge became forfeit.

Ad-Dāraquṭnī related from Sufyān ibn 'Uyaynah from Ziyād ibn Sa'd from az-Zuhrī from Sa'īd ibn al-Musayyab from Abū Hurayrah that the Messenger of Allah ﷺ said, 'The pledge does not become forfeit. He has its gain and bears its loss.' Ziyād ibn Sa'd is one of the trustworthy keepers. This is a good *isnād*. Mālik transmitted from Ibn Shihāb in a *mursal* transmission from Sa'īd ibn al-Musayyab that the Messenger of Allah ﷺ said, 'A pledge does not become forfeit.' Abū 'Umar said, 'As far as I know, that is how it is related by all of those who relate the *Muwaṭṭā'* from Mālik except for Ma'n ibn 'Īsā.'

He connected its transmission, and Ma'n is trustworthy, although I fear that the error in it is from 'Alī ibn 'Abd al-Ḥamīd al-Ghaḍārī from Mujāhid ibn Mūsā from Ma'n ibn 'Īsā. In it he added from 'Abdullāh 'Amrūs from al-Abharī with his *isnād*, 'He has its gain and bears its loss.' Transmitters disagree about this addition. Ibn Abī Laylā, Ma'mar and others removed it.

Ibn Wahb related it and said, 'Yūnus said that Ibn Shihāb said, "Sa'id ibn al-Musayyab used to say, 'The pledge belongs to the one who pledged it. He has its gain and bears its loss.'"' Ibn Shihāb reported that this is part of what Sa'id ibn al-Musayyab said, not what the Prophet ﷺ said. However, Ma'mar did mention it *marfū'* from Ibn Shihāb. Ma'mar is the firmest of those who relate from Ibn Shihāb. 'Alī corroborated it *marfū'* from Yaḥyā ibn Abī Unaysah, who is not strong. The basis of this hadith with the people of knowledge of transmission is that it *mursal*. Although it is connected by various paths, they find fault in them. Furthermore, no one makes this hadith *marfū'*, but they disagree about its interpretation and meaning.

Ad-Dāraquṭnī also related it *marfū'* from Ismā'īl ibn 'Ayyāsh from Ibn Abī Dh'ib from az-Zuhrī from Sa'īd from Abū Hurayrah. Abū 'Umar said that Ismā'īl did not hear it from Ibn Abī Dh'ib, but rather heard it from 'Abbād ibn Kathīr from Ibn Abī Dh'ib. We consider 'Abbād to be weak and he is not used as an authority. We also believe that the hadiths of Ismā'īl are not accepted when they are reported from people other than those of his land. When he relates from Syrians, his hadiths are in order. When he relates from Madinans and others, there are many errors and much confusion in his hadiths.

Growth in the pledge is part of it when it is not distinct, like clarified butter, or progeny, like infants of animals, and fruit. This includes palm shoots and other sorts of produce, fruits, milk and wool. They are not included as part of the pledge unless that is stipulated. The difference is that infants follow mothers in *zakāt*, but that is not the case with wool, milk and the fruit of trees because they do not follow their sources in *zakāt* and do not have the same form or the same idea. They have their own ruling which is not the same ruling as their source. This is not the case with infants and progeny. Allah knows best what is correct regarding that.

It is permitted for someone whose debts encompass all his property to leave a pledge, as long as he has not been declared bankrupt. The pledgee is more entitled to the pledge than the other creditors. Mālik and a group of people stated that. Something different is also related from Mālik which was stated by 'Abd al-'Azīz ibn Abī Salamah: it is that the rest of the creditors are included with him in that. That is of no consequence because the transactions of someone who has not been debarred are sound in all circumstances, whether buying or selling. The creditors dealt with him in buying and selling and deciding. The position of Mālik does not differ in this area. The same is true of the pledge, and Allah knows best.

If you leave things on trust with one another the one who is trusted must deliver up his trust

This is an order from Allah to hand over what was left in trust and not to procrastinate. The command here is mandatory and is connected to the consensus that it is mandatory to pay debts. The judge can confirm that and creditors can compel him to pay it. Furthermore there are sound hadiths which make another person's property unlawful to him. The word for '*amānah*' (leave on trust) is a verbal noun meaning something for which one is responsible. 'His' refers to the one who owes the debt [and left the pledge].

and be fearful of Allah his Lord.

He must not conceal anything that rightfully belongs to someone else.

Do not conceal testimony.

This forbids a witness from causing harm by hiding the fact of his testimony. The prohibition is mandatory and a threat accompanies it. The prohibition applies to when the witness fears that the right will be lost. Ibn 'Abbās said, 'A witness must testify when he is called upon to testify and report when he is asked to report.' If there are several witnesses, it is a *farḍ kifāyah* that they testify. When two have satisfied it, the obligation falls from the rest of them. If they do not do it, then it is incumbent on the remaining witness to go and do it so that there is affirmation. This is known when he is called upon to do it when he says, 'Ensure my right by conveying the testimony you have.' Then it becomes incumbent on him to do it.

If someone does conceal it, his heart commits a crime.

The heart is mentioned since concealment is an action and the heart is that piece of flesh by whose soundness the entire body is sound, as the Prophet ﷺ said. One part of it designates the whole of it. This was mentioned at the beginning of the *sūrah*. Aṭ-Ṭabarī said, 'When a witness resolves not to convey his testimony and abandons performing it with the tongue, then he commits a sin in both ways.' 'His heart commits a crime' is metaphorical. It stresses the real nature of what occurs and indicates the threat. That is part of eloquence and fine use of language in expressing the meaning. It is said that the crime of the heart is the reason for its transformation. When Allah transforms the heart, He makes the person a hypocrite and seals it. We seek refuge from Allah. This was already mentioned at the beginning of the *sūrah*.

Know that Allah's commands concerning testimony and writing are intended to rectify discord and to avoid disputes which might lead to conflict, thereby preventing Shayṭān from enticing people to deny others their rights and exceed what the *Sharī'ah* has defined for them, or not to confine themselves to the amount they are owed. It is for this reason that the *Sharī'ah* forbids unknown sales which would lead to disagreement and conflict and bring about mutual rancour and separation. One aspect of this is Allah's prohibition of gambling and games of chance and drinking wine. Allah says: *'Shayṭān wants to stir up enmity and hatred between you by means of wine and gambling.'* (5:91) Whoever is guided by Allah in respect of His commands and restraints, obtains the good of this world and the *dīn*. Allah Almighty says: *'But if they had done what they were urged to do, it would have been better for them.'* (4:66)

Al-Bukhārī related from Abū Hurayrah that the Prophet ﷺ said, 'If someone takes something from another intending to repay it, Allah will repay it for him, and if someone takes it intending to destroy it, Allah will destroy him.' An-Nasā'ī reported that Maymūnah, the wife of the Prophet ﷺ, used to have a lot of debts, and she was asked, 'Umm al-Mu'minīn, do you incur debts when you have nothing with which to pay them?' She replied, 'I heard the Messenger of Allah ﷺ say, "If anyone takes on a debt intending to pay it, Allah will help him with it."'

Aṭ-Tahāwī, Abū Ja'far aṭ-Ṭabarī and al-Ḥārith ibn Abī Usāmah in his *Musnad* reported from 'Uqbah ibn 'Āmir that the Messenger of Allah ﷺ said, 'Do not frighten people when they are secure.' They asked 'Messenger of Allah, how can that happen?' 'By debts,' he replied.

Al-Bukhārī reported from Anas that the Prophet ﷺ said in a supplication, 'O Allah, I seek refuge with You from worry, sorrow, incapacity, laziness, cowardice, miserliness, heavy debts and the oppression of men.' Scholars say that heavy debts are those which the debtor can find no way to pay. The word for 'heavy' is taken from the Arabic expressions *'ḥiml muḍli'*', an overburdening load, and *'dābah muḍli'*', an animal unable to bear its load. The author of *al-'Ayn* said that.

The Prophet ﷺ said, 'A debt is the disgrace of the *dīn*.' It is related that he said, 'Debts are worry by night and abasement by day.' Our scholars say that debts are disgrace and abasement because they preoccupy the heart and mind, and one is always concerned about paying them. There is abasement to the creditor when he meets him and he continues to endure the burden of the creditor's favour to him by delaying paying it to the end of its term. He may promise to pay and then put it off, or the creditor may abuse him because of it and he will lie, or he may give him an oath and then break it, and other such things. This is why the Prophet ﷺ sought refuge from it. It was said to the Messenger of Allah, 'How often you seek refuge from debts!' He said, 'When a man is in debt, he will speak and lie and promise and break his promise.' Furthermore, sometimes someone may die without paying the debt and then be left in pledge for it, for the Prophet ﷺ said, 'The soul of the believer is pledged in the grave for his debts until they are paid.' All of these things are disgrace in the *dīn* which removes its beauty and perfection. Allah knows best.

When Allah commands people to write down debts, to bear witness and to take pledges, that constitutes a clear text about preserving property and making it grow, refuting ignorant false Sufis and the riffraff who follow them who do not agree with that. They abandon all their wealth and do not leave enough for themselves and their families. Then, when they and their families are in need, they either turn to the generosity of brothers or friends, or take from the wealthy and unjust. This is blameworthy and forbidden. Abu-l-Faraj al-Jawzī said, 'I do not wonder at those who practise asceticism when they are lacking in knowledge.

I do wonder at how people who have knowledge and intellect encourage this and command it when it is contrary to the *Sharīʿah* and logic.' Al-Muḥāsibī talked a lot about this and Abū Ḥāmid al-Ghazālī praised it as well. I think al-Muḥāsibi has more of an excuse than Abū Ḥāmid because Abū Ḥāmid had more *fiqh*, although his entry into *taṣawwuf* obliged him to support what he had entered into.

Al-Muḥāsibī said, 'I heard that when 'Abd ar-Raḥmān ibn 'Awf died, some of the Companions of Messenger of Allah ﷺ said, "We fear for 'Abd ar-Raḥmān because of what he left." Kaʿb said. "Glory be to Allah! What do you fear for 'Abd ar-Raḥmān? He earned well, spent well and left well." That reached Abū Dharr who went out angrily after Kaʿb. He picked up the jawbone of a camel and then went to look for Kaʿb. Kaʿb was told, "Abū Dharr is looking for you." So he ran to 'Uthmān asking him for his help and telling him the story. Abū Dharr tracked down Kaʿb until he came to 'Uthmān's house. When he entered, Kaʿb got up and sat down behind 'Uthmān, fleeing from Abū Dharr. Abū Dharr said to him, "Son of a Jewish woman, do you claim that there is no harm in what 'Abd ar-Raḥmān left! The Messenger of Allah ﷺ went out one day and said, 'The ones with the most will be the ones with the least on the Day of Rising except for those who say such-and-such.'"' Al-Muḥāsibī said, 'In spite of his excellence, 'Abd ar-Raḥmān will still be made to stand in the courtyard on the Day of Rising because of his lawful earnings which he used for the sake of abstinence and acts of charity, and so he will be prevented from hastening to the Garden with the poor and will be have to crawl in behind them.'

Al-Ghazālī mentioned this and supported it by the hadith of Thaʿlabah who was given money and then refused to pay *zakāt*. He said, 'If anyone examines the states of the Prophets and *awliyā'* and their statements, he will not doubt that the absence of wealth is better than its existence, even if it is directed towards good ends, since the least of the consequences of wealth is that attending to it distracts the *himmah* (aspiration) from remembrance of Allah. So a *murīd* must leave his property so that he only has what he needs and not have a dirham to which his heart turns so that he is veiled from Allah.'

Al-Jawzī said, 'All of this is contrary to the *Sharīʿah* and intelligence, and is poor understanding of what is desired in respect of property. Allah honoured and esteemed it and commanded it to be preserved since He made it the support of the human being and that which is the support of the noble human being is also noble. The Almighty says: *"Do not hand over to the simple-minded any property of theirs for which Allah has made you responsible."* (4:5). He forbade property to be surrendered to someone without good sense and says: *"If you perceive that they have sound judgment hand over their property to them."* (4:6) The Prophet ﷺ forbade squandering property and told Sa'd, "It is better to leave rich heirs than to leave them poor, begging from other people," and he said, "Nothing helped me like the property of Abū Bakr." He told 'Amr ibn al-'Āṣ, "The best of property is the good property of a righteous man." He prayed for Anas, "O Allah, make his property and children plentiful and bless him in it." Ka'b said, "One thing I repent of is that I divested myself of my property as *sadaqah* for Allah and His Messenger." He said, "Keep part of your property for yourself. That will be better for you."'

Al-Jawzī continued, 'These hadiths are found in the sound collections and are contrary to what false Sufis believe about a lot of wealth being a veil and a punishment and that having it is contrary to reliance on Allah. It cannot be denied that its temptation is something to be feared, that a lot of people avoid it out of fear of that, that amassing it properly rarely occurs, that the safety of the heart from temptation by it is rare and that it is unusual for a heart to be busy with it while still remembering the Next World. This is why its temptation is feared. As for earning property, when someone confines himself to what will suffice him of what is lawful, that is necessary. As for someone who intends to amass it and have a lot of the lawful, one looks to his intention. If his intention is to boast, that is evil. If he intends a modest income for himself and his family, to save up for changes of fortune and bad times, and intends to expand things for his brothers, enrich the poor and do righteous actions, his intention will be rewarded, and his amassing it with this intention is better than many acts of obedience.

'The intention of many of the Companions was to amass sound wealth for good ends and so they encouraged it and asked for more. When the Prophet ﷺ gave az-Zubayr a land grant, he summoned his horse and ran his horse until it stopped, and then threw his whip and he said, "Give him up to where his whip lands." Sa'īd ibn 'Ubādah said in his supplication, "O Allah, give me expansion." The brothers of Yūsuf said, *"We can get an extra load."* (12:65) Shu'ayb said to Mūsā, *"If you complete ten, then that is up to you."* (28:27) When Ayyūb was healed and golden locusts began to fall on him, he began to collect them in his garment and collected a lot, he was asked, "Are you not full?" He said, "Lord, does a poor man have his fill of Your bounty?"

'This is something embedded in human nature. The words of al-Muḥāsibī are erroneous and indicate lack of knowledge. What he mentioned about Ka'b and Abū Dharr is impossible and forged by the ignorant. Its lack of soundness is concealed because of their attachment to the People [i.e. Sufis]. Its *isnād* is not firm. The truth of the matter is that Abū Dharr died in 25 AH and 'Abd ar-Raḥmān ibn 'Awf died in 32 AH so he lived seven years after Abū Dharr. The actual words of the account indicate that it is forged. How could the Companions say, "We fear for 'Abd ar-Raḥmān?" Is there not a consensus that it is permitted to amass lawful wealth, so what is the sense of fearing for someone because of something which is allowed? Would the *Sharī'ah* permit something and then punish someone for it? This is poor understanding.

'How would Abū Dharr disapprove of 'Abd ar-Raḥmān when 'Abd ar-Raḥmān was far more excellent than him? Is its attribution to 'Abd ar-Raḥmān alone evidence that he did not follow the path of the Companions? Ṭalḥah left three thousand measures and every measure weighed three hundredweight. Az-Zubayr left two hundred and fifty thousand. Ibn Mas'ūd left seventy thousand. Many of the Companions amassed wealth and left it and no one objected to that. As for the words "'Abd ar-Raḥmān will crawl on the Day of Rising," this is proof that the transmitter does not know the hadith. I seek refuge with Allah from 'Abd ar-Raḥmān crawling on the Day of Rising! Do you think that one of the ten promised the Garden, one of the people present at the Battle of Badr, and one of the people of the Shūrā, would have to crawl?

'Then it was 'Umārah ibn Zādhān who related the hadith and al-Bukhārī said that his hadiths are shaky. Aḥmad said that he reported many denounced hadiths from Anas. Abū Ḥātim ar-Rāzī said that he is not authoritative. Ad-Dāraquṭnī said that he is weak.

'The statement, "It is better to abandon lawful wealth than to amass it" is not true. When the intention is sound, then amassing it is better without any disagreement among the scholars. Sa'īd ibn al-Musayyab said, "There is no good in one who does not seek wealth with which to pay his debts and protect his reputation. If he dies, he leaves inheritance for those after him." He himself left four hundred dinars. Sufyān left two hundred. He used to say. "Wealth in this time is an armour." The Salaf continued to praise wealth and collect it for recommended things and to help the poor. Some people shun it since they prefer to devote themselves to worship. They have strong aspiration and are content with only a little. If someone says this, then this small amount is better for him than approaching the business, but he is close to the level of sin.'

Part of what indicates that preserving property and caring for it is correct is that one can fight for it and over it. The Prophet ﷺ said, 'If someone is killed in defence of his property, he is a martyr.' This will be mentioned further in *Sūrat al-Mā'idah*, Allah willing.

لِّلَّهِ مَا فِي ٱلسَّمَٰوَٰتِ وَمَا فِي ٱلْأَرْضِ وَإِن تُبْدُوا۟ مَا فِىٓ أَنفُسِكُمْ
أَوْ تُخْفُوهُ يُحَاسِبْكُم بِهِ ٱللَّهُ فَيَغْفِرُ لِمَن يَشَآءُ وَيُعَذِّبُ مَن يَشَآءُ
وَٱللَّهُ عَلَىٰ كُلِّ شَىْءٍ قَدِيرٌ ﴿٢٨٤﴾

284 Everything in the heavens and everything in the earth belongs to Allah. Whether you divulge what is in yourselves or keep it hidden, Allah will still call you to account for it. He forgives whomever He wills and He punishes whomever He wills. Allah has power over all things.

Whether you divulge what is in yourselves or keep it hidden, Allah will still call you to account for it.

People disagree about this statement and there are five different positions about it:

– One group say that it is abrogated. Ibn 'Abbās, Ibn Mas'ūd, 'Ā'ishah, Abū Hurayrah, ash-Sha'bī, 'Aṭā', Muḥammad ibn Sīrīn, Muḥammad ibn Ka'b, Mūsā ibn 'Ubaydah and a group of Companions and Tābi'ūn said that. This degree of accountability remained until Allah revealed: *'Allah does not impose on any self any more than it can bear.'* (2:286) We find in *Ṣaḥīḥ Muslim* that Ibn 'Abbās said, 'When the *āyah* was revealed: *"Whether you divulge what is in yourselves or keep it hidden, Allah will still call you to account for it,"* something of [fear of that] entered their hearts that had never entered them before. The Prophet ﷺ said, "Say: 'We hear and obey and submit.'" So Allah cast faith into their hearts and then Allah Almighty revealed: *"Allah does not impose on any self any more than it can bear. For it, is what it has earned, and against it is what it has merited. Our Lord, do not take us to task if we forget or make a mistake!"* and He said, "I have done it." *"Our Lord, do not place on us a load like the one You place on those before us!"* and He said, "I have done it." *"Our Lord, do not place on us a load we have not the strength to bear! And pardon us, and forgive us and have mercy on us. You are our Master, so help us against the people of the believers."* (2:286) He said, "I have done it."' One variant has: 'When they did that, Allah abrogated it for them and then revealed: *"Allah does not impose on any self any more than it can bear."*'

– Ibn 'Abbās, 'Ikrimah, ash-Sha'bī and Mujāhid said that it is an *āyah* of judgment specifically about the testimony referred to earlier, which it is forbidden to conceal and for which the person will be called to account. Allah informs us in this *āyah* that a person will be called to account for what he conceals inside himself.

– The *āyah* is about doubt and certainty which comes to the heart. Mujāhid said that.

– It is a general ruling and not abrogated. Allah will call His creatures to account for their actions and for things they did not do, which were settled in themselves and which they concealed, desired and intended. He will forgive the believers and punish the people of disbelief and hypocrisy for that. Aṭ-Tabarī mentioned this position, and related something similar from Ibn 'Abbās. It is related from 'Alī ibn Abī Ṭalḥah that Ibn 'Abbās said, 'It was not abrogated. But when Allah gathers the creatures, He will say, "I will tell you what you concealed in yourselves." He will tell the believers and then forgive them. As for the people of doubt and uncertainty, He will tell them of the denial they concealed. That is what He means when He says: *"He forgives whomever He wills and He punishes whomever He wills,"* and the meaning of His words: *"He will take you to task for the intention your hearts have made"* (2:225) referring to doubt and hypocrisy.'

Aḍ-Ḍaḥḥāk said, 'On the Day of Rising Allah will tell each person what he was concealing so that he knows that he does not have to fear on account of it.' In a report we read, 'Allah Almighty will say on the Day of Rising: "This is the Day on which secrets are revealed and consciences probed. My scribes only record your actions which appear on your limbs and tongues. I know what they do not know and know what they do not report or write down. I will inform you of that and reckon you for it and then I will forgive whoever I wish and punish whomever I wish." So He will forgive the believers and punish the unbelievers.'

This is the soundest position on this matter. It is indicated by the hadith in which the Prophet ﷺ said, 'Allah will pardon My Community for what their selves suggest to them when they do not articulate that nor act on it.' We say that this refers to the judgments of this world, like divorce, emancipation and sales whose rulings are not binding as long as they are not spoken. That which it mentioned in the *āyah* is what is between the servant and Allah in the Next World.

– Al-Hasan said that the *āyah* is one whose ruling is not abrogated. Aṭ-Ṭabarī mentioned that other scholars said things similar to what has been quoted from Ibn 'Abbās, although they added that the punishment, repaying people for what occurs within their selves and is accompanied by thought, is manifested through the misfortunes that befall them in this world, its pains and all the things which are disliked in it. Something similar to this is reported in a chain of transmission from 'Ā'ishah. That is the fifth view. Aṭ-Ṭabarī preferred that it is a judgment whose ruling is not abrogated. Ibn 'Aṭā' said, 'This [that it is not abrogated] is correct. Allah's words: *"Whether you divulge what is in yourselves or keep it hidden..."* refer to things which are within your capacity and ability accompanied by conviction and thought, since the words of the *āyah* include thoughts which worried the

Companions and the Prophet ﷺ and so Allah explained to them what He meant by revealing another *āyah* and stipulated that the ruling is that a person is only obliged to do what he is capable of doing. It is not possible to repel thoughts. They predominate and they are not part of what people are held accountable for. This explanation gave them relief and alleviated their anxiety.'

The rest of the *āyah* is one of judgment and is not abrogated. One thing which refutes the claim of abrogation is that the *āyah* is a report, not an order or instruction, and abrogation does not occur in respect of reports. If someone believes that there is abrogation, it can only be in the ruling which was connected to the Companions when they were alarmed by the *āyah*. That was that the Prophet ﷺ said, 'Say, "We hear and obey."' That conveys the command to be firm in this and cling to Allah and see the kindness of Allah in His forgiveness. If this is the case, the ruling can be abrogated and the *āyah* is similar to Allah's words: *'If there are twenty of you who are steadfast, they will overcome two hundred.'* (8:65) This is also in the form of a report, but the meaning demands: 'Hold to this, be firm on it and steadfast accordingly.' Then it was abrogated after that. As far as I know, the consensus of the people is that this *āyah* about *jihād* was abrogated by a hundred being required to be firm against two hundred. Ibn 'Aṭiyyah said that this *āyah* in *al-Baqarah* is the most similar thing to it. It is said that there is allusion and specification in the words and that the words imply: Allah will call you to account for that if He wishes. According to this, there is no abrogation.

An-Naḥḥās said, 'Part of the best of what is said about this *āyah*, and most similar to the literal meaning, is what Ibn 'Abbās said: it is universal and undefined. Then one adds the hadith of Ibn 'Umar about intimate conversation which al-Bukhārī, Muslim and others transmitted. In Muslim's variant, he said, "I heard the Messenger of Allah ﷺ say, 'On the Day of Rising, the believer will draw near to his Almighty Lord until He puts His veil over him and will have to admit to his wrong actions. He will say, 'Do you admit to this?' He will reply, 'O Lord, I admit to them.' Allah will say, 'I concealed them for you in the world and today I forgive you for them.' He will be given the page containing his good deeds. There will be an announcement about unbelievers and hypocrites in front of people: 'These people lied about Allah.'"'

It is said that the *āyah* was revealed about those who took the unbelievers as friends rather than the believers. It means: 'O believers, if you make known or conceal what is in yourselves about taking the unbelievers as protectors and friends, Allah will take you to account for it.' Al-Wāqidī and Muqātil said that. For evidence of this, they recite Allah's words in *Āl 'Imrān*: 'Say: *"Whether you conceal what is in your breasts or make it known* [in taking the unbelievers as friends], *Allah knows it.'*" (3:29) It is also indicated by the *āyah* before it: *'The believers should not take unbelievers as friends rather than believers.'* (2:28)

This is unlikely because the context of the *āyah* does not demand it. It will be explained in *Āl 'Imrān*, Allah willing. Sufyān ibn 'Uyaynah said, 'I heard that the Prophets used to bring this *āyah* to their people.'

He forgives whomever He wills and He punishes whomever He wills.

Ibn Kathīr, Nāfi'. Abū 'Amr, Ḥamzah and al-Kisā'ī recited in the apocopate form, *yaghfir – yu'adhdhib*, while Ibn 'Āmir and 'Āṣim read it *yaghfiru – yu'adhdhibu*. It is related that Ibn 'Abbās, al-A'raj, Abu-l-'Ālīyah, and 'Āṣim al-Jaḥdarī recited them as *yaghfira – yu'adhdhiba*, implying an elided *'an'*. The truth is that it is added to the meaning as is seen in 2:285. Adding to the word is better because of the resemblance.

An-Naḥḥās said that it is related from Ṭalḥah ibn Muṣarrif without the *fā'* before 'He forgives' as an appositive. Ibn 'Aṭiyyah said that it is recited that way by al-Ju'fī and Khallād. It is related that it is like that in the copy of the Qur'an of Ibn Mas'ūd. Ibn Jinnī said that it is an appositive for *'call you to account'* and it explains the calling to account. [ILLUSTRATIVE POEM OMITTED] An-Naḥḥās said that it is better than the jussive.

ءَامَنَ ٱلرَّسُولُ بِمَآ أُنزِلَ إِلَيۡهِ مِن رَّبِّهِۦ وَٱلۡمُؤۡمِنُونَۚ كُلٌّ ءَامَنَ بِٱللَّهِ وَمَلَٰٓئِكَتِهِۦ
وَكُتُبِهِۦ وَرُسُلِهِۦ لَا نُفَرِّقُ بَيۡنَ أَحَدٖ مِّن رُّسُلِهِۦۚ وَقَالُواْ سَمِعۡنَا وَأَطَعۡنَاۖ
غُفۡرَانَكَ رَبَّنَا وَإِلَيۡكَ ٱلۡمَصِيرُ ٢٨٥ لَا يُكَلِّفُ ٱللَّهُ نَفۡسًا إِلَّا وُسۡعَهَاۚ
لَهَا مَا كَسَبَتۡ وَعَلَيۡهَا مَا ٱكۡتَسَبَتۡۗ رَبَّنَا لَا تُؤَاخِذۡنَآ إِن
نَّسِينَآ أَوۡ أَخۡطَأۡنَاۚ رَبَّنَا وَلَا تَحۡمِلۡ عَلَيۡنَآ إِصۡرٗا كَمَا حَمَلۡتَهُۥ عَلَى
ٱلَّذِينَ مِن قَبۡلِنَاۚ رَبَّنَا وَلَا تُحَمِّلۡنَا مَا لَا طَاقَةَ لَنَا بِهِۦۖ وَٱعۡفُ عَنَّا
وَٱغۡفِرۡ لَنَا وَٱرۡحَمۡنَآۚ أَنتَ مَوۡلَىٰنَا فَٱنصُرۡنَا عَلَى ٱلۡقَوۡمِ
ٱلۡكَٰفِرِينَ ٢٨٦

285 The Messenger believes in what has been sent down to him from his Lord, and so do the believers. Each one believes in Allah and His angels and His Books and His Messengers. We do not differentiate between any of His Messengers. They say, 'We hear and we obey. Forgive us, our Lord! You are our journey's end.' 286 Allah does not impose on any self any more than it can bear. For it is what it has earned; against it, what it has merited. Our Lord, do not take us to task if we forget or make a mistake! Our Lord, do not place on us a load like the one You placed on those before us! Our Lord, do not place on us a load we have not the strength to bear! And pardon us; and forgive us; and have mercy on us. You are our Master, so help us against the people of the unbelievers.

The Messenger believes in what has been sent down to him from his Lord.

It is related from al-Ḥasan, Mujāhid and aḍ-Ḍaḥḥāk that this *āyah* is about the Night Journey (*al-Miʿrāj*). The same *tafsīr* is transmitted from Ibn 'Abbās. Some of them say that the entire Qur'an was brought down to Muḥammad ﷺ by Jibrīl except for this one *āyah*. One of them said, 'It is what he heard during the *Miʿrāj*.' Others say that it was not about the *Miʿrāj* because the Night Journey occurred in Makkah while this entire *sūrah* is Madinan.

As for those who say that this *āyah* is about the Night Journey, they say, 'When the Prophet ﷺ ascended and reached a high place in the heavens, Jibrīl accompanied him until he reached the Lote Tree of the Furthest Limit. Then Jibrīl said to him, "I cannot go beyond this place. No one except you has been commanded to go beyond it." So the Prophet ﷺ went beyond the Lote Tree until he reached what Allah wished. Jibrīl had indicated that the Prophet ﷺ should greet his Lord and so he said. "Greetings are for Allah and prayers and good words." Allah said, "Peace be upon you, O Prophet and the mercy of Allah and His blessings." The Prophet ﷺ desired that his Community should have a share of the greeting and so he said. "Peace be upon us and on the righteous slaves of Allah." Jibrīl and all the people of the heavens said, "I bear witness that there is no god except Allah alone without partner and I bear witness that Muḥammad is His slave and Messenger," and then Allah Almighty said: *"The Messenger believes…"*, meaning that he is thankful and that the Messenger affirms "*what has been sent down to him from his Lord.*" The Prophet ﷺ wanted his Community to share in the honour and said, *"And so do the believers. Each one believes in Allah and His angels and His Books and His Messengers. We do not differentiate between any of His Messengers.*"' This means that they say, 'We believe in all the Messengers and do not disbelieve in any of them and do not differentiate between any of them as the Jews and Christians did.'

So his Lord said to him, 'How do they accept the *āyah*s We have revealed?' That is inherent in His words: '*Whether you divulge what is in yourselves.*' The Messenger of Allah ﷺ said, *'They say, "We hear and obey. Forgive us, our Lord! You are our journey's end."'* That means the source to which they will return. Then Allah said: *'Allah does not impose on any self any more than it can bear,'* i.e. more than it is capable of. *'For it, what it has earned'* of good and *'against it what it has merited'* of evil. At that point Jibrīl said, 'Ask and it will be given to you.' So the Prophet ﷺ said, *'Our Lord, do not take us to task if we forget'* and do something in ignorance *'or make a mistake'* in what we do deliberately. It is said that we do things both forgetfully and in error. Jibrīl said, 'If you are granted that, then error and forgetfulness will be removed from your community. Ask for something else. He said ﷺ, *'Our Lord, do not place on us a load like the one You placed on those before us!'* That was when good things were made unlawful for them because of their wrongdoing. When they sinned at night, they found it written on their doors. Fifty prayers were imposed on them and then Allah lightened it for this community and reduced it after fifty prayers were imposed. Then he said ﷺ, *'Our Lord, do not place on us a load we have not the strength to bear!'* He was saying, 'Do not burden us with actions which we will not be able to do and so incur punishment.' It is said that it means: 'What is hard for us.' That is because if they had been commanded to perform fifty prayers, they would have been able to do that, but it would have been very difficult for them and they would not have been able to persevere in it. *'And pardon us'* and spare us from being transmogrified *'and forgive us'* and do not let us be swallowed up by the earth *'and have mercy on us'* and do not bombard us. *'You are our Master'* and Protector and Preserver, *'so help us against the people of the unbelievers.'* His supplication was answered.

In defining the extent of Allah's help, the Prophet ﷺ reported, 'I was helped by terror going before me for the distance of a month.' It is said that when those going on a military expedition leave their houses with a sincere intention and beat the drums, terror and awe falls into the hearts of the unbelievers the distance of a month away, whether they know that they have set out or not. When the Prophet ﷺ returned from his Night Journey, Allah revealed these *āyahs* so that he could inform his Community of these things.

There is another aspect to the interpretation of this *āyah*. Az-Zajjāj said, 'In this *sūrah*, after Allah has mentioned the obligation of the prayer and *zakāt* and clarified the principles of hajj, the ruling of menstruation, divorce, *īlā'*, the stories of the Prophets and clarified the ruling on usury, He mentions His own worth by saying: *"Everything in the heavens and everything in the earth belongs to Allah."* Then He mentions that all this is affirmed by the Prophet ﷺ and the believers: *"The Messenger believes in what has been sent down to him from his Lord."* This means that the Messenger affirms all of these things which were mentioned as do all of the believers who affirm Allah, His angels, His Books and His Messengers.'

It is said that the reason for its revelation was the *āyah* before it. When the former *āyah* was revealed to the Prophet ﷺ, it was hard on the Companions of the Messenger of Allah, so they went to the Messenger of Allah ﷺ and then knelt and said, 'Messenger of Allah, we have been given as obligations actions we can do: prayer, fasting, *jihād* and *ṣadaqah*, but in this *āyah* Allah has revealed something that it is impossible for us to do.' The Messenger of Allah ﷺ said, 'Do you mean to say what the people of the two Books before you said: "We hear and we disobey"? Say: "We hear and we obey. Forgive us, our Lord! You are our journey's end."' When the people recited it, their tongues were humbled and then Allah revealed this *āyah*: *'The Messenger believes in what has been sent down to him from his Lord...'* When they said that, Allah abrogated the *āyah* and revealed: *'Allah does not impose on any self any more than it can bear. For it, is what it has earned, and against it, is what it has merited. Our Lord, do not take us to task if we forget or make a mistake!'* He said, 'Yes.' *'Our Lord, do not place on us a load like the one You placed on those before us!'* He said, 'Yes.' *'Our Lord, do not place on us a load we have not the strength to bear!'* He said, 'Yes.' *'And pardon us, and forgive us, and have mercy on us. You are our Master, so help us against the people of the unbelievers.'* He said, 'Yes.' Muslim transmitted this from Abū Hurayah.

Our scholars said that the fact that the first variant has 'I have done it' while this one has 'Yes' indicates the hadith was transmitted by its meaning. When the matter was confirmed by their saying 'We hear and obey,' Allah praised them in this *āyah* and removed from them the hardship they experienced about thoughts which occur to them. This favour is the fruit of obedience and devotion to Allah. What happened to the tribe of Israel was the opposite of that. They were censured and made to endure the hardships of abasement, wretchedness and exile because they said, 'We hear and we disobey.' Such is the result of disobedience and recalcitrance towards Allah. We seek refuge with Allah from His vengeance by His grace and generosity!

The Prophet ﷺ was told, 'The house of Thābit ibn Qays is adorned with lamps every night.' He replied, 'Perhaps he is reciting *Sūrat al-Baqarah*.' Thābit was told about this and said, 'I recite: "*The Messenger believes...*" from *Sūrat al-Baqarah*.' It was revealed when the Companions of the Prophet were experiencing hardship because Allah threatened to call them to account for what their selves concealed. They complained about that to the Prophet ﷺ and he said, 'Perhaps you say, "We hear and we disobey" as the tribe of Israel said?' They said, 'We hear and we obey!' and so Allah revealed this *āyah* to him. The Prophet ﷺ said, 'They should believe.'

'*Believe*' means to affirm, as has already been mentioned. That which was sent down is the Qur'an. The reading of Ibn Mas'ūd has the word 'believe' after 'believers': 'and the believers believe...' Nāfi', Ibn Kathīr, 'Āṣim in the transmission of Abū Bakr and Ibn 'Āmir recite '*kutubihi*' (books) in the plural and recite '*kitābihi*' in the singular in *at-Taḥrīm*. Here and in *at-Taḥrīm* Abū 'Amr recites '*kutubihi*' in the plural. Ḥamzah and al-Kisā'ī recite '*kitābihi*' in the singular in both places. If it is in the plural, it means all Books. If it is in the singular, it is the verbal noun which includes all that is written which is sent down from Allah. If it is recited in the singular, it can mean all Books and *kitāb* is a generic noun. So both readings are the same. Allah says: '*Then Allah sent out Prophets bringing good news and giving warning, and with them He sent down the Book* (kitāb).' (2:213)

Most recite 'Messengers' as '*rusulihi*' as well as '*rusulinā*', '*rusulikum*' and '*rusuluka*', except for Abū 'Amr from whom '*ruslihi*' is related. He relates '*ruslinā*', '*ruslikum*' but both '*rusuluka*' and '*rusluka*'. Abū 'Alī said that if someone recites '*rusulikum*', it is the root of the word. If it is *rusl*, then it is as a lightening occurs in singular words like '*unq* and *ṭunb*, and then it is more proper in the plural which is heavier. Makkī said something to that effect.

Most people recite 'differentiate' with the *nūn* of the first person plural. It means: 'They say, "We do not differentiate."' So 'they say' is elided. This usage is seen in other *āyahs* like 13:23 and 3:191. Sa'īd ibn Jubayr, Yaḥyā ibn Ya'mur,

Abū Zur'ah ibn 'Amr ibn Jarīr and Ya'qūb recited it in the third person with *yā'*. This refers back to 'each' (*kull*). Hārūn said that the mode (*ḥarf*) of Ibn Mas'ūd has *'yufarriqūna'*.

'One' (*aḥad*) is in the singular rather than the plural because *'aḥad'* can be used of both the singular and the plural as we see elsewhere, as in 69:47. It is an adjective of one, while the plural is meant. The Prophet ﷺ said, 'Booty was not made to anyone (*aḥad*),' meaning to any of the rulers but you. Ru'bah said:

The affairs of people become your *dīn*.
They do not fear anyone (*aḥad*) but you.

This *āyah* shows that the believers are not like the Jews and Christians who believe in some of the revelation and reject some of it.

They say, 'We hear and we obey.'

This suggests some elision such as 'We hear as those who accept hear.' It is said that 'hear' means 'accept' as in the prayer when it is said, 'Allah hears whoever praises Him,' and so there is no elision. This entails praise of the speaker. Obedience is acceptance of the command.

Forgive us, our Lord!

The word *'ghufrān'* (forgive) is a verbal noun and the object of it is implied, so what is literally 'Your forgiveness' means 'grant us Your forgiveness,' as az-Zajjāj said. Others say that it means, 'We ask (or I ask) for Your forgiveness.'

You are our journey's end.'

This is an affirmation of the Resurrection and the fact that we will stand before Allah. It is related that when this *āyah* was revealed, Jibrīl told the Prophet ﷺ, 'Allah has allowed praise of you and your community. Ask and you will be given,' and the following *āyah* was what he asked.

Allah does not impose on any self any more than it can bear.

Imposition implies a command to do something which is difficult and entails hardship. Al-Jawharī related that. The word *'wus''* (bear) denotes capacity and effort. This is a definite report and it is a declaration from Allah that, from the moment of the revelation of the *āyah*, He has not imposed on His slaves any kind of worship, demanded of the hearts or the limbs, which is not within the capacity of the one on whom it is imposed. Through this *āyah*, anxiety was removed from the

Muslims with regard to the matter concerning their thoughts. There is something related from Abū Hurayrah which conveys the meaning of this *āyah*. He said, 'I would not wish to be anyone whose mother bore him except for Ja'far ibn Abī Ṭālib. I followed him one day when I was hungry. When he reached his house, all he found in it was a churn for butter in which only a few traces remained. He broke it up between us and we began licking what was on it. He said:

> "Allah does not impose on any self more than it can bear,
> and a hand can only be generous with what it has."'

People disagree about whether it is permissible for a ruling about worldly matters to be imposed on someone when it is not within his capacity to carry it out. They do, however, agree that there is no imposition in the *dīn* which is beyond a person's capacity. This *āyah* informs us that such an imposition does not occur in the *Sharī'ah*. Abu-l-Ḥasan al-Ash'arī and a group of *mutakallimūn* say that it is logically permissible for someone to be charged with doing something he is not capable of doing, and that does not detract at all from the tenets of belief (*'aqīdah*) in the *Sharī'ah*. That sort of command can be meant to be a punishment for the person on whom it is imposed, as when someone who made images is ordered to create a barley-seed on the Day of Judgment. Those who say that it is permitted disagree about whether it occurred in respect of the Message of Muḥammad ﷺ or not.

One group say that such an imposition occurred in the case of Abū Lahab, because he was obliged to believe in all of the *Sharī'ah* and yet part of the revelation was that he would never believe because the judgment on him was that his hands would be ruined and he would burn in the Fire. It was announced that he would not believe and so he was charged with believing something which he could not believe. Another group says that such an imposition does not occur at all and report that there is a consensus on that. They say the words: *'He will bum in a Flaming Fire'* (111:3) mean 'He will be brought to it.' Ibn 'Aṭiyyah related that.

The word *'yukallifu'* (impose) is a transitive verb with two objects one of which is elided so that 'worship' or 'something' is implied. By Allah's kindness and blessing to us, even though He imposed on us what is hard and difficult – such as odds of one against ten and *hijrah*, which entails leaving one's homeland and separation from family, homeland and traditions – Allah did not impose on us burdensome hardships or painful matters, such as those He imposed on those before us which involved killing themselves and cutting out the patch soiled by urine on clothes and skins. Rather He made things easy for us and reduced the burden and the chains which He had placed on those before us. To Allah belongs praise, grace, favour and blessing.

For it is what it has earned; against it, what it has merited.

The words refer to good actions and bad actions, according to as-Suddī. The majority of scholars do not disagree with that. Ibn 'Aṭiyyah stated that. It is similar to Allah's words: *'No bearer of a burden can bear the burden of another'* (6:164) and *'What each self earns is for itself alone.'* (6:164) Thoughts and their like are not part of what a human being earns. The expression for good actions is in the words *'for it'* since a person rejoices in earning them and adds them to his property. Bad actions are *'against it'* since they are weights and burdens and hard to bear, as one says, 'I have (lit. for me) property,' and 'There is a debt against me.' The root *kasaba*, which has the basic meaning of acquisition, is repeated and the meaning differs according to the form the word takes [*kasabat* = earned, *iktasabat* = merited]. Ibn 'Atiyyah said, 'It is clear to me regarding this that good actions are part of what is acquired without being a burden since their acquirer is following the path of Allah's command and His *Sharī'ah*. Evil deeds are acquired since their acquirer burdens himself through them by rending the veil which Allah has forbidden. So the *āyah* utilises both usages.'

This *āyah* indicates that it is valid to call people's actions 'acquisitions'. People do not create them. If one were to say that a person created his actions, that is simply metaphorical. Al-Mahdawī and others said that it is said that this *āyah* means that no one is taken to task for the actions of another. Ibn 'Atiyyah said, 'This is sound in itself, but it is not an aspect of this *āyah*.'

Aṭ-Ṭabarī said that the *āyah* is evidence that someone who kills someone else by crushing, choking or drowning is personally responsible in respect of retaliation or blood money as opposed to someone whose blood money is the responsibility of their clan (*'āqilah*). That differs from the literal words of the *āyah*. It indicates that the fact that there is no retaliation against a father does not demand that it is also cancelled for someone who is jointly responsible. It indicates the obligation of the *ḥadd* against the *'āqilah* when they enable someone who is insane. Qāḍī Abū Bakr ibn al-'Arabī said, 'Our scholars mentioned that this *āyah* is about retaliation being mandatory against the partner of a father, differing from Abū Ḥanīfah, and against someone who shares in accidental homicide, differing from ash-Shāfi'ī and Abū Ḥanīfah, because each of them has merited killing. They said that joint participation by someone on whom retaliation is not obliged is not an argument for averting what is averted by doubt.'

Our Lord, do not take us to task if we forget or make a mistake!

This *āyah* means: 'Pardon our wrong actions if we forget and make a mistake or simply forget or simply make a mistake,' as the Prophet ﷺ said, 'Error and forgetfulness have been removed from my Community and from what they are forced to do,' i.e. its being a wrong action in those cases. There is no disagreement that the wrong action is cancelled out. There is disagreement about the rulings connected to that action. Does that cancellation of the action mean that the action has no legal consequences or does it still entail all its legal consequences? There is disagreement about that, and the sound position is that it varies according to the circumstances. It is agreed that some consequences are not cancelled, like penalties, blood money and obligatory prayers, and others are agreed to be cancelled, like retaliation and speaking words which can be considered to be disbelief. There is disagreement about a third category, like eating out of forgetfulness in Ramadan or breaking an oath out of forgetfulness.

Our Lord, do not place on us a load we have not the strength to bear!

This '*load*' is a weighty burden. Mālik and ar-Rabi' say that the word '*iṣr*' (load) denotes a difficult, onerous thing. Sa'īd ibn Jubayr said that it refers to stringent commands and what was hard for the tribe of Israel regarding urine and the like. Aḍ-Ḍaḥḥāk said, 'They endured hard things.' This is similar to what the others said. An-Nābighah said:

> You who protected the side of the mountain from the descent of their riders,
> bearing the burden (*iṣr*) for them after they recognised it.

'Aṭā' said that it refers to being turned into pigs and monkeys. Ibn Zayd also said that. He also said that it means wrong actions for which there is no repentance or expiation.

The word linguistically means 'charge or undertaking', as when Allah says: *'Do you agree and undertake my charge (*iṣrī*) on that condition?'* (3:81) Another form of the word means constriction, wrong action and burdensomeness. The word *iṣār* denotes a short rope which is used to bind loads and the like. The verb means 'to confine.' According to al-Jawharī, place of confinement is called a *ma'ṣīr*.

Ibn Khuwayzimandād said, 'It is possible to infer from the literal meaning of this *āyah* that it refers to the burden which opponents claim that every act of worship entails. That resembles the words of Allah: *"He has not placed any constraint on you in the dīn,"* (22:78) and the words of the Prophet ﷺ: "The *dīn* is ease, so make things easy. Do not make things difficult."' O Allah, be hard on those who are hard on the Community of Muḥammad ﷺ! Aṭ-Ṭabarī said something similar and said that it is used as an argument for lack of injury and constriction.

Qatādah said that Allah's words: *'Our Lord, do not place on us a load we have not the strength to bear,'* mean, 'Do not make things hard for us as You made them hard for those before us.' Aḍ-Ḍaḥḥāk said, 'Do not impose on us actions which we cannot do.' Ibn Zayd said the same. Ibn Jurayj said, 'Do not turn us into apes or pigs.' Sallām ibn Shābūr said, '"What we do not have the strength to bear" refers to lust.' An-Naqqāsh related it from Mujāhid and 'Aṭā'. It is related that Abu-d-Dardā' used to say in his supplication, 'I seek refuge with You from lust against which one cannot resist.' As-Suddī said, 'It is the strengthening of the shackles which were on the tribe of Israel.'

And pardon us; and forgive us; and have mercy on us. You are our Master, so help us against the people of the unbelievers.

'And pardon us' for our wrong actions. One pardons a wrong action by overlooking it and not punishing for it. *'And forgive us'*, meaning conceal our wrong actions. *Ghafr* is covering and concealing. *'Have mercy on us'* means 'Bestow Your mercy on us.' 'You are our Master' means 'You are our Protector and Helper.' This is instructing people on how best to make supplication.

It is related that when Mu'ādh ibn Jabal finished reciting this *sūrah,* he said, 'Āmīn.' Ibn 'Aṭiyyah said, 'It is thought that he related that from the Prophet ﷺ. If that is the case, it is completion. If it is based on analogy with the *Sūrah* of Praise (the *Fātiḥah*) since that is a supplication and this is a supplication, that is good. 'Alī ibn Abī Ṭālib said, "I do not think anyone with intelligence, who has found Islam, will sleep until he has recited both of them."'

Muslim related this idea from Abū Mas'ūd al-Anṣārī who said that the Messenger of Allah ﷺ said, 'If someone recites these two *āyah*s at the end of *al-Baqarah* in the night, they will spare him,' meaning from rising at night to pray.

It is also related from Ibn 'Umar that he heard the Prophet ﷺ say, 'Allah revealed to me two *āyah*s from the treasures of the Garden. He sealed *Sūrat al-Baqarah* with them. The All-Merciful wrote them with His hand a thousand years before He created creation. If someone reads them after *'Ishā'* twice, they will spare him from rising at night to pray: *"The Messenger believes..."* to the end of the *sūrah.*' It is said that they spare him the evil of Shayṭān so that he does not have any power over him.

Abū 'Amr ad-Dānī related from Ḥudhayfah ibn al-Yamān that the Messenger of Allah ﷺ said, 'Allah Almighty wrote a Book a thousand years before He created the heavens and the earth. He sent down from it these three *āyah*s which conclude al-Baqarah. If someone recites them in his house, Shayṭān will not approach his house for three nights.' It is related that the Prophet ﷺ said, 'I was given these *āyah*s at the end of *Sūrat al-Baqarah* from the treasure under the Throne. No Prophet before me was given them.' This is sound.

3. Sūrah Āl 'Imrān
The Family of 'Imrān 1 – 95

الٓمٓ ۝١ ٱللَّهُ لَآ إِلَٰهَ إِلَّا هُوَ ٱلۡحَيُّ ٱلۡقَيُّومُ ۝٢

1 Alif Lām Mīm. 2. Allah, there is no god but Him, the Living, the Self-Sustaining.

There is a consensus that this *sūrah* is Madinan. An-Naqqāsh related that its name in the Torah was '*Ṭaybah*' ['Good']. Al-Ḥasan, 'Amr ibn 'Ubayd, 'Āṣim ibn Abī an-Nujūd, and Abū Ja'far ar-Ru'āsī recited it with a break between *Mīm* and Allāh and so one stops at *Mīm*, just as they also stop at the names of the numbers even if they are connected. Al-Akhfash Sa'īd said that it is permitted to read it with a *kasrah* on the *mīm* since two silent letters meet, but az-Zajjāj says that this is a mistake and the Arabs do not do that because it is heavy. An-Naḥḥās says that the first reading is the common one and the early grammarians discussed it. Sībawayh believed that *Mīm* has a *fatḥah* because of he meeting of two silent letters. They preferred for it to have a *fatḥah* so that one does not join a *kasrah*, a *yā'*, and the *kasrah* before it.

Al-Kisā'ī said when the letters of the alphabet meet, the connective *alif* is elided and takes on the vowel of the *alif* in the following word and so you say, '*Alif Lām Mīma-llāh*', '*Alif Lām Mīmu-dhkur*' and '*Alif Lām Mīmi-qtarabat.*' Al-Farrā' said that the root is '*Alif Lām Mīm. Allāh*' as ar-Ru'asī said. The vowel of the *hamzah* is put on the *mīm*. 'Umar ibn al-Khaṭṭāb recited '*al-Ḥayyu-l-Qayyām*'. Khārijah said that the copy of the Qur'an of 'Abdullāh has '*al-Ḥayyu-l-Qayyum*'.

What scholars said about the letters themselves at the beginning of the *sūrah*s was already discussed in *al-Baqarah*. As '*Allah, there is no god but Him, the Living, the Self-Sustaining*' is an independent sentence, all the views about the letters are possible.

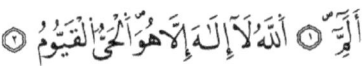

An-Nasā'ī related that 'Umar ibn al-Khaṭṭāb prayed the '*Ishā'* prayer, beginning with *Āl 'Imrān* and recited a hundred *āyah*s in the first *rak'ah* and a hundred in the second. Our scholars say that one should not recite an entire *sūrah* in two *rak'ahs*, but it is allowed if someone does so. In *al-Majmū'ah*, Mālik said that there is no harm in it and it is not a significant matter. The sound position is that it is allowed. The Prophet ﷺ recited *al-A'rāf* in *Maghrib* and divided it between the two *rak'ahs*. An-Nasā'ī transmitted that. Abū Muḥammad 'Abd al-Ḥaqq said that it is sound.

There are various reports about the excellence of this *sūrah*. One report states that it is protection against snakes and a treasure for the destitute, and that it will argue in the Next World on behalf of the one who recites it. If someone recites the end of it in the night, it will be recorded as if he has prayed the entire night. Other things are said as well. Abū Muḥammad ad-Dārimī mentioned in his *Musnad* from Abū 'Ubayd al-Qāsim ibn Salām from 'Ubaydullāh al-Ashja'ī from Mis'ar from Jābir, before what happened to him had happened, from ash-Sha'bī that 'Abdullāh said, '*Āl 'Imrān* is an excellent treasure for someone destitute when he stands in prayer reciting it in the last part of the night.' Muḥammad ibn Sa'īd related from 'Abd as-Salām from al-Jurayrī that Abu-s-Salīl said, 'A man was the target of a blood vendetta and took refuge in the wadi of Majannah, a wadi which no one went into without being bitten by a snake. There were two monks at the edge of the wadi. In the evening, one of them said to his companion, "By Allah, the man is destroyed!" So he began to recite *Sūrah Āl 'Imrān*. They remarked: "He recites *Sūrat Ṭaybah*. Perhaps he will be saved." He was safe in the morning.'

It is reported that Makḥūl said, 'If someone recites *Sūrah Āl 'Imrān* on Friday, the angels pray for him until nightfall.' 'Uthmān ibn 'Affān said, 'If anyone recites the end of *Sūrah Āl 'Imrān* in the night, it will be written for him that he prayed for the whole night.' Ibn Lahī'ah is in its path of transmission. Muslim transmitted from an-Nawwās ibn Sam'ān al-Kilābī: 'I heard the Prophet ﷺ say, "The Qur'an will be brought on the Day of Rising along with the people who acted by it, preceded by *Sūrat al-Baqarah* and *Āl 'Imrān*." The Messenger of Allah ﷺ made three metaphors for these surahs which I have not forgotten: they were like two dark clouds or like canopies with light in them or like two flocks of birds in rows, interceding for the one who recited them.' It is also transmitted that Abū Umāmah said, 'I heard the Messenger of Allah ﷺ say, "Recite the Qur'an. It will come on the Day of Rising to intercede for people who recite it. Recite the two brilliant ones: *al-Baqarah* and *Āl 'Imrān*. They will come on the Day of Rising like two clouds or two canopies, or like two flocks of birds in ranks, interceding for the one who recited them. Recite *Sūrah al-Baqarah*. Using it is a blessing and leaving it is regret, and the sorcerers cannot breach it."' Mu'āwiyah said, 'I heard that "*baṭalah*" are sorcerers.'

There are three statements about why *al-Baqarah* and *Āl 'Imrān* are called 'the two brilliant ones' (*zahrāwayn*). The first is because they are two lights, derived from the essence of the brilliance of flowers. They guide the one who recites them by their brilliant lights, i.e. their meanings. The second is because their recitation will bring great light on the Day of Rising. The third is that they are called that because they are partners in containing the Greatest Name of Allah, as Abū Dāwūd and others mentioned from Asmā' bint Yazīd, who reported that the Messenger of Allah ﷺ said, 'The Greatest Name of Allah is found in these two *āyahs*: *"Your God is one God. There is no god but Him, the All-Merciful, Most Merciful,"* (2:163) and that which is in *Āl 'Imrān* is *"Allah, there is no god but Him, the Living, the Self-Sustaining."*'' Ibn Mājah transmitted it.

Clouds (*ghamām*) are clouds which are piled up and give shade to one's head. That shade is also called *ẓullah*. It means that the person who recites them is in the shade of the reward for them, in the same way that it is said, 'A man is in the shade of his *ṣadaqah*.' 'Interceding' in the hadith means that Allah will create angels who will intercede for them to receive the reward for reciting them, as we find in the hadith: 'If someone recites *'Allah bears witness that there is no god but Him…'* (3:18), Allah will create seventy angels who will ask forgiveness for him until the Day of Rising.' 'With light in them' [in the hadith] is *sharq*, which calls attention to the light because when he ﷺ said 'two dark clouds', it might be imagined to refer to darkness. He ﷺ negated that by mentioning the light in them. Their being 'dark' means that they are dense and so come between those under them and the heat of the sun and its intense rays. Allah knows best.

The reason for the revelation of the beginning of *sūrah* was the arrival of the delegation from Najrān according to Muḥammad ibn Isḥāq. The Christians of Najrān came to the Messenger of Allah ﷺ in Madina in a delegation of sixty riders, including fourteen of their nobles. Among the fourteen were three who were in charge of their affair: the 'Āqib – the leader of the people and the one who decided their policy – whose name was 'Abd al-Masīḥ; the Sayyid – the administrator of their affairs and the one who saw to their transport and arrangements – whose name as al-Ayham; and Abū Ḥārithah ibn 'Alqamah of Banū Bakr ibn Wā'il – their bishop and scholar. They went to the Messenger of Allah ﷺ after the *'Aṣr* prayer. They were wearing silken shawls, cloaks and mantles. The Companions said, 'We have not seen any delegation with such beauty and majesty.' The time of their prayer came and they stood in the mosque of the Prophet ﷺ and prayed to the east. The Prophet ﷺ said, 'Let them be.' They stayed for some days debating with the Messenger of Allah ﷺ about 'Īsā, claiming that he was the son of God and other atrocious, confused statements. The Messenger of Allah ﷺ answered them with cutting arguments but they did not see. The first eighty *āyahs* or so of this *sūrah* were revealed about them, up to the point when the Prophet ﷺ invited them to perform the mutual curse. The full story can be found in Ibn Isḥāq and elsewhere.

نَزَّلَ عَلَيْكَ الْكِتَٰبَ بِالْحَقِّ مُصَدِّقًا لِّمَا بَيْنَ يَدَيْهِ وَأَنزَلَ التَّوْرَىٰةَ وَالْإِنجِيلَ ﴿٣﴾
مِن قَبْلُ هُدًى لِّلنَّاسِ وَأَنزَلَ الْفُرْقَانَ إِنَّ الَّذِينَ كَفَرُوا بِـَٔايَٰتِ اللَّهِ لَهُمْ عَذَابٌ
شَدِيدٌ وَاللَّهُ عَزِيزٌ ذُو انتِقَامٍ ﴿٤﴾

3 He has sent down the Book to you with truth, confirming what was there before it. And He sent down the Torah and the Gospel, 4 previously, as guidance for mankind, and He has sent down the Furqān. Those who reject Allah's Signs will have a terrible punishment. Allah is Almighty, Exactor of Revenge.

The Book is the Qur'an. '*Truth*' is said to mean speaking the truth or the overpowering argument. The Qur'an was sent down in instalments, bit by bit, which is why Allah uses the form '*tanzīl*' (form II), denoting that it occurred time after time. The Torah and Gospel were sent down in one go which is why the form '*anzala*' (form IV) of the verb is used. The *bā'* that is connected to 'truth' is adverbial, modifying 'Book' and is connected to something elided, meaning 'bringing the truth'. It is not connected to 'send down'.

'*What was there before it*' means Revealed Books. Torah means 'light'. It is derived from striking (*warā* or *wariya*) a flint-stone and its root is '*tawraya*', on the measure of *taf'alah or taf'ilah*. Al-Khalīl said that its root is *faw'alah* and the root is *warayah* and the first *wāw* has become a *tā'*. This happens in other Arabic words. It is also said that it is derived from *tarwiyah*, which is alluding to one thing and concealing something else. Most of the Torah consists of allusions and indications rather than explicit clarification, as an historical account. The majority take the first view, as the Almighty says: '*We gave to Musā and Hārūn the Furqān and a shining Light and a Reminder for those who are godfearing.*' (21:48) He means the Torah.

The root of Injīl (Gospel) is the form *if'īl* derived from *najl*, the plural of which is *anājīl*. The root of the Torah is based on concealing (*tawārī*) and the Injīl is a source of knowledge and wisdom. The word *nājilān* is used for parents, since they are a person's root. *Najala* is used for extracting something and so knowledge and wisdom can be extracted from the Injīl. *Najl* is used for a child and descendants since they are brought forth as is said:

To the clan whose ancestor did not bequeath blame
to their children. All are stations and they have progeny (*najl*).

Najl is also used for water which oozes out of the ground. It is used for swampland and it there is the opening (*nijāl*) from which water oozes. So it is called Injīl because by it Allah brings forth that which teaches the truth. *Najlā'* also describes a wide opening in a spring and a spear thrust that makes a wide wound. It is said:

Often a blow with a sharp sword
Is between being open and wide (*najlā'*).

So the Injīl is called that because it is a source of expansion and light for them. *Tanājala* means fighting together and so the people fight about the Injīl from which it takes its name. Shamir related that one of them said that Injīl is a term describing every book full of comprehensive writing. It is said that the verb *najala* means to act and make. It is said that it is from a Syriac word, *evangelion*, as ath-Tha'labī said.

Al-Jawharī said, 'The Injīl is the Scripture of 'Īsā. The word can be masculine or feminine. If it is feminine, it means 'page' and if it is masculine, it means the Book.' Others have said that the Qur'an is also called an 'Injīl' as we find in the story of Mūsā who said, 'O Lord, I see in the Tablets that there are people with "Gospels" (*anājīl*) in their hearts. Make them my community!' Allah Almighty told him, 'That is the community of Aḥmad.' The word 'Gospels' (*anājīl*) therefore meant the Qur'an.

Al-Ḥasan recited *'al-Anjīl'* but the rest have *Injīl*. There are two dialectical forms. It is possible that it is named that because of the manner in which the Arabs arabicise foreign nouns.

'Previously means before the Qur'an. Ibn Fūrak says that *'guidance for mankind'* implies godfearing people as indicated by *'guidance for the godfearing'* (2:3). So the general term is, in fact, specific. *'Furqān'* here is the Qur'an.

إِنَّ ٱللَّهَ لَا يَخْفَىٰ عَلَيْهِ شَيْءٌ فِي ٱلْأَرْضِ وَلَا فِي ٱلسَّمَآءِ ۝

5 Allah – Him from Whom nothing is hidden, either on earth or in heaven.

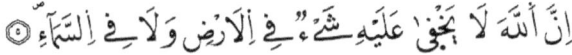

This is a report about Allah's knowledge of all things in detail, and examples of this are numerous in the Qur'an. He knows what was, what is and will be, and what is not. How could 'Īsā be divine or a son of God when many things were hidden from him?

هُوَ ٱلَّذِى يُصَوِّرُكُمْ فِى ٱلْأَرْحَامِ كَيْفَ يَشَآءُ ۚ لَآ إِلَٰهَ إِلَّا هُوَ ٱلْعَزِيزُ ٱلْحَكِيمُ ﴿٦﴾

6 It is He who forms you in the womb however He wills. There is no god but Him, the Almighty, the All-Wise.

It is He who forms you in the womb however He wills.

Here Allah reports about the forming of the human being in the womb. The root of the word for womb (*riḥm*) is mercy (*raḥmah*) because it is part of mutual mercy between people. Form (*ṣūrah*) is derived from *ṣāra*, which is going to something to which one inclines. So a form inclines to a shape or likeness.

This *āyah* exalts Allah and contains a refutation of the Christians of Najrān and that 'Īsā was one of those who create form. This cannot be denied by anyone with intelligence. The Almighty indicates the explanation of formation in the womb in *Sūrat al-Ḥajj* and *Sūrat al-Mu'minūn*. The Prophet ﷺ explained it in the hadith of Ibn Mas'ūd as will be explained, Allah willing. It also refutes the scientists who claim that natural development is an autonomous process. This refutation of them was discussed previously in the commentary on the *Āyah* of *Taḥwīd*. In his *Musnad*, Muḥammad ibn Sanjar reports the following hadith: 'Allah Almighty creates the bones and cartilage of the foetus from the sperm of the man and its fat and flesh and from the liquid of the woman.' This is evidence that the child is a combination of the sperm of the man and the liquid of the mother, as we read explicitly stated in the following *āyah*: *'O mankind, We created you from a male and female.'* (49:13)

We find in *Ṣaḥīḥ Muslim* from Thawbān that a Jew came to the Prophet ﷺ and said, 'I came to ask you about something which none of the people of the earth know except a Prophet or a couple of men.' He asked, 'Will it help you if I tell you?' He answered, 'I will listen with my ears.' He asked him about the genesis of children and the Prophet ﷺ said, 'The emission of the man is white and that of the woman is yellow. When they combine and the sperm of the man dominates that of the woman, it is a male by Allah's permission, and if the liquid of the woman dominates that of the man it is female with Allah's permission.' More of this will be dealt with in *Sūrat ash-Shurā*, Allah willing.

'However He wills' means the child may be beautiful or ugly, black or white, tall or short, happy or wretched, sound or defective, and so forth, to the point

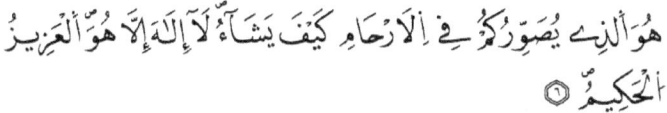

of wretchedness and happiness. It is reported that reciters gathered around Ibrāhīm ibn Adham to listen to the hadiths which he had. He told them, 'I am distracted from you by four things and so I am not free to transmit hadiths.' He was asked, 'What are they?' He answered, 'One is that I reflect on the day of the covenant when Allah said, "Those are in the Garden and I do not care, and those are in the Fire and I do not care." I do not know which of the two groups I will be among on that day. The second is that when I was formed in the womb, the angel entrusted with the wombs said, "O Lord, wretched or happy?" and I do not know what the answer that was given. The third is that when the Angel of Death takes my soul, he will ask, "O Lord, with disbelief or faith?" and I do not know what the answer will be. The fourth is that Allah says: *"Keep yourselves apart today, you evildoers."* (36:59) and I do not know in which of the two groups I will be in.'

There is no god but Him, the Almighty, the All-Wise.

There is no creator or fashioner but Him. That indicates His Oneness; so how can 'Īsā be a creator when he is created? *'The Almighty'* is the One who cannot be overcome and *'the All-Wise'* possesses wisdom or is perfect in what He does. This applies to formation.

هُوَ ٱلَّذِيٓ أَنزَلَ عَلَيۡكَ ٱلۡكِتَٰبَ مِنۡهُ ءَايَٰتٞ مُّحۡكَمَٰتٌ هُنَّ أُمُّ ٱلۡكِتَٰبِ وَأُخَرُ
مُتَشَٰبِهَٰتٞۖ فَأَمَّا ٱلَّذِينَ فِي قُلُوبِهِمۡ زَيۡغٞ فَيَتَّبِعُونَ مَا تَشَٰبَهَ مِنۡهُ ٱبۡتِغَآءَ ٱلۡفِتۡنَةِ
وَٱبۡتِغَآءَ تَأۡوِيلِهِۦۖ وَمَا يَعۡلَمُ تَأۡوِيلَهُۥٓ إِلَّا ٱللَّهُۗ وَٱلرَّٰسِخُونَ فِي ٱلۡعِلۡمِ يَقُولُونَ ءَامَنَّا بِهِۦ
كُلّٞ مِّنۡ عِندِ رَبِّنَاۗ وَمَا يَذَّكَّرُ إِلَّآ أُوْلُواْ ٱلۡأَلۡبَٰبِ ٧

7 It is He who sent down the Book to you from Him: *āyah*s containing clear judgments – they are the core of the Book – and others which are open to interpretation. Those with deviation in their hearts follow what is open to interpretation in it, desiring conflict, seeking its inner meaning. No one knows its inner meaning but Allah. Those firmly rooted in knowledge say, 'We believe in it. All of it is from our Lord.' But only people of intelligence pay heed.

It is He who sent down the Book to you from Him:

Muslim transmitted that 'Ā'ishah said, 'The Prophet ﷺ recited, *"It is He who sent down the Book to you from Him*...(to the end of the *āyah*)." Then the Messenger of Allah ﷺ said, "When you see those who follow what is open to interpretation in it, they are the ones whom Allah has named, so beware of them."' Abū Ghālib said, 'I was walking with Abū Umāmah while he was riding his donkey. When we reached the road to the mosque of Damascus, there were some heads set up. He asked, "Whose heads are these?" The reply was, "Those are the leaders of the Khārijites who were brought from Iraq." Abū Umāmah said, "The dogs of the Fire! The dogs of the Fire! The dogs of the Fire! The worst to be killed under heaven! Bliss to those who killed them and those they killed!" He repeated that three times and then wept. I asked, "Why are you weeping, Abū Umāmah?" He replied, "Out of compassion for them. They were among the people of Islam and then they left it." Then he recited, *"Do not be like those who split up and differed after the Clear Signs came to them."* (3:105) I asked, "Abū Umāmah, are they them?" "Yes," he replied. I asked, "Is that something you say from your opinion or something you heard from the Messenger of Allah ﷺ?" He replied, "Then I would indeed be bold! I would indeed be bold! Rather I heard it from the Messenger of Allah ﷺ more than once, twice, three times, four times, five times, six times, or seven times." He put his fingers in his ears. "Otherwise we are deaf!" He said that three times and then he said, "I heard the Messenger of Allah ﷺ say, 'The tribe of Israel split up into seventy-one sects, one of which will be in the Garden and the rest in the Fire, and this Community will have one more than them. One will be in the Garden and the rest in the Fire.'"'

_āyah_s containing clear judgments – they are the core of the Book – and others which are open to interpretation.

Scholars disagree about the *muḥkamāt* and the *mutashābihāt* verses. There are numerous positions regarding this point. The position taken by Jābir ibn 'Abdullāh and followed by ash-Sha'bī, Sufyān ath-Thawrī and others is that the *muhkamāt* are those *āyah*s of the Qur'an whose interpretation is known and whose meaning and explanation is understood, while there is no way to the knowledge of the *mutashābihāt* verses and knowledge of them is the sole prerogative of Allah rather than His creation. That is things like the time of the Final Hour, the emergence of Ya'jūj and Ma'jūj, the Dajjāl and 'Īsā and the letters at the beginnings of the *sūrah*s.

This is the best that I have heard about the *mutashābihāt*. It was already mentioned at the beginning of *Sūrat al-Baqarah* that ar-Rabī' ibn Khaytham said, 'Allah Almighty revealed this Qur'an and He kept the knowledge of whatever He wishes for Himself...' Abū 'Uthmān said that *muḥkam* is the *Fātihah* of the Book and no prayer is allowed without it. Muḥammad ibn al-Faḍl said that it is *Sūrat al-Ikhlāṣ* because there is only *tawḥīd* in it.

It is said that the whole Qur'an is *muḥkam* since Allah says: *'A Book whose verses are perfectly constructed'* (11:1) and it is said that it is all *mutashābih* since He says: *'a mutashābih Book.'* (39:23) This statement has nothing to do with the meaning of this *āyah*. The first *āyah* refers to the construction and order and that it is truly from Allah. The meaning of the second is that its parts resemble one another and confirm one another. That is not what is meant here. In this *āyah* the word *mutashābih* means containing probability and that whose meaning is ambivalent, as when the Jews said, *'Cows are all much the same for us.'* (2:70) It is possible that it means different species of cows.

What is meant by *muḥkam* is the opposite of this. It is that in which there is no ambiguity and that which can only have one meaning. It is also said that the *mutashābih* can have several meanings. When the possibilities are restricted to one meaning and the rest are invalid, then it is *muḥkam*. The *muḥkam* is always a fundamental from which there are branches, and the *mutashābih* is a branch. Ibn 'Abbās said, 'The *muḥkamāt* are exemplified in the words of Allah in *Sūrat al-An'ām: "Say: 'Come and I will recite to you what your Lord has made unlawful for you'..."* (6:151-153) and in *Al-Isrā'*: *"Your Lord has decreed: that you should worship none but Him, and that you should show kindness to your parents..."* (17:23)' Ibn 'Aṭiyyah remarked, 'This is what I consider to be examples of the *muḥkamāt*.'

Ibn 'Abbās also said, 'The *muḥkamāt* verses are those which abrogate, state the *ḥarām*, the obligations, and what is believed and what is acted upon. The *mutashābihāt* are those which are abrogated and which are advanced and deferred, examples, oaths, and what is believed but not acted upon.' Ibn Mas'ūd and others said that the *muḥkamāt* are abrogating and *mutashābihāt* are abrogated. That was stated by Qatādah, ar-Rabī' and aḍ-Ḍaḥḥāk. Muḥammad ibn Ja'far ibn az-Zubayr said, 'The *muḥkamāt* are those which contain the decisive argument of the Lord, the protection of His slaves, and refute opponents and falsehood. They cannot be altered nor twisted from their place. The *mutashābihāt* can be diverted, twisted and interpreted. Allah tests the slaves through them.' Mujāhid and Ibn Isḥāq said that. Ibn 'Aṭiyyah said, 'This is the best statement about this *āyah*.'

An-Naḥḥās said, 'The best that is said about this is that the *muhkamāt* are self-evident and do not require reference to anything else, such as: *"And no one is comparable to Him"* (112:4) and *"But I am Ever-Forgiving to anyone who turns in repentance."* (20:82) The *mutashābihāt* are *āyahs* like: *"Truly Allah forgives all wrong actions"* (39:53), which refers to His words: *"I am Ever-Forgiving to anyone who turns in repentance"*

(20:82) and *"Allah does not forgive partners being attributed to Him."* (4:48).' What an-Naḥḥās said clarifies what Ibn 'Aṭiyyah preferred.

Linguistically, *muḥkam* is a passive participle from *aḥkama*. *Iḥkām* is exactitude. There is no doubt about that whose meaning is clear and in which there is no uncertainty or vacillation. That is due to the clarity of its individual words and perfect structure which otherwise might result in ambiguity. Allah knows best.

Ibn Khuwayzimandād said, 'There are various aspects to the *mutashābih*. That to which a ruling is connected and on which scholars disagree is which *āyah* abrogates the other. An example of this is found in the words of 'Alī and Ibn 'Abbās about a pregnant woman whose husband dies: they said that she observes the shorter of the two terms. 'Umar, Zayd ibn Thābit, Ibn Mas'ūd and others said that it ends when she gives birth. They said, "The Lesser *Sūrah* of Women (65:4) abrogated the period of four months and ten days." Ibn 'Abbās and 'Ali said that it did not. That was like their disagreement about a bequest to an heir and whether or not it was abrogated. That is when there is a conflict between two *āyahs* about which of them is advanced when abrogation is not known and its preconditions are not met. An example of that is: *"Apart from that He has made all other women lawful for you."* (4:24) That would include combining it with slaves, while the words of Allah: *"Not marrying two sisters at the same time except for what took place in the past"* (4:23) forbid it. The same principle applies when there is an apparent conflict between hadiths or analogies. That is considered to be *mutashābih*. Not part of *mutashābih*, however, is reciting an *āyah* with two readings. Reciting both is like acting by all that they entail as in 5:6.'

We find in al-Bukhārī that Sa'īd ibn Jubayr said, 'A man said to Ibn 'Abbās, "I find things in the Qur'an which seem contradictory to me." He asked, "What are they?" He said: "'*That Day there will be no family ties between them and they will not be able to question one another*' (23:101) and '*They will confront each other, questioning one another.*' (37:27) '*They will not be able to hide a single circumstance from Allah*' (4:42) and '*They say, "By Allah, our Lord, We were not idolaters."*'" (6:23) and in this *āyah* they are hiding something. In *an-Nāzi'āt*: '*He built heaven ... After that He smoothed out the earth.*' (79: 27-30). So Allah mentions the creation of the heaven before the earth. Then He says, '*Do you reject Him who created the earth in two days ... Then He turned to heaven.*' (41:9-11) Here He mentions the creation of the earth before heaven. And He says: '*Allah is Ever-Forgiving, Most Merciful*' (4:100), '*Allah is Almighty, All-Wise*' (4:158) and '*Allah is All-Hearing, All-Seeing.*' (4:134) and He uses the past tense."

'Ibn 'Abbās replied, "'*No family ties between them*' refers to the first blast. Then there will be the second blast and all those who are in the heavens and the earth will swoon except for whomever Allah wishes. There will be no ties between them then and they will not to able to question one another. Then there will be another blast and they will begin to question one another. As for the words: *'We were not idolaters'* and *'They will not be able to hide a single circumstance from Allah,'* Allah will forgive the people of sincerity for their wrong actions and the idolaters will say, 'Let us say, "We were not idolaters."' So Allah will seal their mouths and their limbs will say what they did. Then it will be known that not a single circumstance will be hidden from Allah. Then those who rejected will wish that they had been Muslims. Allah created the earth in two days and then turned to heaven and arranged it into seven heavens in two days. Then He smoothed out the earth and brought forth water and plants from it and created in it mountains, trees and hills and what is between them in another two days. That is His words, *'After that He smoothed out the earth.'* So He created the earth and what is in it in four days and the heaven in two days. His words: *'Allah is Ever-Forgiving, Most Merciful'* mean Himself. He was, and continues to be, like that. Allah did not intend anything except that He did exactly what He desired. Woe to you! The Qur'an is not contradictory! It is all from Allah."'"

Those with deviation in their hearts

In the phrase *'those with deviation in their hearts'* the word *zaygh* means inclination, as when the sun inclines or the eyes incline. It is used for when someone deviates by abandoning the goal they were aiming for, as when Allah says: *'So when they deviated, Allah made their hearts deviate (*azāgha*).'* (61:5) This *āyah* embraces every group: unbelievers, *zindīqs*, the ignorant and those involved in innovation. At the time it was revealed, it was specifically referring to the Christians of Najrān. Qatādah said about this, 'If this is not the Ḥarūriyyah and other Khārijites, I do not know who it is.' This interpretation is reported from Abū Umāmah which is *marfū'*. It is enough for you.

follow what is open to interpretation in it, desiring conflict, seeking its inner meaning.

Our shaykh, Abu-l-'Abbās, said, 'Those who follow the *mutashābihāt* follow them and collect them, seeking to create doubt about the Qur'an and to misguide the common people, as was done by the *zindīqs* and Qarmatians who attacked the Qur'an, or seeking to believe in the literal sense of the *mutashābihāt*, as was done by the anthropomorphists who took literally those words in the Qur'an and Sunnah that are apparently anthropomorphist, to such an extent that they actually believed that the Creator had a physical body and form, a face, eye, hand, side, foot and finger. Allah is exalted above any such ascription! Or they follow it and begin to interpret it and explain its meanings, or do what Ṣabīgh did when he asked 'Umar a lot of questions. So there are four categories of people listed here.

There is no doubt about the disbelief of the first group, and Allah judged that they should be killed without being asked to repent.

The sound position about the second group is that they are unbelievers since there is no difference between them and those who worship idols and forms. They are asked to repent. If they do not repent, they are killed as is done with apostates.

In the case of the third group, there is disagreement about the permissibility of doing that in accordance with the disagreement about the permissibility of interpreting such *āyahs*. It is known that the position of the early generations was not to undertake interpretation (*ta'wīl*) while at the same time they absolutely stated that the literal meaning was impossible. They said, 'Leave it as it has come.' Some believed that interpretation was possible and could be applied to a sound meaning linguistically without making that definitive in any way.

The judgment regarding the fourth group is to strongly discipline them, as was done by 'Umar to Ṣabīgh. Abū Bakr al-Anbārī said, 'The imāms of the early generations used to punish those who asked about the explanation of the obscure letters in the Qur'an because, if the one who asked meant by his question to perpetuate innovation and cause sedition, then he deserves reproach and a strong punishment. If it this was not his aim, he merits rebuke for committing a wrong action since at the time it provided atheistic hypocrites with a means to achieve their desire to weaken the Muslims through doubt and misguidance by diverting the Qur'an from the paths of revelation and true interpretation.'

Referring to that is what Qāḍī Ismā'īl ibn Isḥāq reported from Sulaymān ibn Ḥarb ibn Zayd from Yazīd ibn Ḥāzim from Sulaymān ibn Yasār that Ṣabīgh ibn 'Isl came to Madīnah and began to ask about the *mutashābih* parts of the Qur'an and other things. 'Umar heard about that and sent for him. He was brought and 'Umar had prepared for him some palm branches. When he got there, 'Umar asked, 'Who are you?' He replied, 'I am the slave of Allah, Ṣabīgh.' 'Umar said, 'And I am the slave of Allah, 'Umar.' Then he went to him and hit his head with a branch and split it, and he continued to beat him until the blood ran down his face. He said, 'Enough, *Amīr al-Mu'minīn*! By Allah, what I found in my head has gone!' There are various transmissions about how he was disciplined and that will be mentioned in *Sūrat adh-Dhāriyāt*. Then Allah inspired him to repent and cast that into his heart and he repented.

The meaning of *'seeking conflict'* is to seek out and convey the unclear and uncertain matters to the believers so that they become disunited and people turn to deviation. Az-Zajjāj said that *'seeking its inner meaning'* means to seek the explanation of people's resurrection and revivification, and Allah informs us that the interpretation of that and its time are only known by Him. The evidence for that is the words of the Almighty: *'What are they waiting for but its fulfilment (*ta'wīlahu*)? The Day its fulfilment occurs* (i.e. the Day when they see the resurrection, gathering and punishment they were promised), *those who forgot it before will say, "The Messengers of our Lord came with the Truth."'* (7:53) It means: 'We have been shown the true interpretation of what the Messengers told us' He said, 'So the reciter stops at the words of Allah: *"No one knows its inner meaning but Allah,"* in other words no one knows about the Resurrection but Allah alone.'

No one knows its inner meaning but Allah.

It is said that a group of Jews, including Ḥuyayy ibn Aḥṭab, came to the Messenger of Allah ﷺ and said, 'We heard that *"Alif-Lām-Mīm"* has been revealed to you. If you are speaking the truth, the domain of your kingdom will last seventy-one years because in the reckoning of the letters, *alif* is 1, *lām* is 30 and *mīm* is 40.' Then: *'No one knows its inner meaning but Allah'* was revealed. *Ta'wīl* can mean explanation and it can mean what something refers back to. It is derived from the verb *āla*, meaning 'to refer back to'. Some *fuqahā'* define *ta'wīl* as the production of a probable meaning of a literal expression when there is other evidence to support that departure from its normal meaning. *Tafsīr* is the explanation of the expression itself and *ta'wīl* is to explain the meaning. An example of this is *'rayb'* in 2:2. The *tafsīr* is that it means 'doubt' and its *ta'wīl* is that it means 'no doubt in the believers' or 'it is true in itself and does not admit of any doubt. "Doubt" describes the doubter.'

Those firmly rooted in knowledge

Scholars disagree about this and whether it is a new sentence or connected to what is before it, in which case the *wāw* is connective. Most say that it is a new sentence. This is what Ibn 'Umar, Ibn 'Abbās, 'Ā'ishah, 'Urwah ibn az-Zubayr, 'Umar ibn 'Abd al-'Azīz and others said. It is the position of al-Kisā'ī, al-Akhfash, al-Farrā', Abū 'Ubayd and others. Abū Nuhayk al-Asadī said, 'They used to connect this *āyah* to what is before it, but it is separate. The knowledge of those firmly rooted in knowledge only reaches their words, 'We believe in it. All of it is from our Lord.' 'Umar ibn 'Abd al-'Azīz said something similar. Aṭ-Ṭabarī related the like of it from Yūnus ibn Ashhab from Mālik ibn Anas. According to this, 'they say' is the predicate of 'those firmly rooted'.

Al-Khaṭṭābī said, 'Allah has divided the *āyahs* of His Book one is commanded to believe in and affirm into two parts: *muḥkam* and *mutashābih*. He reported that the *mutashābihāt* of the Book are those whose interpretation Allah alone knows; no one else knows their interpretation. Then Allah praised those who are firmly rooted in knowledge since they say, "We believe in it." If it had not been for the soundness of their faith, they would not deserve praise.' The position of most scholars is to have a full stop in this *āyah* after Allah's words: *'except Allah.'* That is related from Ibn Mas'ūd, Ubayy ibn Ka'b, Ibn 'Abbās and 'Ā'ishah. It is related that Mujāhid said that the words '*those firmly rooted in knowledge*' are connected to what is before it and mean that they too know it.

One of the linguists used this as evidence and said that the meaning is: 'Those firmly rooted in knowledge know it, saying, "We believe."' making 'they say' an adverb. Most linguistic scholars, however, deny that and think that it is unlikely because the Arabs do not elide both the verb and the object, and do not use an adverb in the form of a *ḥāl* without the verb. If that had been permitted, it would be permitted to say, "Abdullāh riding,' meaning "Abdullāh came riding.' That is permitted when the verb is mentioned and is used adverbially. What most scholars say – confirmed by the schools of the grammarians – is more appropriate than the isolated statement of Mujāhid. It is also not permitted for Allah to negate something in respect of His creation and then affirm it for Himself and then be a partner in that. Do you not see that Allah says: *'Say: "No one in the heavens and the earth knows the Unseen except Allah"'* (2:65), *'He alone will reveal it at its proper time'* (7:187) and *'All things are passing except His Face'* (28:88). All of this is part of what only Allah knows and no one else shares it with Him. That is like His words: *'No one knows its inner meaning except Allah.'* If the *wāw* connected to '*firmly rooted*' had been for the order, there would be no point in the words: *'All of it is from our Lord.'* Allah knows best.

What al-Khaṭṭābī said about not taking the view of Mujāhid – that '*firmly rooted*' is added to the name of Allah and they are included in knowledge of the *mutashābihāt* – is related from Ibn 'Abbās. In Mujahid's view in addition to their knowledge of it, they say, '*We believe in it.*' Ar-Rabī', Muḥammad ibn Ja'far ibn az-Zubayr, al-Qāsim ibn Muḥammad and others also said that. According to that 'say' is an adverb. [POEM TO ILLUSTRATE} Those who take this view argue that Allah praised them for being firm in knowledge, so how could He praise them for being ignorant? Ibn 'Abbās said, 'I am one of those who know its interpretation.' Mujāhid recited this *āyah* and also said, 'I am one of those who know its interpretation.' The Imam of the Ḥaramayn, Abu-l-Mu'ālī, related that from him.

Some scholars, however, refer this back to the first statement and say, 'It implies that what is meant by stopping at "*except Allah*" means that no one knows the interpretation of the *mutashābihāt* except Allah, while those firmly rooted in knowledge know some of it and say, "*We believe in it. All is from our Lord*" by the proofs which are set up in the verses which are *muḥkam*, and those who refer to them are made firm. When they know the interpretation of some of them but not others, they say, "We believe in it. All of it is from our Lord, and our knowledge does not encompass the hidden things in His sound *Sharī'ah*. Its knowledge is with Allah."' If someone says, 'Some explanation is obscure even for those "*firmly rooted*", so that Ibn 'Abbās said, "I do not know what is meant by *al-awwāh* or *ghislīn*,"' the answer is 'This is not necessary because Ibn 'Abbās learned it after that and explained it.' The answer is more definitive than that. That is because Allah did not say that everyone '*firmly rooted*' must have this knowledge. If one person does not know it, another can teach him.

Ibn Fūrak preferred that the '*firmly rooted*' know the interpretation and are firm in that. The Prophet ﷺ said to Ibn 'Abbās, 'O Allah, give him understanding in the *dīn* and teach him interpretation (*ta'wīl*),' i.e. 'teach him the meanings of Your Book.' If you look at it in this way, the stop could be after '*firmly rooted in knowledge*.' Shaykh Abu-l-'Abbās Aḥmad ibn 'Umar said, 'This is sound. Calling them "*firmly rooted*" demands that they know more than the *muḥkam* which is known equally by all of those who understand the words of the Arabs. In what way would they be "*firmly rooted*" if they only knew what everyone knows?'

There are different categories of *mutashābihāt*. Some are definitively only known by Allah, such as the matter of the *rūḥ* and the Last Hour, and no one is given knowledge of these things, not Ibn 'Abbās or anyone else. As for those which can have several senses linguistically and different forms in Arabic, their correct interpretation can be known and one can remove incorrect interpretations, such as Allah's words about 'Īsā being, '*a spirit from Him*,' (4:181) and similar things. No one should be called '*firmly rooted*' unless they know a lot of this type of interpretation according to what they are enabled to discover. As for those who say that the *mutashābih* things are abrogated, on that basis it is correct to include the '*firmly rooted*' in the knowledge of interpretation, but it is not valid to consider the *mutashābihāt* to be only of this category.

Rusūkh is firmness in a thing. That which is firm is described as '*rāsikh*'. Its root in physical bodies is the firm rootedness of mountains and trees in the earth. A poet said:

Love was firm in my heart for Laylā.
Its signs refuse to alter.

In the same way, faith can be firmly rooted in the heart. The verb is *rasakha, yarsakhu*. Some said that a pool is firm (*rasakha*) when its water settles. Ibn Fāris related that. It is a word which has opposite meanings. *Rasakha*, *raṣakha*, *raṣuna* and *rasaba* are all confirmed. The Prophet ﷺ was asked about those '*firmly rooted in knowledge*' and said that it is: '…whoever fulfils his oath, speaks the truth and whose heart is straight.' If it is asked how there can be something *mutashābih* in the Qur'an when Allah says: '*We have sent down the Reminder to you so that you can make clear to mankind what has been sent down to them*' (16:44) and how it can be that He did not make all of it clear, the answer is that there is wisdom in that – and Allah knows best – in displaying the superiority of scholars. If all of it had been clear, their superiority in relation to one another would not appear. That is how it is done when someone makes a classification: he makes some of it clear and some of it unclear, and a place is left for experience because when the existence of something is of no importance, its radiance is little. Allah knows best.

All of it is from our Lord.'

This refers to the Book of Allah, and all its parts, both those that are clear and those that are open to interpretation.

But only people of intelligence pay heed

and say this and believe and stop where it stops and do not follow the *mutashābihāt*. *Lubb* is intelligence and the *lubb* of anything is its core which is why it is used to denote the intellect. '*Ūlū*' is the plural of *dhū*.

رَبَّنَا لَا تُزِغْ قُلُوبَنَا بَعْدَ إِذْ هَدَيْتَنَا وَهَبْ لَنَا مِن لَّدُنكَ رَحْمَةً إِنَّكَ أَنتَ الْوَهَّابُ ﴿٨﴾

8 'Our Lord, do not make our hearts swerve aside after You have guided us. And give us mercy from You. You are the Ever-Giving.

'Our Lord, do not make our hearts swerve aside'

Something is elided and 'they say' is implied here. This is talking about

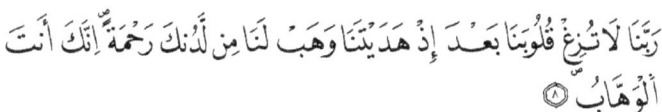

about those firmly rooted in knowledge. It is possible that it means: 'Say, "O Muḥammad."' It is said that the swerving of the heart is towards corruption and inclination away from the *dīn*. Do they fear that, when they have been guided, Allah will turn them to corruption? The answer is that they asked, after Allah had guided them, for Him not to test them by actions which would be burdensome for them which they would be unable to do like those referred to in His words: *'If We had directed them kill themselves or leave their homes.'* (4:64) Ibn Kaysān said, 'They asked not to swerve lest Allah would make their hearts swerve as in His words: *"So when they deviated, Allah made their hearts deviate"* (61:5), in other words, "Make us firm in the guidance You have granted to us. Otherwise we might swerve and deserve our hearts to swerve."'

It is said that this is separate from what came before it. That is because after Allah mentioned the people who swerve, He taught His slaves to call on Him so that they would not be among the censured party who are mentioned: the people who do swerve. We find in the *Muwaṭṭā'* that Abū 'Abdullāh aṣ-Ṣanābiḥī is reported to have said, 'I arrived in Madīnah during the caliphate of Abū Bakr aṣ-Ṣīddiq and I prayed *maghrib* behind him. He recited the *Umm al-Qur'ān* and two of the shorter *sūrahs* from the *Mufaṣṣal* in the first two *rak'ahs*. Then he stood up in the third and I drew so near to him that my clothes were almost touching his clothes. I heard him reciting the *Umm al-Qur'ān* and this *āyah: "Our Lord, do not make our hearts swerve aside after You have guided us, and give us mercy from You. You are Ever-Giving."'* Scholars say that his recitation of this *āyah* was a kind of *qunūt* and supplication since that was at the time of the Riddah. *Qunūt* is permitted in *maghrib* according to a group of people of knowledge, and it is also permitted in every prayer when a terrible matter comes upon the Muslims which alarms them and because of which they fear for themselves.

At-Tirmidhī related that Shahr ibn Ḥawshab said, 'I asked Umm Salamah, "*Umm al-Mu'minīn*, what was the most frequent supplication used by the Messenger of Allah ﷺ when he was with you?" She replied, "His most frequent supplication was, 'O Overturner of hearts, make my heart firm in your *dīn*.' I said, 'Messenger of Allah, the supplication you use the most is "O Overturner of hearts, make my heart firm in your *dīn*!"' He said, 'Umm Salamah, there is no human being whose heart is not between two of Allah's fingers. If He wishes, He makes him go straight, and, if he wishes, He makes him swerve.'" Mu'ādh recited, *"Our Lord, do not make our hearts swerve aside after You have guided us."*' He said that it is a *ḥasan* hadith. This is evidence against the Mu'tazilites who say that Allah does not misguide His slaves. If there had not been swerving away from Him, it would not be permitted ask Him for what is not possible in respect of Him to be repelled. Abū Wāqid and al-Jarrāḥ recited '*tazigh*' with the action attributed to the hearts. This is desire for Allah. Both readings mean that swerving is created by Allah and He makes them swerve.

And give us mercy from You.

This means 'directly from You and Your presence,' as a favour from You, not on account of anything that has come from us or any action of ours. This involves submission and casting off. There are four dialectical forms of '*ladun*': *ladun*, which is the most eloquent; *ladu*; *laduni*, and *ladna*. Some false Sufis and esoteric *zindīqs* grab on to this *āyah* and others like it and say: 'You see, knowledge is what Allah gives direct without any need for acquisition or studying of books. Pages are but a veil.' This is refuted as will be explained elsewhere. The *āyah* means: 'Give us a blessing which issues from Your mercy' because mercy is one of the attributes of the Essence and so a direct gift of it is inconceivable. The verb for give is *wahaba*, *yahabu*. The root is *yahibu*. It is an error if someone says that the root is *yawhaba*.

رَبَّنَآ إِنَّكَ جَامِعُ ٱلنَّاسِ لِيَوْمٍ لَّا رَيْبَ فِيهِ إِنَّ ٱللَّهَ لَا يُخْلِفُ ٱلْمِيعَادَ ٩

9 Our Lord, You are the Gatherer of mankind to a Day of which there is no doubt. Allah will not break His promise.'

It means: 'You are the Resurrector and Reviver of them after they have been dispersed.' It is affirmation of the resurrection on the Day of Rising. Az-Zajjāj said, 'This is the interpretation which the '*firmly rooted*' know and affirm. Those who follow what is open to interpretation about the business of the resurrection disagree about it to the point that they end up denying it.' '*Rayb*' is doubt and was discussed in *Sūrat al-Baqarah*. *Mi'ād* is the form *mif'āl* from *wa'd*.

إِنَّ ٱلَّذِينَ كَفَرُوا۟ لَن تُغْنِىَ عَنْهُمْ أَمْوَٰلُهُمْ وَلَآ أَوْلَٰدُهُم مِّنَ ٱللَّهِ شَيْـًٔا ۖ وَأُو۟لَٰٓئِكَ هُمْ
وَقُودُ ٱلنَّارِ ١٠

10 As for those who disbelieve, their wealth and children will not help them against Allah in any way. They are fuel for the Fire,

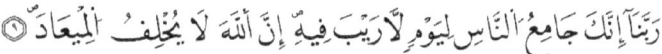

The meaning is clear: neither their wealth nor children will avail them against Allah's punishment in any way. As-Sulamī recited '*yughnā*' (rather than '*tughnā*')

because of the sentence structure indicating something coming between the noun and the verb. Al-Ḥasan recited '*yughnī*' in order to make it lighter. The '*min*' means 'in the face of' (*'inda*) according to Abū 'Ubaydah.

They are fuel for the Fire.

'*Waqūd*' (fuel) is a name for firewood. This was already mentioned in *Sūrat al-Baqarah*. Al-Ḥasan, Mujāhid and Ṭalḥah ibn Muṣarrif read it as *wuqūd* which is a verbal noun, meaning 'fuel for the burning of the Fire'. In Arabic, *wāw* can have the vowel *ḍammah*. *Wuqūd* is the verbal noun for the burning of a fire from the verb *waqada*.

Ibn al-Mubārak transmitted from the hadith of al-'Abbās ibn 'Abd al-Muṭṭalib that the Messenger of Allah ﷺ said, 'This *dīn* will be victorious until the seas are crossed and you plunge into the sea on horses in the way of Allah Almighty. Then there will come some people who recite the Qur'an and when they recite it, they will say, "Who knows the most recitation among us? Which of us has the most knowledge?" He turned to his Companions and asked, "Do you think that there is any good in those people?" "No," they answered. He said, "Those are from you and they are from this community, and they are fuel for the Fire."'

كَدَأْبِ ءَالِ فِرْعَوْنَ وَالَّذِينَ مِن قَبْلِهِمْ كَذَّبُوا بِـَٔايَٰتِنَا فَأَخَذَهُمُ اللَّهُ بِذُنُوبِهِمْ
وَاللَّهُ شَدِيدُ الْعِقَابِ ﴿١١﴾

11 as was the case with the people of Pharaoh and those before them. They denied Our Signs so Allah seized them for their wrong actions. Allah is fierce in retribution.

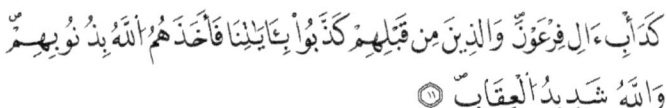

Da'b designates 'custom, habit and business.' The verb *da'aba yad'abu* means to exert oneself and toil, and Form IV means to pursue a journey with energy. It is used for making a camel travel hard. *Dā'ibān* means night and day. Abū Ḥātim said, 'I heard Ya'qūb say, "*ka-da'ab*" with a *fatḥah* on the *hamzah*. He asked me, a young boy at that time, "On what basis is it permitted to say '*ka-da'ab*'?" I told him, "I think that it comes from the verb *da'iba, yad'abu, da'b*." He accepted that from me and was surprised at my ability in spite of my youth. I do not know whether it is said or not.' An-Naḥḥās said that this is an error and that one never says '*da'iba*', but rather '*da'aba*'. That is what the grammarians have said, including al-Farrā' who related it in *Kitāb al-Maṣādir*. *Da'abah* is also permitted because it contains a throat letter. There is disagreement about the *kāf*. It is said that it is in the nominative, implying, 'Their custom is like that of the people of Pharaoh,' meaning that 'what the unbelievers are doing to you is like what the people of Pharaoh did to Mūsā.' Al-Farrā' said that the meaning is: 'The Arabs have disbelieved like the people of Pharaoh disbelieved.'

An-Naḥḥās said that 'like' cannot be connected to 'disbelieve' because 'disbelieve' is in the connective. It is said that it is connected to 'seized them', in other words, 'Allah seized them like He seized the people of Pharaoh.' It is also said that it is connected to the phrase *'their wealth and children will not help them'*, meaning that wealth will not help them like wealth and children did not help the people of Pharaoh. This is a rebuttal directed at those who failed to go out to perform *jihād*, claiming that they were distracted by wealth and family. It can also refer to them being fuel for the Fire and the similarity lies in burning.

This idea is supported by the *āyah*: *'A most evil torment engulfed Pharaoh's people – the Fire, morning and night, to which they are exposed; and on the Day the Hour takes place: "Admit Pharaoh's people to the harshest punishment!"'* (40:45-46) The first position is the most likely and more than one scholar has said that. Ibn 'Arafah said that the expression '*...the case with the people of Pharaoh*' means 'the custom of the people of Pharaoh'. He said, 'Those unbelievers made a habit of abandoning and harassing the Prophet ﷺ just as the habit of the people of Pharaoh was to harass the Prophets.' Al-Azharī said that it means that. The words in *al-Anfāl: 'Such was the case with Pharaoh's people'* (8:52), mean what happened to the people of Pharaoh. It means that they will be repaid with killing and capture in the same way that the people of Pharaoh were repaid with drowning and destruction.

'Our Signs' can refer to the *āyahs* recited in the Qur'an or the signs which are set up in creation as evidence of His Oneness.

قُل لِّلَّذِينَ كَفَرُوا۟ سَتُغْلَبُونَ وَتُحْشَرُونَ إِلَىٰ جَهَنَّمَ ۚ وَبِئْسَ ٱلْمِهَادُ ١٢

12 Say to those who disbelieve: 'You will be overwhelmed and crowded into Hell. What an evil resting-place!'

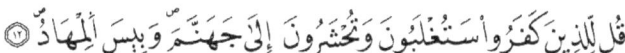

This refers to the Jews. Muḥammad ibn Isḥāq said, 'When the Messenger of Allah ﷺ defeated Quraysh at Badr and came back to Madīnah, he gathered the Jews and said, "Company of Jews! Be warned by Allah of what happened to Quraysh at Badr before the same thing as befell them befalls you. You know that I am a sent Prophet. You will find that in your Book and in Allah's covenant with you." They said, "Muḥammad, do not be deluded by the fact that you killed some foolish people who have no knowledge of war and grasped your opportunity to defeat them! By Allah, if you fight us, you will find out that we are the true people!" Then Allah revealed this.'

Another variant reads it with *yā'* instead of *tā'*, meaning 'They (Quraysh) will be overwhelmed.' *'You will be crowded into Hell'* means in the Next World. This is transmitted from 'Ikrimah and Sa'īd ibn Jubayr from Ibn 'Abbās. In Abū Ṣāliḥ's variant from him is that it was revealed when the Jews were happy with what happened in the Battle of Uḥud. This coincides with the reading of Nāfi' who has a *yā'* referring to Quraysh in both verbs: 'They will be overwhelmed and crowded.'

What an evil resting-place!

This means Hell, taking the *āyah* literally. Mujāhid said, 'It means: "what you have prepared for yourselves is evil,"' as if the meaning was 'Evil are your actions which have led you to Hell.'

قَدْ كَانَ لَكُمُۥٓ ءَايَةٞ فِي فِئَتَيْنِ اِ۬لْتَقَتَا فِئَةٞ تُقَٰتِلُ فِي سَبِيلِ اِ۬للَّهِ وَأُخْرَىٰ كَافِرَةٞ
تَرَوْنَهُم مِّثْلَيْهِمْ رَأْيَ اَ۬لْعَيْنِ وَاللَّهُ يُؤَيِّدُ بِنَصْرِهِۦ مَن يَشَآءُ إِنَّ فِي ذَٰلِكَ لَعِبْرَةٗ
لِّأُوْلِي اِ۬لْأَبْصَٰرِ ١٣

13 There was a sign for you in the two parties which met face to face, one party fighting in the Way of Allah and the other unbelievers. You saw them as twice their number with your own eyes. Allah reinforces with His help whoever He wills. There is instruction in that for people of insight.

There was a sign for you in the two parties

The reason that the verb is *kāna* and not *kānat* is that 'sign' (*āyah*) is not a true feminine. It is said that it refers to the clarification, in other words 'you have clarification,' indicating the meaning rather than the actual words. It is like the words of Imru' al-Qays:

White, beautiful, tender,
Like the shoot of a bean-tree breaking out with leaves.

He did not use the feminine form of 'breaking out' because it refers to the stalk. Al-Farrā' said that it is masculine because of the adjective. When the adjective comes between the noun and the verb, then the verb is masculine. This usage was mentioned in *al-Baqarah* (2:180).

The two parties referred to are the Muslims and the idolaters at the Battle of Badr. Most recite '*fi'atun*' in the nominative, meaning one of the parties. Al-Ḥasan and Mujāhid recite it in the genitive and 'the other' is an appositive. Ibn Abī 'Ablah recite both in the accusative, and Ahmad ibn Yaḥyā said that it is permitted as an adverbial *ḥāl*, meaning the two different parties meet: one believing and one disbelieving.

A group of people is called a *fi'ah* (party) because one returns (*yufā'*) to it in times of difficulty. Az-Zajjāj that said *fi'ah* is a group, taken from '*fa'w*', which means to cleave the head with the sword. The verb is used for cleaving through a person. There is no disagreement that this refers to the two groups in the Battle of Badr, but there is disagreement about who is addressed here. It is said that it might be the believers that are addressed and it might be the unbelievers. It is also possible that it is the Jews of Madīnah who are being addressed. Each view has those who espouse it. If it is addressed to the believers, it is meant to strengthen their souls and encourage them to advance against twice their number as indeed happened.

You saw them as twice their number with your own eyes.

Abū 'Alī said that the seeing here is actually seeing with the eyes. Makkī and al-Mahdawī said that it what the eye sees. Nāfi' reads it with a *tā'* as 'You saw them' while the rest read it with a *yā'*: 'They saw them.' The majority believe that the subject in 'you see them' is the believers and 'them' refers to the unbelievers. Abū 'Amr disliked reciting it with *tā'* and said, 'If it had been like that, it would have been twice their number.' An-Naḥḥās said, 'That is not necessary, but it can be twice the number of your companions.' Makkī said that 'you saw' is addressed to the Muslims and 'them' refers to the idolaters. This would mean that it would have to be 'twice your number' and that is not permitted because it differs from the script, but the words can move from the second person to the third person as in other places in the Qur'an like 10:22 and 30:39 in which Allah returns to the third person. So the 'them' can refer to the idolaters, i.e. 'O believers, you see the idolaters as twice their number.' This is an unlikely meaning because Allah would not make the idolaters multiply in the eyes of the Muslims. Rather He tells us that He reduces their number in the eyes of the believers, and so the meaning would be: 'O believers, you saw the idolaters as twice your number when they were three times your number.' So Allah lessened them in the eyes of the Muslims and showed them to be only twice their number to strengthen their spirits. They knew that a hundred of them would overcome two hundred of the unbelievers. He lessened the number of the Muslims in the eyes of the idolaters so that they would be bold and the judgment of Allah would be carried out on them.

It is possible that the pronoun 'their' refers to the Muslims, in other words you, the Muslims, saw yourselves as twice your number. Allah did that to strengthen their spirits in the encounter. The first view is more likely. That is indicated by the words of Allah: *'Remember when Allah showed you them in your dream as only a few'* (8:43) and *'Remember when Allah made you see them as few when you met them.'* (8:44) It is related that Ibn Mas'ūd said, 'I asked a man beside me, "Do you see seventy?" He said, "I think that there are a hundred." When we took captives, they told us that they were a thousand.'

Aṭ-Ṭabarī reported that some people said, 'Allah made the number of believers increase in the eyes of the unbelievers so that they were twice their size.' Aṭ-Ṭabarī thought this weak. Ibn 'Aṭiyyah said, 'That is rejected for several reasons. Rather Allah made the idolaters seem less in the eyes of the believers as was stated.' According to this interpretation, 'You saw' refers to the unbelievers, i.e. 'You, O unbelievers, saw the Muslims as twice their number.' Al-Farrā' said that it means: 'You saw them as twice your number when they were three times your number.' This is unlikely and not known linguistically. Az-Zajjāj says that it is an error because we understand the 'like' of a thing to be the same size as it and 'twice' to be two times as many.

Ibn Kaysān said, 'Al-Farrā' explains it in the following manner: 'It is as when you say when you have a slave, "He needs another one like him." You need him and one like him and you say, "I need two like him." So you need three. The meaning is different to what you say and to the language. So in this case al-Farrā' is saying that the number of the idolaters was three times that of the Muslims in the Battle of Badr. He imagined that it was not permitted for them to see them except as the same number as them. This is highly unlikely and meaningless. Allah made them see them as other than their actual number for two reasons. One is that their best interests lay in that because the hearts of the believers were strengthened by it. The other is that it was a Sign for the Prophet ﷺ. The Battle of Badr will be mentioned later, Allah willing.

If it is recited with *yā'*, Ibn Kaysān said that 'them' refers to 'the unbelievers' and 'their number' refers to 'the party fighting in the Way of Allah' as indicated by the context. That is confirmed by the words: *'Allah reinforces with His help whomever He wills.'* This, as we said, would mean that the idolaters were three times the number of the Muslims and appeared as only twice their number in their eyes. He said that the seeing refers to the Jews. Makkī said that the seeing refers to the party fighting in the Way of Allah and the group seen were the unbelievers. This means that the party fighting in the Way of Allah saw the unbelievers as twice the number of the believers while the unbelievers were actually three times their number, but Allah made them appear as less to them and 'you' is addressed to the Jews. Ibn 'Abbās and Ṭalḥah recited *'yurawnahum'* and as-Sulamī has it with a *tā'* and *ḍammah* in the passive.

زُيِّنَ لِلنَّاسِ حُبُّ الشَّهَوَاتِ مِنَ النِّسَاءِ وَالْبَنِينَ وَالْقَنَاطِيرِ الْمُقَنْطَرَةِ
مِنَ الذَّهَبِ وَالْفِضَّةِ وَالْخَيْلِ الْمُسَوَّمَةِ وَالْأَنْعَامِ وَالْحَرْثِ ذَٰلِكَ
مَتَاعُ الْحَيَاةِ الدُّنْيَا وَاللَّهُ عِنْدَهُ حُسْنُ الْمَآبِ ﴿١٤﴾

14 To mankind the love of worldly appetites is painted in glowing colours: women and children, and heaped-up mounds of gold and silver, and grazing horses with fine markings, and livestock and fertile farmland. All that is merely the enjoyment of the life of this world. The best homecoming is in the presence of Allah.

To mankind the love of worldly appetites is painted in glowing colours:

'Painted in glowing colours' means 'adorned', and people disagree about who is the adorner is. One group say that it is Allah who adorns, and that is the apparent meaning of what 'Umar ibn al-Khaṭṭāb said, and which al-Bukhārī mentioned. We read in the Revelation: *'We made everything on the earth an adornment for it.'* (18:7) When 'Umar said, 'Now, O Lord, when You have adorned it for us!' there was revealed: *'Say, "Shall I tell you of something better than that?"'* (3:15)

Another group said, 'The adorner is Shayṭān.' This is the apparent position of al-Ḥasan. He said, 'Who then makes it seem attractive? No one is stronger in censure of it than its Creator.' So the adornment of Allah is by bringing into existence and preparation for use and producing natures disposed to these things. The adornment of Shayṭān is by whispering, deceit and making it seem good to them to take in an improper way. This *āyah*, according to both views, is a warning for all people. That contains rebuke for the contemporaries of Muḥammad ﷺ: the Jews and others.

Most recite *'zuyyina'* in the passive tense with 'love' in the nominative. Aḍ-Ḍaḥḥāk and Mujāhid recited *'zayyana'* with 'love' in the accusative. The vowel on 'appetites' is different when it is a noun or an adjective. *Shahawāt* is the plural of *shahwah*. A man who is *shahwān* is greedy for something. Something which is *shahīy* is desirable. Following appetites is ruin and obeying them is destruction. We find in *Ṣaḥīḥ Muslim* that the Prophet ﷺ said: 'The Garden is surrounded by disliked things and the Fire is surrounded by appetites.' Anas related it from the Prophet ﷺ. The point of this illustration is that the Garden is only obtained by crossing the deserts of disliked things and putting up with them. One is only saved from the Fire by abandoning one's appetites and weaning the self from them. It is related that the Prophet ﷺ said, 'The Path of the Garden is sorrow on a hill and the Path of the Fire is easy on the flat.' It means that the Path to the Garden is difficult to travel since it goes by the tops of the hills and the Path to the Fire is easy without hardness and exposure.

women

He begins with women because men's lower selves often look longingly at them. They are the snares of *shayṭān* and temptation for men. The Messenger of Allah ﷺ said, 'I have not left after me any trial greater for men than women.' Al-Buhkārī and Muslim transmitted it. The trial of women is greater than all other things.

It is said that there are two kinds of trial in women and only one in children. As for the two in women, one is that it can lead to severing of kinship because the woman may order her husband to cut himself off from his mother and sisters. The second is the trial of amassing both lawful and unlawful property. As for children, the single trial is amassing wealth for them. 'Abdullāh ibn Mas'ūd reported that the Messenger of Allah ﷺ said, 'Do not put your women in upper rooms nor teach them writing.' The Messenger of Allah ﷺ cautioned them in this way because to put them in upper rooms is to be on the look out for men and there is no protection or concealment for them in that because they are close to men and constitute a trial and temptation for them, and because they are created from men, and so they desire men. Man has lust created in him and she is the focus of it. Therefore, neither of them is safe from the other. The comment about teaching writing is on account of temptation. The Prophet ﷺ is reported by Abū Hurayrah as saying, 'You should have a woman with religion. May your hands be dusty.' Muslim transmitted it from Abū Hurayrah. We find in the *Sunan* of Ibn Mājah that Ibn 'Umar reported that the Messenger of Allah ﷺ said, 'Do not marry women for their beauty. Their beauty might ruin you. Do not marry them for their wealth. Their wealth might make you oppress them. Marry them for their *dīn*. A black slavegirl with religion would be better for you even if she has a split nose.'

and children

Banūn is the plural of *ibn* (son). Allah reported that Nūḥ said, *'My son is part of my family.'* The diminutive is *bunayy* as Luqmān said. It is reported that the Prophet

ﷺ asked al-Ash'ath ibn Qays. 'Do you have any children by Ḥamzah's daughter?' He answered, 'Yes, and I wish that had a bowl of food which I could give her from those that remain of the Banū Jabalah.' The Prophet ﷺ said, 'If you say that, they are the fruit of the hearts and delight of the eyes. They are also a source of cowardice, miserliness and sorrow.'

and heaped-up mounds of gold and silver

Qanāṭir is the plural of *qinṭār*. It is a large heap of money as Allah says: '*...and have given your original wife a large amount.*' (4:20) It is said that it is the name of a measure, like *riṭl* and *rub'*. It is also used when something reaches that weight, meaning that it is equal to it. The verb is used for a man who has a lot of wealth such that it reaches that level. Az-Zajjāj said, '*Qinṭār* is derived from the verb meaning to make something firm. A bridge is called *qanṭarah* because it is firmly made. So it is as if the *qintār* were a contract of property.' Ṭarafah said:

Like the bridge of the Romans, her lord swears
that she will be surrounded until it is strengthened with bricks.

Scholars disagree about exactly how much it is and there are several positions regarding it. Ubayy ibn Ka'b related that Prophet ﷺ said, 'A *qinṭār* is 1200 *ūqiyyahs*.' Mu'ādh ibn Jabal, 'Abdullāh ibn 'Amr, Abū Hurayrah and a group of scholars said that, and Ibn 'Aṭiyyah said that it is the soundest position, but the *qinṭār* varies in different lands according to the size of the *ūqiyyah*. It is said to be 12,000 *ūqiyyahs*. In his sound *Musnad*, al-Bustī transmitted from Abū Hurayrah that the Messenger of Allah ﷺ said, 'A *qinṭār* is 12,000 *ūqiyyahs*. It is better than what is between heaven and the earth.' Abū Hurayrah also took that view. We find in the *Musnad* of Abū Muḥammad ad-Dārimī that Abū Sa'īd al-Khudrī said, 'Whoever recites ten *āyahs* in the night will be written among those who remember. Whoever recites a hundred *āyahs* will be written among the obedient. Whoever recites from five hundred to a thousand *āyahs* will have the reward of a *qinṭār* in the morning.' He was asked, 'What is the *qinṭār*?' and he replied, 'Enough gold to fill a bull's hide.' It is *mawqūf*. Abū Naḍrah al-'Abdī said that.

It is said to be derived from Syriac. An-Naqqāsh said that al-Kalbī said that it is Greek. Ibn 'Abbās, aḍ-Ḍaḥḥāk and al-Ḥasan said that is 1200 *mithqāls* of silver. Al-Ḥasan says that that is *marfū'*. Ibn 'Abbās also said that it is 12,000 dirhams of silver and 1000 dinars of gold, which is the blood money for a Muslim man. That is reported from al-Ḥasan and aḍ-Ḍaḥḥāk. Sa'īd ibn al-Musayyab said that it is 80,000. Qatādah said it is 100 *riṭls* of gold or 80,000 dirhams of silver. Abū

Ḥamzah ath-Thumālī said that the *qinṭār* in North Africa and Andalusia is 80,000 *mithqāls* of gold or silver. As-Suddī said that it is 4000 *mithqāls*. Mujāhid said that is 70,000 *mithqāls*. That is related from Ibn 'Umar. Makkī related one view that a *qinṭār* is forty *ūqiyyahs* of gold or silver. Ibn Sīdah said that in *al-Muḥkam*. He said, 'The *qinṭār* is a thousand *mithqāls*.' Ar-Rabī' ibn Anas said, 'A *qinṭār* is a lot of wealth piled up.' This was known among the Arabs. Part of it is the above-mentioned *āyah*: '*...and have given your original wife a large amount.*' (4:20) Part of that is the hadith: 'Ṣafwān ibn Umayyah had a *qinṭār* in the Jāhiliyyah as did his father.' This refers to his wealth. Al-Ḥakam said that it is what is between heaven and earth.

'Heaped up': there is disagreement about the meaning of *muqanṭarah*. Aṭ-Ṭabarī and others said that it means multiplied, as if a *qinṭār* is 3 and *muqanṭarah* is 9. It is related that al-Farrā' said that it is the plural of the plural and so it is 9. As-Suddī said that it means minted (i.e. dirhams and dinars.) Makkī says that it means 'complete'. Al-Harawī said that the form is a verbal usage. One of them said that *qanṭarah* is used for a bridge because the density of its structure. Ibn Kaysān and al-Farrā' said that it is not less than nine *qinṭārs*. It is said that it indicates the presence of ready and available wealth. We find in the *Ṣaḥīḥ* of al-Bustī from 'Abdullāh ibn 'Umar that the Messenger of Allah ﷺ said, 'Anyone who prays at night with ten *āyahs* will not be written among the heedless. Anyone who prays at night with a hundred will be written among the obedient. Anyone who prays at night with a thousand will be written among the *muqanṭirīn*.'

'Gold and silver': *dhahab* (gold) is a feminine noun. Its plurals are *dhihāb* and *dhuhūb*. *Dhahaba* describes someone taking a good direction (*madhhab*). *Dhahab* is also a measure used in Yemen. The verb *dhahiba* describes a man who sees a gold mine and is astonished (*dhahiba*). *Fiḍḍah* (silver) is well known and its plural is *fiḍaḍ*. *'Dhahab'* is derived from *dhahāb* (departure) and silver (*fiḍḍah*) from *infaḍḍa*, which means 'to be scattered'. The derivation makes one aware of the fact that they will disappear and are not firm as we see in the world. How excellent is what one of them said about this:

'The Fire' is the last thing that the dinar says.
'Worry' is the end of the dirham.
Even if he is wary, between them a man
has his heart tormented by the Fire and worry.

grazing horses with fine markings,

The word for horses is *khayl*. Ibn Kaysan said that he was told by Abū 'Ubaydah that the singular is *khā'il*. A horse is called that because it is proud (*ikhtāla*) in its gait. Others said that it is a collective noun without a singular and one horse is '*faras*'. We find in a hadith from 'Alī that the Prophet ﷺ said: 'Allah created the horse from the wind which is why it flies without wings.' Wahb ibn Munabbih said, 'He created it from the south wind.' Wahb said, 'There is no glorification, *takbīr* or *shahādah* said by the owner of a horse but that it hears it and answers with the like of it.' More mention of horses will come in *Sūrat al-Anfāl*. It is reported in a tradition, 'Allah showed Ādam all the animals and he was told, "Choose one of them." He chose the horse. He was told, "You have chosen your might."' This is the source of the name *khayl*. They are also called *khayl* because they are marked with might. If anyone rides one, he is exalted by Allah's gift to him and by it is arrogant (*ikhtāla*) towards the enemies of Allah. A horse is called '*faras*' because covers (*iftarasa*) the distance of the air like a lion and captures it. It crosses the distance with its hooves as if it swallowed it up. It is called an Arabian horse because it was brought after Ādam to Ismā'īl as a reward for raising the foundations of the House. Ismā'īl was an Arab. It was a gift from Allah to him and so the horse was called 'Arabian'.

The Prophet ﷺ said, 'Shayṭān will not enter a house with a noble horse in it.' A horse is called 'noble' when it is free of defects. Abū Qatādah said that the Prophet ﷺ said, 'The best of horses are black ones with white blazes and a white spot on the nose, then black ones with white blazes and white legs, except on an offside one. If it is not black, then a bay one with these markings.' At-Tirmidhī transmitted it from Abū Qatādah. It is reported in the *Musnad* of ad-Dārimī that a man said, 'Messenger of Allah, I want to buy a horse. What sort should I buy?' He answered ﷺ, 'Buy a black one with a white spot on the nose and white legs, except on an offside one, or a bay with these markings. You will get booty and be safe.' An-Nasā'ī reported from Anas: 'There was nothing which the Messenger of Allah ﷺ loved more, after women, than horses.' The imams related from Abū Hurayrah that the Messenger of Allah ﷺ said, 'There are three kinds of horses: those which are a reward for a man, those which are a protection for a man and those which contain a burden for a man.' It is so famous that it need not be mentioned. The rulings concerning horses will be mentioned adequately in *al-Anfāl* and *an-Naḥl*.

'With fine markings' (*musawwamah*) means grazing in the meadows and pasture according to Sa'īd ibn Jubayr. One uses *sāma* to mean camels and sheep grazing where they like. The verb from which the noun is taken means to release animals to graze and so they are called '*musawwamah*'. We find in the *Sunan* of Ibn Mājah that 'Alī said, 'The Messenger of Allah ﷺ forbade letting animals graze (*sawm*)

before sunrise and to slaughter animals with milk.' '*Sawm*' means grazing here. Allah says: '*...among which you graze* (tusīmūna) *your herds.*' (16:10) Al-Akhṭal said:

Someone like Ibn Baz'ah or another like him,
more fitting for is the son of the camel herder.

Sawām are any grazing animals. It is also said that it means made ready for *jihād*. Ibn Zayd said that.

Mujāhid said that it means 'marked and beautiful.' 'Ikrimah said, 'They are marked by beauty,' and an-Naḥḥās preferred that, taking it from the words 'a handsome (*wasīm*) man'. Ibn 'Abbās said that it means marked with colours, (like blazes) on their faces. It then comes from *sīmā* which is a sign. This is what al-Kisā'ī and Abu 'Ubaydah said. All of this is allowed by the term: they are freely grazing, ready for war and marked so that they are recognised from other horses when grazing. Abū Zayd said that the basis for that is putting a piece of wool or a marker to distinguish them from other horses which are grazing. The linguist Ibn Fāris said in *al-Mujmal* that they are released with riders on them. Al-Mu'arrij said that it means branded. Al-Mubarrad said that they are known in the lands. Ibn Kaysān said that it means piebald. All of the ideas are similar in respect of demarcation.

and livestock

An'ām it is used for camels and all grazing animals according to Ibn Kaysān whereas *na'am* is only for camels. Al-Farrā' said that the word is masculine rather than feminine while al-Harawī says that it can be either. *An'ām* are livestock: camels, cattle, sheep and goats. *Na'am* are just camels. Ibn Mājah reports from 'Urwa al-Bāriqī: 'Camels are might for their people, sheep are blessing and good is tied up in the forelocks of horses until the Day of Rising.' Ibn 'Umar reports that the Messenger of Allah ﷺ said, 'Sheep are among the animals of the Garden.' Abū Hurayrah said: 'The Messenger of Allah ﷺ instructed the rich to have sheep and the poor to have chickens.' He said that when the rich have chickens Allah gives permission for the destruction of the cities. Umm Hāni' reported that the Prophet ﷺ said to her, 'Keep sheep. There is blessing in them.' He transmitted it from Abū Bakr ibn Abī Shaybah from Wakī' from Hisham ibn 'Urwah from his father from Umm Hāni' with a sound *isnād*.

fertile farmland.

Ḥarth is a word used for all land that is tilled. It is a verbal noun used for designation. *Ḥaratha* is the verb used when someone ploughs the land for farming. *Ḥirāthah* is used for the cultivation of grains, gardens and other types of agriculture. Using it the hadith states: 'Cultivate for this world as if you were going to live forever.' We find in a hadith from 'Abdullāh: 'Cultivate this Qur'an,' i.e. study it thoroughly, and Ibn al-A'rabī said that *ḥarth* is studying in depth. Another hadith states: 'The truest of names is al-Ḥārith', because the one who cultivates earns. *Iḥtirāth* means to acquire wealth. *Miḥrāth* is kindling for a fire and *ḥarāth* is the thread of the bow-string. *Aḥratha* is to make a camel lean. We find in the hadith of Mu'āwiyah: 'What did your watering camels do?' The answer was, 'We made them lean on the Day of Badr.' Abū 'Ubayd said that it means 'we made them lean'.

We find in *Ṣaḥīḥ al-Bukhārī* that Abū Umāmah al-Bāhilī said that he saw a ploughshare and some agricultural implements and remarked, 'I heard the Messenger of Allah ﷺ say, "Whenever this enters a house abasement enters it."' It is said that abasement is what adheres to those involved agricultural labour on account of the duties due on the land which are demanded by rulers. Al-Muhallab said, 'The meaning of this hadith, and Allah knows best, is to encourage elevated circumstances and seeking one's provision from the noblest of crafts. That is because the Messenger of Allah ﷺ feared that his community would become preoccupied with farming and abandon riding horses and doing *jihād* in the Way of Allah because they were too occupied with agriculture, and then those nations who ride horses and live off what they bring them would conquer them. Therefore, he encouraged people to gain their livelihood from *jihād* rather than gravitating to cultivation of the earth and humble occupations. Do you not see that 'Umar said, 'Imitate the people of Ma'd (who were energetic) and wear coarse clothing. Cut off stirrups and leap onto horses. Then the camel-herders will not defeat you.' He commanded them to keep horses and train their bodies by leaping onto them. We find in the two *Ṣaḥīḥ* collections from Anas ibn Mālik, however, that the Prophet ﷺ said, 'If any Muslim plants a plant or sows a crop and a bird, person or animal eat from it, it is *ṣadaqah* for him.'

Scholars say that Allah mentioned four types of wealth, and each type of wealth is the source of wealth for a certain group of people. Gold and silver enrich merchants. Fine horses are the wealth of kings. Flocks are the wealth of the people of the desert, and farmland is the wealth of the people of estates. So the trial of each group lies in the category by which he enriches himself. Women and children apply to all off them.

All that is merely the enjoyment of the life of this world.

This means that what they enjoy in it will vanish and not remain. Consequently one should be abstinent in this world and desire the Next World. Ibn Mājah and others reported from Ibn 'Umar that the Messenger of Allah ﷺ said, 'This world is enjoyment, and the best of its enjoyment is a righteous woman.' We find in a hadith: 'Make do with little of this world and Allah will love you,' referring to enjoying rank and wealth beyond what is absolutely necessary. The Prophet ﷺ said, 'The son of Ādam only has a right to these three things: a house in which to live, a garment with which to clothe his nakedness, and plain bread and water.' At-Tirmidhī transmitted it from al-Miqdām ibn Ma'dikarīb. Sahl ibn 'Abdullāh was asked, 'What makes it easy for a person to leave this world and all appetites?' He replied, 'His busying himself with that he is commanded to do.'

The best homecoming is in the presence of Allah.

Ma'āb is a place of return from the verb *āba, ya'ūbu*. A poet said:

Everyone absent returns
but the one absent through death does not return.

The root of *māb* is *ma'wab* and the vowel of the *wāw* has been changed into a *hamzah* and the *alif* has replaced the *wāw* as in the word *maqāl*. The entire *āyah* is meant to show the smallness and insignificance of this world and to encourage hope for a good return to Allah in the Next World.

قُلْ أَؤُنَبِّئُكُم بِخَيْرٍ مِّن ذَٰلِكُمْ لِلَّذِينَ اتَّقَوْا عِندَ رَبِّهِمْ جَنَّاتٌ
تَجْرِي مِن تَحْتِهَا الْأَنْهَارُ خَالِدِينَ فِيهَا وَأَزْوَاجٌ مُّطَهَّرَةٌ وَرِضْوَانٌ
مِّنَ اللَّهِ وَاللَّهُ بَصِيرٌ بِالْعِبَادِ ﴿١٥﴾

15 Say, 'Shall I tell you of something better than that?' The godfearing will have Gardens with their Lord, with rivers flowing under them, remaining in them timelessly, for ever, and purified wives, and the Pleasure of Allah. Allah sees His slaves:

The question ends at 'that'. 'The godfearing' is an advanced predicate and 'Gardens' is in the nominative by the inceptive. It is said that it ends at 'with their Lord' and 'Gardens' is in the nominative by an implied inceptive. It implies: 'those are Gardens.' By this interpretation 'Gardens' can be in the genitive instead of 'better'. That is not permitted in the first interpretation.

Ibn 'Aṭiyyah said, 'This *āyah* and the one before it are like the words of the Prophet ﷺ: "A woman can be married for four reasons: her wealth, her lineage, her beauty, and her religion. Seek the one with religion. May your hands be in the dust!" Muslim and others transmitted it. "Seek the one with religion" is an illustration of this *āyah*. Allah mentioned this *āyah* as solace for lack of this world and to strengthen the souls in abandoning it.' The meaning of the words in this *āyah* were already discussed in *al-Baqarah*.

Riḍwān (pleasure) is a verbal noun derived from *riḍā*. That is because when the people of the Garden enter it, Allah will say to them, 'Do you want me to give you more?' and they will answer, 'Our Lord, what is better than this?' He will say, 'My pleasure so that I will never be angry with you again.' Muslim transmitted it. *'Allah sees His slaves'* is a promise and a threat.

ٱلَّذِينَ يَقُولُونَ رَبَّنَآ إِنَّنَآ ءَامَنَّا فَٱغْفِرْ لَنَا ذُنُوبَنَا وَقِنَا عَذَابَ
ٱلنَّارِ ﴿١٦﴾ ٱلصَّٰبِرِينَ وَٱلصَّٰدِقِينَ وَٱلْقَٰنِتِينَ وَٱلْمُنفِقِينَ
وَٱلْمُسْتَغْفِرِينَ بِٱلْأَسْحَارِ ﴿١٧﴾

16 those who say, 'Our Lord, we believe, so forgive us our wrong actions and safeguard us from the punishment of the Fire.' 17 The steadfast, the truthful, the obedient, the givers, and those who seek forgiveness before dawn.

'*Those*' is an appositive for the prior 'godfearing'. It can be in the nominative, meaning, 'they are those,' or in the accusative for praise. '*Our Lord*' means 'O Our Lord'. '*We believe*' is 'We assent and confirm'. Then there is a prayer for forgiveness,

The '*steadfast*' are those who refrain from disobedience and their lower appetites. It is also said that it refers to being steadfast in acts of obedience. The '*truthful*' are those who are true in both word and deed. The '*qānitīn*' are the obedient. The '*givers*' are those who spend in the Way of Allah. This was discussed in full in *Sūrat al-Baqarah*.

In this *āyah* Allah Almighty explains the states of the godfearing who are promised the Garden. There is disagreement about the meaning of *'those who seek forgiveness before dawn.'* Anas ibn Mālik said that they are those who ask for forgiveness. Qatādah said that they are simply those who pray at that time. There is no contradiction here. Both groups both pray and ask for forgiveness. Dawn is singled out for mention because it is a time when the prayer is most likely to be accepted and a time when it is answered. The Messenger of Allah ﷺ said in the explanation of the words of the Almighty reporting from Ya'qūb to his sons: *'I will ask my Lord for forgiveness for you'* (12:98), that he delayed that until dawn. At-Tirmidhī transmitted it.

The Prophet ﷺ asked Jibrīl, 'Which part of the night is best for being heard?' He replied, 'I do not know, but the Throne trembles at dawn.' 'Dawn' is either *saḥar* or *saḥr*. Az-Zajjāj said, '*Saḥar* is the time when the night retreats until the second dawn rises.' Ibn Zayd said that it is the last sixth of last night.

The soundest of what is related by the Imāms is from Abū Hurayrah that the Prophet ﷺ said, 'Allah descends to the lowest heaven every night when the first third of the night has passed and says, "I am the King. I am the King. Who is there who calls on Me so that I can answer him? Who is there who asks me so that I can give to him? Who is there who asks My forgiveness so that I can forgive him?" That continues until dawn rises.' (Muslim) There is disagreement about its interpretation. The best of what is said on it is what has come in an-Nasā'ī from Abū Hurayrah and Abū Sa'īd: 'The Messenger of Allah ﷺ said, "Allah waits until the end of the first half of the night and then commands a caller who says, 'Is there a caller who can be answered? Is there someone who asks for forgiveness so that he can be forgiven?'"' Abū Muḥammad 'Abd al-Ḥaqq says that it is sound and removes any ambiguity and clarifies any possibility. There is something elided after 'first half of the night' which is 'an angel descends'. Success is by Allah. We dealt with this in *Kitāb al-Asnā*.

Additional point: Asking forgiveness is recommended and Allah praises those who ask forgiveness in this *āyah* and others, as in: *'They would seek forgiveness before dawn.'* (51:18) Anas ibn Mālik said, 'We were instructed to ask forgiveness seventy times at dawn.' Sufyān ath-Thawrī said, 'I have heard that in the first part of the night a caller calls for the obedient to stand, and they stand and pray until dawn. At dawn there is a call: "Where are those who ask for forgiveness?" and so those people ask for forgiveness. Other people rise and pray and join them. When dawn has entered, there is another call: "Will the heedless not rise?" and they rise from their beds like the dead are brought out of their graves.'

It is related that Anas said that he heard the Prophet ﷺ say, 'Allah said, "I intended to punish the people of the earth and when I looked at those making My houses flourish, those who love one another for My sake, those who pray *tahajjud* at night and those who ask for forgiveness at dawn, I averted the punishment from them."' Makḥūl said, 'When there are fifteen men in a community asking forgiveness of Allah every day twenty-five times, Allah will not seize that community with a general punishment.' Abū Nu'aym mentioned that in *al-Ḥilyah.* Nāfi' said, 'Ibn 'Umar used to pray at night. He would ask, "Nāfi', is it dawn yet?" "No," I would answer. He would continue to pray and then ask that question. When I said, "Yes," he would sit asking for forgiveness.' Ibrāhīm ibn Ḥāṭib related that his father said, 'I heard a man in the corner of the mosque at dawn say, "O Lord! You commanded me and I obeyed. This is dawn, so forgive me." I looked and it was Ibn Mas'ūd.'

All the reports indicate that asking forgiveness should be done with the tongue and presence of the heart, and it does not mean, as Ibn Zayd said, those who pray the *Ṣubḥ* prayer in the group. Allah knows best. Luqmān said to his son, 'My son, do not let the cock be cleverer than you, calling at dawn while you are still asleep.'

The preferred form of asking forgiveness is reported by al-Bukhārī via Shaddād ibn Aws from the Prophet ﷺ: 'The best way to ask forgiveness is to say, "O Allah, You are my Lord. There is no god but You. You created me and I am Your slave. I comply with Your covenant and Your promise as much as I can. I seek refuge with you from the evil of what I have done. I acknowledge my sin, so forgive me. No one can forgive sins but You alone."' He continued, 'Anyone who says this during the day having confidence in it and dies on that day before evening will be among the people of the Garden. Anyone who says it during the night having confidence in it and dies before morning will be among the people of the Garden.' It is only in his Collection.

Abū Muḥammad 'Abd al-Ghanī ibn Sa'īd related from Ibn Lahī'ah from Abū Ṣakhr from Abū Mu'āwiyah from Sa'īd ibn Jubayr from aṣ-Ṣahbā' al-Bakrī from 'Alī ibn Abī Ṭālib that the Messenger of Allah ﷺ took 'Alī's hand and said, 'Shall I teach you some words which, if you say them and your sins are as many as the tracks of ants, or the tracks of tiny ants, Allah will forgive you for them and you will be completely forgiven. They are: "O Allah, there is no god but You. Glory be to You. I have done evil and wronged myself, so forgive me. None can forgive wrong actions but You alone."'

شَهِدَ ٱللَّهُ أَنَّهُۥ لَآ إِلَٰهَ إِلَّا هُوَ وَٱلْمَلَٰٓئِكَةُ وَأُو۟لُوا۟ ٱلْعِلْمِ قَآئِمًۢا
بِٱلْقِسْطِ ۚ لَآ إِلَٰهَ إِلَّا هُوَ ٱلْعَزِيزُ ٱلْحَكِيمُ ﴿١٨﴾

18 Allah bears witness that there is no god but Him, as do the angels and the people of knowledge, upholding justice. There is no god but Him, the Almighty, the All-Wise.

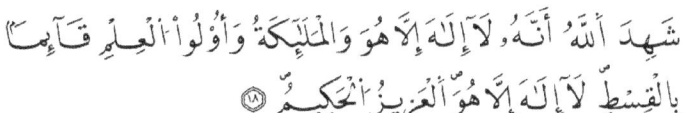

Sa'īd ibn Jubayr said, 'There were three hundred and sixty idols around the Ka'bah, and when this *āyah* was revealed, they fell down in prostration.' Al-Kalbī said, 'When the Messenger of Allah ﷺ appeared in Madīnah, two of the rabbis of Syria travelled to him and when they saw Madīnah, one of them said to the other, "This city closely resembles the description of the city of the Prophet who will come at the end of time!" When they went to the Prophet ﷺ, they recognised him by his description and asked him, "Are you Muḥammad?" "Yes," he replied. "You are Aḥmad?" they asked, and he said, "Yes." They said, "We ask you about the clear testimony. If you tell it to us, we will believe in you and affirm you." The Messenger of Allah ﷺ said to them, "Ask me." They said, "Tell us the greatest testimony in the Book of Allah." So Allah Almighty revealed to His Prophet ﷺ, *"Allah bears witness that there is no god but Him, as do the angels and the people of knowledge, upholding justice,"* and the two men became Muslim and affirmed the Messenger of Allah ﷺ.'

It is said that '*the people of knowledge*' means the Prophets. Ibn Kaysān said, 'It is the Muhājirūn and Anṣār.' Muqātil said, 'It is the believers of the People of the Book,' and as-Suddī and al-Kalbī said that it is all believers. That is most likely because it is general.

This *āyah* is evidence of the excellence of knowledge and the nobility and excellence of scholars. If anyone had been nobler than scholars, Allah would have connected them to His name and the name of his angels, as He did scholars. He said to His Prophet ﷺ about the excellence of knowledge: *'Say: "Lord, increase me in knowledge."'* (20:114) If there had been anything nobler than knowledge, then Allah would have commanded His Prophet ﷺ to ask for increase in it. The Prophet ﷺ said, 'Scholars are the heirs of the Prophets,' and 'Scholars are the trustees of Allah over His creation.' This honour for scholars is immense and their place in the *dīn* is important.

Ḥāfiẓ Abū Muḥammad 'Abd al-Ghanī transmitted from Barakah ibn Nashīṭ, who is 'Ankal ibn Ḥakārik, while the commentary is that of Barakah ibn Nashīṭ who was a *ḥāfiẓ*, from 'Umar ibn al-Mu'ammil from Muḥammad ibn Abi-l-Khaṣīb from 'Ankal from Muḥammad ibn Isḥāq from Sharīk from Abū Isḥāq from al-Barā' that the Messenger of Allah ﷺ said, 'The people of knowledge are the heirs of the Prophets. The people of the heavens love them and the fish in the sea ask for their forgiveness from the time they die up until the Day of Rising.' There is also a hadith about this from Abu-d-Dardā' that Abū Dāwūd transmitted.

Ghālib al-Qaṭṭān reported, 'I came to Kufa to trade and camped near al-A'mash and I used to go and visit him. On the night when I wanted to go to Basra he was standing doing *tahajjud* reciting this *āyah: "Allah bears witness that there is no god but Him*...(to) *Islam."* (3:18-19) Al-A'mash said, "I testify to what Allah testified and I entrust to Allah this *shahādah*, and it is in Allah's custody for me. The *dīn* with Allah is Islam." He repeated that several times. I went to him and said good-bye and then said, "I heard you recite this *āyah*. What have you heard about it? I have been with you for a year and you did not convey it to me." He said, "By Allah, I will tell it to you in a year's time." I got up and wrote that day on his door. When a year had passed, I said, "Abū Muḥammad, the year has passed." He said, "Abū Wā'il reported to me from 'Abdullāh ibn Mas'ūd that the Messenger of Allah ﷺ said, 'The one who has it will be brought on the Day of Rising and Allah will say, "My slave entrusted it to me and I am more entitled to fulfil it. Admit My slave to the Garden."'""

Abu-l-Faraj al-Jawzī said that Ghālib is Ghālib ibn Khaṭṭāf al-Qaṭṭān. He related this hadith from al-A'mash and it is *mu'ḍal* (perplexing). Ibn 'Adī said that it is weak. Aḥmad ibn Ḥanbal said that Ghālib ibn Khaṭṭāf al-Qaṭṭān is very trustworthy. Ibn Ma'īn said that he is trustworthy and Abū Ḥātim is righteous and truthful. You have enough proof of his integrity and trustworthiness in the fact that both al-Bukhārī and Muslim transmit from him in their books.

A hadith is reported from Anas in which the Prophet ﷺ said, 'If someone recites: *"Allah bears witness that there is no god but Him, as do the angels and the people of knowledge, upholding justice. There is no god but Him, the Almighty, the All-Wise"* when he goes to sleep, Allah will create 70,000 angels asking forgiveness for him until the Day of Rising.' It is said that whoever affirms this testimony firmly in his heart has established justice. It is related that Sa'īd ibn Jubayr said, 'There were three hundred and sixty idols around the Ka'bah. Each sub-tribe of the Arabs had one or two idols. When this *āyah* was revealed, the idols fell in prostration to Allah.'

Allah bears witness that there is no god but Him,

'Allah bears witness' means 'explains and informs.' Someone testifies before a judge when he makes it clear and informs about someone who owes something and who is owed it. Az-Zajjāj said, 'The witness is the one who informs about the thing and makes it clear. So Allah directs us to His Oneness by what He created and made clear.' Abū 'Ubaydah said that it means, 'Allah decides,' i.e. informs. Ibn 'Aṭiyyah, however, says that this is rejected for various reasons.

Al-Kisā'ī recited *'annahu'* and later *'anna'd-dīn'*. Al-Mubarrad said, 'What it implied is: "The *dīn* with Allah is Islam which is that there is no god but Allah."' A *bā'* which would normally be in the sentence (*bi-anna*) is elided. Islam explains the meaning of *tawḥīd*. According to al-Kisā'ī, Ibn 'Abbās recited '*innahu, anna'd-dīn'*, implying 'Allah bears witness that the *dīn* in the sight of Allah is Islam.' Then he begins a new sentence. Abū "l-Muhallab, a reciter, recited '*shuhadā'a lillāh'* in the accusative for the *ḥāl*, but '*shuhadā'u*' is also reported from him. Shu'bah related from 'Āṣim from Zirr that Ubayy related that the Prophet ﷺ used to recite, 'The *dīn* with Allah is the Ḥanīfiyyah, not Judaism, Christianity or Magianism.' Abū Bakr al-Anbārī said, 'It is evident to anyone with discrimination that these words spoken by the Prophet ﷺ are explanation and some of those who transmitted the hadith included it in the Qur'an.'

'Upholding' is in the accusative for the *ḥāl* which reinforces His Name in *'Allah bears witness'* or '*but Him'*. Al-Farrā' said that it is in the accusative for the break and so it is like the root, *al-qā'im*. When the *alif-lām* is cut off, then it is in the accusative. The reading of 'Abdullah has '*al-qā'imu bi'l-qisṭ'* as an adjective. *Qisṭ* is justice.

'There is no god but Him' is repeated because the first is in the position of a claim and testimony and the second is in the position of a ruling. Ja'far aṣ-Ṣādiq said, 'The first is a description and *tawḥīd* and the second is the notice and information, i.e. "Say: 'There is no god but Allah, the Almighty, the All-Wise.'"'

إِنَّ ٱلدِّينَ عِندَ ٱللَّهِ ٱلْإِسْلَٰمُ ۗ وَمَا ٱخْتَلَفَ ٱلَّذِينَ أُوتُوا۟ ٱلْكِتَٰبَ إِلَّا مِنۢ
بَعْدِ مَا جَآءَهُمُ ٱلْعِلْمُ بَغْيًۢا بَيْنَهُمْ ۗ وَمَن يَكْفُرْ بِـَٔايَٰتِ ٱللَّهِ فَإِنَّ ٱللَّهَ سَرِيعُ
ٱلْحِسَابِ ﴿١٩﴾

19 The *dīn* with Allah is Islam. Those given the Book only differed after knowledge had come to them, envying one another. As for those who reject Allah's Signs, Allah is swift at reckoning.

The *dīn* with Allah is Islam.

In this *āyah* '*dīn*' means obedience and religion (*millah*). Islam means faith and acts of obedience. Abu-l-'Āliyah said that and most *mutakallimūn* believe that. The basis for the different names for faith (*īmān*) and Islam is based on the hadith of Jibrīl. They can be used as synonyms, and so each of them is used for the other as we see in the hadith about the delegation of 'Abd al-Qays in which he ﷺ commanded them to believe in Allah alone. He asked, 'Do you know what faith is?' They answered, 'Allah and His Messenger know best.' He said, 'It is to testify that there is no god but Allah and that Muḥammad is the Messenger of Allah, perform the prayer, pay *zakāt*, fast Ramadān and to pay a fifth of booty.' It is the same when he ﷺ says, 'There are about seventy branches of faith: the least of which is to remove something harmful from the road and the highest of which is the words: "There is no god but Allah."' At-Tirmidhī transmitted it. Muslim added, 'Modesty is a branch of faith.' They also blend together, so that one is used and the other is meant, just as this *āyah* includes affirmation and actions, and as the Prophet ﷺ said, 'Faith is affirmation with the heart, expression on the tongue and implementation of the pillars.' Ibn Mājah transmitted it. It has already been mentioned. What is true is the first statement where the basic facts and the Sharī'ah are concerned. Anything further than that is just elaboration and Allah knows best.

Those given the Book only differed after knowledge had come to them.

Allah reports about the disagreement of the People of the Book and that it occurred when they already had knowledge of the truth and that it was due to envy and seeking this world. Ibn 'Umar and others said that. There is change in the normal linguistic order here. Al-Akhfash said that means: those who were given the Book only differed out of envy of one another after knowledge had come to them.

Muḥammad ibn Ja'far ibn az-Zubayr said, 'It is the Christians who are being referred to in this *āyah*. It is to rebuke the Christians of Najrān.' Ar-Rabī' ibn Anas said, 'What is meant are the Jews.' The expression '*those given the Book*' includes both Jews and Christians. They only differed about the Prophethood of Muḥammad ﷺ '*after knowledge had come to them,*' meaning the clarification of his description and Prophethood in their Books. It is also said that it means: 'those who were given the Gospel only differed about 'Īsā, and split into sects, after the knowledge had reached them that Allah is one and 'Īsā is the slave of Allah and His Messenger.'

'*Baghyan*' is in the accusative for the direct object or as a *ḥāl* modifying 'those'. Allah knows best.

فَإِنْ حَآجُّوكَ فَقُلْ أَسْلَمْتُ وَجْهِيَ لِلَّهِ وَمَنِ اتَّبَعَنِ ۗ وَقُل لِّلَّذِينَ أُوتُوا الْكِتَٰبَ
وَالْأُمِّيِّۦنَ ءَأَسْلَمْتُمْ ۚ فَإِنْ أَسْلَمُوا فَقَدِ اهْتَدَوا ۖ وَّإِن تَوَلَّوْا فَإِنَّمَا عَلَيْكَ
الْبَلَٰغُ ۗ وَاللَّهُ بَصِيرٌ بِالْعِبَادِ ٢٠

20 If they argue with you, say, 'I have submitted myself completely to Allah, and so have all who follow me.' Say to those given the Book and those who have no Book, 'Have you become Muslim?' If they become Muslim, they have been guided. If they turn away, you are only responsible for transmission. Allah sees His slaves.

If they argue with you, say, 'I have submitted myself (lit. my face) completely to Allah'

This means: 'If they argue using false statements and errors, then base yourself on what you are duty bound to believe and convey, and Allah will help you.' *'My face'* means 'myself' as in the hadith, 'I (literally "my face") have prostrated to the One who created me and formed me.' It is said that here 'face' means intention. This was already discussed in full in *al-Baqarah*. The first is more likely. 'Face' is used to designate the entire Essence since it is the noblest part of the person and the focus of the senses. A poet said:

I have submitted myself ('my face') to the One to Whom
the clouds bearing rain submit.

Proficient *mutakallimūn* say that His words *'the Face of your Lord will remain'* (55:27) mean the Essence. It is said that it is action by which His pleasure (face) is intended.

In *'who follow me'* the 'who' is in the position of the nominative, added to the 'I' in 'I have submitted', meaning 'those who follow me have submitted'. It is possible that it is added to the nominative pronoun without stressing the gap between them. Nāfi', Abū 'Amr and Ya'qūb keep the *yā'* in 'follow me' as in the root. The rest elide it, following the written Qur'an where it is written without a *yā'*.

Say to those given the Book and those who have no Book, 'Have you become Muslim?'

"Those given the Book" means the Jews and Christians and *"those who have no Book"* means those who have no Scripture, in other words the Arab idolaters. *'Have you become Muslim?'* is a question which needs affirmation and also implies a command, meaning, 'Become Muslim.' Aṭ-Ṭabarī and others said that. Az-Zajjāj says that it is a threat, and this is good because the meaning then is: 'Have you become Muslim or not?' The expression is then used in the past tense to stress the report about them being guided. It is said that the words *'you are only responsible for transmission'* were abrogated by *jihād*. Ibn 'Aṭiyyah said that this requires having knowledge of the history of its revelation. As for the apparent meaning of the revelation of these *āyahs* about the delegation of Najrān, the meaning is: 'You must convey what has been revealed to you about fighting and other things.'

إِنَّ ٱلَّذِينَ يَكْفُرُونَ بِـَٔايَٰتِ ٱللَّهِ وَيَقْتُلُونَ ٱلنَّبِيِّـِٔنَ بِغَيْرِ حَقٍّ
وَيَقْتُلُونَ ٱلَّذِينَ يَأْمُرُونَ بِٱلْقِسْطِ مِنَ ٱلنَّاسِ فَبَشِّرْهُم بِعَذَابٍ
أَلِيمٍ ﴿٢١﴾ أُو۟لَٰٓئِكَ ٱلَّذِينَ حَبِطَتْ أَعْمَٰلُهُمْ فِى ٱلدُّنْيَا وَٱلْءَاخِرَةِ
وَمَا لَهُم مِّن نَّٰصِرِينَ ﴿٢٢﴾

21 As for those who reject Allah's Signs, and kill the Prophets without any right to do so, and kill those who command justice, give them news of a painful punishment. 22 They are the ones whose actions come to nothing in this world or the Next World. They will have no helpers.

As for those who reject Allah's Signs and kill the Prophets

Abu-l-'Abbās al-Mubarrad said, 'Some of the tribe of Israel had Prophets come to them and call them to Allah, but they killed them. Some believers came afterwards and commanded them to submit and they killed them too. It was about them that this *āyah* was revealed.' So Ma'qil ibn Abī Miskīn said, 'The Prophets used to come to the tribe of Israel without a Book and they killed them. Some people who followed them stood and commanded justice and were killed.' Ibn Mas'ūd reported that the Messenger of Allah ﷺ said, 'Evil are people who kill other people who command to justice. Evil are people who do not command the right and forbid the wrong. Evil are people among whom a believer has to dissemble.' Abū 'Ubaydah ibn al-Jarrāḥ reported that the Prophet ﷺ said, 'The tribe of Israel killed forty-three Prophets at the beginning of the day in one hour; one hundred and twelve of the worshippers of the tribe of Israel rose and commanded the right and forbade the wrong and they killed them all at the end of the day. They are mentioned in this *āyah*.' Al-Mahdawī and others mentioned this. Shu'bah related from Abū Isḥāq from Abū 'Ubaydah that 'Abdullāh said, 'The tribe of Israel used to kill seventy Prophets on a single day and then set up their vegetable market at the end of the day. If someone says that those who were being warned about this did not actually kill a Prophet, the answer is that they agreed with those who did the killing and so they were in the same position as them. They also sought the Prophet ﷺ and his Companions and wanted to kill them. Allah says about them: *"When those who disbelieve were plotting against you to imprison you or kill you."* (8:30)'

This *āyah* indicates that commanding the right and forbidding the wrong was mandatory for past nations. It is the lesson of the Message and the caliphal task of

Prophethood. Al-Ḥasan reported that the Messenger of Allah ﷺ said, 'Whoever commands the right or forbids the wrong is Allah's caliph on His earth and the caliph of His Messenger and the caliph of his Book.' Durrah bint Abī Lahab said, 'A man came to the Prophet ﷺ when he was on the minbar and asked, "Who is the best of people, Messenger of Allah?" He replied, "The one who commands the right and forbids the wrong, has the most fear of Allah, and maintains his ties of kinship."'

We read in the Revelation: *'The men and women of the hypocrites are as bad as one another. They command what is wrong and forbid what is right.'* (9:67) Then Allah says: *'The men and women of the believers are friends of one another. They command what is right and forbid what is wrong.'* (9:71) Allah made the fact of commanding the right and forbidding the wrong the measure of the difference between the believers and the hypocrites. This indicates that the most specific of the believer's qualities is commanding the right and forbidding the wrong, and their summit is calling to Islam and fighting for it. Commanding the right is not suitable for everyone. The ruler undertakes it since he establishes the *ḥudūd* and he punishes according to his opinion and imprisons, exiles or banishes. In every town he sets up a strong righteous man with knowledge and trustworthiness and commands him to see that the *ḥudūd* are carried out, but without excess. Allah says: *'...those who, if We establish them firmly on the earth, will establish the prayer and pay zakāt, and command the right and forbid the wrong.'* (22:41)

The people of the *Sunnah* say that it is not a precondition for the one who forbids the wrong to be upright, as opposed to innovators who say, 'Only the upright can do it.' This is discarded because justice is only found in a few people while commanding the right and forbidding the wrong is general to all people. If they counter with the words of Allah: *'Do you order people to devoutness and forget yourselves?'* (2:44) and: *'It is abhorrent to Allah that you should say what you do not do'* (61:3) and the like, they are told, 'Censure here is about committing what is forbidden, not forbidding the wrong. There is no doubt that the prohibition is uglier when it comes from someone who does what is prohibited than from someone who does not do it.' That is why he will go around in Hell like a donkey around a millstone as we explained in *al-Baqarah* (2:44).

The Muslims agree about what Ibn 'Abd al-Barr mentioned: that when there is something wrong, it is an obligation on everyone who is able to do it to change it. If changing it is only a matter of censure which does not lead to harm that should not prevent them from changing it. If someone cannot change it physically, then they should do so with their tongue. If they cannot do that, then with their heart if they can do no more than that. If someone objects with their heart, they have done what they must do if they cannot do more than that.

The hadiths from the Prophet ﷺ very often stress commanding the right and forbidding the wrong, but that is limited to one's ability. Al-Ḥasan said, 'If someone speaks to a believer, he hopes for a good result. If he speaks to someone ignorant, it is to teach him. If someone draws his sword or whip and says, "Fear me! Fear me!" then you should have nothing to do with him.' Ibn Mas'ūd said, 'It is enough for a man, when he sees something objectionable which he cannot change, that Allah knows that he dislikes it in his heart.' Ibn Lahī'ah related from al-A'raj from Abū Hurayrah that the Messenger of Allah ﷺ said, 'It is not lawful for a believer to humble himself.' They asked, 'Messenger of Allah, what is humbling oneself?' He replied, 'Exposing himself to affliction which he cannot bear.' Ibn Mājah transmitted this from 'Alī ibn Zayd ibn Jid'ān from al-Ḥasan ibn Jundub from Ḥudhayfah from the Prophet ﷺ. Something can be said about both transmissions.

It is related that one of the Companions said, 'When a man sees something wrong which he cannot do anything about, he should say three times, "O Allah, this is wrong." Then he has done what he must.' Ibn al-'Arabī claimed that if someone hopes to remove a wrong but fears that if he does that he will be beaten or killed, most scholars say that he is permitted to embark on that in the face of that uncertainty. If he does not hope to remove it, then what is the point? Then he added, 'What I believe is that if someone is sincere in his intention, he should embark on doing it without caring about the consequences.' This differs from the consensus which Abū 'Umar mentioned. This *āyah* indicates that it is permitted to command the good and forbid the wrong even if one fears being killed. The Almighty says: *'Command what is right and forbid what is wrong and be steadfast in the face of all that happens to you.'* (31:17) This alludes to being harmed.

The Imāms relate that Abū Sa'īd al-Khudrī said, 'I heard the Messenger of Allah ﷺ say, "Whoever of you sees something wrong should change it with his hand; if he cannot, then with his tongue; if he cannot, then with his heart, and that is the weakest form of belief."'

Scholars say that changing with the hand is for the rulers, with the tongue for the scholars and with the heart for the weak, i.e. common people. If the wrong can be removed with the tongue by forbidding it, then one should do that. If the only way to achieve it is through punishment and killing, it should be done. If it can be removed without killing, then it is not permissible to kill. This is taken from the words of the Almighty: *'Fight the attackers until they revert to Allah's command.'* (49:9) That is the basis for what scholars say about when a person defends himself against someone who attacks their person, or property, or the person and property of someone else: someone may do that and nothing can be held against him. If Zayd sees 'Umar trying to take Bakr's property, he must defend it if the owner is unable to do so or is not happy about it. It is said that the people of any town containing the following four individuals are protected from affliction: a just ruler who does not wrong, a scholar who is on the path of guidance, shaykhs who command the right and forbid the wrong and encourage seeking knowledge and the Qur'an, and women who are covered and do not display themselves in the way they used to in the Jāhiliyyah.

Anas ibn Mālik said, 'The Messenger of Allah ﷺ was asked, "When will we abandon commanding the right and forbidding the wrong?" He replied, "When there appears among you what appeared among earlier communities." We asked, "Messenger of Allah, what appeared among the nations before us?" He replied, "When power is in the hands of your young people, lewdness in your great people, and knowledge in your base people."' Zayd said that this means that knowledge is with the impious. Ibn Mājah transmitted it. More about this will come in *al-Mā'idah*, Allah willing. The meaning of the expression '*come to nothing*' was mentioned in *al-Baqarah*.

أَلَمْ تَرَ إِلَى الَّذِينَ أُوتُوا نَصِيبًا مِّنَ الْكِتَابِ يُدْعَوْنَ إِلَىٰ كِتَابِ
اللَّهِ لِيَحْكُمَ بَيْنَهُمْ ثُمَّ يَتَوَلَّىٰ فَرِيقٌ مِّنْهُمْ وَهُم مُّعْرِضُونَ ﴿٢٣﴾

23 Do you not see those who have been given a portion of the Book being invited to let Allah's Book be the judge between them? But then a group of them turn away.

Ibn 'Abbās said, 'This *āyah* was revealed because the Messenger of Allah ﷺ entered the Jewish study house where there was a group of Jews and called them to Allah. Nu'aym ibn 'Umar and al-Ḥārith ibn Zayd asked him, "What religion are you following, Muhammad?" The Prophet ﷺ replied, "I follow the religion of Ibrāhīm." They said, "Ibrahīm was a Jew." The Prophet ﷺ said, "Bring the Torah. It is between us and you." They refused and this *āyah* was revealed.'

An-Naqqāsh mentioned that it was revealed because a group of Jews denied the Prophethood of Muḥammad ﷺ. The Prophet ﷺ told them, 'Bring the Torah. There is a description of me in it.' They refused. Most recite 'judge' as '*yaḥkuma*' while Abū Ja'far Yazīd ibn al-Qa'qā' recited '*yuḥkama*'. The first reading is better because of what is in 45:29.

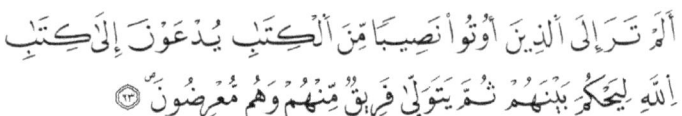

This *āyah* contains proof of the obligation of someone summoned to present his case before the judge because he has been called to the Book of Allah. If he does not do it, he opposes what is specifically incumbent on him in terms of restraining people by discipline. This occurs with us in Andalusia and the Maghrib, but not in Egypt. This ruling is explained in *Sūrat an-Nūr: 'When they are summoned to Allah and His Messenger so that he can judge between them, a group of them immediately turn away ... No, it is simply that they are wrongdoers.'* (24:48-50)

Az-Zahrāwī reported from al-Ḥasan that the Messenger of Allah ﷺ said, 'If someone's opponent calls him to a Muslim judge and he does not respond, he is a wrongdoer with no right.' Ibn al-'Arabī said that this hadith is false but the words 'he is a wrongdoer' are sound but the words 'with no right' are not sound. It is possible that it means he is based on something that is not right. Ibn Khuwayzimandād al-Mālikī said, 'It is mandatory for everyone who is summoned to the assembly of the judge to respond as long as he does not know the judge to be impious or known to have enmity towards the claimant or defendant.'

It contains evidence that the laws of the Sharī'ahs that came before us are binding on us except for what we know to be abrogated, and it is mandatory for us to judge by the laws of the Prophets before us as will be clarified. We do not read the Torah or act on what is in it because it is not in the possession of those who are trustworthy regarding it and because they have changed it. If we know that something in it has not been altered or changed, then it would be permitted for us to recite it. It is related that 'Umar said to Ka'b, 'If you know that it is the Torah which was revealed to Mūsā ibn 'Imrān, I will recite it.' He knew what had not been changed in it and that is why he called them to judge by it. It is said that the *āyah* was revealed about that and Allah knows best.

ذَٰلِكَ بِأَنَّهُمْ قَالُوا۟ لَن تَمَسَّنَا ٱلنَّارُ إِلَّآ أَيَّامًا مَّعْدُودَٰتٍ ۖ وَغَرَّهُمْ فِى
دِينِهِم مَّا كَانُوا۟ يَفْتَرُونَ ٢٤

24 That is because they say, 'The Fire will only touch us for a number of days.' Their inventions have deluded them in their *dīn*.

This indicates their turning away, turning their backs and being deluded in what they said, as in their words, *'We are Allah's children and His loved ones.'* (5:18) The meaning of the expression *'a number of days'* was discussed in *al-Baqarah*.

فَكَيْفَ إِذَا جَمَعْنَاهُمْ لِيَوْمٍ لَا رَيْبَ فِيهِ وَوُفِّيَتْ كُلُّ نَفْسٍ مَا كَسَبَتْ وَهُمْ
لَا يُظْلَمُونَ ﴿٢٥﴾

25 But how will it be when We gather them all together for a Day about which there is no doubt? Every self will be paid in full for what it earned. They will not be wronged.

This is addressed to the Prophet ﷺ and his community by way of restraint and wonder: 'How will they be, or what will they do, when they are gathered on the Day of Rising and the falseness of those lies they told in this world is unmasked and they are repaid for what they earned by their disbelief, audacity and wrongdoing?' The *lām* connected to 'Day' means 'on (a Day)' according to al-Kisā'ī. The Basrans say that it means 'for the reckoning of a Day'. Aṭ-Ṭabarī said: 'for what will happen on a Day.'

قُلِ اللَّهُمَّ مَالِكَ الْمُلْكِ تُؤْتِي الْمُلْكَ مَنْ تَشَاءُ وَتَنْزِعُ الْمُلْكَ مِمَّنْ تَشَاءُ
وَتُعِزُّ مَنْ تَشَاءُ وَتُذِلُّ مَنْ تَشَاءُ بِيَدِكَ الْخَيْرُ إِنَّكَ عَلَىٰ كُلِّ شَيْءٍ قَدِيرٌ ﴿٢٦﴾

26 Say, 'O Allah! Master of the Kingdom! You give sovereignty to whomever You will You take sovereignty from whomever You will. You exalt whomever You will You abase whomever You will. All good is in Your hands. You have power over all things.

'Alī reported that the Prophet ﷺ said, 'When Allah wanted to reveal the *Fātiḥah* of the Book, the *Āyat al-Kursī*, and *"Say, 'O Allah! Master of the Kingdom …'* to *'… without any reckoning',"* they were suspended from the Throne and there was no veil between them and Allah. They said, "Our Lord, do not send us down to the abode of wrongdoing and to those who disobey You." Allah said, "By My Sight and My Majesty, no one will recite you after every prayer, but that I will make him dwell in the Preserve of Sanctity for doing that and look at him with My hidden Eye seventy times day and grant seventy of his needs every day, the least of which is forgiveness, and give him refuge from every enemy and help him, and nothing but death keeps him from entering the Garden."'

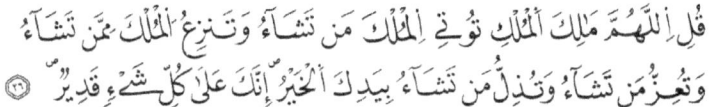

Mu'ādh ibn Jabal said, 'One day I was prevented from being with the Prophet ﷺ and did not pray *Jumu'ah* with him. He asked, "Mu'ādh! What kept you from the *Jumu'ah* prayer?" I answered, "Messenger of Allah, I owe the Jew, Yuḥannā ibn Bārā, an *ūqiyyah* of gold and he is waiting for me at my door. I feared he would keep me from you." He said, "Mu'ādh, do you want Allah to settle your debt for you?" "Yes," I replied. He said, "Say every day: *'Say, "O Allah! Master of the Kingdom …to… without any reckoning"* (3:27), You are the All-Merciful and Most Merciful to this world and the Next. You give of them to whomever You wish and deny them to whomever You wish. Settle My debt for me!" Even if you owe the like of this world in gold, Allah will settle it for you.'"

Ḥāfiẓ Abū Nu'aym transmitted that 'Aṭā' al-Khurasānī reported that Mu'ādh ibn Jabal said, 'The Messenger of Allah ﷺ taught me some *āyahs* of the Qur'an – or words – which are such that there is no Muslim on the earth who uses them for supplication when he is distressed by debt, but that Allah will settle it for him and alleviate his worry. I reckon that he mentioned it from the Prophet ﷺ.' It is a *gharīb* hadith of 'Aṭā' who has it *mursal* from Mu'ādh.

Ibn 'Abbās and Anas ibn Mālik said, 'When the Messenger of Allah ﷺ conquered Makkah and promised his community the kingdoms of Persia and Byzantium, the hypocrites and Jews said, "Unlikely! Unlikely! How can Muḥammad lay claim to Persia and Byzantium! They are too mighty and unassailable for that! Are not Makkah and Madīnah enough for Muḥammad so that now he desires the kingdoms of Persia and Byzantium?" Then Allah revealed this *āyah.'*

It is said that it was revealed to refute the falsehood of the Christians of Najrān when they said that 'Īsā was God. That is because it is evident to every person with a sound nature that 'Īsā did not possess any of these qualities. Ibn Isḥāq said, and Allah knows best, that this *āyah* is about their obstinacy and disbelief and that 'Īsā was given Signs from Allah as proof of his Prophethood that took the form of bringing the dead to life and other things while Allah alone is the One who does these things as He says: *'You give sovereignty to whomever You will. You take sovereignty from whomever You will. You exalt whomever You will. You abase whomever You will,'* and *'You merge the night into the day. You merge the day into the night. You bring the living from the dead. You bring out the dead from the living. You provide for whomever You will without any reckoning.'* If 'Īsā had been God, he would have done that and that would have been considered a sign.

Say, 'O Allah! Master of the Kingdom!

Grammarians disagree about *'Allahumma'* while they agree that the *hā'* has a *ḍammah*, the *mīm* is double with a *fatḥah* and that it is vocative. It is also found with a single *mīm* as we see in a poem of al-A'shā. Al-Khalīl, Sībawayh and all the Basrans say that the root is: *'Yā 'llāhu'* and when the verb is used without the vocative particle *'yā'*, they replace it with this doubled *mīm*. These two *mīms* replace the two letters *yā-alif.* The *ḍammah* on the *hā'* is the *ḍammah* of the noun which is in the singular vocative. Al-Farrā' and the Kufans believe that the root is *'Yā 'llāhu ummanā bi-khayr'* (O Allah, lead us in good) and there is elision and the two words mixed together. The *ḍammah* on the *hā'* is the *ḍammah* of *'ummanā'* and when the *hamzah* is elided, then the vowelling moves. An-Naḥḥās says that according to the Basrans this is a grave error and that the best position on that is what al-Khalīl and Sībawayh said. Az-Zajjāj said, 'It is impossible to omit the *ḍammah,* which indicates the singular vocative, and the *ḍammah* of *'umm'* to be put onto the name of Allah. This is denial of the name of Allah Almighty.' Ibn 'Aṭiyyah said, 'This is an error on the part of az-Zajjāj. He claimed that he had never heard, *"Yā Allāhu umm"* and that the Arabs do not say, *"Ya-llahumma."*'

The Kufans say that the vocative particle is added to *'Allahumma'* as *'Yā Allahumma'* and quote poems illustrating that. [Poetry] They state that if the *mīm* had replaced the vocative particle, they would not be together. Az-Zajjāj said, 'This is aberrant and it is not known who said it. One does not abandon what is in the Book of Allah and all the collection of the Arabs.' [POETRY] The Kufans said that a single *mīm* is added to some words, but not a double *mīm.*

Some grammarians say that what the Kufans said is an error because if it had been as they said, it would be necessary to only say *'Allahumma'* alone because there is a supplication with it, but you say, *'Allahumma-r-Razzāq'.* If it had been as they claim, then the two would have been separated.

An-Naḍr ibn Shumayl said, 'Whoever says, *"Allahumma"* has called on Allah with all His Names.' Al-Ḥasan said, '*"Allahumma"* is a comprehensive supplication.'

Qatādah said, 'I heard that the Prophet ﷺ asked Allah to give his community the kingdom of Persia and Allah revealed this *āyah.*' Muqātil said, 'The Prophet ﷺ asked Allah to give him the kingdoms of Persia and Byzantium as part of his community and Allah taught him to make this supplication.'

'Master' is a second vocative according to Sībawayh. It is like Allah's words: *'Say: "O Allah, Originator of the heavens and the earth."'* (39:46) He says that it cannot describe *'Allahumma,'* but Muḥammad ibn Yazīd and Ibrāhīm ibn as-Sarī az-Zajjāj disagreed and said that in syntax it is an adjective of the name of Allah and the same is true of 39:46.

The word *'mulk'* here means Prophethood according to Mujāhid. It is said it means victory, and it is said that it means wealth and slaves. Az-Zajjāj said that it refers to the master of people and what they own. It is said that it means the Master of this world and the Next. It is also said that sovereignty means faith and Islam, meaning, 'You give it to whomever You wish.' The same is true of what follows as there is some natural elision in the words. [Poetry] Az-Zajjāj says that it means that Allah does whatever He wishes with people.

You exalt whomever You will. You abase whomever You will.

'Exalt' means to make high, overcoming and conquering as in the phrase: *'He got the better of me* ('azzanī) *with his words.'* (38:23) *'Abase'* is to cause to be overcome, overpowered and conquered. Ṭarafah said:

> A man slow in noble affairs, quick in what is unseemly,
> humiliated in the gathering of the men, an outcast.

All good is in Your hands.

This means that all good and evil is in Your hands, and there is some elision in the words. It is said that 'good' is singled out because it is what people supplicate for and desire. An-Naqqāsh said that it means victory and booty.

The people of indications said that Abū Jahl was very wealthy but was cast into the well at Badr. The poor – Ṣuhayb, Bilāl and Khabbāb – had no wealth; their wealth was faith. *'Say: "O Allah! Master of the Kingdom! You give sovereignty to whomever You will."'* The Messenger was an orphan in the care of Abū Ṭālib in the beginning and then he later called to the bodies thrown into the pit: 'O 'Utbah! O Shaybah! *"You exalt whomever You will and You abase whomever You will."'* He was referring to Ṣuhayb and Bilāl. 'Do not believe that We denied you in this world because We hate you.'

You have power over all things.

His blessing is universal and He gives blessing to whomever He wishes.

تُولِجُ ٱلَّيْلَ فِي ٱلنَّهَارِ وَتُولِجُ ٱلنَّهَارَ فِي ٱلَّيْلِ وَتُخْرِجُ ٱلْحَىَّ مِنَ ٱلْمَيِّتِ وَتُخْرِجُ
ٱلْمَيِّتَ مِنَ ٱلْحَىِّ وَتَرْزُقُ مَن تَشَآءُ بِغَيْرِ حِسَابٍ ٢٧

27 You merge the night into the day. You merge the day into the night. You bring out the living from the dead. You bring out the dead from the living. You provide for whoever You will without any reckoning.'

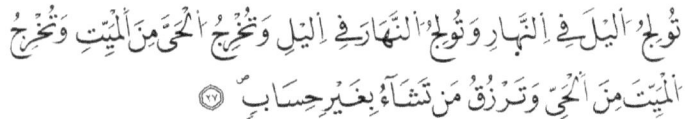

Ibn 'Abbās, Mujāhid, al-Ḥasan, Qatāda and as-Suddī said that *'merging the day into the night…'* means 'We put the decrease of one into the lengthening of the other and so if the night has fifteen hours, which is longer, the day has nine hours, which is shorter.' *'Merge the day into the night'* is the same. That is what al-Kalbī said, and it is related from Ibn Mas'ūd. It is also possible that the words simply mean that the night and day follow one another. One goes and then the other comes.

Commentators disagree about the meaning of *'You bring out the living from the dead.'* Al-Ḥasan said that it means: 'bring the believer out from the unbeliever and the unbeliever from the believer.' Something similar is related from Salmān al-Fārisī. Ma'mar related from az-Zuhrī that the Prophet ﷺ went to his wives and found a woman of beautiful appearance there. He asked, 'Who is this?' They answered, 'One of your aunts.' He asked, 'Who is she?' They replied, 'Khālidah bint al-Aswad ibn 'Abd Yaghūth.' The Prophet ﷺ said, 'Glory be to the One who brings the living from the dead!' She was a righteous woman and her father was an unbeliever.

What is meant by this is the death of the heart of the unbeliever and life of the heart of the believer, and so life and death are used metaphorically. Some scholars believe that life and death here are real. 'Ikrimah said, 'It is the emergence of the live chick from the egg which is dead, and the emergence of the egg, which is dead, from the live chicken.' Ibn Mas'ūd said that it is the sperm, which is dead, that emerges from the man who is alive, and the man who emerges living from it when it itself is dead. 'Ikrimah and as-Suddī also said, 'It is the grain from ear and the ear from the grain. The kernel emerges from the palm tree and the palm tree emerges from the kernel. Life is likened to the palm and the ear.' *'You provide for whoever You will'* means without constriction or stinting, as in 'He gives without reckoning.'

لَا يَتَّخِذِ الْمُؤْمِنُونَ الْكَافِرِينَ أَوْلِيَاءَ مِن دُونِ الْمُؤْمِنِينَ وَمَن يَفْعَلْ
ذَٰلِكَ فَلَيْسَ مِنَ اللَّهِ فِي شَيْءٍ إِلَّا أَن تَتَّقُوا مِنْهُمْ تَقِيَّةً وَيُحَذِّرُكُمُ اللَّهُ
نَفْسَهُ وَإِلَى اللَّهِ الْمَصِيرُ ﴿٢٨﴾

28 The believers should not take unbelievers as friends rather than believers. Anyone who does that has nothing to do with Allah at all – unless it is because you are afraid of them. Allah advises you to be afraid of Him. Allah is the final destination.

The believers should not take unbelievers as friends rather than believers.

Ibn 'Abbās said, 'Allah forbade the believers to be friendly towards the unbelievers and take them as friends.' This accords with His words: *'Do not take any outside yourselves as intimates.'* (3:118) The words: *'He has nothing to do with Allah'* means that he is not part of the party of Allah or among His friends. It is like the words in *Surah Yusuf*: '*...ask the town*' (12:82). Then Allah makes an exception:

unless it is because you are afraid of them.

Mu'ādh ibn Jabal and Mujāhid said, 'This is *taqiyyah* in the Path of Islam before the Muslims were strong. Today, however, Allah has made Islam strong so that there is no need to dissemble before the enemy.' Ibn 'Abbās said, 'It is that someone says something with his tongue while his heart is in fact at peace in faith. Such a person should not be killed and does not commit a wrong action.' Al-Ḥasan said, '*Taqiyyah* is permissible for human beings until the Day of Rising but *taqiyyah* may not be used as a justification for killing.' Jābir ibn Zayd, Mujāhid and aḍ-Ḍaḥḥāk recited '*taqiyyah*' rather than '*tuqāh*'.

It is said that if a believer is abiding among the unbelievers, he can flatter them with his tongue, if he fears for himself, as long as his heart is at peace with faith. *Taqiyyah* is only lawful when there is fear of being killed, amputation or great injury. If someone is forcibly compelled to disbelief, the sound position is that he can be firm and refuse to articulate disbelief, but it is permitted for him to do that as will come in *an-Naḥl*, Allah willing. Ḥamzah and al-Kisā'ī pronounce '*tuqāh*' with *imālah* while the rest make it emphatic. The root of '*tuqāh*' is '*wuqayah*' on the measure *fu'alah* and the *wāw* has been changed into a *tā'* and the *yā'* into an *alif*.

Aḍ-Ḍaḥḥāk reported from Ibn 'Abbās that this *āyah* was revealed about 'Ubādah ibn aṣ-Ṣāmit al-Anṣārī, who was a godfearing man who had been at the Battle of Badr. He had an alliance with the Jews. When the Prophet ﷺ went out on the Day of the Parties, 'Ubādah said, 'Prophet of Allah, I have five hundred men of the Jews with me. I thought that they should come out with me and I can use them to defeat the enemy.' Allah revealed, '*The believers should not take...*' It is also said that it was revealed about 'Ammār ibn Yāsir when he said some of what the unbelievers forced him to say as will be mentioned in *an-Naḥl*.

Allah advises you to beware of Him.

Az-Zajjāj said, 'Allah cautions you about Himself." The Almighty says, quoting the words of Sayyidina 'Isa: '*You know what is in my self but I do not know what is in Your Self.*' (5:116) It means: 'You know what I have and what my reality is but I do not know what You have and what Your reality is.' Others say that it means to be afraid of His punishment. '*You know what is in my self*' is what is concealed of me. '*Allah is the final destination*' means that the end will be Allah's repayment of one's actions. This affirms the Resurrection.

قُلْ إِن تُخْفُوا مَا فِي صُدُورِكُمْ أَوْ تُبْدُوهُ يَعْلَمْهُ اللَّهُ وَيَعْلَمُ مَا فِي السَّمَاوَاتِ
وَمَا فِي الْأَرْضِ وَاللَّهُ عَلَىٰ كُلِّ شَيْءٍ قَدِيرٌ ﴿٢٩﴾

29 Say, 'Whether you conceal what is in your breasts or make it known, Allah knows it. He knows what is in the heavens and what is on earth. Allah has power over all things.'

He knows the secrets in the hearts and what they contain as well as what is in the heavens and the earth. He is the Knower of the unseen worlds and nothing whatsoever is hidden from Him.

يَوْمَ تَجِدُ كُلُّ نَفْسٍ مَّا عَمِلَتْ مِنْ خَيْرٍ مُّحْضَرًا وَمَا عَمِلَتْ مِن سُوءٍ تَوَدُّ لَوْ أَنَّ بَيْنَهَا
وَبَيْنَهُ أَمَدًا بَعِيدًا وَيُحَذِّرُكُمُ اللَّهُ نَفْسَهُ وَاللَّهُ رَءُوفٌ بِالْعِبَادِ ﴿٣٠﴾

30 On the Day that each self finds the good it did, and the evil it did, present there in front of it, it will wish there were an age between it and then. Allah advises you to beware of Him. Allah is Ever-Gentle with His slaves.

The word *'Day'* is in the accusative as it is governed by the verb in *'Allah advises you'* while some say it is connected to *'Allah is the final destination'* or to *'Allah has power over all things.'* It is possible for it to be a stop and imply an elided 'Remember the day...' It is like Allah's words: *'Allah is Almighty, Exactor of Revenge. On the Day the earth is changed.'* (14:47-48) The word *'present'* is a *ḥāl* modifying an elided pronoun from the connective *mā*. It implies: 'On the Day each self finds the good it did present.' This is on the basis that the verb *wajada* means 'to find', as one finds a lost camel. The second *mā* is added to the first, and the words *'it will wish'* is a *ḥāl* modifying the second *mā*.

If you make *'tajid'* mean 'you know', then *'present'* is the second object, and *'wish'* is also in the position of a second object. It would imply: On the Day that each self knows the repayment for what it did present before it.' It is permitted for the second *mā* to be in the nominative by the inceptive and *'wish'* to be in the nominative as the predicate of the inceptive and it is not permitted then for *mā* to mean repayment because *'wish'* is then nominative. If it had been in the past tense, it could be repayment and the words would mean: 'Any evil you did, you will wish that there had been an age between it and that,' in other words like the distance between the east and west. When the future has *mā* as a precondition, it is only in the jussive. It would imply the elision of a *fā'*, and would imply: whatever evil it did, *then* it would wish. Abū 'Alī said, 'In my view it is analogous to what al-Farrā' said about His words, exalted is He, "*If you obeyed them you would* then *be idolators*" (Sūrat al-An'ām 6:121) that it is based on the elision of the *fā'*.'

'Amad' (age) is the end and the plural is *āmād*. 'One says, 'He overcame the leader (*istawla-l-amad*).' An-Nābighah said:

Except one like you or one you precede
as the steed comes first when overcoming the leader.

Amad also means anger, and the verb *amida* is to be angry.

قُلۡ إِن كُنتُمۡ تُحِبُّونَ ٱللَّهَ فَٱتَّبِعُونِي يُحۡبِبۡكُمُ ٱللَّهُ وَيَغۡفِرۡ لَكُمۡ ذُنُوبَكُمۡۚ وَٱللَّهُ
غَفُورٞ رَّحِيمٞ ٣١

31 Say, 'If you love Allah, then follow me and Allah will love you and forgive you for your wrong actions. Allah is Ever-Forgiving, Most Merciful.'

Ḥubb and *maḥabbah* mean 'love' as does *'ḥibb'*, which can also mean 'beloved' like *khidn* and *khadīn*. Both *aḥabba* and *ḥabba* are verbs meaning 'to love'. When one says *aḥabbahu* the one loved is *muḥabb* and when one says *ḥabbahu, yaḥibbuhu* the one loved is *maḥbūb*. Al-Jawharī said that this is aberrant because a passive participle does not have a *kasrah* on the middle letter. Abu-l-Fatḥ said, 'The root in it is *ḥabuba* and the *bā'* is silent and elided into the second. Ibn ad-Dahhān Sa'īd said that there are two dialectical usages of *ḥabba*: *ḥabba* and *aḥabba*. The evidence that here it is *aḥabba* is that the same form is also used in 5:54 and 3:31. *Ḥabba* relates to *fa'ula* because of the saying *ḥabīb* and to *fa'ila* because of the saying *maḥbūb*. There is no active participle of *ḥabba* and so one never says, 'I am a *ḥābb*.' The passive participle of the IV form only occurs rarely, such as his words:

...with me he has the rank of the honoured beloved (*muḥabb*).

Abu Zayd cited *ḥababtuhu uḥibbuhu* and recited:

For by Allah if not for his dates I would not have loved (*ḥababtuhu*) him
and he was not less than 'Uwayf and Hāshim.

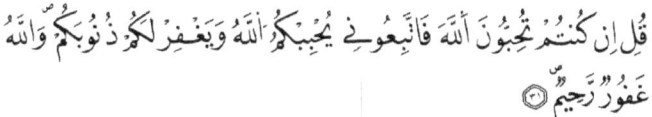

And he recited:

By your life, I and the demands of a great metropolis
are like the one who grows in distance because of what he loves (*ḥabba*).

Al-Aṣma'ī cited *fatḥah* on the letter of the present/future along with *yā'* alone (*yaḥabbu*).

Ḥubb is also the name for a jar in Persian which has been arabicised. Its plural is *ḥibāb* and *ḥibabah*. Al-Jawharī said that.

The *āyah* was revealed about the delegation of Najrān when they claimed that what they alleged about 'Īsā was out of love for Allah. Al-Ḥasan and Ibn Jurayj said that it was revealed about some of the People of the Book who said, 'We are those who love our Lord.' It is related that the Muslims then said, 'O Messenger of Allah, by Allah, we love our Lord,' and so Allah revealed this.

Ibn 'Arafah said, 'Love (*maḥabbah*) with the Arabs means desire for the thing while aiming for it.' Al-Azharī said, 'A person's love for Allah and His Messenger is to obey them and follow their commands. Allah says: *"If you love Allah, then follow me."* Allah's love for the slave is shown by His blessing them with forgiveness. When Allah says: *"Allah does not love the unbelievers,"* (3:32) He means that He will not forgive them.'

Sahl ibn 'Abdullāh said, 'The sign of love of Allah is love of the Qur'an. The sign of love of the Qur'an is love of the Prophet ﷺ. The sign of the love of the Prophet ﷺ is love of the Sunnah. The sign of love of Allah, love of the Qur'an, love of the Prophet and love of Sunnah is love of the Next World. The sign of love of the Next World is that one loves oneself. The sign of love of oneself is to hate this world. The sign of hatred of this world is to only take from it enough provision to suffice your needs.'

It is related from Abu-d-Dardā' that the Messenger of Allah ﷺ said about: *'Say, "If you love Allah, then follow me and Allah will love you"'*: that it constituted piety, *taqwā*, humility and abasement of the self. Abū 'Abdullāh at-Tirmidhī transmitted it.

It is related that the Prophet ﷺ said, 'Anyone who wants Allah to love him must speak the truth, hand over trusts to their owners and not harm his neighbour.' We find in *Ṣaḥīḥ Muslim* that Abū Hurayrah reported that the Messenger of Allah ﷺ said, 'When Allah loves a person, He calls out to Jibrīl and says, "I love so-and-so, so love him," and so Jibril loves him. Then a call goes out among the people of heaven, "Allah loves so-and-so, so love him!" and the people of heaven love him. Then acceptance is placed in the earth for him. When He hates a person, He calls out to Jibrīl and says, "I hate so-and-so, so hate him." So Jibrīl hates him. Then a call goes out among the people of heaven, "Allah hates so-and-so, so hate him!"

and they hate him. Then hatred is placed in the earth for him.' More of this will be mentioned in *Sūrat Maryam,* Allah willing.

Abū Rajā' al-'Uṭāridī recited *'yaḥbubkum'*. 'Forgive you' is added to 'love you'. Maḥbūb related that Abū 'Amr ibn al-'Alā' elided the *rā'* at the end of *'yaghfir'* into the *lām* of *'lakum'*. An-Naḥḥās stated that al-Khalīl and Sībawayh do not permit the *rā'* to be elided into the *lām*. Abū 'Amr is too esteemed to err about such matters. Perhaps he lowered the vowel as he does in many places.

قُلْ أَطِيعُوا۟ ٱللَّهَ وَٱلرَّسُولَ ۖ فَإِن تَوَلَّوْا۟ فَإِنَّ ٱللَّهَ لَا يُحِبُّ ٱلْكَٰفِرِينَ ٣٢

32 Say, 'Obey Allah and the Messenger.' Then if they turn away, Allah does not love the unbelievers.

Part of the clarification of this will come in *an-Nisā'*. The phrase: *'...if they turn away'* is a precondition but not inflected because it is in the past tense. It implies: if they turn to their disbelief and turn away from obeying Allah and His Messenger. The clause: *'Allah does not love the unbelievers'* means that He is not pleased with their actions and will not forgive them.

He said *'fa-inna-llāha'* and not *'innahu'* because when the Arabs exalt something, they mention it again as Sībuwayh quotes:

I do not see death. Nothing gets ahead of death.
  Death disturbs both the wealthy and poor.

إِنَّ ٱللَّهَ ٱصْطَفَىٰٓ ءَادَمَ وَنُوحًا وَءَالَ إِبْرَٰهِيمَ وَءَالَ عِمْرَٰنَ عَلَى ٱلْعَٰلَمِينَ ٣٣

33 Allah chose Ādam and Nūḥ and the family of Ibrāhīm and the family of 'Imrān over all other beings –

Allah chose Ādam and Nūḥ

'Iṣṭafā' means 'to choose'. This implies: 'Allah chose their *dīn*,' which is the *dīn* of Islam. Az-Zajjāj says, 'He chose them for Prophethood over the people of their times.'

It is said that the name 'Nūḥ' is derived from *nāḥa* (to mourn). It is a foreign name but is inflected normally because it has three letters. He was the Shaykh of the Messengers and the first Messenger whom Allah sent to the people of the earth after Ādam. He prohibited marriage with daughters, sisters, aunts and all close relatives. Some historians said that Idrīs was before him, but that is weak as will be explained in *Sūrat al-A'rāf*.

and the family of Ibrāhīm and the family of 'Imrān over all other beings

The meaning of *'āl'* (family) was discussed in *al-Baqarah*. We find in al-Bukhārī that Ibn 'Abbās said, 'The family of Ibrāhīm and the family of 'Imrān include the believers of the family of Ibrāhīm, the family of 'Imrān, the family of Yāsīn and the family of Muḥammad. Allah says: *"The people with the strongest claim to Ibrāhīm are those who followed him and this Prophet and those who believe."* (3:68)' It is said that the family of Ibrāhīm is Ismā'īl, Isḥāq, Ya'qūb and the Tribes, and that Muḥammad ﷺ was part of the family of Ibrāhīm. It is said that the family of Ibrāhīm was just himself and the same is true of the family of 'Imrān. Affirming this is the words of the Almighty: *'...certain relics left by the families of Mūsā and Hārūn.'* (2:248) We also find in a hadith, 'I was given one of the flutes of the family of Dāwūd.' A poet said:

Do not weep for a dead person after the death
of the one loved by 'Alī, 'Abbās and the family of Abū Bakr.

Another said:

He suffers from the mention of Laylā's family (*āl*),
as a healthy person suffers from a sting.

He means the one who remembers Laylā herself.

It is said that the family of 'Imrān is the family of Ibrāhīm, and it is said that it means 'Īsā because his mother was the daughter of 'Imrān. It is said that it was 'Imrān himself. Muqātil said that 'Imrān was the father of Mūsā and Hārūn, and his name was 'Imrān ibn Yaṣhur ibn Qāhāt ibn Lāwī ibn Ya'qūb. Al-Kalbī says that 'Imrān was the father of Maryam, and he was a descendant of Sulaymān. As-Suhaylī says that he was 'Imrān ibn Mātān whose wife was Ḥannah. He singled out these Prophets for mention because the Prophets and Messengers are according to their genus and their genus is from their offspring. 'Imrān is not declined because of the *'ān'* at the end of it.

The phrase *'over all other beings'* refers to the people of their time according to commentators. Abū 'Abdullāh Muḥammad ibn 'Alī at-Tirmidhī al-Ḥakīm says that it means all creatures. It is said that it means all creatures until the Day the Trumpet is sounded. That is because the Prophets and Messengers are the elect of creation. Muḥammad ﷺ exceeds the rank of being chosen because he is also a beloved and a mercy. The Almighty says: *'We only sent you as a mercy to the worlds.'* (21:107) The other Messengers are created for mercy while the character of Muḥammad ﷺ himself was mercy. That is why he was security for creatures: when Allah sent him, creation was safe from the punishment until the time the

Trumpet is sounded. The other Prophets did not have this position. That is why the Prophet ﷺ said, 'I am a guiding mercy.' So he said that he himself was mercy for creation from Allah and from Allah for creation.

It is said that Ādam was chosen by Allah for five things. The first was his creation by the Hand of Allah in the best form. The second was that He taught him all the names. The third was the command to the angels to prostrate to him. The fourth was that He let him live in the Garden. The fifth is that He made him the father of mankind.

Allah chose Nūḥ for five things. The first was that He made him the father of mankind because all the rest were drowned and only his descendants remained. The second was his long life. It is said, 'Bliss to the one who lives a long life and has good actions.' The third that He answered his prayer about the unbelievers and believers. The fourth is that He carried him in the ship. The fifth is that he was the first to abrogate laws, because before this it was not forbidden to marry aunts.

Allah also chose Ibrāhīm for five things. The first was that He made him the father of the Prophets because it is related that a thousand Prophets descended from him. The second is that He took him as a friend. The third is that He saved him from the Fire. The fourth is that He made him an imam for people. The fifth is that He tested him with instructions and gave him success in carrying them out.

Since Mūsā and Hārūn were the sons of 'Imrān, Allah chose them since He sent manna and quail down for his people, which no other Prophet had. If it is the father of Maryam, He chose Maryam to bear 'Īsā without a father which happened to no one else in the world. Allah knows best.

ذُرِّيَّةً بَعْضُهَا مِنۢ بَعْضٍ وَٱللَّهُ سَمِيعٌ عَلِيمٌ ﴿٣٤﴾

34 descendants one of the other. Allah is All-Hearing, All-Knowing.

The meaning of '*descendants*' was already discussed in *al-Baqarah*. It is in the accusative for the *ḥāl* as al-Akhfash said, meaning descendants from the descendants of others. The Kufans say that there is a stop. Az-Zajjāj says that it is an appositive, i.e. He chose some of their descendants from others.

The words '*one of the other*' can either refer to actual descent or to the fact that they help one another. We see the same usage in 9:67 were the hypocrites assist one another in misguidance as al-Ḥasan and Qatādah said. It is also said that it refers to being selected and chosen and given Prophethood. It is said that it is actual physical descendants of one another, but this is the weakest view.

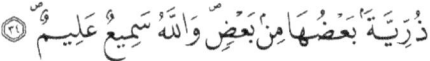

إِذْ قَالَتِ ٱمْرَأَتُ عِمْرَٰنَ رَبِّ إِنِّى نَذَرْتُ لَكَ مَا فِى بَطْنِى مُحَرَّرًا فَتَقَبَّلْ مِنِّىٓ ۖ إِنَّكَ أَنتَ ٱلسَّمِيعُ ٱلْعَلِيمُ ﴿٣٥﴾ فَلَمَّا وَضَعَتْهَا قَالَتْ رَبِّ إِنِّى وَضَعْتُهَآ أُنثَىٰ وَٱللَّهُ أَعْلَمُ بِمَا وَضَعَتْ وَلَيْسَ ٱلذَّكَرُ كَٱلْأُنثَىٰ ۖ وَإِنِّى سَمَّيْتُهَا مَرْيَمَ وَإِنِّىٓ أُعِيذُهَا بِكَ وَذُرِّيَّتَهَا مِنَ ٱلشَّيْطَٰنِ ٱلرَّجِيمِ ﴿٣٦﴾

35 Remember when the wife of 'Imrān said, 'My Lord, I have pledged to You what is in my womb, devoting it to Your service. Please accept my prayer. You are the All-Hearing, the All-Knowing.' 36 When she gave birth, she said, 'My Lord! I have given birth to a girl' – and Allah knew very well what she had given birth to, male and female are not the same – 'and I have named her Maryam and placed her and her children in Your safekeeping from the accursed Shayṭān.'

Remember when the wife of 'Imrān said.

Abū 'Ubaydah said that the '*when*' is redundant. Muḥammad ibn Yazīd said: 'It implies "remember when".' Az-Zajjāj said, 'The meaning is: "He chose the family of 'Imrān when the wife of 'Imrān said..."' She was Ḥannah bint Fāqūd ibn Qunbul, the mother of Maryam and grandmother of 'Īsā. It is not an Arabic name and Ḥannah is not known in Arabic as a woman's name. However, we do find Abū Ḥannah al-Badrī, but it is said that his name is Abū Ḥabbah, and that is sounder. His name was 'Āmir. Dayr Ḥannah is in Syria and there is another place called that which Abū Nuwās mentions in a poem.

Ḥabbah is frequently used as a name in Arabic. That includes Abū Ḥabbah al-Anṣārī, and Abu-s-Sanābil ibn Ba'kak mentions Ḥabbah in the hadith of Subay'ah. Khannah is only known in the daughter of Qāḍī Yaḥyā ibn Aktham. She was the mother of Muḥammad ibn Naṣr. Jannah is only known in Abū Jannah, the maternal uncle of Dhu-r-Rummah the poet. All of that is in the book of Ibn Mākūlā.

My Lord, I have pledged to You what is in my womb, devoting it to Your service.

The meaning of *nadhr* (pledge, vow) was already discussed. A vow is something which a person imposes on himself which he was not obliged to do. It is said that when she was pregnant the mother of Maryam said, 'If Allah saves me and I give birth to what is in my womb, I will devote him to Him.' *'Laka'* means 'to Your service.' *'Muḥarrar'* is an adverbial *ḥāl* or an adjective of something elided.

It means: 'I have pledged to You what is in my womb as a boy devoted to You.'

The first is more consistent with the commentary, context and syntax. In respect of syntax, it is putting the adjective in place of what is described which is not permitted in certain places while it is permitted metaphorically in other places. In respect of commentary, it is said that the reason for what 'Imrān's wife said was that she was old and had not given birth. They were the people of a house devoted to Allah and one day she was sitting in the shade of a tree and saw a bird feeding its young and she felt tender and yearned for a child because of seeing that bird. She prayed to Allah to give her a child and she vowed that she would give up the child to serve Him, meaning that he would be a servant of the temple devoted to worship of Allah. That was permitted in their law, and the children were bound to fulfil the vow of their parents. She bore a girl, and a girl was not fitting for temple service either because of being subject to menstruation and the impurity involved or because of not being cut out for mixing with men. She had hoped that it would be a boy that she could devote to His service.

Ibn al-'Arabī said, 'There is no disagreement that 'Imrān's wife did not impose an actual vow on her pregnancy because she was free. There is no disagreement that a person cannot make a vow on behalf of their child, whatever their circumstances. If the one making a vow is a slave, nothing he says in that respect is affirmed. If he is free, it is not sound that he should dictate his child's future. The same is true of a woman. So in what way was it a vow? Allah knows best, but people desire a child for company, help and solace, so this woman asked for a child for company and solace. When Allah granted her that, she vowed to abandon her share of the child's company. That was based on serving Allah. This is the vow of the free pious ones. She wanted him to be devoted from both aspects, free from the servitude of this world and being occupied with it. One of the Sufis said to his mother, "Mother, let me belong to Allah, to worship Him and learn knowledge." She said, "Yes." So he set out until he had an insight and then he returned to her and knocked on the door. She said, "Who is it?" He told her, "Your son, so-and-so." She answered, "We left you to Allah and will not return to you."'

Muḥarrar (devoting) is derived from *ḥurriyah* (freedom), the opposite of slavehood. From this root comes *taḥrīr* (editing) of a book, which is to purify it of confusion and unsoundness. Khaṣīf related from 'Ikrimah and Mujāhid that *muḥarrar* is someone who is sincerely devoted to Allah with nothing of this world sullying him. This is a known linguistic usage. Someone who is sincere is called '*ḥurr*' and '*muḥarrar*' which both have the same meaning.

When she gave birth, she said, 'My Lord! I have given birth to a girl.'

Ibn 'Abbās said, 'She said this because only males are accepted in fulfilment of the vow she had made and Allah had accepted Maryam.' It is said she raised her until she was grown up and then sent her. Ashhab related that from Mālik. It is said that she put her in her wrapping and sent her to the temple and fulfilled her vow straightaway. Perhaps they did not have segregation then as was also the case at the beginning of Islam. Al-Bukhārī and Muslim reported that a black woman used to sweep the mosque in the time of the Prophet ﷺ and then died.

Allah knew very well what she had given birth to.

If it is read as *waḍa'tu* ('I have given birth to'), it is connected to the rest of her words. That is the reading of Abū Bakr and Ibn 'Āmir. It contains the idea of submission to Allah, humility and to put Him above having anything hidden from Him. It is not a report because Allah's knowledge of everything is confirmed in the heart of the believer. She said that to exalt Allah. In the reading of the majority (*waḍa'at*), it is part of the words of Allah. It implies that it is after: *'I have placed her and her children in Your safekeeping from the accursed Shayṭān.'* Allah knew very well what she had given birth to. Al-Mahdawī said that. Makkī said that it is information from Allah to us by way of confirmation. Allah knew what Maryam had given birth to, whether or not she said it. This is strengthened by the fact that, if it is part of the words of Maryam, it is like the words, 'You know best what I have given birth to' because she called to Him at the beginning of her words: *'My Lord, I have given birth to a girl.'* It is related from Ibn 'Abbās as *'waḍa'ti* ('You have given birth to'), and so this was said to her.

male and female are not the same

Some of the Shāfi'īs use this as evidence that if a woman obeys her husband and has intercourse in the daytime in Ramaḍān, they are not the same with regard to the obligation of *kaffārah*. Ibn al-'Arabī said, 'This is foolishness. This is a report about a Law before you and they do not say that. This righteous woman intended to clarify her situation. She had vowed her son to the service of the temple. When she found it was a girl, she excused herself to her Lord for things being different to what she had intended.'

'I have named her Maryam'

An-Naḥḥās said that 'Maryam' is not inflected because it is a foreign noun which means 'servant of the Lord' in their language. The words: *'her children'* refer to 'Īsā; the word *'dhurriyah'* can be used for both the plural and singular. We find in *Ṣaḥīḥ Muslim* from Abū Hurayrah that the Messenger of Allah ﷺ said, 'Every child who is born is pricked by Shayṭān on the day he is born and so it cries out – except for Maryam and her son.' Then Abū Hurayrah added, 'Recite, if you like: *"I have placed her and her children in Your safekeeping."*'

Our scholars said, 'The point of this hadith is that Allah answered the supplication of Maryam's mother. Shayṭān pricks all of the children of Ādam, even the Prophets and *awliyā'*, except for Maryam and her son. A veil was put between them and the prick hit the veil but none of it pierced through it.' Our scholars observed, 'Even if that was the case, it is false that only the two of them are singled out for it, nor does this oblige that the prick of Shayṭān causes misguidance and error in the person pricked. That is a false supposition. Shayṭān often presented forms of corruption and error to the Prophets and *awliyā'*, but Allah protected them from what Shayṭān cast as He says: *"You have no authority over any of My slaves."* (15:42) Moreover, each of the descendants of Ādam has a companion from the *shayṭāns* assigned to him as was stated by the Messenger of Allah ﷺ. So even if Maryam and her son were protected from the prick, they were not protected from Shayṭān clinging and being attached to them. Allah knows best.

فَتَقَبَّلَهَا رَبُّهَا بِقَبُولٍ حَسَنٍ وَأَنۢبَتَهَا نَبَاتًا حَسَنًا وَكَفَلَهَا زَكَرِيَّآءُ كُلَّمَا دَخَلَ
عَلَيْهَا زَكَرِيَّآءُ الْمِحْرَابَ وَجَدَ عِندَهَا رِزْقًا قَالَ يَٰمَرْيَمُ أَنَّىٰ لَكِ هَٰذَا قَالَتْ
هُوَ مِنْ عِندِ اللَّهِ إِنَّ اللَّهَ يَرْزُقُ مَن يَشَآءُ بِغَيْرِ حِسَابٍ ﴿٣٧﴾ هُنَالِكَ
دَعَا زَكَرِيَّآءُ رَبَّهُ قَالَ رَبِّ هَبْ لِي مِن لَّدُنكَ ذُرِّيَّةً طَيِّبَةً إِنَّكَ سَمِيعُ الدُّعَآءِ ﴿٣٨﴾

37 Her Lord accepted her with approval and made her grow in health and beauty. And Zakariyyā became her guardian. Every time Zakariyyā visited her in the Upper Room, he found food with her. He said, 'Maryam, how did you come by this?' She said, 'It is from Allah. Allah provides for whoever He wills without any reckoning.' 38 Then and there Zakariyyā called on his Lord and said, 'O Lord, grant me by Your favour an upright child. You are the Hearer of Prayer.'

Her Lord accepted her with approval and made her grow in health and beauty.

This means 'He let her travel the path of the fortunate' as Ibn 'Abbās said. Some people say that it refers to caring for her upbringing. Al-Ḥasan said that it means He did not punish her for a moment, night or day.

The phrase: *'He made her grow in health and beauty'* means that Allah made her physique proportionate without lack or excess. In a single day, she grew the amount a child would normally grow in a year. *'Qabūl'* (accepted) and *'nabāt'* (grow) are verbal nouns other than the ones that would normally be used with a verb in Forms IV and V. [Illustrative poems omitted] The copy of the Qur'an of Ibn Mas'ūd has *'anzala-l-malā'ikata tanzīlan'* because *nazzala* and *anzala* mean the same. Al-Mufaḍḍal said that it means, 'He made her grow beautifully.' It is more fitting to take the meaning we mentioned. The root of approval (*qabūl*) is *qubūl* because it is a verbal noun like *dukhūl* and *khurūj*, and the *fatḥah* is used in few letters, like *walū'* and *wazū'*. It is only these three. Abū 'Amr, al-Kisā'ī and the imams said that. Az-Zajjāj allowed *qubūl* based on the root.

Zakariyyā became her guardian.

He adopted her. Abū 'Ubaydah said that he was responsible for her care. The Kufan reading is '*kaffala*' (Form II) which is transitive, taking two objects, and means: 'Zakariyyā was made her guardian,' by Allah who decreed that and made it easy for him. Ubayy's copy of the Qur'an has the verb in Form IV (*akfalahā*) which has a similar meaning to Form II. It is also transitive, and the two verbs before it are also in Form IV. So Allah is speaking about Himself and what he did with her. That is why it is in Form II.

The rest read it as *kafala*, ascribing the action to Zakariyyā and so Allah informs us that Zakariyyā undertook her care and guardianship as indicated by His words: *'...which of them would be the guardian of Maryam'* (3:44). Makkī said that it is preferred because Form II derives from Form I because when when Allah made Zakariyyā her guardian, he became her guardian at Allah's command and because what he did was by Allah's will and decree. So the two readings are intermeshed.

Hārūn ibn Mūsā ibn Kathīr and Abū 'Abdullāh al-Muzanī related '*kafilahā*'. Al-Akhfash said that one can say *kafala, yakfulu*, and *kafila, yakfalu*, and I have not heard *kafula* although it has been mentioned.

Ḥafṣ, Ḥamzah and al-Kisā'ī recite Zakariyyā without *maddah* or *hamzah* while the rest have a *maddah* and *hamzah* as Zakariyā'. The people of Hijaz say Zakariyyā'. The people of Najd elide the *alif* and say 'Zakariyy'. There are four dialectical usages. Abū Ḥātim said 'Zakariyyu' without inflection because it is a foreign name. This is an error because a name with a *yā'* in it like this is inflected, like *kursiyy* and Yaḥyā. If it is read with a *maddah* and short, it is not inflected because there is a feminine *alif* in it, it is foreign and definite.

Every time Zakariyyā visited her in the Upper Room, he found food with her.

The word *miḥrāb* linguistically denotes the noblest place in an assembly, and it will be dealt with more fully in *Sūrah Maryam*. Tradition tells us that she was in an upper room and that Zakariyyā visited her by way of a ladder. 'Adī ibn Zayd said:

When I came to the lady of the *miḥrāb*,
I only reached her by climbing a ladder.

Abū Ṣāliḥ related from Ibn 'Abbās that 'Imrān's wife became pregnant when she was old and made a vow that the child would be devoted to the temple. 'Imrān said to her, 'What on earth have you done? What if it is a girl?' They were both distressed about that. Then 'Imrān died while Ḥannah was pregnant and she bore a girl and Allah accepted her. Only boys were devoted to the temple, so the rabbis used their reeds, with which wrote they down the Revelation, to draw lots for her care. Zakariyyā became her guardian and found a place for her. When she was older, he arranged an upper room for her which was reached by a ladder. He hired a wet-nurse for her and she used to lock the door and only Zakariyyā went to her until she was an adult. When she menstruated, he moved her to his house and she stayed with her aunt, the wife of Zakariyyā, as al-Kalbī says. Muqātil says that her sister was the wife of Zakariyyā. When she was pure and had purified herself, he took her back to the room. Some of them say that she did not menstruate but was free from that.

When Zakariyyā visited her, he found her with winter fruit in the summer and summer fruit in the winter. He said: *'Maryam, how did you come by this?' She answered, 'It is from Allah.'* That made Zakariyyā yearn for a child and he said, 'The One who brings her this can also give me a child.'

The preposition *'annā'* means 'from where' as Abū 'Ubaydah said. An-Naḥḥās said, 'This is somewhat negligent because *'ayna'* asks about place and *'annā'* asks about direction and method. It means: 'From where and how did this come to you?' Al-Kumayyat distinguished between them:

How (*annā*) and from where (*ayna*) did rapture affect you
when there is no youthful passion or doubt?

As for the words: *'Allah provides…'* It is possible that Maryam said this or that it is Allah speaking. That was the reason for the supplication of Zakariyyā to ask for a child.

Then and there Zakariyyā called on his Lord.

'There' (*hunālika*) can be used for time and place although its basic use is in reference to place. Al-Mufaḍḍal ibn Salamah said that *hunālika* is about time and *hunāka* is about place, but one can be used in place of the other.

grant me by Your favour an upright child.

The word '*hab*' means 'give'. *Dhurriyyah* can be singular or plural, male or female. Here it is singular. This is indicated by Allah's words: '*...give me an heir* (walī) *from You*' (19:5) where He uses the singular, not the plural *awliyā'*. '*Ṭayyibah*' is in the feminine because of '*dhurriyah*'. This sort of usage is seen in:

Your father another khalīfah bore him
And you are a khalifah with that perfection.

Where *khalīfah* is referred to with a feminine verb (*waladat*).

It is related from Anas that the Prophet ﷺ said, 'If a man dies leaving righteous offspring, Allah will give him the same reward for their actions without that diminishing their rewards at all.' The derivation of *dhurriyyah* was discussed in *al-Baqarah*. '*Ṭayyibah*' here means righteous and blessed. The words: '*You are the Hearer of prayer*' means 'You accept the prayer.' We find confirmation of that in the expression: 'Allah hears whoever praises Him.'

This *āyah* is evidence that one can ask for a child. It is the *sunnah* of the Messengers and those who are true. The Almighty says: '*We sent Messengers before you and gave them wives and children too.*' (11:38) We find in *Ṣaḥīḥ Muslim* that Sa'd ibn Abī Waqqāṣ said that 'Uthmān ibn Maz'un wanted to be celibate and the Messenger of Allah ﷺ forbade it. He said, 'If he had permitted it, we would have castrated ourselves.' Ibn Mājah transmitted from 'Ā'ishah that the Messenger of Allah ﷺ said: 'Marriage is part of my *Sunnah*, and whoever does not act by my *Sunnah* is not with me. Marry. I will have more numbers than other nations by you. If someone is wealthy, he should marry. If he has no wealth, he should fast. It is a shield.' This is a refutation of those who say that someone who wants a child is stupid. Allah reports that Ibrāhīm said: '*Make me highly esteemed among the later peoples*' (26:84) and He says: '*Those who say, 'Our Lord, give us joy in our wives and children.*' (25:74)

Al-Bukhārī has a chapter on asking for children. The Prophet ﷺ asked Abū Ṭalḥah when his son died, 'Did you make love to your wife in the night?' 'Yes,' he answered. He said, 'May Allah bless you in the result of your night.' She became pregnant. We find in al-Bukhārī that Sufyān said that a man of the Anṣār said, 'I saw nine children, all of whom recited the Qur'an.' There is also a chapter on 'Supplication for many children with blessing.' Anas ibn Mālik said that Umm

Sulaym said, 'Messenger of Allah, pray to Allah for your servant Anas.' He said, 'O Allah, give him much wealth and many children and bless him in what You give him.' The Prophet ﷺ said, 'O Allah, forgive Abū Salamah, elevate his rank among the guided and give him successors among his descendants.' Al-Bukhārī and Muslim transmitted it. The Prophet ﷺ said, 'Marry a loving fertile woman. I will have the largest of the nations by you.' Abū Dāwūd transmitted it.

There are many reports like this which encourage people to seek to have children since a person hopes to gain benefit by that in his life and after his death. The Prophet ﷺ said, 'When one of you dies, his actions come to an end except for three,' and he mentioned 'a righteous child who prays for him.' If there had only been this hadith, that would have been enough.

Since this is established, it is obligatory for the human being to make supplication to his Creator to guide his children and spouse to success, guidance, righteousness and chastity and that they help him in his *dīn* and in worldly things so that he has great benefit from them in this world and the Hereafter. Do you not see that Allah says: '*...make him, my Lord, pleasing to You*' (19:6) and '*...give us joy in our wives and children.*' (25:74) The Messenger of Allah ﷺ prayed for Anas: 'O Allah, give him much wealth and many children and bless him in it.' Al-Bukhārī and Muslim transmitted this. That is enough.

فَنَادَتْهُ الْمَلَائِكَةُ وَهُوَ قَائِمٌ يُصَلِّي فِي الْمِحْرَابِ أَنَّ اللَّهَ يُبَشِّرُكَ بِيَحْيَىٰ
مُصَدِّقًا بِكَلِمَةٍ مِّنَ اللَّهِ وَسَيِّدًا وَحَصُورًا وَنَبِيًّا مِّنَ الصَّالِحِينَ ﴿٣٩﴾

39 The angels called out to him while he was standing in prayer in the Upper Room: 'Allah gives you the good news of Yaḥyā, who will come to confirm a Word from Allah, and will be a leader and a celibate, a Prophet and one of the righteous.'

The angels called out to him

Ḥamzah and al-Kisā'ī recited '*fa-nādāhu*' with the *alif* for the masculine and *imālah* because its root is a *yā'*. Ibn 'Abbās and Ibn Mas'ūd read it with an *alif* and Abū 'Ubayd preferred it. It is related from Jarīr that Mughīrah ibn Ibrāhīm said that 'Abdullāh [ibn Mas'ūd] used the masculine for the angels throughout the Qur'an. Abū 'Ubayd said, 'We think that he preferred that in order to be different from the idolaters who said that the angels were the daughters of Allah.'

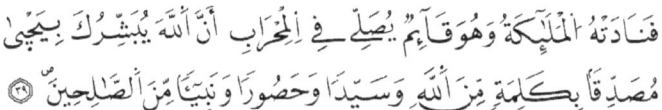

An-Naḥḥās said, 'This argument is worthless because the Arabs use both feminine and masculine verbs with "men" as well as with "women", so how can that be used as an argument in the Qur'an? If it had been permitted to use this in the Qur'an as an argument against them, it would have been permitted for them to use in argument the words of Allah: *"When the angels said* (qālat)." The argument against them is: *"Were they present at their creation* (hum)?" (43:19) So how can they say that they are female when it is known that this is mere opinion and whim?" *'Nādāhu'* is permitted in the masculine plural and *nādāthu* is permitted because 'group' is feminine.

Makkī said, *'Malā'ikah* (angels) is a broken plural for sentient beings and the feminine is used as it is for those who are not sentient. Using the feminine *hiya*, you say, "They (*hiya*) are men. They are palm stumps. They are camels." You use the feminine and say, "The Bedouins said." This is strengthened by its usage here and elsewhere in the Qur'an (6:93, 13:23) So both masculine and feminine are good.

As-Suddī said that it was Jibrīl alone, and that is found in the reading of Ibn Mas'ūd. It says in *an-Naḥl: 'He sends down angels with the Rūḥ'* (16:2) and He means Jibrīl and the *Rūḥ* is the revelation. It is permitted in Arabic to use the plural for a single person. We see that in the Revelation (3:173) where the plural refers to Nu'aym ibn Mas'ūd. It is also said that all the angels called to him. That is what is most apparent. It means that the call came from them.

while he was standing in prayer in the Upper Room: 'Allah gives you the good news of Yaḥyā

'Anna-llāh' means *'bi-anna-llāh'*. Ḥamzah and al-Kisā'ī read *'inna,'* meaning 'The angels say that Allah…' The people of Madīnah read *'yubashshiruka'* while Ḥamzah reads *'yabshuruka'*. The same is true of Ḥumayd ibn al-Qays al-Makkī who has *'yubshiruka'*. The meaning is the same. They are three dialectal possibilities with the same meaning. The evidence for the first is the majority recitation that this is in the past tense or a command. There are many examples of this in the Qur'an. The second reading which is that of 'Abdullāh ibn Mas'ūd which is from *bashara, yabshuru*, which is the dialect of Tihāmah. [Poetry] The third is from *abshara, yubshiru*. [Poetry]

The name of Yaḥyā in the first Book was Ḥayā. Sārah was given her name by Ibrāhīm. In Arabic it means, 'does not give birth'. When he was given the good news of Isḥāq, he called her Sārah and Jibrīl gave her that name. She asked, 'Ibrāhīm, why did you omit a letter of my name [i.e. Sarai].' Ibrāhīm asked Jibrīl about that and he said, 'That letter will be added to the name of a descendant of hers among the best of Prophets. His name is Ḥayā and he will be called Yaḥyā.' An-Naqqāsh mentioned it. Qatādah said that he was called Yaḥyā because Allah gave him life with faith and Prophethood. Some of them said that he is called that because Allah revived people through his guidance. Muqātīl said that it is derived from the name of Allah, *al-Ḥayy* (the Living). It is said that it was because he revived the relatives of his mother.

who will come to confirm a Word from Allah.

The 'Word' is 'Īsā according to most commentators. 'Īsā is called a 'Word' because he was brought into existence by the word of Allah 'Be' without a father. Abu-s-Sammāl al-'Adawī recited '*kilmah*' throughout the Qur'an which is a classical dialectal form. It is said that he is called a Word because people are guided by him as they are guided by the words of Allah. Abū 'Ubaydah said, 'a Word from Allah' is 'a Book from Allah'. The Arabs call a *qaṣīdah* (ode) a 'word'. Many other things are said, but the first is the best known among most scholars.

Yaḥyā was the first to believe in and affirm 'Īsā. He was three years older than 'Isā, or six months is also said. They were cousins. When Zakariyyā heard his testimony, he went to him and embraced him while he was wrapped in a cloth. Aṭ-Ṭabarī said, 'When Maryam was pregnant with 'Īṣā, her sister was also pregnant with Yaḥyā. She visited her sister and said, "Maryam! Do you know that I am pregnant?" Maryam replied, "Do you know that I am also pregnant?" She said to her, "I felt what is in my womb prostrating to what is in your womb."' As-Suddī said that is acknowledgement of His words: '*...confirm a Word from Allah.*'

A 'leader' (*sayyid*) is one who leads his people and whose word is accepted. Its root is *saywid*. This indicates the permission to call a human being '*sayyid*' as one can also use '*azīz* (mighty) or *karīm* (generous) for someone. Indeed, it is related that the Prophet ﷺ said to the tribe of Qurayzah, 'Rise for your *sayyid*.'

We find in al-Bukhārī and Muslim that the Prophet ﷺ said about al-Ḥasan, 'This grandson of mine is a leader and perhaps, by him, Allah will put things right between two great parties of Muslims,' and that took place. When 'Alī was slain, more than 40,000 gave allegiance to him, including many who had not joined his father and those who broke their allegiance with him. For about seven months he was Caliph in Iraq and the lands beyond Khorasan. Then he went to Mu'āwiyah with the people of the Hijaz and Iraq while Mu'āwiyah went to him with the people of Syria. When the groups saw one another at a place called Maskin in Sawad in the region of Anbar, al-Ḥasan did not want to fight because he knew that neither side would be victorious until many of the other side had been slain and in that way the Muslims would be destroyed. He handed over authority to Mu'āwiyah with certain stipulations that he made, one of which was that he would have authority after Mu'āwiyah died. Mu'āwiyah was bound by all of that and the words of the Prophet ﷺ were verified: 'This son of mine is a leader...' There is no greater leader than one made a leader by Allah and His Messenger.

Qatādah said that '*sayyid*' means a leader in knowledge and worship. Ibn Jubayr and aḍ-Ḍaḥḥāk said, 'In knowledge and fear of Allah.' Mujāhid said, 'a noble leader.' Ibn Zayd said, 'One who is not overcome by anger.' Az-Zajjāj said, 'One who is above his peers in every type of good.' This is comprehensive. Al-Kisā'ī said, 'A *sayyid* among goats is one advanced in years.' A hadith has, '...a two-year-old sheep is better than a *sayyid* goat.' [Poetry]

'Celibate' (*ḥaṣūr*) is derived from *ḥaṣr*, meaning confinement. The verbs *ḥaṣara* and *aḥṣara* means 'to confine'. Ibn Mayyādah says:

> The shunning of Laylā was not that she kept herself far away
> From you and work did not detain (*aḥṣaratka*) you.

A she-camel that is *ḥaṣūr* has a narrow opening to a teat. A man who is *ḥaṣūr* does not go to women, as if he was held back from them. *Ḥaṣūr* and *ḥāṣir* are used for a man who is confined to bed and does not go out. One says, 'The people drank, but so-and-so was niggardly (*ḥuṣira*) with them.' [Poetry] We find in the Revelation: '*We have made Hell a prison* (ḥaṣīr) *for the unbelievers.*' (17:8) *Ḥaṣīr* is where the king sits because he is veiled from others. [Poetry] Yaḥyā was celibate because he did not approach women, as if he was kept from what men normally do, as Ibn Mas'ūd and others said, the form *fa'ūl* often having a passive meaning, as *ḥalūb* means 'milked'. [Poetry] Ibn Mas'ūd, Ibn 'Abbās, Ibn Jubayr, Qatādah, 'Aṭā, and others said that it means he does not approach women although he is able to do so.

This is the soundest of the various views for two reasons. The first is that it is praise for him, and praise is given for an acquired trait which is not generally innate. The second is because it expresses an active choice, meaning that he restrained himself from his appetites. [POEM ON VERB FORM] This might have been part of his Divine Law. Our Law, however, stipulates marriage as was already mentioned. Ibn 'Abbās, Sa'īd ibn al-Musayyab and aḍ-Ḍaḥḥāk said that *ḥaṣūr* refers to someone who has been castrated. Abū Ṣāliḥ related that Abū Hurayrah said that he heard the Messenger of Allah ﷺ say, 'Every human being will meet Allah with a sin that he has committed, for which He will either punish him or show mercy to him, except for Yaḥyā the son of Zakariyyā. He was a leader, celibate, a Prophet and one of the righteous.' It is said that it means he kept himself from disobeying Allah.

As for the expression '*one of the righteous*,' az-Zajjāj said that the righteous person is the one who practises what Allah has imposed on him and gives people their rights.

قَالَ رَبِّ أَنَّىٰ يَكُونُ لِي غُلَامٌ وَقَدْ بَلَغَنِيَ الْكِبَرُ وَامْرَأَتِي عَاقِرٌ قَالَ كَذَٰلِكَ اللَّهُ يَفْعَلُ مَا يَشَاءُ ﴿٤٠﴾

40 He said, 'My Lord, how can I possibly have a son when I have reached old age and my wife is barren?' He said, 'It will be so. Allah does whatever He wills.'

It is said that 'Lord' here means Jibrīl, and he asked Jibrīl how he could have a son. This is the view of al-Kalbī. Some say that he means Allah. '*Annā*' means 'how'. There are two points contained in this question. One is that he asked how he could have a son when he and his wife were of an age when they could not conceive, and the second is that he was asking if he would be given a son from his barren wife or from another woman. It is said that he meant: 'How can this be the case when I and my wife are in this state' out of humility.

It is related that the time between his supplication and the good news was forty years, and he was ninety when he received the good news and his wife was a similar age. Ibn 'Abbās and aḍ-Ḍaḥḥāk said that he was 120 and his wife was ninety, since the word, '*barren*', means too old to conceive. *'Āqir* (barren) can describe a man or woman. The verb is *'aqara. 'Uqr* and *'aqārah* mean 'barrenness. It is said that someone is 'barren' because it wounds (*'aqara*) lineage. Barrenness (*'uqr*) in a woman occurs when she is too old to conceive. *'Āqir* is used for a large tract of sand where nothing grows. *'Uqr* refers to the bride-price given to a woman when intercourse with her is a result of dubiousness (or likeness (i.e. to his wife)). It is also used for a cock's egg. *'Uqr* is a hearth. The *'uqr* of a fire is the middle of it and the *'aqr* of a basin is the end of it where camels stand when they arrive. It is a word with multiple meanings.

The '*kāf*' in '*kadhālika*' means: 'Allah does whatever He wishes like that.' *Ghulām* (son) is derived from *ghulmah*, which is intense desire for intercourse. [Poetry] It denotes a youth whose moustache has started to grow, or it is used for a boy up to the age of seventeen. The plurals are *ghilmah* and *ghilmān*. *Ghaylmān* is a youth or a girl as well as being a male tortoise. The verb *ightilama* describes the sea when its waves are clashing.

قَالَ رَبِّ ٱجْعَل لِّىٓ ءَايَةً قَالَ ءَايَتُكَ أَلَّا تُكَلِّمَ ٱلنَّاسَ ثَلَٰثَةَ أَيَّامٍ إِلَّا رَمْزًا ۗ
وَٱذْكُر رَّبَّكَ كَثِيرًا وَسَبِّحْ بِٱلْعَشِىِّ وَٱلْإِبْكَٰرِ ﴿٤١﴾

41 He said, 'My Lord, appoint a Sign for me.' He said, 'Your Sign is that you will not speak to people for three days, except by gesture. Remember your Lord much and glorify Him in the evening and after dawn.'

He said, 'My Lord, appoint a Sign for me.'

When he was given the good news of a son and did not think that it was not within Allah's power to bring that about, he asked for a sign by which to recognise the soundness of the matter and that it was truly from Allah, and so Allah punished him by afflicting him with the inability to speak to people after the angels had spoken to him. Most commentators have said, 'It was not an illness or muteness' which would be a form of punishment. Ibn Zayd said, 'When Zakariyyā's wife became pregnant with Yaḥyā, he could not speak to anyone. Although he recited the Qur'an and invoked Allah, he was unable to converse with anyone.'

except by gesture.

Linguistically, *ramz* (gesture) means to indicate with the lips, but it is also used for indication with the eyebrows, eyes and hands. Its basis is movement. It is said he sought that sign for increased reassurance, meaning, 'Complete the blessing by giving me a sign so that the sign will be an increase of blessing and honour.' Then he was told, 'Your Sign is that you will not speak to people for three days,' meaning that he would be unable to speak for three days. This is evidence that this was said to him after the angels gave him the good news. The words: *'I created you before, when you were nothing.'* (19:9) mean: 'I brought you into existence by My power. In the same way I will bring a son into existence for you.' An-Naḥḥās preferred this view. He said, 'Qatādah's statement about Zakariyyā being punished by not being able to speak is rejected because Allah did not inform us that he had sinned nor did He forbid him to do that. His words means: "Give me a sign to indicate the existence of a child since that is hidden from me."'

'Ramz' is in the accusative as a separated exception according to al-Akhfash, Al-Kisā'ī says that the verb is *ramaza*, *yarmuzu* and *yarmizu*. It is also recited as *'ramazan'* and *'rumuzan'* whose singular is *rumzah*.

This *āyah* is evidence for a gesture being able to take the place of words, which is found a lot in the *Sunnah*. The strongest example is found in the ruling of the

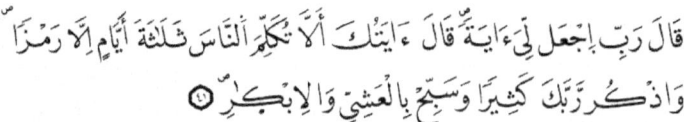

Prophet ﷺ in the case of the black woman when he asked her, 'Where is Allah?' and she indicated heaven with her head. He said, 'Free her. She is a believer.' So this shows that Islam can be confirmed by gesture, and it is the basis of religion by which blood and life are protected and the Garden and salvation from the Fire are merited. The judgment is that her belief was confirmed in the same way that it would have been if she had expressed it verbally. Therefore gesture must be similarly admissible in every other area of the *dīn*. This is the view of most *fuqahā'*.

Ibn al-Qāsim related from Mālik that when a mute person makes a gesture indicating divorce, it is binding. In the case of a man who becomes ill and his tongue is disabled, ash-Shāfi'ī said that he is like a mute person in respect of taking a wife back and divorce. Abū Ḥanīfah said, 'It is permitted if the gesture is well known. If it is not, then it is void.' That judgment is not based on analogy, but on *istiḥsān*. Analogy would entail it being invalid because he does not speak nor is his gesture understood. Abu-l-Ḥasan ibn Baṭṭāl said, 'In saying this, Abū Ḥanīfah referred to the fact that he did not know of any sunnah which permitted gestures in different rulings in the *dīn*.' Al-Bukhārī attempted to deal with this matter in his chapter, 'Chapter of gestures in divorce and other matters.' 'Aṭā' said that the words: *'You will not speak to people'* meant that he should fast for three days because when they fasted they only spoke by gesture. This, however, is unlikely, and Allah knows best.

Some people say that it is permissible for the Qur'an to be abrogated by the *Sunnah*. Zakariyyā was forbidden to speak when he was able to do so, and this was abrogated by the words of the Prophet ﷺ, 'There is no silence in the day until night.' Most scholars say that it is not abrogated because Zakariyyā was prevented from speaking by some disability which kept him from having the power to speak even though he was healthy. That is what most scholars say. Many scholars believe that the hadith means that there should be no silence where remembrance of Allah is concerned. As for prattle, there is no benefit in it and silence in respect of that is good.

Remember your Lord much and glorify Him in the evening and after dawn.'

He commands him to not abandon *dhikr* in spite of his tongue being restrained according to the first view. The meaning of *dhikr* was already discussed in *al-Baqarah*.

Muḥammad ibn Ka'b al-Quraẓī said, 'If anyone had had a licence to abandon *dhikr*, it would have been Zakariyyā since Allah says: "*You will not speak to people for three days, except by gesture. Remember your Lord much...*" and there might also have been a licence in battle but Allah says: *"When you meet a troop, stand form and remember Allah repeatedly."* (8:45) Aṭ-Ṭabarī mentioned it.

The word *'glorify'* here means 'pray' as the prayer is called glorification since it disconnects Allah from evil. *'Evening'* (*'ashiy*) is the plural of *'ashīyah*. It is also said that it is a singular. Mujāhid said that it is the time from after midday until sunset. In the *Muwaṭṭā'*, al-Qāsim ibn Muḥammad said, 'None of the people I met prayed *Ẓuhr* until well after noon.' *Ibkār* is from dawn until mid-morning.

وَإِذْ قَالَتِ ٱلْمَلَٰٓئِكَةُ يَٰمَرْيَمُ إِنَّ ٱللَّهَ ٱصْطَفَىٰكِ وَطَهَّرَكِ وَٱصْطَفَىٰكِ عَلَىٰ نِسَآءِ ٱلْعَٰلَمِينَ ﴿٤٢﴾

42 And when the angels said, 'Maryam, Allah has chosen you and purified you. He has chosen you over all other women.

Maryam, Allah has chosen you and purified you.

The words *'purified you'* refer to purification from disbelief, as Mujāhid and al-Ḥasan said. Az-Zajjāj said it means of all impurities: menstruation, lochia and other things. Allah *'chose her'* to give birth to 'Īsā over all the women of her time. Al-Ḥasan, Ibn Jurayj and others say that it means over all women until the Trumpet is sounded, and that is sound as we will explain. That is the position of az-Zajjāj and others.

The word *'chosen'* is repeated because the first time it means chosen for worship and the second chosen to bear 'Īsā. Muslim reports that Abū Mūsā said that the Prophet ﷺ said, 'There are many perfect men, but the only perfect women are Maryam daughter of 'Imrān, and Āsiyah, the wife of Pharaoh. 'Ā'ishah is preferred to other women like *tharīd* over other types of food.' Our scholars said that 'perfect' means complete. The perfection of each thing is according to what it is. Absolute perfection belongs only to Allah. There is no doubt that the most perfect human beings are the Prophets, then the *awliyā'*, then the truly sincere, then the martyrs and then the righteous. If this is confirmed, then it is said that the perfection mentioned in the hadith means Prophethood which would necessitate that Maryam and Āsiyyah were Prophets, and that is indeed said. The sound position is that Maryam was a Prophet because Allah gave Revelation to her by means of an angel in the same way that He gave Revelation to the other Prophets. This will be further discussed in *Sūrat Maryam*. As for Āsiyyah, there is no clear evidence of her Prophethood, but of her *ṣīddiqiyyah* and excellence, as will be explained in *at-Taḥrīm*.

It is related by sound paths from Abu Hurayrah that the Prophet ﷺ said, 'The best of the women of this world are four: Maryam bint 'Imrān, 'Āsiyyah bint Muzaḥam, Khadījah bint Khuwaylid and Fāṭimah bint Muḥammad.' Ibn 'Abbās reported that the Prophet ﷺ said, 'The best of the women of the Garden are: Khadījah bint Khuwaylid, Fāṭimah bint Muḥammad, Maryam bint 'Imrān and 'Āsiyyah bint Muzaḥam, the wife of Pharaoh.' Another path has: 'After Maryam, the mistress of the women of the people of the Garden will be Fāṭimah and Khadījah.'

The apparent meaning of the Qur'an and the hadiths demands that Maryam is the best of all the women of the world from Ḥawwā' to the last woman alive when the Final Hour comes. The angels conveyed to her Revelation from Allah containing responsibility, information and good news, as was conveyed to other Prophets, and so she is a Prophet, and a Prophet is better than a *walī*. Therefore she is better than all other women, first and last. Next in excellence is Fāṭimah and then Khadījah according to what is related by Ibn 'Abbās whereby the Messenger of Allah ﷺ said: 'The mistress of the women of the world is Fāṭimah, then Khadījah and then Āsiyyah.' This is a good hadith which gives rises to ambiguity.

Allah singled out Maryam for things He did not give to any other woman: the Spirit of Absolute Purity spoke to her, purified her, blew into her shirt and approached her for that breath. That happened to no other woman. She believed the words of her Lord and did not ask for any sign as proof of the good news as Zakariyyā had done. That is why Allah called her *ṣiddīqah* in the Revelation when He says *'a woman of truth'* (5:75) and: *'She confirmed the words of her Lord and His Books and was one of the obedient'* (66:12). Allah testified that she was a woman of truth and affirmed the words of the good news and testified that she was one of the obedient.

The good news was received by Zakariyyā and he then considered his old age and the barrenness of his wife and asked for a sign. Maryam received the good news of a boy and then considered her virginity and not being touched by a mortal. She was told, '*That is how it is*,' and she said nothing more and affirmed the words of her Lord and did not ask for any sign as proof. What other woman has possessed these qualities? This is why it is related that she will be among the forerunners to the Garden with the Messengers. The Prophet ﷺ said, 'If I were to take an oath, I would carry it out. Only about a dozen men will enter the Garden before the forerunners of my community. They include Ibrāhīm, Ismā'īl, Isḥāq, Ya'qūb, the tribes [i.e. Yūsuf and his brothers], Mūsā, 'Īsā and Maryam bint 'Imrān.' Allah knows best.

It is incumbent on someone who follows outward knowledge, and takes outward matters as proof of inward matters, to acknowledge the words of the Messenger of Allah ﷺ, 'I am the master of the children of Ādam, and it is no boast' and, 'On the Day of Rising the Banner of Praise will be in my hands and the keys of honour will be in my hands. I will be the first to speak, the first to intercede, the first to give good news and the first… and the first…' He only gained this leadership over the Messengers in this world by something immense inwardly. That is also the case with Maryam. She only obtained Allah's testimony in Revelation to her being a woman of truth and affirmation in words by her rank of proximity. Those who say that she was not a Prophet said that her seeing of the angel Jibrīl was the same as his being seen by the Companions in the form of Diḥyah al-Kalbī when he asked about Islam and faith. That did not make the Companions Prophets. The first view is clearer and more frequently taken. Allah knows best.

يَٰمَرۡيَمُ ٱقۡنُتِي لِرَبِّكِ وَٱسۡجُدِي وَٱرۡكَعِي مَعَ ٱلرَّٰكِعِينَ ٤٣

43 Maryam, obey your Lord and prostrate and bow with those who bow.'

This means to stand a long time in prayer, as Mujāhid said. Qatādah said that it is to be constant in obedience. The meaning of *qunūt* has already been discussed. Al-Awzā'ī said, 'When the angels said that to her, she stood in the prayer until her feet were swollen and ran with blood and pus.' Prostration is mentioned before bowing because the conjunction '*wāw*' does not necessarily imply sequence in time. The disagreement about this was mentioned in *al-Baqarah* (2:158). It is also said that that was the order in their religion (that prostration preceded bowing). *'Bow with those who bow'* means to pray like them, even if she did not pray with them. It is said that it means the group prayer. This was also already discussed in *al-Baqarah*.

ذَٰلِكَ مِنۡ أَنۢبَآءِ ٱلۡغَيۡبِ نُوحِيهِ إِلَيۡكَۚ وَمَا كُنتَ لَدَيۡهِمۡ إِذۡ يُلۡقُونَ
أَقۡلَٰمَهُمۡ أَيُّهُمۡ يَكۡفُلُ مَرۡيَمَ وَمَا كُنتَ لَدَيۡهِمۡ إِذۡ يَخۡتَصِمُونَ ٤٤

44 This is news from the Unseen which We reveal to you. You were not with them when they cast their reeds to see which of them would be the guardian of Maryam. You were not with them when they quarrelled.

This is news from the Unseen which We reveal to you.

This is referring to what Allah mentioned about Zakariyyā, Yaḥyā and Maryam. The words: *'We reveal to you'* are evidence of the Prophethood of Muḥammad ﷺ since he was reporting about Zakariyyā and Maryam without having read the previous Books and the People of the Book confirmed it. *'This'* alludes back to what has just been mentioned. Revelation (*waḥy*) is sending the Message to the Prophet ﷺ and can mean inspiration and indication and the like. Its linguistic root means 'to inform in secret' which is why inspiration is called *waḥy*. Usage of it is found in the *āyah: 'When I inspired the Disciples…'* (5:111) and: *'Your Lord revealed to the bees.'* (16:68) It is said that the words: *'inspired the Disciples'* means 'commanded them.' The verb is *waḥā* and *awḥā* and *ramā* and *armā* which mean the same. Al-'Ajjāj said:

> He revealed to it to remain stable and it remained.

Waḥy can also mean speed as we see in the hadith: 'Speed. Speed. (*al-waḥy. al-waḥy.*)' Ibn Fāris says that it means indication, writing and the message and all that entails informing whatever it is. *Waḥiyy* is quick and *waḥā* is voice.

You were not with them when they cast their reeds to see which of them would be the guardian of Maryam.

'You, Muḥammad, were not in their presence.' Reeds (*aqlām*), the plural of *qalam*, are so-called because they have been cut (*qalama*). It is said that it refers to their arrows. It is also said that it was the reeds with which they wrote the Torah, which is more excellent, since Allah forbade drawing arrows in 5:3, saying that it is 'deviance', although doing that is permissible in a different way to the way they were used in the Jāhiliyyah for gambling.

Zakariyyā said, 'I am more entitled to care for her because I am married to her maternal aunt.' He was married to Ashya' bint Fāqūd, the sister of Ḥannah bint Fāqūd, the mother of Maryam. The tribe of Israel said, 'We are more entitled. She is the daughter of our scholar.' So they drew lots. Each one brought his reed and they put them into a river and the one whose reed remained would be the guardian. The Prophet ﷺ said, 'The reeds were carried away and that of Zakariyyā rose to the top.' It was a sign for him because he was a Prophet at whose hands Signs appeared. Something else is also said in respect of the grammar of the sentence which gives the meaning: 'they were looking to see which of them would be the guardian.'

Some of our scholars use this as evidence that drawing lots is a permissible practice. It is a principle in our *Sharī'ah* for all of those who desire fairness in dividing things up. It is a *sunnah* according to the majority of *fuqahā'*, when the evidence is equal on both sides, in order to be fair, to calm hearts and to remove suspicion with respect to the allotting. No one is preferred over the other when that for which lots are drawn is the same type of thing, following the Book and the *Sunnah*. Abū Ḥanīfah and his people reject drawing lots and reject the hadiths about it and claim that there is no sense to it because it is like drawing arrows which Allah has forbidden. Ibn al-Mundhir related that Abū Ḥanīfah permitted it, saying, 'Lots are not proper by analogy, but we abandon analogy in that case and take the traditions and the *Sunnah*.'

Abū 'Ubayd points out, 'Three Prophets made use of the practice of drawing lots: Yūnus, Zakariyyā, and our Prophet, Muḥammad ﷺ.' Ibn al-Mundhir said, 'The allowance for employing the practice of drawing lots is like a consensus among the people of knowledge when deciding how things should be divided between partners and there is no sense in rejecting it.' At the end of the chapter on testimony, al-Bukhārī has 'Chapter on drawing lots in difficult cases and the words of Allah: '...*when they cast their reeds*.'' He includes the hadith of an-Nu'mān ibn Bashīr: 'The example of someone who thinks little of the limits of Allah and falls into them is like some people who draw lots on a boat...' This hadith will be discussed in *al-Anfāl* and in *az-Zukhruf*. Al-Bukhārī also has the hadith of Umm al-Alā' when the Anṣār drew lots for the lodging of the Muhājirūn, and the lot of 'Uthmān ibn Maẓ'ūn went to them, and the hadith of 'Ā'ishah which says: 'When the Messenger of Allah ﷺ wanted to travel, he would draw lots between his wives, and he would travel with whichever wife had her lot drawn.'

The transmission from Mālik varies about someone drawing lots to determine which wife goes on a journey with him. Sometimes he says that one draws lots based on the hadith and sometimes he says that he should travel with the one who is most fitted to that journey. There is the hadith of Abū Hurayrah in which the Messenger of Allah ﷺ says, 'If people knew what a reward there was for the call and the first row, and could find nothing but drawing lots for it, they would draw lots.' There are many hadiths regarding this matter and the methodology of drawing of lots is described in the books of *fiqh*. Abū Ḥanīfah argues that the discussion of lots in the case of Zakariyyā and the wives of the Prophet ﷺ was in a context when they would in fact consent without lots being drawn and so it was permitted. Ibn al-'Arabī says that this is weak because the point of drawing lots is to extract a hidden ruling in a case where there is a dispute. That is not the case when there is mutual consent. It is not valid for anyone to say that lots take the place of mutual consent. Lots are never drawn when there is mutual consent. It is always when there is a dispute and begrudgement.

According to ash-Shāfiʿī and those who take his position, the description of the methodology of drawing lots is that small pieces of equal size are cut and on each piece the name of the person with a share is written. Then they are placed inside equal-sized nutshells without cracks and left to dry a little. Then a man who was not present puts them in a cloth and covers them with it. Then they are extracted from that. When the name of a man comes out, he is given the portion drawn for him.

The *āyah* also indicates that a maternal aunt is more entitled to guardianship than all other relatives except the grandmother. The Prophet ﷺ judged that custody of the daughter of Ḥamzah should go to Jaʿfar who was married to her maternal aunt, saying, 'The maternal aunt is in the position of the mother.' This was already mentioned in *al-Baqarah.*

Abū Dāwūd transmitted that 'Alī said, 'Zayd ibn Ḥārithah went to Makkah and brought Ḥamzah's daughter. Jaʿfar said, "I will take her. I am more entitled to my uncle's daughter and I am married to her maternal aunt. A maternal aunt is [like the] mother." 'Alī said, "I am more entitled to my uncle's daughter. I am married to the daughter of the Messenger of Allah ﷺ and so I am more entitled to her." Zayd said, "I am more entitled to her. I went to her, travelled with her and brought her." The Messenger of Allah ﷺ came out and the story was told to him. He said, "I judge that the girl should be with Jaʿfar. She will be with her maternal aunt and the maternal aunt is like the mother."' Ibn Abī Khaythamah mentioned that Zayd ibn Ḥārithah was the executor of Ḥamzah. So according to this, the maternal aunt has more entitlement than the executor. When the cousin is her husband, that does not prevent the maternal aunt from taking custody, even if he is not a *maḥram* of the girl.

إِذْ قَالَتِ ٱلْمَلَٰٓئِكَةُ يَٰمَرْيَمُ إِنَّ ٱللَّهَ يُبَشِّرُكِ بِكَلِمَةٍ مِّنْهُ ٱسْمُهُ ٱلْمَسِيحُ
عِيسَى ٱبْنُ مَرْيَمَ وَجِيهًا فِى ٱلدُّنْيَا وَٱلْءَاخِرَةِ وَمِنَ ٱلْمُقَرَّبِينَ ﴿٤٥﴾ وَيُكَلِّمُ ٱلنَّاسَ
فِى ٱلْمَهْدِ وَكَهْلًا وَمِنَ ٱلصَّٰلِحِينَ ﴿٤٦﴾

45 When the angels said, 'Maryam, Allah gives you good news of a Word from Him. His name is the Messiah, 'Īsā, son of Maryam, of high esteem in this world and the Next, and one of those brought near. 46 He will speak to people in the cradle, and also when fully grown, and will be one of the righteous.'

This *āyah* indicates the Prophethood of Maryam. The *'When'* is either connected to *'quarrelled'* or to *'you were not with them.'* Abu-s-Sammāl recitation of *'bi-kalmati'* was already mentioned. *'His name'* uses the masculine, not the feminine pronoun (for 'word') because *'word'* here refers to *'son'*. Messiah (*Masīḥ*) is a title of 'Īsā, and means 'truthful' according to Ibrāhīm an-Nakha'ī. It is said to be an arabicised word and its root has a *shīn*. So it has various meanings. Ibn Fāris says that *masīh* is sweat and also means truthful. A dirham which is *masīḥ* is smooth, without engraving. *Masḥ* means sexual intercourse. A place which is described as *amsaḥ* is bare. *Masḥā'* is a human with thin thighs and buttocks. Someone is described as having traits (*masḥah*) of beauty. *Masā'iḥ* are good bows, the singular being *masīḥah*. [Poetry]

They disagree about the origin of the term *masīḥ* in respect of 'Īsā. It is said that he brushed through (*masaḥa*) the earth, in that he came to it but did not remain. Ibn 'Abbās said that he did not wipe over (*masaḥa*) anyone with a defect without that healing him, which is why he was called *Masīḥ*. According to this it has the meaning of an active participle. It is said that that was because he was anointed (*masīḥ*) with the oil of blessings. The Prophets used to be anointed with it and it had a fragrant scent. When he was anointed with it, it was known that he was a Prophet. It is said that it was because beauty touched him and showed on him. It is said that he was called that because he was cleansed with purity from wrong actions.

Abu-l-Haytham said, '*Masīḥ* is the opposite of *masīkh*. It is said that Allah smoothed (*masaḥa*) the creation of a person with good blessed character and transformed (*masakha*) someone's creation into something ugly and blameworthy.' Ibn al-A'rabī said, 'The *Masīh* is truthful and the *Maskhīh* is one-eyed which is why he is the Dajjāl.' Abū 'Ubayd said, 'The root of *masīh* in Hebrew is *mashiḥā* and has been Arabicised.' The Dajjāl is a called a Messiah because one of his eyes is smoothed over (*mamsūḥ*). Some people call him *Mashīkh* rather than *Masīh* although the first is better known. He is called that because he will travel (*yasīhu*) around in the land and will enter all towns except for Makkah, Madīnah and Jerusalem. The Dajjāl will cause trial (*miḥnah*) in the land while the son of Maryam brought a gift (*minḥah*). A poet said:

The Messiah (*Masīh*) will kill the Messiah (*Mashīkh*).

We find in *Saḥīḥ Muslim* from Anas ibn Mālik that the Messenger of Allah ﷺ said, 'There is no land where the Dajjāl will not go except for Makkah and Madīnah.' The hadith of 'Abdullāh ibn 'Amr has 'except the Ka'bah and Jerusalem.' Abū

Ja'far aṭ-Ṭabarī mentioned it. Abū Ja'far aṭ-Ṭaḥāwī added, 'the mosque of aṭ-Ṭūr'. He related it from Junādah ibn Abī Umayyah from one of the Companions of the Prophet from the Prophet ﷺ.

We find in the hadith of Abū Bakr ibn Abī Shaybah from Samurah ibn Jundub that the Prophet ﷺ said, 'He will be victorious over the entire world except for the Ḥaram and Jerusalem. He will lay siege to the believers in Jerusalem.' We find in *Saḥīḥ Muslim*: 'When things are like that, Allah will send the Messiah, son of Maryam and he will descend at the white minaret in the east of Damascus, wearing two yellow garments with his hands on the wings of two angels. When he bows his head, it will seem as if drops are falling from his head. When he raises his head, drops like pearls will fall. Any unbeliever who catches the scent of his breath will die, and his breath will go as far as he can see. He will search for him [the Dajjāl] and will catch him at the gate of Ludd and kill him.'

Finally it is said that there is no derivation for 'Messiah' because Allah named him that and so 'Īsā and *Masīḥ* are interchangeable. 'Īsā is a foreign name which is why it is not inflected. If it is Arabicised, it is not inflected in the definite or indefinite because it ends with an *alif.* They would say that it is from the verb *'āsa, ya'ūsu*, which is to manage.

of high esteem in this world and the Next, and one of those brought near.

Wajīh (*of high esteem*) means honoured with high rank and value. According to al-Akhfash, it is in the accusative for the *ḥāl*. The plural is *wujahā'* or *wijahā'*. *'One of those brought near'* means brought near to Allah and is added to the words *'of high esteem'*.

He will speak to people in the cradle, and also when fully grown, and will be one of the righteous,'

'Cradle' (*mahd*) is a place where a child lies during the time of his infancy. The verb means to arrange a matter and smooth it. We find in the Revelation: '... *making the way easy* (yamhadūna) *for themselves.'* (30:44) The verb *imtihada* (Form VIII) is used with something high, like a camel's hump. The word '*kahl*' (*fully grown*) refers to the period between being a boy and being an old man. The term *kahlah* is used for a woman. Form VIII of the verb is used for a meadow when it is in full bloom. It is said that he spoke to people in the cradle as a sign, and spoke to them when fully grown with Revelation and the Message.

Abu-l-Abbās said, 'He spoke to them in the cradle to prove his mother's innocence. He said, *"I am the slave of Allah."* (19:30)' The expression *'when fully grown'* is said to refer to the fact that when Allah makes him descend from heaven, he will be thirty-three. He will be fully grown and will say to them, *'I am the slave of Allah'* as he said in the cradle. So both ages are signs and proofs.

Al-Mahdawī said, 'The point of the *āyah* is that Allah informs them that 'Isā will speak to them in the cradle and live until he is fully grown. That is because the norm was that someone who spoke in the cradle did not survive for long.' Az-Zajjāj said that it means 'he will speak to them when fully grown.' Al-Farrā' and al-Akhfash said that it is added to *'of high esteem'*. It is said that it means that he will speak to people as a child and when fully grown.

Ibn Jurayj related that Mujāhid said that the word *'kahl'* means being forbearing, but an-Nahhās said that this is not recognised as a linguistic usage. Those who study language say that it means the age of forty. Some of them say that one is a child until the age of sixteen, a youth until the age of thirty-two and then mature at thirty-three, as al-Akhfash said. The words among *'among the righteous'* is supplementary to *'of high esteem'* and means 'among the righteous worshippers.'

Abū Bakr ibn Abī Shaybah mentioned from 'Abdullāh ibn Idrīs from Ḥuṣayn that Hilāl ibn Yasāf said, 'Only three people spoke in the cradle: 'Īsā, the child in the story of Yūsuf, and the child in the story of Jurayj.' We find in *Ṣaḥīḥ Muslim* from Abū Hurayrah that the Prophet ﷺ said, 'Only three spoke in the cradle: 'Īsā ibn Maryam, the child in the story of Jurayj, and the infant who was being suckled by his mother when a tyrant [passed].'

It was reported from Ṣuhayb in the story of the story of the Trench: 'A woman was brought to be thrown in the fire on account of her faith with an infant.' It has in a version other than that in Muslim: 'She held back from being thrown into it and the child said, "Mother, be steadfast! You are following the truth!"'

Aḍ-Ḍaḥḥāk said, 'Six spoke in the cradle: the witness for [the Prophet] Yūsuf, the child of the hairdresser of the wife of Pharaoh, 'Īsā, Yaḥyā, the child in the story of Jurayj, and child in the story of the tyrant.' He did not mention the Trench. If that is included, it is seven. There is no contradiction between this and the words of the Prophet ﷺ, 'Only three spoke in the cradle.' He reported about what he knew that had been revealed to him at that time. Then later Allah informed him about whatever further He wished and he reported that.

The story about Yūsuf will be dealt with later, Allah willing. The story about Jurayj, the one about the tyrant, and the story about the Trench are found in *Ṣaḥīḥ Muslim*. The story of the Trench will be found in *Sūrat al-Burūj*, Allah willing.

As for the story of the hairdresser of Pharaoh's wife, al-Bayhaqī mentioned from Ibn 'Abbās that the Prophet ﷺ said, 'When I was taken on the Night

Journey, a pleasant fragrance reached me and I asked, "What is this fragrance?" They said, "It is the fragrance of the hairdresser of Pharaoh's daughter and her children. [While she was combing her hair], the comb fell from her and she said, 'In the Name of Allah.'" Pharaoh's daughter asked, 'My father?' She answered, 'My Lord, your Lord and your father's Lord.' She said, 'Do you have a Lord other than my father?' She replied, 'Yes, my Lord, your Lord and your father's Lord is Allah.' He summoned her and demanded, 'Do you have a Lord other than me?' 'Yes,' she answered, 'my Lord and your Lord is Allah.' He ordered a hollow brass cow to be heated up and then commanded that she be thrown into it. She said, 'I have something to request of you.' 'What is it?' he asked, She said, 'Put my bones and those of my children in the same place.' He said, 'I will grant that to you because of what I owe you.' He gave the command and they were thrown one by one into it until it reached the suckling babe. It said, 'Mother! Do not hold back! We are following the truth.'"" Then he said, 'Four spoke when they were infants: this one, the witness of Yūsuf, the child with Jurayj and 'Īsā ibn Maryam.'

قَالَتْ رَبِّ أَنَّىٰ يَكُونُ لِي وَلَدٌ وَلَمْ يَمْسَسْنِي بَشَرٌ قَالَ كَذَٰلِكِ اللَّهُ يَخْلُقُ مَا
يَشَاءُ إِذَا قَضَىٰ أَمْرًا فَإِنَّمَا يَقُولُ لَهُ كُن فَيَكُونُ ﴿٤٧﴾

47 She said, 'My lord! How can I have a son when no man has ever touched me?' He said, 'It will be so.' Allah creates whatever He wills. When He decides on something, He just says to it, 'Be!' and it is.

She addressed Jibrīl because he is the one who appeared to her as the messenger of her Lord saying, 'I am your Lord's messenger to give you a pure son.' When she heard that, she asked about how that would occur without sexual intercourse, noting that the normal means of conception was through sexual intercourse either in marriage or fornication. Stressing that, her words are reported in *Sūrat Maryam*: *'I am not an unchaste woman'* (19:20) because the words *'no man has ever touched me'* include both the lawful and the unlawful. It is said that she did not think that anything was impossible for Allah's power, but she wanted to know how that would occur: by a future husband or by Allah's direct creation. When Jibrīl said, *'It will be so! Your Lord says, "That is easy for Me to do"'* (19:9), he breathed into the collar and sleeve of her shift, as Ibn Jurayj says.

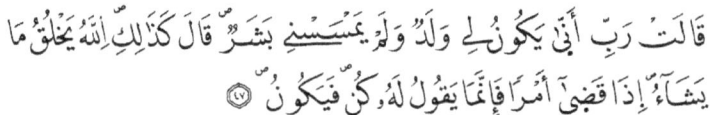

Ibn 'Abbās said that Jibrīl touched the sleeve of her shift with his finger and breathed into it and she conceived immediately. Various other things are said as well, and this will be discussed in *Sūrat Maryam*, Allah willing.

One of them said that Jibrīl breathed into her womb and it attached itself. One of them said that it is not permitted that the creation be from the breath of Jibrīl because then the child would be part angel and part human, but rather the reason for that is that when Allah Almighty created Ādam and took the covenant from his progeny, he put some of the fluid in the loins of fathers and some in the wombs of mothers. When the two fluids meet, a child is produced. Allah gave Maryam both fluids: some in her womb and some in her spine. Jibrīl breathed into her to stimulate her desire because as long as a woman does not have her desire ignited, she does not become pregnant. When that happened by Jibrīl's breath, the fluid in her spine descended into her womb and the two fluids mixed and the foetus was attached. That is why Allah then says: *'When He decides on something,'* meaning when He wants to create something. This was discussed in *al-Baqarah*.

وَيُعَلِّمُهُ ٱلْكِتَٰبَ وَٱلْحِكْمَةَ وَٱلتَّوْرَىٰةَ وَٱلْإِنجِيلَ ﴿٤٨﴾ وَرَسُولًا إِلَىٰ بَنِىٓ
إِسْرَٰٓءِيلَ أَنِّى قَدْ جِئْتُكُم بِـَٔايَةٍ مِّن رَّبِّكُمْ ۖ إِنِّىٓ أَخْلُقُ لَكُم مِّنَ ٱلطِّينِ
كَهَيْـَٔةِ ٱلطَّيْرِ فَأَنفُخُ فِيهِ فَيَكُونُ طَيْرًۢا بِإِذْنِ ٱللَّهِ ۖ وَأُبْرِئُ ٱلْأَكْمَهَ
وَٱلْأَبْرَصَ وَأُحْىِ ٱلْمَوْتَىٰ بِإِذْنِ ٱللَّهِ ۖ وَأُنَبِّئُكُم بِمَا تَأْكُلُونَ وَمَا
تَدَّخِرُونَ فِى بُيُوتِكُمْ ۚ إِنَّ فِى ذَٰلِكَ لَءَايَةً لَّكُمْ إِن كُنتُم مُّؤْمِنِينَ ﴿٤٩﴾

48 He will teach him the Book and Wisdom, and the Torah and the Gospel, 49 as a Messenger to the tribe of Israel, saying: 'I have brought you a Sign from your Lord. I will create the shape of a bird out of clay for you and then breathe into it and it will be a bird by Allah's permission. I will heal the blind and the leper, and bring the dead to life, by Allah's permission. I will tell you what you eat and what you store up in your homes. There is a Sign for you in that if you are believers.

He will teach him the Book and Wisdom,

Ibn Jurayj said that the Book refers to writing and script. It is said that the Book is other than the Torah and the Gospel which Allah taught 'Īsā.

as a Messenger to the tribe of Israel, saying:

'As a Messenger' either means, 'We will make him a Messenger' or 'He will speak to them as a Messenger.' It is also said that it is joined to the words *'of high esteem.'* Al-Akhfash said, 'If you wish, you can make the *wāw* before Messenger interpolated while the word "Messenger" is a *ḥāl* modifying *hā'* (him). It implies: "He will teach him the Book as a Messenger."' We find in a long hadith reported by Abū Dharr: 'The first of the Prophets of the tribe of Israel was Mūsā and the last was 'Īsā.'

I will create the shape of a bird out of clay for you and then breathe into it and it will be a bird by Allah's permission.

It means: 'I will form and fashion it for you.' Al-A'raj and Abū Ja'far recited 'shape' as '*ka-hayyati*' while the rest have it as '*ka-hay'ati*' with a *hamzah*. The word '*ṭayr*' (bird) can be masculine or plural. 'Breathe into it' means into part of it or into the clay. It became a bird. 'Bird' is read as *ṭā'ir* or *ṭayr*.

Wahb said, 'It flew as long as the people were looking at it. When they stopped looking at it, it fell down dead so as to distinguish the action of creation from the action of Allah.' It is said that he only created a bat which has the full form of the bird so as to be more extensive in power because it has teats, teeth and ears. It menstruates, becomes pure and gives birth.'

It is said that they asked for the creation of a bat because it is the most wondrous of all creation. Among its wonders is that it is flesh and blood, flies without feathers, reproduces as mammals reproduce, without eggs like other birds, and it produces milk. It is not seen in the light of day or in darkest night, but at sunset and dawn. It laughs like a human being and menstruates like a human being. It is said that the people asked him for a sign out of their obstinacy, saying, 'Create a bat for us and put a spirit into it if you are telling the truth.' So he took some clay and fashioned a bat from it and then breathed into it and it flew in the sky. The fashioning and breathing was from 'Īsā and the creation was from Allah, in the same way that the breathing [into Maryam] was from Jibrīl, and the creation was from Allah.

I will heal the blind and the leper, and bring the dead to life, by Allah's permission.

Ibn 'Abbās and Abū 'Ubaydah said that *akmah* is someone who is born blind. Ibn Fāris also said that. Suwayd said:

His eyes were blind (*akmah*) so that they were white.

Mujāhid said that *akmah* is the one who can see in the day but not at night. 'Ikrimah said that *akmah* means someone who is dim-sighted, but linguistically it refers to blindness. The verb is *kamiha, yakmahu, kamah.* Form II is also used to mean to make blind.

A leper (*abraṣ*) is someone suffering from white leprosy which is a whiteness that shows on the skin. *Abraṣ* also means the moon. '*Sāmm abraṣ*' is an albino. These two ailments are mentioned because medicine was important in the time of 'Īsā and so Allah showed them that type of miracle.

He brought four individuals back to life: a friend of his, the son of the old woman, the daughter of a tax-collector, and Sām ibn Nūḥ. Allah knows best. The friend had died some days before and He prayed to Allah and he rose by Allah's permission, lived and had a child. The son of the old woman had passed by him being carried on a bed and he prayed to Allah and he got up, wrapped in his shroud, and carried the bed on his shoulder and returned to his family. He went to the daughter of the tax-collector in the night and prayed to Allah for her. She lived and had children.

When they saw that, they said, 'He has brought back to life those who have recently died. Perhaps they were not dead but in a stupor.' So he brought to life Sām ibn Nūḥ. He said, 'Show me his grave.' He went out with the people to his grave and he prayed to Allah and he came out of his grave, white-haired. 'Īsā asked him, 'Why is your hair white when there was no white hair in your time?' He answered, 'Spirit of Allah, you summoned me and I heard a voice saying, "Respond to the Spirit of Allah!" I thought that the Day of Rising had come and terror of that turned my hair white.' He asked him about the wresting of the soul at death. He said, 'Spirit of Allah, the bitterness of the wresting has not left my throat.' He had died more than four thousand years earlier. He told the people, 'Affirm him. He is a Prophet.' Some people believed him and said that he was a Prophet and some said that it was sorcery.

It is related from Ismā'īl ibn 'Ayyāsh from Muḥammad ibn Ṭalḥah from a man that when 'Īsā wanted to bring the dead to life, he would pray two *rak'ah*s and recite *Surat al-Mulk* (67) in the first and *Surat as-Sajdah* (32) in the second. When he finished, he praised Allah and then invoked his seven names: 'O Ancient! O Hidden! O Constantly Abiding! O Unique! O Odd! O One! O Everlasting Sustainer!' Al-Bayhaqī mentioned it and said that its *isnād* is not strong.

I will tell you what you eat and what you store up in your homes.

That is because when he brought the dead back to life, they asked for another sign and said, 'Tell us what we eat in our houses and store up for the tomorrow.' He told them in detail: 'You, you ate such-and-such, and you, you ate such-and-such and stored up such-and-such.' Mujāhid, az-Zuhrī and as-Sakhtiyānī recited *'mā tadhkharūna'*. Sa'īd ibn Jubayr and others said, 'He used to tell the children in the school what they stored up until their fathers forbade them to sit with him.' Qatādah said, 'He told them what they ate from the table and what they secretly stored from it.'

وَمُصَدِّقًا لِّمَا بَيْنَ يَدَيَّ مِنَ ٱلتَّوْرِيٰةِ وَلِأُحِلَّ لَكُم بَعْضَ ٱلَّذِے حُرِّمَ
عَلَيْكُمْ وَجِئْتُكُم بِـَٔايَةٍ مِّن رَّبِّكُمْ فَاتَّقُواْ ٱللَّهَ وَأَطِيعُونِ ﴿٥٠﴾
إِنَّ ٱللَّهَ رَبِّے وَرَبُّكُمْ فَاعْبُدُوهُ هَٰذَا صِرَٰطٌ مُّسْتَقِيمٌ ﴿٥١﴾

50 I come confirming the Torah I find already there, and to make lawful for you some of what was previously forbidden to you. I have brought you a Sign from your Lord. So have *taqwā* of Allah and obey me. 51 Allah is my Lord and your Lord so worship Him. That is a straight path.'

The word *'confirming'* is an adverbial *ḥāl* joined to 'Messenger'. *'What I find already there'* is what came before him. It is said that 'Īsā made lawful to them what they had been forbidden in the Torah because of their wrong actions, such as eating fat and animals with claws. It is said that he made lawful for them what their rabbis had forbidden them that was not actually forbidden in the Torah. Abū 'Ubaydah said that *'some'* can mean 'all'. [Poetry] This is wrong theoretically and linguistically and wrong in the context because 'Īsā allowed them certain foods that Mūsā had forbidden them, such as eating fat and others things, but did not make lawful for them killing, stealing or fornication. The evidence for this is what is related from Qatādah: "Īsā brought what was more lenient than Mūsā because Mūsā brought the prohibition of camels and fat and 'Īsā made some of that lawful.'

An-Nakha'ī recited *'ḥaruma'*. 'Some' means 'all' which something is added to it which indicates it as we see in the words of the poet:

You have destroyed Abū Mundhir. Let some of us remain.
Inside you some evil is easier than other kinds.

In the words *'I have brought you a Sign from your Lord'* the singular for *'sign'* is used although they are several, and so it is generic. They are all proofs of his Prophethood.

فَلَمَّآ أَحَسَّ عِيسَىٰ مِنْهُمُ ٱلْكُفْرَ قَالَ مَنْ أَنصَارِىٓ إِلَى ٱللَّهِ ۖ قَالَ
ٱلْحَوَارِيُّونَ نَحْنُ أَنصَارُ ٱللَّهِ ءَامَنَّا بِٱللَّهِ وَٱشْهَدْ بِأَنَّا مُسْلِمُونَ ﴿٥٢﴾

52 When 'Īsā sensed unbelief on their part, he said, 'Who will be my helpers to Allah?' The disciples said, 'We are Allah's helpers. We believe in Allah. Bear witness that we are Muslims.

When 'Īsā sensed unbelief on their part,

This means on the part of the tribe of Israel. The word *'sensed'* here means knew and found, as az-Zajjāj said. Abū 'Ubaydah says that it means 'recognised'. The root of that is knowing about the existence of the thing by touching it, so 'sensing' is knowledge of the thing. Allah says: *'Do you see* (sense) *a trace of any one of them?'* (19:98) The word *'ḥass'* means killing. Allah says: *'…when you were slaughtering them (*taḥussūnahum*) by His permission.'* (3:152) There is also the hadith about the locusts: 'The cold killed (*ḥassahu*) them.' *'Unbelief'* here means disbelief in Allah. It is said that it means hearing words of disbelief from them. Al-Farrā' said, 'They wanted to kill him.'

he said, 'Who will be my helpers to Allah?'

This is asking for help against them. As-Suddī, ath-Thawrī and others said, 'The meaning is "with Allah".' Allah knows best. Al-Ḥasan said, 'It means, "Who will be my helpers on the Path to Allah" because he called them to Allah.' It is said that it means, 'Who will add their help to that of Allah?' These are two excellent views. He asked for help to defend his people and make the Call to Islam public. Al-Ḥasan and Mujāhid said that. This is the custom of Allah for His Prophets and *awliyā'*. Lūṭ said: *'If only I had the strength to combat you or could take refuge in some powerful support'* (11:80). He meant a clan and companions to help him.

The disciples said, 'We are Allah's helpers. We believe in Allah.

The helpers are those who help Allah's Prophet and His *dīn*. The 'disciples' are the companions of 'Īsā, who were twelve men according to al-Kalbī and Abū Rawq. There is disagreement about why they were called *'ḥawwāriyyūn'*. Ibn 'Abbās said that they were called that because of the whiteness of their garments and that they were fishermen. Ibn Abī Najīḥ and Ibn Arṭāh said that they were fullers and were called that because of the whiteness of their garments. 'Aṭā' said, 'Maryam exposed 'Īsā to various types of work. The last of these was that of the disciples who were fullers and dyers. 'Īsā's teacher wanted to travel and he told

'Īsā, 'I have many garments of different colours. I have taught you how to dye, so dye them.' 'Īsā heated one pot and put all the garments in it and said, 'By Allah's permission, be what I want from you.' The fuller arrived while all the garments were in the pot. When he saw it, he said, 'You have ruined them!' Then 'Īsā brought a red garment, a yellow one, a green one, and other colours and his dye was written on each of them. The fuller was astonished and realised that that was from Allah. He summoned the people to him and they believed in him. So they are the Disciples.

Qatādah and aḍ-Ḍaḥḥāk said they were called that because they were the elite companions of the Prophet because of the purity of their hearts. It is said that they were kings and each king prepared food and invited people to come to it. 'Īsā was seated at a bowl whose contents did not decrease. The king asked him, 'Who are you?' 'Īsa son of Maryam,' he answered. He said, 'I leave you this kingdom of mine and will follow you.' He went with those with him and they were the disciples. Ibn 'Awn said that.

The root of *ḥawar* linguistically is whiteness. The verb *ḥawwara* is used for bleaching a garment. *Huwwārā* is white food. The verb *iḥwarra* means to become white. A bowl that is *muḥawwarah* is whitened. *Ḥawārī* also means 'helper' as the Messenger of Allah ﷺ said, 'Every Prophet has a helper, and my helper is az-Zubayr.' *Ḥawāriyyāt* means women because of their whiteness. [Poetry]

رَبَّنَآ ءَامَنَّا بِمَآ أَنزَلْتَ وَاتَّبَعْنَا ٱلرَّسُولَ فَٱكْتُبْنَا مَعَ ٱلشَّٰهِدِينَ ٥٣

53 Our Lord, we believe in what You have sent down and have followed the Messenger, so write us down among the witnesses.'

It means that they say: 'We believe in what is in Your Book and what has appeared of Your judgment.' The Messenger is 'Īsā. '*The witnesses*' are the community of Muhammad ﷺ as Ibn 'Abbas stated. It means: 'Confirm our names with their names and place us among them.' It is also said that it means: 'Write us down with those who testify that Your Prophets told the truth.'

وَمَكَرُوا وَمَكَرَ ٱللَّهُ وَٱللَّهُ خَيْرُ ٱلْمَٰكِرِينَ ٥٤

54 They plotted and Allah plotted. But Allah is the best of plotters.

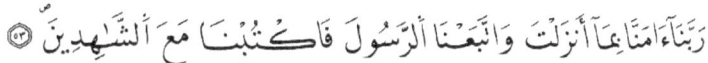

The people who '*plotted*' were the unbelievers of the tribe of Israel in whom he sensed unbelief, in other words they plotted to kill him. That was when 'Īsā and his mother were expelled by his people from among them and he returned to them with the Disciples. He proclaimed the call among them and they wanted to kill him and plotted to assassinate him. That was their plotting. The plotting of Allah is when He draws on His slaves from where they do not know, as al-Farrā' and others said. Ibn 'Abbās said: 'Whenever they commit an error, He renews blessing for them.' Az-Zajjāj said, 'It is Allah's repaying them for their plotting. He named it by the original action which led to it.' We have examples of that in 2:15 and 4:142. This was already discussed in *al-Baqarah*.

The linguistic root of *makr* (plot) is using stratagems and deceit. *Makr* is a plump shank and a type of garment. *Makr* is a type of plant. It is said that it is russet as Ibn Fāris said.

It is said that Allah's plotting was casting the shape of 'Īsā on someone else while raising 'Īsā to Him when the Jews agreed to kill him. They entered the house and he fled from them and Jibrīl took him up from the window to heaven. Their ruler told a vile man among them called Yahūdhā, 'Go in and kill him. He entered by the window and did not find 'Īsā there. Allah then made him resemble 'Īsā. When he came out looking like 'Īsā', they seized him, killed him and crucified him. Then they said, 'His face is like that of 'Īsā, but his body is like that of our fellow! If this is our fellow, then where is 'Īsā? If this is 'Īsā, where is our fellow?' They began to fight among themselves and killed one another. This is what is meant by the *āyah* although other things are said as well.

Mākir is an active participle from *makara, yamkuru*. Some scholars consider 'the Best of plotters' to be one of the names of Allah Almighty and say in supplication, 'O Best of plotters, plot for me and not against me.' The Prophet ﷺ used to say in his supplication, 'O Allah, plot for me and not against me!' We have mentioned this in *Kitāb al-Asnā*. Allah knows best.

إِذْ قَالَ ٱللَّهُ يَٰعِيسَىٰٓ إِنِّى مُتَوَفِّيكَ وَرَافِعُكَ إِلَىَّ وَمُطَهِّرُكَ مِنَ ٱلَّذِينَ كَفَرُوا۟
وَجَاعِلُ ٱلَّذِينَ ٱتَّبَعُوكَ فَوْقَ ٱلَّذِينَ كَفَرُوٓا۟ إِلَىٰ يَوْمِ ٱلْقِيَٰمَةِ ثُمَّ إِلَىَّ
مَرْجِعُكُمْ فَأَحْكُمُ بَيْنَكُمْ فِيمَا كُنتُمْ فِيهِ تَخْتَلِفُونَ ﴿٥٥﴾

55 When Allah said, "Īsā, I will take you back and raise you up to Me and purify you of those who disbelieve. And I will place the people who follow you above those who disbelieve until the Day of Rising. Then you will all return to Me, and I will judge between you regarding the things about which you differed.

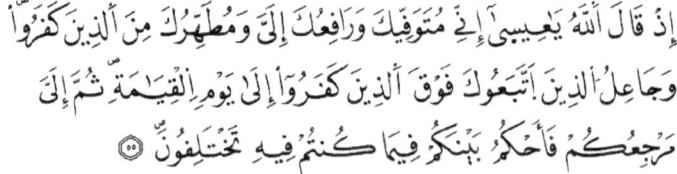

When Allah said, "Īsā, I will take you back and raise you up to Me

The order here is not sequential as is stated by a group of people with grasp of meanings, including aḍ-Ḍaḥḥāk and al-Farrā'. They say that the *wāw* does not entail time sequence. It means: 'I will raise you to Me, purify you of those who disbelieve and make you die after you descend from heaven' as in His words: *'And were it not for a prior word from your Lord, and a specified term, it would inevitably have already taken place.'* (20:129) A poet said:

O palm tree from a root,
    May the mercy and peace of Allah be on you!

And the order of the words is reversed.

Al-Ḥasan and Ibn Jurayj said that 'take back' means to take and raise to heaven without him dying. You use the same verb for taking property from a person. Wahb ibn Munabbih said, 'Allah made 'Īsā die for three hours and then raised him to heaven.' This, however, is unlikely because of the sound reports from the Prophet ﷺ about his descent and killing of the Dajjāl as we explained in *Kitāb at-Tadhkirah*. Ibn Zayd said that 'take back' and 'raise' mean the same and he has not yet died. Ibn Abī Ṭalḥah related from Ibn 'Abbās that it means: 'make you die'. Ar-Rabī' ibn Anas said that it is the 'death' of sleep. The Almighty says: *'It is He who takes you back to Himself at night.'* (6:60) This means that He makes you sleep because sleep is the brother of death. The Prophet ﷺ was asked, 'Is there sleep in the Garden?' 'No,' he answered, 'sleep is the brother of death and there is no death in the Garden.' Ad-Dāraquṭnī transmitted it. The sound position is that Allah raised him to heaven without that being through death or sleep, as was stated by al-Ḥasan and Ibn Zayd. Aṭ-Ṭabarī preferred it and it is sound from Ibn 'Abbās. Aḍ-Ḍaḥḥāk said that.

Aḍ-Ḍaḥḥāk said, 'The story is that 'Īsā gathered the Disciples in a room. There were twelve of them. The Messiah entered by a niche in the room and Iblīs informed all the Jews about that. About four thousand of them met and attacked the door of the room. The Messiah said to the Disciples, "Which of you will go out and be killed and be with me in Paradise?" One man said, "I will, Prophet of Allah." He gave him a woollen shirt and turban and handed him his staff and he was made to look like 'Īsā. He went out to the Jews and they crucified and killed him. Allah robed the Messiah in feathers, clothed him in light and cut him off from the pleasure of food and drink, and he flew with the angels.'

Abū Bakr ibn Abī Shaybah mentioned from Abū Mu'āwiyah from al-A'mash from al-Minhāl from Sa'īd ibn Jubayr that Ibn 'Abbās said, 'When Allah Almighty wanted to raise 'Īsā to heaven, he came out to his twelve Companions from part of the room with his head dripping with water. He said to them, "One of you will deny me twelve times after he has believed in me." Then he asked, "Which of you will take on my resemblance and be killed in my place and be with me in my degree?" One of their youngest stood and said, "I will!" 'Īsā said, "Sit down." Then he repeated the request and the young man stood and said, "I will!" 'Īsā said, "Sit down." Then he repeated the request yet again and the young man stood and said, "I will!" He said, "Yes then. It will be you." So Allah made him resemble 'Īsā.' Allah Almighty raised 'Īsā to heaven from an aperture in the room. Some of the Jews came, looking for him, and seized the one who looked like him and killed him and then crucified him. One of them denied him twelve times after having believed in him. They split into three groups. One group said, "God was among us for as long as he wished and then ascended to heaven." They are the Jacobites. Another group said, "The son of God was among us for as long as he wished and then Allah raised him to heaven." They are the Nestorians. Another group said, "The slave of Allah and His Messenger was among us for as long as he wished and then Allah raised him to Him." They are the Muslims. The two unbelieving groups fought the Muslim group and killed them. Islam remained extinct until Allah sent Muḥammad ﷺ. Allah revealed: *"One faction of the tribe of Israel believed and the other disbelieved. So We supported those who believed..."* (61:14) This means that their forefathers believed in the time of 'Īsā and *"...against their enemy"* means by making their *dīn* triumph over that of the unbelievers *"... and they became victorious."*'

We find in *Ṣaḥīḥ Muslim* from Abū Hurayrah that the Messenger of Allah ﷺ said, 'By Allah, the son of Maryam will descend as a just judge and will break the crosses, kill the pigs and remove the *jizyah*, and there will be so much wealth that no one will have to strive for it. Rancour, mutual hatred and mutual envy will be removed. People will be invited to receive wealth and no one will accept it.' He also related that the Prophet ﷺ said, 'By the One Who has my soul in His hand, the son of Maryam will say the *talbiyah* for ḥajj or *'umrah* or both at the ravine of ar-Rawḥā'.'

He will not bring a new Law and so abrogate our *Sharī'ah*, but he will renew what has fallen into misuse of it. It is as we find in *Ṣaḥīḥ Muslim* from Abū Hurayrah that the Messenger of Allah ﷺ said, 'How will you be when the son of Maryam descends among you and your imam is from you?' Ibn Abī Dhi'ib said, 'Do you know what is meant by "your imam is from you?"' The transmitter asked him to tell him and he said, 'He will lead you by the Book of your Almighty Lord and the Sunnah of your Prophet ﷺ.' We further clarified this in *Kitāb at-Tadhkirah*.

The root of *'mutawaffīka'* is *'mutawaffiyuka'* and the *ḍammah* is elided because it is heavy. It is the predicate of *inna*, and '*raise you*' is added to it as is '*purify you*' and '*place*'. '*Jā'ilu*' is permitted to be '*jā'ilun*'. It is said that there is a complete stop at 'purify you of those who disbelieve.' An-Naḥḥās said that it is a good position.

The you in '*the people who follow you*' refers to Muḥammad ﷺ. The words '*...above those who believe*' means by the proof and establishing the evidence. '*The people who follow you*' is addressed to Muḥammad ﷺ, although aḍ-Ḍaḥḥāk and Muḥammad ibn Abān say that the Disciples are meant. Allah knows best.

فَأَمَّا ٱلَّذِينَ كَفَرُوا۟ فَأُعَذِّبُهُمْ عَذَابًا شَدِيدًا فِى ٱلدُّنْيَا وَٱلْءَاخِرَةِ
وَمَا لَهُم مِّن نَّٰصِرِينَ ﴿٥٦﴾ وَأَمَّا ٱلَّذِينَ ءَامَنُوا۟ وَعَمِلُوا۟ ٱلصَّٰلِحَٰتِ
فَنُوَفِّيهِمُۥٓ أُجُورَهُمْ وَٱللَّهُ لَا يُحِبُّ ٱلظَّٰلِمِينَ ﴿٥٧﴾ ذَٰلِكَ نَتْلُوهُ عَلَيْكَ
مِنَ ٱلْءَايَٰتِ وَٱلذِّكْرِ ٱلْحَكِيمِ ﴿٥٨﴾

56 As for those who disbelieve, I will punish them with a harsh punishment in this world and the Next World. They will have no helpers.' 57 As for those who believe and do right actions, We will pay them their wages in full. Allah does not love wrongdoers. 58 That is what We recite to you of the Signs and the wise Reminder.

They will be punished in this world by killing, crucifixion, capture and the payment of *jizyah,* and in the Next World by the Fire.

إِنَّ مَثَلَ عِيسَىٰ عِندَ ٱللَّهِ كَمَثَلِ ءَادَمَ خَلَقَهُۥ مِن تُرَابٍ ثُمَّ قَالَ
لَهُۥ كُن فَيَكُونُ ﴿٥٩﴾ ٱلْحَقُّ مِن رَّبِّكَ فَلَا تَكُن مِّنَ ٱلْمُمْتَرِينَ ﴿٦٠﴾

59 The likeness of 'Īsā in Allah's sight is the same as Ādam. He created him from earth and then He said to him, 'Be!' and he was. 60 It is the truth from your Lord so do not be among the doubters.

This is evidence for the validity of using analogy. The comparison between 'Īsā and Ādam was based on the fact that, like Ādam, 'Īsā was created without a father not that he was created from dust. The one resembles the other, even if there is a great difference between them, in that single attribute. Ādam was created from dust and 'Īsā was not, and there is a difference between them in this respect. But the similarity between them was that they were both created without a father and because the basis of their creation was dust. Ādam was not created from dust itself, but the dust became mud and then clay, and then he was created from that. Similarly, 'Īsā went from one state to another and then became a human being without a father.

This *āyah* was revealed about the delegation of Najrān when they denied the words of the Prophet ﷺ: "Īsā is the slave of Allah and His Word.' They said, 'Show us a slave created without a father!' The Prophet ﷺ replied, 'Ādam. Who was his father? Do you then wonder at Īsā not having a father? Ādam had neither father nor mother.' That is referred to by the words of Allah: *'Every time they come to you with a difficult point, We bring you the truth and the best of explanations.'* (25:33)

It is also related that when the Prophet ﷺ invited them to Islam, they said, 'We were Muslims before you,' he said, 'You lie. Three things keep you from Islam: your statement that Allah has had a son, your eating pork and your bowing to the cross.' They asked, 'So who was 'Isā's father?' Then Allah revealed this *āyah* up until *'upon the liars.'* (3:61)

When he invited them to mutually curse one another, they said to one other, 'If you do it, the wadi will be filled with fire against you.' They asked, 'Do you offer us something else?' He said, 'It is either Islam, *jizyah*, or war.' They agreed to pay *jizyah*.

The words end at *'Ādam'*. The verb *'was* (yakūn)' is in the future tense while the past tense is meant as is understood from the meaning. Al-Farrā' said that *'It is the truth from your Lord'* is in the nominative by an implied 'It is'. It is a new sentence whose predicate is 'from your Lord'. It is said that it is an active participle, i.e. 'The truth has come to you.'

Do not be among the doubters

This is addressed to the Prophet ﷺ, but what is meant is his community because he had no doubts about the story of 'Īsā.

فَمَنْ حَآجَّكَ فِيهِ مِنۢ بَعْدِ مَا جَآءَكَ مِنَ ٱلْعِلْمِ فَقُلْ تَعَالَوْا۟ نَدْعُ أَبْنَآءَنَا
وَأَبْنَآءَكُمْ وَنِسَآءَنَا وَنِسَآءَكُمْ وَأَنفُسَنَا وَأَنفُسَكُمْ ثُمَّ نَبْتَهِلْ
فَنَجْعَل لَّعْنَتَ ٱللَّهِ عَلَى ٱلْكَٰذِبِينَ ٦١

61 If anyone argues with you about him after the knowledge that has come to you, say, 'Come then! Let us summon our sons and your sons, our women and your women, ourselves and yourselves. Then let us make earnest supplication and call down the curse of Allah upon the liars.'

If anyone argues with you about him after the knowledge that has come to you,

'If, Muḥammad, anyone argues with you and debates with you about 'Īsā after you know that he is the slave and Messenger of Allah.'

say, 'Come then! Let us summon our sons and your sons, our women and your women, ourselves and yourselves. Then let us make earnest supplication and call down the curse of Allah upon the liars.'

The form *'ta'ālaw'* was used for someone respected and with a high position and then was used to ask anyone to come forward. It will be further explained in *al-A'nām*. This shows that the term *'sons'* can refer to grandsons since the Prophet ﷺ brought al-Ḥasan and al-Ḥusayn with Fāṭimah walking behind and 'Alī behind her. He said to them, 'If I supplicate, then say, "Āmīn."' *Ibtihāl* is intense supplication as Ibn 'Abbās said. Abū 'Ubaydah and al-Kisā'ī said that it is to curse one another. The root of *ibtihāl* is striving in supplication with curses and other things. Labīd said:

Time looked at the mature masters of his people
and strove (*ibtihala*) [to destroy them].

Bahl means cursing, and a small amount water. *Abhala* (Form IV) is to leave someone to himself or to his own will. Form I is used in the same way. Ibn 'Abbās said that it is about the delegation of Najrān. Their leaders were the *'Āqib* (leader), the *Sayyid* (master) and Ibn Ḥarith.

This *āyah* is one of those informing about the Prophethood of Muḥammad ﷺ because when he invited them to mutual cursing, they refused and were content to pay the *jizyah* after their leader told them if they engaged in mutual cursing, the wadi would have been filled with fire against them and that Muḥammad is a Prophet with a Message. He told them that they knew that he had brought definitive information deciding what is true about 'Īsā. So they did not accept the mutual curse and went to their land having agreed to pay the *jizyah*: every year a thousand fine robes in Ṣafar and a thousand in Rajab. The Messenger of Allah ﷺ made peace with them on that basis.

Most scholars said that what the Prophet ﷺ said about al-Ḥasan and al-Ḥusayn, '...*let us summon our sons and your sons*' and about al-Ḥasan, 'This son of mine is a master', are specifically for al-Ḥasan and al-Ḥusayn: the Prophet ﷺ called them his sons rather than anyone else since he ﷺ said, 'Every cause and lineage will be cut off on the Day of Rising except for my lineage and cause.' That is why some of the people of ash-Shāfi'ī say about someone who makes a bequest to the child of a certain person who had no children, but had grandchildren from a son and from a daughter, that the bequest goes to the child of the son, but not of the daughter. That is the position of ash-Shāfi'ī. This will be further dealt with in *al-An'ām* and *az-Zukhruf*, Allah willing.

إِنَّ هَٰذَا لَهُوَ ٱلْقَصَصُ ٱلْحَقُّ ۚ وَمَا مِنْ إِلَٰهٍ إِلَّا ٱللَّهُ ۚ وَإِنَّ ٱللَّهَ لَهُوَ ٱلْعَزِيزُ
ٱلْحَكِيمُ ﴿٦٢﴾ فَإِن تَوَلَّوْا۟ فَإِنَّ ٱللَّهَ عَلِيمٌۢ بِٱلْمُفْسِدِينَ ﴿٦٣﴾

62 This is the true account: there is no other god besides Allah. Allah – He is the Almighty, the All-Wise. 63 And if they turn away, Allah knows the corrupters.

'This' indicates the Qur'an and the stories it contains. It is called an *'account'* because the meanings follow one another in it, as *qaṣṣa* can also mean 'to follow'. In the phrase *'there is no other god besides Allah,' 'min'* is added for stress. The Almighty (*al-'Azīz*) is the One Who cannot be overcome and the All-Wise (*al-Ḥakīm*) is the One with wisdom. This has already been discussed.

قُلْ يَٰٓأَهْلَ ٱلْكِتَٰبِ تَعَالَوْا۟ إِلَىٰ كَلِمَةٍ سَوَآءٍۭ بَيْنَنَا وَبَيْنَكُمْ أَلَّا نَعْبُدَ إِلَّا
ٱللَّهَ وَلَا نُشْرِكَ بِهِۦ شَيْـًٔا وَلَا يَتَّخِذَ بَعْضُنَا بَعْضًا أَرْبَابًا مِّن دُونِ ٱللَّهِ ۚ فَإِن
تَوَلَّوْا۟ فَقُولُوا۟ ٱشْهَدُوا۟ بِأَنَّا مُسْلِمُونَ ﴿٦٤﴾

64 Say, 'People of the Book! come to a proposition which is the same for us and you – that we should worship none but Allah and not associate any partners with Him and not take one another as lords besides Allah.' If they turn away, say, 'Bear witness that we are Muslims.'

Say, 'People of the Book! come to a proposition which is the same for us and you

According to al-Ḥasan, Ibn Zayd and as-Suddī, this is addressed to the people of Najrān. According to Qatādah, Ibn Jurayj and others, it is addressed to the Jews of Madīnah. They are addressed in that way because they turned their rabbis into Lords in the way they obeyed them. It is also said that it is addressed to both the Jews and the Christians. The Prophet ﷺ also quoted this *āyah* in his letter to Heraclius. He said, 'In the Name of Allah, the All-Merciful, Most Merciful. From Muḥammad, the Messenger of Allah, to Heraclius, ruler of Byzantium. Peace be upon whomever follows the guidance. I invite you to Islam. Become Muslim and you will be safe. Become Muslim and Allah will double your reward. If you turn away, then you bear the sin of your subjects. "'*People of the Book! come to a proposition which is the same for us and you – that we should worship none but Allah and not associate any partners with Him and not take one another as lords besides Allah.' If they turn away, say, 'Bear witness that we are Muslims.'*"'

The word *sawā'* means justice and fairness. Qatādah said that. Zuhayr said:

Show me a course of action with no unfairness in it,
in which we are equal.

Al-Farrā' said, 'Both *siwā* and *suwā* have the meaning of equality.' It is used in 20:58. He said that the reading of 'Abdullāh has '*'adl'* instead of *'sawā'*'. The reading of Qa'nab has '*kilmah*'. It means: 'Respond to what we invite you to. It is a just, upright proposition which does not deviate at all from the truth,' which He, *ta'ālā*, explained by his words: '*that we should worship none but Allah.*'

and not take one another as lords besides Allah

'An' [collected to *allā*] is in the genitive for the appositive for *'proposition'* or in the nominative by an implied inchoative. It means: 'We only worship Allah' or it is explanative without any place. [OMISSION] Al-Kisā'ī and al-Farrā' said that the phrase *'not associate any partners with Him and not take'* is in the jussive, imagining that there is no *'an'* at the beginning of the words.

It means, 'We do not follow others in their making anything lawful or unlawful except regarding what Allah Himself has made lawful.' It is similar to Allah's words: '*They have taken their rabbis and monks as lords besides Allah.*' (9:31) It means: 'They raised them to the station of their Lord by accepting their making things *ḥarām* or *ḥalāl* which Allah had not.' This indicates the falsity of the position of pure *istiḥsān* which is not based on any legal proof. Aṭ-Ṭabarī said, 'It is like the rulings by *istiḥsān* of Abū Ḥanīfah in the determinations he made without any clear reliance on a source.' It also refutes the Rāfidite Shi'ites who say that one must accept the position of the Imām without any legal clarification: he can make lawful what Allah has made unlawful without explaining what he has relied on in the Sharī'ah in doing that. *Arbāb* (lords) is the plural of *rabb*. The word '*besides*' (*dūn*) means 'other than'.

If they turn away, say, 'Bear witness that we are Muslims.'

'If they turn away' from what they are being called to, *'say, "Bear witness that we are Muslims,"'* meaning, 'we are ascribed to the *dīn* of Islam, obeying its judgments

and acknowledging that Allah has given us favours and blessings in respect of that without taking anyone else as a Lord, not 'Īsā, 'Uzayr or the angels, because they are temporal beings just as we are. We do not accept any of the prohibitions made by the monks prohibiting things which Allah has not prohibited to us. If we did that, we would be accepting them as lords.' 'Ikrimah said that the meaning of '*take*' here is 'prostrate to'. It was already mentioned that prostration to people had existed until the time of the Prophet ﷺ and then the Prophet forbade Mu'ādh to prostrate to him as was explained in *al-Baqarah*. Anas ibn Mālik said, 'We asked, "Messenger of Allah, shall we bow to each other?" "No," he answered. We asked, "Shall we embrace one another?" "No," he replied, "shake hands."' Ibn Mājah transmitted it in the *Sunan*. This will be further dealt with in *Sūrat Yūsuf*, as will touching a copy of the Qur'an without being pure in *al-Wāqi'ah*.

يَٰٓأَهْلَ ٱلْكِتَٰبِ لِمَ تُحَآجُّونَ فِىٓ إِبْرَٰهِيمَ وَمَآ أُنزِلَتِ ٱلتَّوْرَىٰةُ وَٱلْإِنجِيلُ
إِلَّا مِنۢ بَعْدِهِۦٓ ۚ أَفَلَا تَعْقِلُونَ ﴿٦٥﴾

65 'People of the Book! why do you argue concerning Ibrāhīm when the Torah and Gospel were only sent down after him? Why do you not use your intellect?

The root of '*lima*' (why) is '*limā*' and the final *alif* has been elided to differentiate between the interrogative and the report. These *āyah*s were revealed because of the claim of each group of the Jews and Christians that Ibrāhīm was following their religion. Allah said that they were lying because Christianity and Judaism only emerged after him. Az-Zajjāj says that this *āyah* is the clearest argument against the Jews and the Christians since both the Torah and Gospel were revealed after Ibrāhīm and the name of their religions is not found in either Scripture while the name Islam is found in every Scripture. It is said that there were a thousand years between Ibrāhīm and Mūsā and a thousand between Mūsā and 'Īsā. The words '*Why do you not use your intellect?*' refutes their argument and invalidates their position. Allah knows best.

هَٰٓأَنتُمْ هَٰٓؤُلَآءِ حَٰجَجْتُمْ فِيمَا لَكُم بِهِۦ عِلْمٌ فَلِمَ تُحَآجُّونَ فِيمَا لَيْسَ
لَكُم بِهِۦ عِلْمٌ ۚ وَٱللَّهُ يَعْلَمُ وَأَنتُمْ لَا تَعْلَمُونَ ﴿٦٦﴾

66 You are people arguing about something of which you have knowledge. Why do you argue about something of which you have no knowledge? Allah knows; you do not know.'

You are people arguing about something of which you have knowledge.

This means about Muḥammad ﷺ because they knew him from his description in their Books and then they used a false argument.

Why do you argue about something of which you have no knowledge?

This refers to their spurious claim about Ibrāhīm being a Jew or a Christian. The root of '*hā antum*' is '*a antum*' and the first *hā'* replaces the *hamzah* because they are sisters as Abū 'Amr ibn al-'Alā' and al-Akhfash said. An-Naḥḥās said that this is a good position. Qunbul reads from Ibn Kathīr: '*ha'ntum*'. The best view is that the *hā'* replaces the *hamzah*. It is possible that the *hā* is to call attention to it, and it is added to '*antum*' and the *alif* is elided because it is used so frequently. There are two dialectal forms for '*hā'ulā'*': extended and short. [Omission]

This *āyah* contains evidence for the prohibition of someone arguing about something about which he has no knowledge and the prohibition of the one with no accurate information. The command to debate is for those with knowledge and certainty, as Allah says: '*Argue with them in the best way.*' (16:125)

It is reported that a man came to the Prophet ﷺ to disown his son and said, 'Messenger of Allah, my wife has given birth to a black boy.' The Messenger of Allah ﷺ asked, 'Do you have camels?' 'Yes,' he replied. He asked, 'What is their colour?' 'Red,' he said. He asked, 'Are there any ash-coloured ones among them?' 'Yes,' he replied. 'Where does that come from?' he asked. He said, 'Because of a throw-back.' The Messenger of Allah ﷺ said, 'This child may be a throw-back.' This is reality of debate and the end of how the Messenger of Allah ﷺ was making guidance clear.

مَا كَانَ إِبْرَٰهِيمُ يَهُودِيًّا وَلَا نَصْرَانِيًّا وَلَٰكِن كَانَ حَنِيفًا مُّسْلِمًا وَمَا
كَانَ مِنَ ٱلْمُشْرِكِينَ ﴿٦٧﴾

67 Ibrāhīm was neither a Jew nor a Christian, but a man of pure natural belief – a Muslim. He was not one of the idolaters.

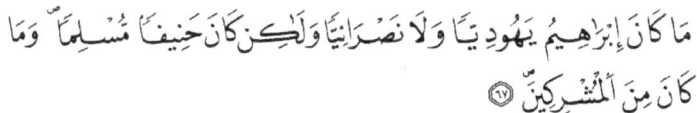

Allah put him above their false claims and made it clear that he was following the Islamic Ḥanīfiyyah religion and was not an idolater. A *ḥanīf* is someone who unifies Allah, makes ḥajj, sacrifices, circumcises and faces *qiblah.* The derivation of Ḥanīf was mentioned in *al-Baqarah.* Linguistically a Muslim is someone who submits to the command of Allah and obeys Him. The meaning of Islam was also adequately discussed in *al-Baqarah.*

إِنَّ أَوْلَى ٱلنَّاسِ بِإِبْرَٰهِيمَ لَلَّذِينَ ٱتَّبَعُوهُ وَهَٰذَا ٱلنَّبِىُّ وَٱلَّذِينَ ءَامَنُوا۟
وَٱللَّهُ وَلِىُّ ٱلْمُؤْمِنِينَ ﴿٦٨﴾

68 The people with the strongest claim to Ibrāhīm are those who followed him and this Prophet and those who believe. Allah is the Protector of the believers.

Ibn 'Abbās said, 'The leaders of the Jews said, "By Allah, Muḥammad, you know that we are the people most entitled to the religion of Ibrāhīm, more than you or any others. He was a Jew and you only envy us." Then Allah revealed this *āyah.*' '*Awlā*' means 'more entitled'. It is said that it means with help and assistance. It is also said that it means with the proof. *'Those who followed him'* are those following his religion and *Sunnah. 'This Prophet'* is singular to show esteem for him. A similar example of using the singular for this purpose is in 55:68, and this was already discussed extensively in *al-Baqarah.*

Walī means helper. Ibn Mas'ūd reported that the Prophet ﷺ said, 'Every Prophet has protectors among the Prophets and my protector among them is my forefather and the Friend of my Lord.' Then he recited this.

وَدَّت طَّآئِفَةٌ مِّنْ أَهْلِ ٱلْكِتَٰبِ لَوْ يُضِلُّونَكُمْ وَمَا يُضِلُّونَ إِلَّآ أَنفُسَهُمْ
وَمَا يَشْعُرُونَ ﴿٦٩﴾

69 A group of the People of the Book would love to misguide you. They only misguide themselves but they are not aware of it.

This was revealed about Mu'ādh ibn Jabal, Ḥudhayfah ibn al-Yaman, and 'Ammār ibn Yāsir when the Jews of the Banū an-Naḍīr, Qurayẓah and Qaynuqā' invited them to their religion. This *āyah* is similar to: *'Many of the People of the Book would love it if they could make you revert to being unbelievers after you have believed, showing their innate envy.'* (2:109). '*Min*' is either partitive, meaning 'some of them', or it is generic meaning 'all'.

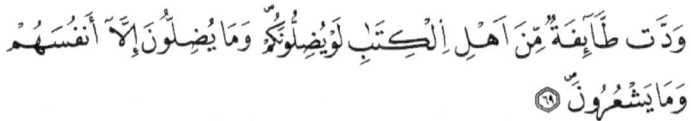

The words '*...to misguide you*' means they want you to disobey by turning from Islam and opposing it. Ibn Jarīr said that it means 'to destroy you.' An example of that is the words of al-Akhṭal:

You were the mote in a disturbed frothing wave
which the flood casts aside and is completely lost (*dalla ḍalālan*).

The words '*...they are not aware*' mean that they will not misguide them, or that they do not know the soundness of Islam, which they should learn because its proofs are evident and arguments radiant. Allah knows best.

يَٰٓأَهْلَ ٱلْكِتَٰبِ لِمَ تَكْفُرُونَ بِـَٔايَٰتِ ٱللَّهِ وَأَنتُمْ تَشْهَدُونَ ﴿٧٠﴾

70 People of the Book! why do you reject Allah's Signs when you yourselves are there as witnesses?

In other words, when you are witnessing the soundest of the signs which you find in your Books, as Qatādah and as-Suddī said. It is also said that it means: 'When you are witnessing something identical to the signs of the Prophets which you affirm.'

يَٰٓأَهْلَ ٱلْكِتَٰبِ لِمَ تَلْبِسُونَ ٱلْحَقَّ بِٱلْبَٰطِلِ وَتَكْتُمُونَ ٱلْحَقَّ وَأَنتُمْ تَعْلَمُونَ ﴿٧١﴾

71 People of the Book! why do you mix truth with falsehood and knowingly conceal the truth?

Mixing is muddling. This was mentioned in *al-Baqarah* as well as the meaning of the previous *āyah* and the one before it. 'Conceal' can also be '*taktumū*' as the answer to the question, and '*knowingly*' (literally 'and you know') is a sentence in the position of a *ḥāl*.

وَقَالَت طَّآئِفَةٌ مِّنْ أَهْلِ ٱلْكِتَٰبِ ءَامِنُوا۟ بِٱلَّذِىٓ أُنزِلَ عَلَى ٱلَّذِينَ ءَامَنُوا۟
وَجْهَ ٱلنَّهَارِ وَٱكْفُرُوٓا۟ ءَاخِرَهُۥ لَعَلَّهُمْ يَرْجِعُونَ ﴿٧٢﴾

72 A group of the People of the Book say, 'At the beginning of the day, you should claim to believe in what was sent down to those who believe, and then at the end of the day, you should reject it, so that hopefully they will revert.

This was revealed about Ka'b ibn al-Ashraf, Mālik ibn aṣ-Ṣayf and others. They said to the lowly among their people, 'Believe in what was revealed to those who believe at the beginning of the day.' '*Wajh*' is used for beginning because it is its best part and the first of what is confronted. A poet said:

Luminous in the beginning (*wajh*) of the day,
like an ocean pearl, slipped from its string.

Another said:

Whoever is happy at the killing of Mālik
should go to our women at the beginning (*wajh*) of the day.

The position of Qatādah is that they did that to make the Muslims uncertain. The word *tā'ifah* means a group. The word is derived from the noun *ṭāfa* and it is used in the singular.

The *āyah* means: The Jews said to one another, 'Display belief in Muḥammad at the beginning of the day and then reject him at the end of it. If you do that, doubt will appear in those who follow him in his religion, and they will revert from his religion to your religion. They will say, "The People of the Book must have better knowledge of it than we do."' It is said that the meaning is: 'Believe in his prayer towards Jerusalem at the beginning of the day, for it is the truth, and reject his other prayer at the end of the day towards the Ka'bah. Hopefully they will revert to your *qiblah*.' Ibn 'Abbās and others said that. Muqātil said that it means that they came to Muḥammad ﷺ at the beginning of the day and then came away from him and told the lowly ones, 'It is true. Follow him.' Then they added, 'Until we look in the Torah.' Then they returned at the end of that day and said, 'We looked in the Torah and it is not him.' They desired to confuse the lowly by that and make them doubt.

وَلَا تُؤْمِنُوٓا۟ إِلَّا لِمَن تَبِعَ دِينَكُمْ قُلْ إِنَّ ٱلْهُدَىٰ هُدَى ٱللَّهِ أَن يُؤْتَىٰٓ أَحَدٌ مِّثْلَ
مَآ أُوتِيتُمْ أَوْ يُحَآجُّوكُمْ عِندَ رَبِّكُمْ قُلْ إِنَّ ٱلْفَضْلَ بِيَدِ ٱللَّهِ يُؤْتِيهِ مَن يَشَآءُ
وَٱللَّهُ وَٰسِعٌ عَلِيمٌ ﴿٧٣﴾

73 Do not trust anyone except for those who follow your dīn.' Say, 'Allah's guidance is true guidance. But you think it is impossible for anyone to be given the same as you were given, or to argue with you before your Lord.' Say, 'All favour is in Allah's Hand and

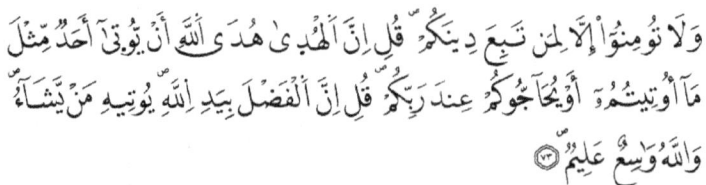

He gives it to whomever He wills. Allah is All-Encompassing, All-Knowing.

Do not trust anyone except for those who follow your dīn.'

This is a prohibition. This is something the Jews said to one another; their leaders said it to their lesser people. As-Suddī said, 'It is what the Jews of Khaybar said to the Jews of Madīnah.'

This *āyah* is the most problematic *(ashkāl)* in the *sūrah*. It is related from al-Ḥasan and Mujāhid that the meaning is: 'Do not believe anyone except those who follow your *dīn* and do not believe that they will argue with you before your Lord because they have no proof. You have a sounder *dīn* than them.' The phrase *'or to argue'* is in the position of the genitive and means 'by their arguing with you'. It means: 'Do not affirm them. They have no argument that anyone else has been given anything like we have been given such as the Torah, the manna and quails, the parting of the sea and other similar signs and marks of distinction.'

Allah's guidance is true guidance.

This is interposed between the two statements.

But you think it is impossible for anyone to be given the same as you were given, or to argue with you before your Lord.'

Al-Akhfash said that import of *'to be given'* is: 'Only believe those who follow your religion and do not believe that anyone will be given the like of what you were given and do not believe that they can argue with you.' It is said that it means that the Jewish scholars said: 'Do not believe that any but those who follow your religion will be given the like of what you were given.' The stress here is their denial that anyone could be given the like of what they were given since the Jewish scholars told them, 'Do not believe that anyone but those who follow your religion will be given the like of what you have been given,' stressing the denial of their statement. That is because the Jewish scholars told them, 'Do not believe that anyone but those who follow your religion will be given the like of what you were given,' meaning that no one else will be given the like of what you have been given. So the wording is according to the order. *'An'* is in the position of the nominative and it implies: 'to affirm or confirm that anyone can be given the like of what you were given,' *'An'* can be in the position of the accusative with a verb implied, which is stronger in Arabic because it is more proper to have a question with a verb. It implies: 'Do you affirm that someone can be given?' or disseminate or mention that?

Ibn Kathīr, Ibn Muḥayṣin and Ḥumayd recited it with *maddah*. Abū Ḥātim said that *'ān'* means *'a li'an'* and the *lām* of the genitive has been elided to lighten the word and the *maddah* has been replaced as we see in 69:14.

According to this reading, it is possible that the words *'argue with you'* refers to the believers and *'aw'* means *'an'* because they are particles of uncertainty and repayment and can be used in place of each other. In that case the *āyah* implies: 'O believers, if they argue with you before your Lord, then say, "O Muḥammad, the true guidance is that of Allah and we follow it."'

If it is read without *maddah*, the first negative indicates their denial when they say, 'Do not believe.' So it means that the Jewish scholars said to them, 'Do not believe that anyone will be given the like of what you have been given, they have neither faith nor proof.' So it is added to the idea of knowledge, wisdom, the Book, the argument, manna and quails, splitting the sea and other qualities and miracles. It means: 'Only you have these things, so do not believe anyone other than those who follow your religion will bring the like of what you have been given.'

There is a change in the normal word order according to this reading and the *lām* is extra. Ibn Jurayj said that it means: 'Only believe those who follow your *dīn*, disliking anyone to be given the like of what you have been given.' Yet another says that it means: 'Do not speak about what your Books contain of Muḥammad's description to anyone except those who follow your religion so that it will not be a way for the idolaters to come to believe him.'

Al-Farrā' said that it is possible that the words of the Jews stop at 'your *dīn*' and then Allah says to Muḥammad ﷺ, *'Say: "Allah's guidance is true guidance,"'* i.e. the true clarification is that of Allah. Then *'But you think it is impossible for anyone to be given the same as you were given'* is to convey the idea that no one will be given the like of what you were given. [Omission]

It is also possible that the entire *āyah* is addressed to the believers to make their hearts firm and focus their inner eyes so that they do not fall into doubt when the Jews try to confuse them and tell lies about their *dīn*. It would then mean: 'Do not believe, believers, other than those follow your *dīn*. Do not believe that they can be given the like of what you have been given of excellence and the *dīn*, and do not believe that those who oppose you can argue with you in the presence of your Lord. Guidance is Allah's guidance and all favour is in His Hand.'

Aḍ-Daḥḥāk said, 'The Jews said, "We will argue with those who oppose our religion in the presence of our Lord," and Allah made it clear that they will be refuted and punished, and that the believers will be the victors and debate with their opponents on the Day of Rising.' We find in a report that the Messenger of Allah ﷺ said, 'The Jews and Christians will argue with us before our Lord, and will say, "You gave us one reward and gave them two rewards!" Allah will say, "Were you wronged in your rights at all?" "No," they will reply. He will say, "That is My bounty which I give to whomever I will."'

Our scholars say that if they had known that that was by the grace of Allah, they would not argue with you in the presence of our Lord. So Allah informed His Prophet ﷺ, 'They will argue with you on the Day of Rising in the presence of your Lord.' Then He said, 'Now tell them: *"All favour is in Allah's Hand and He gives it to whomever He wills. Allah is All-Encompassing, All-Knowing."'* Ibn Kathīr recites *'ān yu'tā'* with *maddah* for the interrogative. [Poetry] The rest have it without *maddah.* Sa'īd ibn Jubayr recited *'in yu'tā'* with a negative meaning, and it is part of the words of Allah as al-Farrā' stated. It means: 'Say, Muḥammad, "Allah's guidance is true guidance. If anyone is given the like of what you have been given or argues with you before your Lord falsely (meaning the Jews) who say, "We are better than you."' [GRAMMATICAL POINTS OMITTED] Al-Ḥasan recited *'an yu'tiya'* meaning, 'that anyone one gives someone the like of what you are given' and the object is elided.

Two things are said about *'Say, "Allah's guidance is true guidance."'* One is that guidance (*hudā*) is guiding to good and direction (*dalāla*) is directing to Allah by the Hand of Allah which He gives to His Prophets. So do not deny He can give to other than you the like of what He gave you. If they deny that, say: *'All favour is in Allah's Hand and He gives it to whomever He wills.'* The second point is that the guidance is Allah's guidance which He gives to the believers in affirming Muḥammad ﷺ, and nothing else. Some of the people of subtle indications say about this *āyah*, 'Only keep the company of those who agree with you in your states and paths.' Allah knows best.

يَخۡتَصُّ بِرَحۡمَتِهِۦ مَن يَشَآءُۗ وَٱللَّهُ ذُو ٱلۡفَضۡلِ ٱلۡعَظِيمِ ٧٤

74 He picks out for His mercy whoever He wills. Allah's favour is indeed immense.'

The word *'mercy'* here refers to Prophethood and guidance, as al-Ḥasan, Mujāhid and others said. Ibn Jurayj said that it means Islam and the Qur'an. Abū 'Uthmān said, 'It is the most beautiful statement since through it, the one with hope hopes and the one with fear fears.

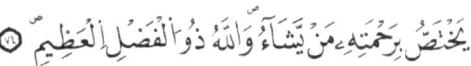

وَمِنْ أَهْلِ ٱلْكِتَٰبِ مَنْ إِن تَأْمَنْهُ بِقِنطَارٍ يُؤَدِّهِۦٓ إِلَيْكَ وَمِنْهُم مَّنْ
إِن تَأْمَنْهُ بِدِينَارٍ لَّا يُؤَدِّهِۦٓ إِلَيْكَ إِلَّا مَا دُمْتَ عَلَيْهِ قَآئِمًا ذَٰلِكَ بِأَنَّهُمْ
قَالُوا۟ لَيْسَ عَلَيْنَا فِى ٱلْأُمِّيِّۦنَ سَبِيلٌ وَيَقُولُونَ عَلَى ٱللَّهِ ٱلْكَذِبَ
وَهُمْ يَعْلَمُونَ ﴿٧٥﴾

75 Among the People of the Book there are some who, if you entrust them with a pile of gold, will return it to you. But there are others among them who, if you entrust them with just a single dinar, will not return it to you, unless you stay standing over them. That is because they say, 'We are under no obligation where the gentiles are concerned.' They tell a lie against Allah and they know it.

Among the People of the Book there are some

This refers to Jews such as 'Abdullāh ibn Salām. The *'others among them'* refers to Jews such as Finḥāṣ ibn 'Āzūrā'. A man entrusted him with a dinar and then he cheated him. It is also said that it refers to Ka'b ibn al-Ashraf and his people.

Ibn Waththāb and al-Ashhab al-'Uqaylī recited *'in tīmnahu'* following the dialect of those who recite *'nista'īn'*. It is the dialect of Bakr and Tamīm. Nāfi' and al-Kisā'ī recite *'yu'ddihī'* with a *yā'*. Abū 'Ubayd said that Abū 'Amr, al-A'mash, 'Āṣim and Ḥamzah in the transmission of Abū Bakr agree that there is a stop on the *hā'* and recite *'yu'dddih'*. An-Naḥḥās said that the *sukūn* on the *hā'* is only permitted in poetry by some grammarians. Some of them do not permit it at all. He thought that it was an error on the part of those who recite it, thinking that the apocative is reflected on the *hā'*. Abū 'Amr is too esteemed to think something like that. What is sound is that he has a *kasrah* on the *hā'* which is the reading of Yazīd ibn al-Qa'qā'. Al-Farrā' said, 'The position of some Arabs is that the *hā'* is in the jussive when there is a vowel preceding it.' [POETRY OMITTED] It is said that there can be a *sukūn* on the *hā'* here because it is in the jussive and it is a faded *hā'*. Abu-l-Mundhīr Sallām and az-Zuhrī recite *'yu'addihu'* with a *ḍammah* on the *hā'* and without a *wāw*. Qatādah,_umayd and Mujāhid recite *'yu'addihū'* with a *wāw*. [MORE ON THIS]

Allah is saying that the People of the Book include both those who are treacherous and those who are trustworthy. The believers cannot distinguish between them and so they should avoid all of them. The People of the Book are singled out for mention, even if some of the believers are like that, because treachery is more frequent among them, and so the words are about what predominates, and Allah knows best.

Qinṭār was already explained. A dinar weighs 24 *qīrāṭ*s, and the *qīrāṭ* is three medium grains of barley and so it is 72 grains. That is agreed upon. If someone is mindful when it is a lot and discharges it, then it is more likely that he will be the same with a little. If someone is treacherous about a little or refuses to give it, that will be more likely when there is a lot. This is the clearest evidence of the principle of what is implied by the words, and there is great disagreement about it among scholars of legal principles.

Allah mentioned two groups: those who pay readily and those who only pay when they are forced to do so. There are also people who do not pay even if you stand over them. Allah mentioned both groups because they are usual while the third is rare. The words deal with what is usual. Ṭalḥah ibn Muṣarraf, Abū 'Abd ar-Raḥmān as-Sulamī and others recited '*dimtu*' which is the dialect of Azd as-Sarāh.

Abū Ḥanīfah used the words, *'unless you stay standing over them'* as evidence for staying close to debtors while the other scholars reject that. It was discussed in *al-Baqarah*. Some of our Baghdādī scholars used this as evidence for imprisoning debtors since if a debtor can be pursued and kept from transacting, it is also permitted to imprison him.

It is said that the meaning is 'You confront him and intimidate him and make him embarrassed.' Modesty is in the eyes. Do you not see what Ibn 'Abbās said, 'Do not seek something you need from the blind. Modesty is in the eyes. If you seek something you need from your brother, look at him directly in the face so that he is embarrassed and gives it.' It is said that *'standing'* is sticking to him. It is also said that 'standing' refers to constant asking, not physical standing.

The root of dinar is *dinnār* and one of the *nūn*s has been changed into a *yā'* to lighten the word because it is so frequently used. That is indicated by the plural, *danānīr*, and the diminutive *dunaynīr*.

Trusts are of immense importance in the *dīn*. Part of what shows this is that trusts and kinship will stand at the sides of the Sirāṭ, as is stated in *Ṣaḥīḥ Muslim*, and only someone who was conscientious about both of them will be able to cross it. Muslim related that Ḥudhayfah said that the Prophet ﷺ told them about the removal of trust and said, 'A man will go to sleep and trustworthiness will be taken from his heart and just its trace will remain.' That was mentioned in full in *al-Baqarah*.

In Ibn Mājah, Ibn 'Umar reported that the Prophet ﷺ said, 'When Allah

Almighty wants to destroy someone, He strips away modesty from him. When modesty is stripped from him, you only meet him as hateful and hated. When you only meet him as hateful and hated, trustworthiness is stripped from him. When trustworthiness is stripped from him, you only meet him as treacherous and perfidious. When you only meet him as treacherous and perfidious, then mercy is stripped from him. When mercy is stripped from him, you only meet him as accursed and cursed. When you only meet him as accursed and cursed, then the halter of Islam is removed from him.' The Prophet ﷺ said, 'Return the trust to the one who entrusted it to you and do not betray the one who betrays you.' Allah knows best.

There is no granting of legal integrity to the People of the Book as a whole, nor to some of them, on the basis of this *āyah*, contrary to what some believe about that, because there are impious Muslims to whom trust is given, and who are entrusted with a lot of wealth, and that is not considered to be a reason for deeming them to be upright. The method of establishing legal integrity and witnessing is not satisfied by merely discharging a trust in property in transactions and deposits. Do you not see their words: *'We are under no obligation where the gentiles are concerned'* (3:75)? How can one consider as just someone who believes that our property and honour are fair game? If that had been enough to establish their legal integrity, their testimony against Muslims would have been allowed.

That is because they say, 'We are under no obligation where the gentiles are concerned.'

The subject of *'they say'* is the Jews. It is said that when the Jews gave allegiance to the Muslims, they said, *'We are under no obligation where the gentiles are concerned,'* in other words, 'There is no barrier stopping us from wronging them since they differ from us.' They claimed that that is in their Book. Allah says that they are lying and refuted them, saying that, on the contrary, they should be punished for their lies and thinking it to be lawful to take other people's property. Abū Isḥāq az-Zajjāj says, 'The sentence ends with *'No'* and *'The truth is, if people honour their contracts…'* is a new sentence.

It is said that the Jews used to contract debts with the Arabs and when those with the rights asked for their rights, the Jews said, 'You have "*no way against us*" because you left your *dīn* and so your debt is cancelled for us.' They claimed that it was the ruling of the Torah and here Allah refutes them, saying that it is not as they say. Allah told them, *'No,'* refuting their claim that: *'We are under no obligation where the gentiles are concerned.'* Then He says: *'The truth is, if people honour their contracts and are godfearing,'* fearing *shirk*, they are not among the liars, but Allah and His Messenger love them.

A man said to Ibn ʿAbbās, 'We deliberately take a portion of the property of the people of the *dhimmah* in the form of a chicken or a sheep and we say, "There is no harm in that."' He said, 'This is like what the People of the Book said: "*We are under no obligation where the Gentiles are concerned.*" If they have paid the *jizyah*, their property is not lawful for you except with their consent.' ʿAbd ar-Razzāq mentioned it from Maʿmar from Abū Isḥāq al-Hamdānī from Ṣaʿṣaʿah.

They tell a lie against Allah and they know it.

This indicates that an unbeliever is not worthy of having his testimony accepted because Allah has described him as being a liar. It also refutes the unbelievers who make *ḥalāl* and *ḥarām* other than what Allah has made *ḥalāl* and *ḥarām*, and put that in their *Sharīʿah*. Ibn al-ʿArabī said, 'From this is deduced a refutation of those who give judgment based on the principle of *istiḥsān* without any proof. I do not know of any of the people of the qiblah who say this.' We find in a tradition: 'When this *āyah* was revealed, the Prophet ﷺ said, "There is nothing in the *Jāhiliyyah* which is not under my feet except for trusts. They must be discharged to both the pious and impious."'

بَلَىٰ مَنْ أَوْفَىٰ بِعَهْدِهِۦ وَٱتَّقَىٰ فَإِنَّ ٱللَّهَ يُحِبُّ ٱلْمُتَّقِينَ ٧٦

76 No, the truth is, if people honour their contracts and are godfearing, Allah loves the godfearing.

These are those who fear Allah and do not lie and do not make *ḥalāl* what has made *ḥarām*. Allah loves those people. The meaning of that has already been discussed. The personal pronoun *hā'* connected to 'contract' can refer to Allah, or it is possible that it is refers to those who honour, and fear disbelief, treachery and breaking contracts. *ʿAhd* (contract) is a verbal noun.

إِنَّ ٱلَّذِينَ يَشْتَرُونَ بِعَهْدِ ٱللَّهِ وَأَيْمَٰنِهِمْ ثَمَنًا قَلِيلًا أُو۟لَٰٓئِكَ لَا خَلَٰقَ
لَهُمْ فِى ٱلْءَاخِرَةِ وَلَا يُكَلِّمُهُمُ ٱللَّهُ وَلَا يَنظُرُ إِلَيْهِمْ يَوْمَ ٱلْقِيَٰمَةِ وَلَا يُزَكِّيهِمْ
وَلَهُمْ عَذَابٌ أَلِيمٌ ٧٧

77 Those who sell Allah's contract and their own oaths for a paltry price, such people will have no portion in the Next World and on the Day of Rising Allah will not speak to them or look at them or purify them. They will have a painful punishment.

The Imāms related that al-Ash'ath ibn Qays said, 'There was some land that was shared between me and a Jewish man, and he disavowed me, so I took him to the Prophet ﷺ. The Messenger of Allah ﷺ asked me, "Do you have a clear proof?" I answered, "No." He said to the Jew, "Swear." I said, "Messenger of Allah, then he will swear and make off with my property." Then Allah revealed: *"Those who sell Allah's contract and their own oaths for a paltry price..."*'

The Imāms also related from Abū Umāmah that the Messenger of Allah ﷺ said, 'If anyone takes the right of a Muslim by his oath, Allah will make the Fire obligatory for him and deny him the Garden.' A man said to him, 'Even if it is something insignificant, Messenger of Allah?' He said, 'Even if it is only an arak stick.' Allah not looking at them on the Day of Rising was dealt with in *al-Baqarah.*

This *āyah* and the hadiths indicate that the outward judgment of a judge does not make property lawful inwardly if the one who is given the judgment knows it to be false. The Imāms related from Umm Salamah that the Messenger of Allah ﷺ said, 'Litigants come to me and it may be that one of them is more eloquent in his argument than the other and so, because of that, I give judgment about some right, which actually belongs to his brother, in his favour. By doing that I cut out for him a piece of the Fire which he will bring on the Day of Rising, so he should not take it.'

There is no disagreement about this among the Imāms. Abū Ḥanīfah is excessive, saying, 'The judgment of a judge based on false testimony allows marriage for the one who was forbidden it,' as was mentioned in *al-Baqarah.* He claimed that if there are two false witnesses that a man has divorced his wife and the judge decides based on their testimony, she is lawful for the one who marries her knowing that to be false. This is abhorrent and not in keeping with explicit hadiths. It protects property and does not consider it to be lawful based on false rulings. Would property be protected, but not sexual relations? The falsity of this will be dealt with in the *āyah* about the *li'ān.* Allah knows best.

وَإِنَّ مِنْهُمْ لَفَرِيقًا يَلْوُۥنَ أَلْسِنَتَهُم بِالْكِتَٰبِ لِتَحْسَبُوهُ مِنَ الْكِتَٰبِ
وَمَا هُوَ مِنَ الْكِتَٰبِ وَيَقُولُونَ هُوَ مِنْ عِندِ اللَّهِ وَمَا هُوَ مِنْ عِندِ اللَّهِ
وَيَقُولُونَ عَلَى اللَّهِ الْكَذِبَ وَهُمْ يَعْلَمُونَ ﴿٧٨﴾

78 Among them is a group who distort the Book with their tongues so that you think it is from the Book when it is not from the Book. They say, 'It is from Allah,' but it is not from Allah. They tell a lie against Allah and they know it.

This means a group of the Jews. Abū Jaʿfar and Shaybah recited *'yuluwūna'* indicating frequency. It means that they alter words and make them mean other than what is intended. The root of *layy* is to incline. One can incline with the hand or with the head. Allah says elsewhere: *'twisting them with their tongues'* (4:46) which means displaying obstinacy about the truth and turning away from it to something else. The same verb used in the phrase: *'…refusing to turn back for anyone'* (3:153) means to turn to him when they were climbing. One says *lawā ʿalayhi*, meaning to turn towards and stand. *Layy* is bending. The verb is *lawā*, *yalwī*, *layy* and *liyān*. [Poetry] We find in hadith, 'The twisting of the finder exposes his honour and exposes him to punishment.' *Alsinah* (tongues) is the plural of *lisān* if it is masculine, and if it is feminine it is *alsun*.

مَا كَانَ لِبَشَرٍ أَن يُؤْتِيَهُ اللَّهُ الْكِتَٰبَ وَالْحُكْمَ وَالنُّبُوَّةَ ثُمَّ يَقُولَ لِلنَّاسِ
كُونُوا عِبَادًا لِّي مِن دُونِ اللَّهِ وَلَٰكِن كُونُوا رَبَّٰنِيِّينَ بِمَا كُنتُمْ
تَعْلَمُونَ الْكِتَٰبَ وَبِمَا كُنتُمْ تَدْرُسُونَ ﴿٧٩﴾

79 It is not right for any human being that Allah should give him the Book and judgment and Prophethood, and then that he should say to people, 'Be worshippers of me rather than Allah.' Rather he will say, 'Be people of the Lord because of your knowledge of the Book and because you study.'

'Mā kāna' means 'he should not'. We see this usage in 4:92, 19:35, and 24:16. *'Bashar'* (human being) can be used for both the plural and the singular because it is a verbal noun. Here it is ʿĪsā who is indicated according to aḍ-Ḍaḥḥāk and as-Suddī, and the Book is the Qur'an, and judgment is knowledge and understanding. It is also said that it is judgments, meaning that Allah does not permit lying to be

part of Prophethood. If a human being were to do that, Allah would strip him of the signs of Prophethood. It is, however, possible for a Prophet to say to people, '*Be people of the Lord*.' This *āyah* was revealed about the Christians of Najrān. As we said, it is related that the cause of the revelation of the entire *sūrah* up to *āyah* 121 was the arrival of the Christians of Najrān, but the Jews are mixed with them because they denied and were obstinate like them.

Rabbāniyyūn is connected to the word '*Lord*' (*rabb*). A *rabbānī* is the one who instructs (*rabbā*) people with a little knowledge before it becomes great. It is as if he were imitating the Lord in making matters easy. That idea is related from Ibn 'Abbās. Some have said that root is '*rabbiyy*' and the *alif-nūn* are added for stress.

Al-Mubarrad said, 'The *rabbāniyyūn* are the masters of knowledge, and the singular is *rabbān*. It it comes from a root meaning "to put right".' It means that they manage the affairs of people and put them right. The *alif* and *nūn* is for stress as in words like *rayyān* and '*aṭshān*. Then the *ḍammah* of the ascription is added to it as is seen in other words. A poet said:

If I am a pledgee in the air, I am put there
by the *rabbānī* hadith scholars.

'*Rabbānī*' means a scholar with knowledge of the *dīn* of the Lord who acts on his knowledge, because if he does not act on it, then he is not a scholar. This idea was discussed in *al-Baqarah*.

Abū Razīn says that it means 'wise scholars'. Shu'bāh related from 'Āṣim from Zirr that 'Abdullāh ibn Mas'ūd is reported as saying that it means the wise among the scholars, and Ibn Jubayr says that it is godfearing sages. Aḍ-Ḍaḥḥāk said, 'No one should abandon the memorisation of the Qur'an,' and quoted this verse. Ibn Zayd said that it refers to rulers and rabbis. Mujāhid said that they are higher than the rabbis. An-Nahhās approves of this, saying that *aḥbār* are rabbis and a *rabbānī* is the one who also has insight into political matters.

The Arabs use the verb *rabba* for putting people's affairs right and attending to them. Such a person is *rābb* and *rabbānī*. Abū 'Ubaydah said, 'I heard a scholar say "The *rabbānī* is the one who knows the lawful and unlawful, commands and prohibitions, and knows the news of the community, past and present."'

When Ibn 'Abbās died, Muḥammad ibn al-Ḥanafiyyah said, 'Today the *rabbānī* of this community has died.' It is related that the Prophet ﷺ said, 'There is no believer, male or female, free or slave, but that it is their duty to Allah Almighty to learn the Qur'ān and understanding in the *dīn*.' Then he recited: '*Be people of the Lord...*' Ibn 'Abbās related it.

because of your knowledge of the Book and because you study.'

The people of Madīnah and Abū 'Amr read *ta'lamūna*, 'what you know' which corresponds with 'study'. Abū Ḥātim preferred this reading. Abū 'Amr said that it is confirmed by 'study' (*tadrusūna*) in Form I, not '*tudarrisūna*' meaning 'teach'. Ibn 'Āmir and the people of Kufa read it '*tu'allimūna*', meaning 'teach'. Abū 'Ubayd preferred it because it combines the two meanings. Makkī said that Form II is more eloquent because every teacher has knowledge, but not everyone with knowledge is a teacher. Form II indicates both whereas Form I only indicates knowledge. So it is more emphatic and coveys greater censure. The reading with Form I finds evidence in the words of Ibn Mas'ūd who said that *rabbāniyyūn* means the wise among the scholars. So it is unlikely that one would say: 'be wise scholars because of what you teach.' Al-Ḥasan said, 'Be wise scholars by your knowledge.' Abū Ḥaywah recited '*tudrisūna*' from Form IV and Mujāhid recited '*ta'allimūna*'.

وَلَا يَأْمُرَكُمْ أَن تَتَّخِذُوا۟ ٱلْمَلَٰٓئِكَةَ وَٱلنَّبِيِّـۧنَ أَرْبَابًا ۗ أَيَأْمُرُكُم
بِٱلْكُفْرِ بَعْدَ إِذْ أَنتُم مُّسْلِمُونَ ۝٨٠

80 He would never command you to take the angels and Prophets as Lords. Would He command you to disbelieve after being Muslim?

Ibn 'Āmir, 'Āṣim and Ḥamzah recited '*lā ya'murakum*' as joined to the previous 'give.' This is strengthened because the Jews asked the Prophet ﷺ, 'Do you want us to take you as a Lord, Muḥammad?' Then Allah revealed the two verses. 'He' here can refer to 'a human being': 'No human being would command,' meaning 'Īsā or 'Uzayr. The rest recite it as '*lā ya'murukum*' as a new sentence separate from the previous words. So the pronoun refers to Allah: 'Allah would never command...' This is strengthened by the reading in the copy of the Qur'an of 'Abdullah: '*lan ya'murukum*' which indicates a new sentence and the pronoun refers to Allah. Makkī mentioned it. Sībuwayh and az-Zajjāj said that. Ibn Jurayj and a group said: Muḥammad ﷺ would not command you (*lā ya'murkum*). This is the reading of Abū 'Amr, al-Kisā'ī and the people of the two *Ḥarams*.

He would not command taking the angels and Prophets as Lords. The Christians esteem Prophets and angels to the extent that they turn them into Lords.

Would He command you to disbelieve after being Muslim?

This expresses denial and astonishment. Allah forbade the Prophets from making people slaves so that they would deify them. But people are obliged to respect them. It is confirmed that the Prophet ﷺ said, 'None of you should say, "my slave" (*'abdī*) or "my slavegirl" (*amatī*), but he should say, 'my lad' or 'my girl. None of you should say "my lord", but should say "my master".' We do find in the Revelation in *Surah Yusuf*: *'Mention me when you are with your Lord.'* (12:42) This usage will be explained there, Allah willing.

وَإِذْ أَخَذَ ٱللَّهُ مِيثَٰقَ ٱلنَّبِيِّـۧنَ لَمَآءَاتَيْنَٰكُم مِّن كِتَٰبٍ وَحِكْمَةٍ ثُمَّ جَآءَكُمْ
رَسُولٌ مُّصَدِّقٌ لِّمَا مَعَكُمْ لَتُؤْمِنُنَّ بِهِۦ وَلَتَنصُرُنَّهُۥ ۚ قَالَ ءَأَقْرَرْتُمْ
وَأَخَذْتُمْ عَلَىٰ ذَٰلِكُمْ إِصْرِى ۖ قَالُوٓاْ أَقْرَرْنَا ۚ قَالَ فَٱشْهَدُواْ وَأَنَا۠ مَعَكُم
مِّنَ ٱلشَّٰهِدِينَ ﴿٨١﴾

81 Remember when Allah made a covenant with the Prophets: 'Now that I have given you a share of the Book and Wisdom, and then a messenger comes to you confirming what is with you, you must believe in him and help him.' He asked, 'Do you agree and undertake my commission on that condition?' They replied, 'We agree.' He said, 'Bear witness, then. I am with you as one of the witnesses.'

Remember when Allah made a covenant with the Prophets:

It is said that Allah made a covenant with the Prophets that they should affirm one another and command belief in one another. That is the meaning of helping by confirmation. This is the position of Sa'īd ibn Jubayr, Qatādah, Ṭāwus, as-Suddī and al-Ḥasan. It is the literal meaning of the *āyah*. Ṭāwus said, 'Allah made a covenant with the first of the Prophets to believe in what the last brings.' Ibn Mas'ūd recited, 'When Allah made a covenant with those who were given the Book.' Al-Kisā'ī said, 'It is possible that it means: when He made a covenant with those who were with the Prophets.' The Basrans said, 'When Allah made a covenant with the Prophets, He made one with those who were with them because they followed them and affirmed them.' So *mā* in *limā* means 'which'. Sībawayh said, 'I asked al-Khalīl ibn Aḥmad about "*When Allah made a covenant...*" and he said, "when" means "which".' An-Naḥḥās said, 'According to al-Khalīl's view, it implies "to that which I gave you" and the pronoun *hā'* is elided because of the length of the word. '*Min*' clarifies the genus. This is like the position of al-Akhfash. Al-Mahdawī said that '*comes to you*' and what follows it is a sentence added to a connective and they refer to something described which is elided. It implies: 'Then a Messenger comes to you, confirming it.'

Then a Messenger comes to you confirming what is with you, you must believe in him and help him.'

Here the Messenger is Muḥammad ﷺ according to 'Alī and Ibn 'Abbās. Even though the indefinite is used, it indicates someone specific, a usage also seen in 16:112-113. So Allah made a covenant with all the Prophets to believe in Muḥammad ﷺ and help him if they were to meet him. He commanded them to take on that contract on behalf of their communities.

The *lām* connected to *'you must believe'* is the apodosis of the oath which is taking the covenant since it is like an oath. It is like saying, 'I took your covenant that you should do such-and-such.' It is as if you were asking for an oath. The oath and its apodosis are separated by a particle which is '*limā*' in the reading of Ibn Kathīr as will come. Those who read it as '*lamā*' make it accept the oath, which is making the covenant. The *lām* connected to the words *'you must believe'* is the apodosis of an elided oath, implying, 'By Allah, you must believe!'

Al-Mubarrad and az-Zajjāj said that *'mā'* is a precondition to which the *lām* of realisation is added as it is added to *in*. It means 'I have given you both of them' and *mā* is in the accusative and 'I have given' is jussive. 'Comes to you' is added to it and the *lām* is the apodosis of the repayment as we also see in 16:86. Al-Kisā'ī said that '*believe in it*' is the support of the oath and it is connected by the first *lām*.

The people of Kufa recite '*limā*' which means 'which' and is connected to 'take', meaning that Allah made a covenant with them because of what He gave them of the Book and Wisdom. Then a Messenger comes to them confirming what is with them so that they believe in him after the covenant, because taking the covenant has the meaning of making someone swear an oath. An-Naḥḥās said that Abū 'Ubaydah said that this is a good position and the meaning is: 'When Allah made a covenant with those who were given the Book: "You should believe in him since I have told you about him in the Torah."'

It is also said that there is some elision in the words and it means: 'When Allah made a covenant with the Prophets: "Teach people what has come to you of the Book and Wisdom and to oblige people to believe."' This elision is indicated by *'Do you undertake My commission on that condition?'* It is also said that '*limā*' means 'after', meaning 'after what I have given you of the Book and Wisdom.'

Sa'īd ibn Jubayr reads *'lammā'* ('when I have given'). It is possible that the root is '*lamā*' and '*min*' is added according to the view of those who think that its addition is mandatory. The *nūn* has changed into a *mīm* and there are three *mīms*, one of which is elided. The people of Madīnah recite 'We have given you' (*ātaynākum*) whereas the others have 'I have given' (*ātaytukum*) in the singular. Not all Prophets were given the Book, only some, but the generality takes precedence here and it applies to the Prophets who were not given the Book because they were given wisdom and Prophethood. Those not given a Book are commanded to take the Book of those before them and so they are included in the description of those who were given the Book.

He asked, 'Do you agree and undertake my commission on that condition?'

The verb *'agree'* is derived from *iqrār* (affirm). The *'commission'* (*iṣr* and *aṣr*) is the contract. Linguistically it means a burden. It is called that because it involves prohibition and making things difficult.

He said, 'Bear witness, then.'

The verb *'bear witness'* means 'know', as Ibn 'Abbās said. Az-Zajjaj said that it means 'make clear' because the witness is the one who verifies the claim of the claimant. It is said that it means: 'Bear witness against yourselves and your followers.' Sa'id ibn al-Musayyab said, 'Allah says to the angels: bear witness against them.'

فَمَن تَوَلَّىٰ بَعْدَ ذَٰلِكَ فَأُولَٰٓئِكَ هُمُ ٱلْفَٰسِقُونَ ﴿٨٢﴾

82 Any who turn away after that are deviators.

Any from the nations of the Prophets who turn away from faith after taking the covenant. Those are the one who have left faith. Someone who is *fāsiq* is someone who goes out.

أَفَغَيْرَ دِينِ ٱللَّهِ تَبْغُونَ وَلَهُۥٓ أَسْلَمَ مَن فِى ٱلسَّمَٰوَٰتِ وَٱلْأَرْضِ طَوْعًا وَكَرْهًا
وَإِلَيْهِ تُرْجَعُونَ ﴿٨٣﴾ قُلْ ءَامَنَّا بِٱللَّهِ وَمَآ أُنزِلَ عَلَيْنَا وَمَآ أُنزِلَ عَلَىٰٓ
إِبْرَٰهِيمَ وَإِسْمَٰعِيلَ وَإِسْحَٰقَ وَيَعْقُوبَ وَٱلْأَسْبَاطِ وَمَآ أُوتِىَ
مُوسَىٰ وَعِيسَىٰ وَٱلنَّبِيُّونَ مِن رَّبِّهِمْ لَا نُفَرِّقُ بَيْنَ أَحَدٍ مِّنْهُمْ وَنَحْنُ لَهُۥ
مُسْلِمُونَ ﴿٨٤﴾

83 Is it other than the dīn of Allah that you desire, when everything in the heavens and earth, willingly or unwillingly, submits to Him and to Him you will be returned? 84 Say, 'We believe in Allah and what has been sent down to us and what was sent down to Ibrāhīm, Ismā'īl and Isḥāq and Ya'qūb and the Tribes, and what Mūsā and 'Īsā and all the Prophets were given by their Lord. We do not differentiate between any of them. We are Muslims submitted to Him.'

Is it other than the dīn of Allah that you desire.

Al-Kalbī said that Ka'b ibn al-Ashraf and his people took an argument they were having with the Christians to the Prophet ﷺ and asked, 'Which of us is more entitled to the *dīn* of Ibrāhīm?' He replied, 'Neither of the parties have his *dīn*.' They said, 'We are not satisfied with your verdict and we will not take your *dīn*.' Then this was revealed. Abū 'Amr reads it with *yā'* (they desire, they return) and with *tā'* (you desire, you return). He said the first is specific and the second general and so there is a distinction. Ḥafṣ and others read them both in the third person and the rest with *tā'* on both as second person. Allah knows best.

willingly or unwillingly, submits to Him and to Him you will be returned?

The words *'submits to Him'* mean surrenders, obeys, is humble and subjected. Every creature is obedient and submits because it is created in a form that it cannot depart from. Qatādah said, 'The believer submits willingly and the unbeliever, at death, unwillingly and that does not help him, since the Almighty says: *"But when they saw Our violent force, their faith was of no use to them."* (40:85)' Mujāhid said, 'The submission of the unbeliever is proved unwilling by his prostrating to other than Allah while his shadow prostrates to Allah. Allah says: *"Do they not see the things Allah has created, casting their shadows to the right and the left, prostrating themselves before Allah in complete humility?"* (16:48) and: *"Everyone in heaven or earth prostrates to Allah, willingly or unwillingly."* (13:15)' It is said that the meaning is that Allah created creation as He wills: some of them handsome, some ugly, tall and short, healthy and sick, but all have no choice but to obey. The healthy obeys and loves that, and the sick obeys and submits even if he dislikes that. Willingly is submitting with ease and unwillingly is with hardship and rejection on the part of the self. *'Ṭaw''* and *'karh'* (willingly and unwillingly) are two verbal nouns used adverbially.

Anas ibn Mālik reported that the Messenger of Allah ﷺ said about this, 'The angels obey Him in heaven and the Anṣār and 'Abd al-Qays on the earth.' The Prophet ﷺ also said, 'Do not curse my Companions. My Companions have submitted out of fear of Allah while other people submit out of fear of the sword.'

'Ikrimah said that 'willingly' implies without need of proof and 'unwillingly' means compelled by the evidence of *tawḥīd.* This is indicated by Allah's words: *'If you asked them who created them, they would say, "Allah!"'* (43:87) and: *'If you ask them, "Who created the heavens and the earth and made the sun and moon subservient?" they will say, "Allah."'* (29:63) Al-Ḥasan said, 'It is general, but its meaning is specific.' He also said that the sentence ends at *'everything in the heavens submits to Him,'* and then Allah says: *'and the earth, willingly or unwillingly.'* He said that the unwilling are the hypocrites whose knowledge does not benefit them. Mujāhid said that Ibn 'Abbās said, 'When someone's animal is difficult or baulks, recite this *āyah* in its ear.'

وَمَن يَبْتَغِ غَيْرَ ٱلْإِسْلَٰمِ دِينًا فَلَن يُقْبَلَ مِنْهُ وَهُوَ فِى ٱلْءَاخِرَةِ مِنَ
ٱلْخَٰسِرِينَ ﴿٨٥﴾

85 If anyone desires anything other than Islam as a dīn, it will not be accepted from him, and in the Next World he will be among the losers.

Mujāhid and as-Suddī said, 'This *āyah* was revealed about al-Ḥārith ibn Suwayd, the brother of al-Ḥulās ibn Suwayd. He was one of the Anṣār. He apostatised from Islam along with twelve men, and they joined the unbelievers in Makkah and this *āyah* was revealed about them. Then he sent to his brother desiring to repent.' That was related from Ibn 'Abbās and others. Ibn 'Abbās said he became Muslim after this was revealed.

and in the Next World he will be among the losers

Hishām said that it means that he will be one of the losers in the Next World. Were it not for that, there would be a separation between the connection and what is connected to. This was already discussed in *al-Baqarah* (2:130).

كَيْفَ يَهْدِى ٱللَّهُ قَوْمًا كَفَرُوا۟ بَعْدَ إِيمَٰنِهِمْ وَشَهِدُوٓا۟ أَنَّ ٱلرَّسُولَ
حَقٌّ وَجَآءَهُمُ ٱلْبَيِّنَٰتُ وَٱللَّهُ لَا يَهْدِى ٱلْقَوْمَ ٱلظَّٰلِمِينَ ﴿٨٦﴾

86 How can Allah guide a people who have disbelieved after having believed? They bore witness that the Messenger was true and that the Clear Signs had come to them. Allah does not guide people who are wrongdoers.

Ibn 'Abbās said, 'A man of the Anṣār became Muslim and then apostasised, became an idolater and then regretted it. He sent to his people to ask the Prophet ﷺ if he could repent. His people went to the Messenger of Allah ﷺ and asked, "Is it possible for him to repent?" Then it was revealed: *'How can Allah guide a people who have disbelieved after having believed…'* (3:86-89) He sent to him and he became Muslim.' An-Nasā'ī transmitted it. One variant reports that a man of the Anṣār became Muslim and then apostasised and joined the idolaters and Allah revealed this. His people sent those *āyah*s to him and when he had read them, he said, 'By Allah, my people would not lie to me about the Messenger of Allah ﷺ and the Messenger of Allah ﷺ would not lie about Allah, and Allah Almighty is the most truthful of the three.' So he repented and returned. The Messenger of Allah ﷺ accepted that from him and let him be.

Al-Ḥasan says that it was revealed about the Jews because they were given the good news of the Prophet ﷺ and prayed for him against the unbelievers. Then when he was sent, they were stubborn and rejected and so Allah revealed, *'The repayment of such people …'*

It is said that the word '*how*' introduces a question which implies denial, meaning *'Allah will not guide…'*. It is the same as Allah's words: *'How could any of the idolaters possibly have a treaty with Allah and with His Messenger?'* (9:7) which means that they do not have a treaty. A poet says:

How can I sleep on a bed
    When there are people all over it?

Allah does not guide people who are wrongdoers.

The literal meaning of the *āyah* would be that someone who disbelieves after becoming Muslim cannot be guided by Allah and Allah does not guide wrongdoers. We know, however, that many apostates became Muslims and were guided by Allah and many wrongdoers repented of the injustice they inflicted. Therefore, it actually means: 'Allah does not guide them as long as they remain in their disbelief and injustice and do not accept Islam.' When they become Muslim and repent, Allah gives them success in that, and Allah knows best.

أُولَٰٓئِكَ جَزَآؤُهُمْ أَنَّ عَلَيْهِمْ لَعْنَةَ ٱللَّهِ وَٱلْمَلَٰٓئِكَةِ وَٱلنَّاسِ
أَجْمَعِينَ ﴿٨٧﴾ خَٰلِدِينَ فِيهَا لَا يُخَفَّفُ عَنْهُمُ ٱلْعَذَابُ وَلَا هُمْ يُنظَرُونَ ﴿٨٨﴾
إِلَّا ٱلَّذِينَ تَابُوا۟ مِنۢ بَعْدِ ذَٰلِكَ وَأَصْلَحُوا۟ فَإِنَّ ٱللَّهَ غَفُورٌ رَّحِيمٌ ﴿٨٩﴾

87 The repayment of such people is that Allah's curse is on them and that of the angels and of all mankind. 88 They will be under it for ever. Their punishment will not be lightened. They will be granted no reprieve. 89 Except for those who, after that, repent and put things right. Truly Allah is Ever-Forgiving, Most Merciful.

This is when they remain with their disbelief. The meaning of the curse was mentioned in *al-Baqarah*. They will not be granted a delay. 'Those who repent' refers to al-Ḥārith ibn Suwayd, as we already stated. Included in the exception are all those who return sincerely to Islam.

إِنَّ ٱلَّذِينَ كَفَرُوا۟ بَعْدَ إِيمَٰنِهِمْ ثُمَّ ٱزْدَادُوا۟ كُفْرًا لَّن تُقْبَلَ
تَوْبَتُهُمْ وَأُو۟لَٰٓئِكَ هُمُ ٱلضَّآلُّونَ ﴿٩٠﴾

90 Those who disbelieve after having believed and then increase in their unbelief, their repentance will not be accepted. They are the misguided.

Qatādah, 'Aṭā' al-Khurasānī and al-Ḥasan said that this was revealed about the Jews who rejected 'Īsā and the Gospel and then further disbelieved in Muḥammad ﷺ and the Qur'an. Abu-l-'Āliyah said, 'It was revealed about the Jews and Christians who rejected Muḥammad ﷺ after their belief in his attribute and description. They *'increase in their unbelief'* by remaining in their unbelief, or by the wrong actions they acquired. This last is what aṭ-Ṭabarī prefers. He believes that it is about the Jews.

Their repentance will not be accepted.

This is problematic since Allah says, *'It is He Who accepts repentance from His slaves and pardons evil acts.'* (42:25) It is said to mean: 'Their repentance will not be accepted at the point of death.' An-Naḥḥās said this is a good position, as Allah says: *'There is no repentance for people who persist in doing evil until death appears to them and who then say, "Now I repent."'* (4:18) It is related from al-Ḥasan, Qatādah and 'Aṭā, and the Prophet ﷺ said, 'Allah accepts the repentance of the slave as long as he is not in his death throes.' This will be discussed in *an-Nisā'*.

It is said that the words *'their repentance will not be accepted'* refer to the good they may have done before they disbelieved because their disbelief cancels those actions. It is said that it means when they turn from their disbelief to another disbelief, but their repentance will be accepted when they return to Islam.

Quṭrub said that this *āyah* was revealed about some of the people of Makkah. They said, 'We will wait for death to befall Muḥammad. If it seems good to us to return to our people, we will do so,' and Allah revealed this, meaning that their repentance will not be accepted while they remain in disbelief. It is not accepted because their resolve is not genuine. Allah accepts all repentance when resolve is genuine.

إِنَّ ٱلَّذِينَ كَفَرُواْ وَمَاتُواْ وَهُمْ كُفَّارٌ فَلَن يُقْبَلَ مِنْ أَحَدِهِم مِّلْءُ ٱلْأَرْضِ
ذَهَبًا وَلَوِ ٱفْتَدَىٰ بِهِۦٓ أُوْلَٰٓئِكَ لَهُمْ عَذَابٌ أَلِيمٌ وَمَا لَهُم مِّن نَّٰصِرِينَ ٩١

91 As for those who disbelieve and die unbelievers, the whole earth filled with gold would not be accepted from any of them if they were to offer it as a ransom. They will have a painful punishment. They will have no helpers.

The word *mil'* designates the amount which will fill a thing and *mal'* is the verbal noun for filling a thing. The *wāw* before '*if they were to offer*' is interpolated and redundant. The *āyah* means: the whole earth filled with gold would not be accepted from anyone if he were to try and ransom himself with it. Some grammarians, however, say that the *wāw* is not interpolated because it indicates a meaning which is: 'the whole earth filled with gold would not be accepted from anyone at all, even if he were to try and ransom himself with it.'

According to al-Farrā', 'gold' is in the accusative for explanation. [EXPLANATION] Al-Kisā'ī said that it is in the accusative by an implied '*min*', i.e. *'min dhahab'*. We see this in 5:95.

We find in *Bukhārī* and *Muslim* that Anas ibn Mālik reported that the Prophet ﷺ said, 'An unbeliever will be brought on the Day of Rising and will be told, "Do you think that if you had the entire earth filled with gold, you could ransom yourself with it?" "Yes," he will reply. He will be told, "Less than that was asked of you."'

لَن تَنَالُوا۟ ٱلْبِرَّ حَتَّىٰ تُنفِقُوا۟ مِمَّا تُحِبُّونَ ۚ وَمَا تُنفِقُوا۟ مِن شَىْءٍ فَإِنَّ ٱللَّهَ
بِهِۦ عَلِيمٌ ﴿٩٢﴾

92 You will not attain true goodness until you give of what you love. Whatever you give away, Allah knows it.

You will not attain true goodness until you give of what you love.

The Imāms related that Anas said, 'When this *āyah* was revealed, Abū Ṭalḥah said, "Our Lord asks us for our property and I testify to you, Messenger of Allah, that I have made my land over to Allah!" The Messenger of Allah ﷺ said, "Give it to your relatives, Ḥassān ibn Thābit and Ubayy ibn Ka'b."' We find in *al-Muwaṭṭā'*, 'The property I love the best is Bayruḥā'.' It faced the mosque. The Messenger of Allah ﷺ used to enter it and drink from its good water.

This *āyah* is evidence for taking the literal and general meaning of words. The Companions did not understand any further meaning than that of the actual words (*faḥwā al-khiṭāb*) when the *āyah* was revealed. When Abū Ṭalḥah heard the words, 'You will not attain true goodness until you give,' he did not need to wait until it clarified how Allah wishes His slaves to spend by another *āyah* or *sunnah* which elucidated that. They loved many things. It is similar to what Zayd ibn Ḥārithah did. He used to love a horse of his called Sabal and said, 'O Allah! You know that I have no property which I love more than this horse of mine!' He took it to the Prophet ﷺ and said, 'Take it in the way of Allah.' He ﷺ said to Usāma ibn Zayd, 'Take it.' Zayd felt disturbed by that, so the Messenger of Allah ﷺ said, 'Allah has accepted it from you.' Asad ibn Mūsā mentioned it.

Ibn 'Umar freed Nāfi'. 'Abdullāh ibn Ja'far gave a thousand dinars. Ṣafiyyah bint Abī 'Ubaydah said, 'I think that was his interpretation of the words of Allah: *"You will not attain true goodness until you give of what you love."*'

Shibl related from Abū Najīḥ that Mujāhid said that 'Umar ibn al-Khaṭṭāb wrote to Abū Mūsā al-Ash'arī asking him to buy a slavegirl from the captives of Jalūlā' for him when Ctesiphon was conquered. Sa'd ibn Abī Waqqāṣ said, "Umar summoned her and liked her. He said, "Allah says: *'You will not attain true goodness until you give of what you love.'*" He freed her.'

Ath-Thawrī related that he heard that the *umm walad* of ar-Rabī' ibn Khaytham said, 'When a beggar came to him, he told me to give sugar to the asker. He loved sugar.' Sufyān said that he was interpreting the words of this *āyah*.

It is reported that 'Umar ibn 'Abd al-'Azīz bought some bags of sugar and gave them away as *ṣadaqah*. He was asked, 'Why didn't you give their value?' He replied, 'Because I love sugar and want to give of what I love.' Al-Ḥasan said, 'You will not obtain what you love except by abandoning what you desire and you will not get what you hope for except by steadfastness in enduring what you dislike.'

There is disagreement about the interpretation of the word *birr* (true goodness). It is said that it means the Garden, as is reported by Ibn Mas'ūd, Ibn 'Abbās, 'Aṭā', Mujāhid, 'Amr ibn Maymūn and as-Suddī. It implies: 'You will not obtain the reward of *birr* until you give of what you love.' *Nawāl* [which comes from the root, 'to obtain'] is giving. It means: 'You will not reach the Garden and be given it until you spend of what you love.'

It is also said that *birr* means righteous action, as we see in the sound hadith, 'You must give *ṣadaqah*. It leads to *birr* and *birr* leads to the Garden.' This was already mentioned in *al-Baqarah*. 'Aṭiyyah al-'Awfī said, 'It means obedience.' 'Aṭā' said, 'You will not obtain the honour of the *dīn* and *taqwā* until you give *ṣadaqah* while you are healthy and greedy, hoping for life and fearing poverty.'

Al-Ḥasan said that the word *'you give'* here indicates obligatory *zakāt*. Mujāhid and al-Kalbī said that it was abrogated by the *Āyah* of Zakāt. It is said that it means: 'until you give of what you love in the way of good in *ṣadaqah* and other acts of obedience.' This is a more general understanding.

An-Nasā'ī reported that Ṣa'ṣa'ah ibn Mu'āwiyah said, 'I met Abū Dharr and said, "Relate to me!" He said, "All right. The Messenger of Allah ﷺ said, 'There is no Muslim who spends two types of all his property in the Way of Allah without the chamberlains of the Garden greeting him, calling him to what he has.'" I asked, "How is that?" He said, "If it is a camel, then it is two camels, or if a cow, then two cows."'

Abū Bakr al-Warrāq said, 'This *āyah* is used as evidence for *futuwwah*, implying that Allah is saying that you will not obtain My goodness to you except by being good to your brothers and spending on them from your property and rank. When you do that, then you will obtain My goodness and kindness.' Mujāhid said, 'This is like His words: *"They give food, despite their love of it, to the poor."* (76:8)' and: *'Whatever you give away, Allah knows it'* and will repay you for it.

كُلُّ ٱلطَّعَامِ كَانَ حِلًّا لِّبَنِىٓ إِسْرَٰٓءِيلَ إِلَّا مَا حَرَّمَ إِسْرَٰٓءِيلُ عَلَىٰ نَفْسِهِۦ
مِن قَبْلِ أَن تُنَزَّلَ ٱلتَّوْرَىٰةُ ۗ قُلْ فَأْتُوا۟ بِٱلتَّوْرَىٰةِ فَٱتْلُوهَآ إِن كُنتُمْ صَٰدِقِينَ ﴿٩٣﴾
فَمَنِ ٱفْتَرَىٰ عَلَى ٱللَّهِ ٱلْكَذِبَ مِنۢ بَعْدِ ذَٰلِكَ فَأُو۟لَٰٓئِكَ هُمُ ٱلظَّٰلِمُونَ ﴿٩٤﴾

93 All food was lawful for the tribe of Israel except what Israel made unlawful for himself before the Torah was sent down. Say, 'Bring the Torah and read it out if you are telling the truth.' 94 So any who, after this, invent a lie against Allah are indeed wrongdoers.

Israel is Ya'qūb. In at-Tirmidhī, Ibn 'Abbās reported that the Jews said to the Prophet ﷺ, 'Tell us what Israel made unlawful for himself.' He said, 'He lived in the desert and suffered from sciatica and did not find anything which he liked to eat except camel flesh and milk. That is what he made unlawful.' They said, 'You spoke the truth.' It is said that he swore that if he were free of it he would leave the food and drink he loved most, and that was camel flesh and milk.

Ibn 'Abbās, Mujāhid, Qatādah and as-Suddī said, 'When he was fleeing from his brother Esau, Ya'qūb came from Harran making for Jerusalem. He was a strong and violent man. On the way he encountered an angel and thought he was a thief and he started to fight him. The angel touched Ya'qūb's thigh and climbed to heaven while Ya'qūb was looking at him and suddenly sciatica erupted [in his leg]. He had great suffering from it and could not sleep for the pain. He spent the night crying out and swore that if Allah healed him, he would not eat sinew or any food containing sinew, and so he forbade it to himself. After that his sons used to remove sinews from meat. The reason that the angel touched Ya'q'ub was that he had vowed that if Allah were to give him twelve sons and he were to reach Jerusalem sound, he would sacrifice the last of them. Aḍ-Ḍahhāk said that that was to bring him out of his vow.

They disagree about whether Ya'qūb's making things unlawful was by his own *ijtihād* or by permission from Allah. The first is the sound position because Allah ascribed that to him. When a Prophet uses his *ijtihād* in something, his followers are obliged to follow it because Allah has confirmed him in that, in the same way that they must follow him when he receives revelation. The same is true of what he gives permission for and uses his *ijtihād* to decide. He must use his *ijtihād* when he is able to do that. If he did not have permission to make a thing unlawful, he would not embark on making anything lawful or unlawful. In a sound transmission, our Prophet ﷺ made honey unlawful to himself and his slavegirl Māriah. Allah did not confirm the prohibition and revealed: *'Why do you make unlawful what Allah has made lawful for you?'* (66:1) This will be dealt with in *at-Taḥrīm*. Aṭ-Ṭabarī said, 'It is possible to say that the generality of His words in 66:1 indicate that it is not specific to Māriah. Ash-Shāfi'ī related that *kaffārah* is obliged for that without the meaning being understood. He made it specific to the text. Abū Ḥanīfah thought that was a principle for forbidding anything permissible and took it to be like an oath.'

Say, 'Bring the Torah and read it out if you are telling the truth.'

Ibn 'Abbās said, 'When Ya'qūb had sciatica, the doctors told him to avoid camel flesh and so he forbade it for himself. The Jews said, "We forbid camel meat for ourselves because Ya'qūb forbade it and Allah sent down its prohibition in the Torah." So Allah revealed this *āyah*.' Aḍ-Ḍaḥḥāk said, 'Allah called them liars and refuted them, saying, "Muḥammad, say: *'Bring the Torah and read it out if you are telling the truth.'* (3:93)" The Almighty said: *"So any who, after this, invent a lie against Allah are indeed wrongdoers."*'

Az-Zajjāj said, 'This *āyah* contains the greatest proof of the Prophethood of Muḥammad, our Prophet ﷺ. He reports that it is not in their Book and commands them to bring the Torah which they refused to do, showing by that that they knew that what he said was by revelation.'

'Aṭiyyah al-'Awfī said, 'That was forbidden them because Ya'qūb forbade it to them. That was when Ya'qūb suffered from sciatica and said, "By Allah, if Allah heals me of it, none of my children will ever eat it!"' [*'Irq an-nasā* is sciatica and *'irq* is sinew or sciatic vein.] Al-Kalbī said, 'Allah did not forbid it in the Torah. He forbade it after the Torah had been revealed because of their wrongdoing and disbelief. When the tribe of Israel committed a major wrong action, Allah forbade them good food or poured out punishment on them, which is death. That is referred to in the words of the Almighty: *"Because of wrongdoing on the part of the Jews, We made unlawful for them some good things which had previously been lawful for them"* (4:160) and: *"We made unlawful for the Jews every animal with an undivided hoof..."* (6:146)'

Ibn Mājah has a chapter in his *Sunan*: 'Treating Sciatica' in which Hishām ibn 'Ammār and Rāshid ibn Sa'īd ar-Ramlī related from al-Walīd ibn Muslim from Hishām ibn Hishām that Anas ibn Sīrīn heard Anas ibn Mālik say that he heard the Messenger of Allah ﷺ say, 'The cure for sciatica lies in melting the tail of a Bedouin's sheep which should then be divided into three parts. One part should be drunk each day on an empty stomach.' Ath-Tha'labī also transmitted in his *Tafsīr* from Anas ibn Mālik who said that the Messenger of Allah ﷺ said about sciatica: 'Take the tail of medium sized Bedouin ram, cut it into small pieces, remove its liquid, divide it into three parts and then ingest one part on an empty stomach for three days.' Anas said, 'I told this to more than a hundred people and they were healed by Allah's permission.' Shu'bah said that a Shaykh related to him in the time of al-Ḥajjāj ibn Yūsuf about sciatica, 'I swear to you by Allah Most High, if you do not stop, I will cauterise you with fire or shave you with a razor!' Shu'bah said, 'I tested it. You say it and wipe over the site.'

قُلْ صَدَقَ ٱللَّهُ فَٱتَّبِعُوا۟ مِلَّةَ إِبْرَٰهِيمَ حَنِيفًا وَمَا كَانَ مِنَ ٱلْمُشْرِكِينَ ﴿٩٥﴾

95 Say, 'Allah speaks the truth, so follow the religion of Ibrāhīm, a man of pure natural belief. He was not one of the idolaters.'

In other words, 'O Muḥammad, Allah speaks the truth: that is not forbidden in the Torah.' Then He commands him to follow his *dīn*. He refuted their false claim about him being an idolater.

TABLE OF CONTENTS FOR *ĀYATS*

Surat al-Baqarah

254 You who believe! give away some of what We have provided for you... 1
255 Allah, there is no god but Him, the Living, the Self-Sustaining... 2
256 There is no compulsion where the *dīn* is concerned... 12
257 Allah is the Protector of those who believe... 15
258 What about the one who argued with Ibrāhīm about his Lord... 16
259 Or the one who passed by a town which had fallen into ruin... 20
260 When Ibrāhīm said, 'My Lord, show me how ... 28
261 The metaphor of those who spend their wealth in the Way of Allah... 33
262 Those who spend their wealth in the Way of Allah... 39
264 You who believe! do not nullify your *ṣadaqah*... 41
265 The metaphor of those who spend their wealth... 44
266 Would any of you like to have a garden of dates and grapes... 47
267 You who believe! give away some of the good things you have earned...50
268 Shayṭān promises you poverty and commands you to avarice... 56
269 He gives wisdom to whomever He wills... 57
270 Whatever amount you spend or vow you make, Allah knows it... 59
271 If you make your *ṣadaqah* public, that is good. But if you conceal it... 60
272 You are not responsible for their guidance, but Allah guides... 64
273 It is for the poor who are held back in the Way of Allah... 67
274 Those who give away their wealth by night and day... 73
275-9 Those who practise usury will not rise from the grave except... 74
280 If someone is in difficult circumstances, there should be a deferral... 95
281 Be fearful of a Day when you will be returned to Allah... 98
282 You who believe! when you take on a debt for a specified period... 100
283 If you are on a journey and cannot find a writer... 127
284 Everything in the heavens and everything in the earth... 140
285-6 The Messenger believes in what has been sent down to him... 144

Sūrah Āli 'Imrān

1-3 Alif Lām Mīm. ... 154
3-4 He has sent down the Book to you with truth... 157
5 Allah – Him from Whom nothing is hidden, either on earth or... 158

6 It is He who forms you in the womb however He will... 159
7 It is He who sent down the Book to you from Him... 160
8 'Our Lord, do not make our hearts swerve aside after You have guided us...169
9 Our Lord, You are the Gatherer of mankind to a Day of which... 171
10 As for those who disbelieve, their wealth and children will not help... 171
11 as was the case with the people of Pharaoh and those before them... 172
12 Say to those who disbelieve: 'You will be overwhelmed... 173
13 There was a sign for you in the two parties which met face to face... 174
14 To mankind the love of worldly appetites is painted... 177
15 Say, 'Shall I tell you of something better than that?' ... 184
16-17 those who say, 'Our Lord, we believe, so forgive us... 185
18 Allah bears witness that there is no god but Him... 187
19 The *dīn* with Allah is Islam... 190
20 If they argue with you, say, 'I have submitted myself... 191
21-22 As for those who reject Allah's Signs... 193
23 Do you not see those who have been given a portion of the Book... 196
24 That is because they say, 'The Fire will only touch us for a number... 197
25 But how will it be when We gather them all together for a Day... 198
26 Say, 'O Allah! Master of the Kingdom! You give sovereignty... 198
27 You merge the night into the day. You merge the day into the night... 201
28 The believers should not take unbelievers as friends... 202
29 Say, 'Whether you conceal what is in your breasts or make it known... 204
30 On the Day that each self finds the good it did, and the evil it did... 204
31 Say, 'If you love Allah, then follow me and Allah will love you... 205
32 Say, 'Obey Allah and the Messenger.' Then if they turn away... 207
33 Allah chose Ādam and Nūḥ and the family of Ibrāhīm... 207
34 descendants one of the other. Allah is All-Hearing, All-Knowing. 209
35-36 Remember when the wife of 'Imrān said, 'My Lord... 210
37-38 Her Lord accepted her with approval... 213
39 The angels called out to him while he was standing in prayer... 217
40 He said, 'My Lord, how can I possibly have a son... 221
41 He said, 'My Lord, appoint a Sign for me.' He said, 'Your Sign is that you will not speak to people for three days, except by gesture. Remember your Lord much and glorify Him in the evening and after dawn.' 222
42 And when the angels said, 'Maryam, Allah has chosen you and purified you. He has chosen you over all other women.224
43 Maryam, obey your Lord and prostrate and bow with those who bow.' 226
44 This is news from the Unseen which We reveal to you... 226
45 When the angels said, 'Maryam, Allah gives you good news... 229

Glossary

Abū Ḥātim: Sahl ibn Muḥammad al-Jushanī as-Sijistānī, d. 255/869, a prominent Basran philologist.
Abū Isḥāq: Ibrāhīm ibn as-Sarī az-Zajjāj, author of *I'rab al-Qur'ān*.
Abū Ja'far: aṭ-Ṭabarī.
Abū 'Ubayd: al-Qāsim ibn Sallām al-Harawī or al-Baghdādī, d. 224/838.
Abū 'Ubaydah: Ma'mar ibn al-Muthanna at-Taymī, d. 209/824, author of *Majāz al-Qur'ān*, the first book on the linguistic analysis of the Qur'an.
Āmīn: *'Ameen'*, a compound of verb and noun meaning 'Answer our prayer' or 'So be it'.
Amīr al-Mu'minīn: 'the Commander of the Believers', the caliph.
'āmm: generally applicable, used in reference to a Qur'anic ruling.
Anṣār: the "Helpers", the people of Madīnah who welcomed and aided the Prophet ﷺ.
'aqīdah: creed, dogma or tent of faith firmly based on how things are.
'āqilah: the paternal kinsmen of an offender who are liable for the payment of blood money.
'arīyah: a kind of sale by which the owner of an *'arīyah* is allowed to sell fresh dates while they are still on the palms by means of estimation, in exchange for dried plucked dates.
'Aṣr: the mid-afternoon prayer.
athar: pl. *āthār*, lit. impact, trace, vestige; synonym of *khabar*, but usually reserved for deeds and precedents of the Companions.
awliyā': the plural of *walī*.
āyah: a verse of the Qur'an.
Āyat al-Kursī: the Throne Verse, 2:255.
'ayn: ready money, cash.
Banū: lit. sons, meaning a tribe or clan.
Baqī' al-Gharqad: the cemetery of Madīnah.
Bilqīs: the Queen of Saba' or Sheba.
Dajjāl: the false Messiah whose appearance marks the imminent end of the world. The root in Arabic means 'to deceive, cheat, take in'.

ḍammah: the Arabic vowel 'u'.
Dāwūd: the Prophet David.
dhimmah: obligation or contract, in particular a treaty of protection for non-Muslims living in Muslim territory.
dhimmī: a non-Muslim living under the protection of Muslim rule.
Dhu-l-Ḥijjah: the twelfth month of the Muslim calendar, the month of the hajj.
Dhu-l-Qa'dah: the eleventh month of the Muslim calendar.
dīn: the life-transaction, lit. the debt between two parties, in this usage between the Creator and created.
Fajr: the dawn prayer.
faqīh: pl. *fuqahā'*, a man learned in knowledge of fiqh who by virtue of his knowledge can give a legal judgment.
farḍ kifāyah: a collective obligation, something which is obligatory for the community as a whole and is satisfied if one adult performs it.
fat-ḥah: the Arabic vowel 'a'.
Fātiḥah: "the Opener," the first sūrah of the Qur'an.
fatwā: an authoritative statement on a point of law.
fiqh: the science of the application of the Sharī'ah. A practitioner or expert in fiqh is called a *faqīh*.
fisq: deviant behaviour, leaving the correct way or abandoning the truth, disobeying Allah, immoral behaviuor.
fuqahā': plural of *faqīh*.
Furqān: discrimination, that which separates truth from falsehood.
futuwwah: chivalry, placing others above one's self, as manifested in generosity, altruism, self-denial, and indulgence for people's shortcomings.
gharīb: a hadith which has a single reporter at some stage of the isnād.
ḥabal al-ḥabalah: a forbidden business transaction in which a man buys the unborn offspring of a female animal.
ḥadd: Allah's boundary limits for the lawful and unlawful. The ḥadd punishments are specific fixed penalties laid down by Allah for specified crimes.
hadith: reported speech of the Prophet ﷺ.
ḥāfiẓ: pl. *ḥuffāẓ*, someone who has memorised the Qur'an.
hajj: the annual pilgrimage to Makka which is one of the five pillars of Islam.
ḥāl: In Arabic grammar, a circumstantial adverb in the accusative case which describes something happening at the same time as the action or event mentioned in the main clause.

ḥalāl: lawful in the Sharī'ah.
hamzah: the character in Arabic which designates a glottal stop.
harām: unlawful in the Sharī'ah.
ḥaram: Sacred Precinct, a protected area in which certain behaviour is forbidden and other behaviour necessary. The area around the Ka'bah in Makkah is a *ḥaram*, and the area around the Prophet's Mosque in Madīnah is a *ḥaram*. They are referred to together as al-Ḥaramayn, 'the two Ḥarams'.
ḥarbī: a belligerent.
ḥarf: pl. *aḥruf*, one of the seven modes or manners of recitation in which the Qur'an was revealed.
Hārūn: the Prophet Aaron, the brother of Mūsā.
ḥasan: good, excellent, often used to describe a hadith which is reliable, but which is not as well authenticated as one which is ṣaḥīḥ.
Hijrah: emigration in the way of Allah. Islamic dating begins with the Hijrah of the Prophet Muḥammad ﷺ from Makkah to Madīnah in 622 AD.
ḥimā: a place of pasturage and water prohibited to the public. It was used for animals paid as zakat and mounts for jihad.
ḥubayq: a small, poor quality date.
Hūd: the Prophet sent to the people of 'Ād.
ḥudūd: plural of *ḥadd*.
Iblīs: the personal name of the Devil. He is also called Shayṭān or the 'enemy of Allah'.
Ibrāhīm: the Prophet Abraham.
'Īd: a festival, either the festival at the end of Ramadan or at the time of the Hajj.
iḍāfah: a possessive construction in Arabic in which the first noun is indefinite and the second usually definite. It is used to indicate possession. The first word is termed '*muḍāf*' and the second is '*muḍāf ilayhi*'.
ijtihād: to exercise personal judgment in legal matters.
īlā': a vow by a husband to abstain from sexual relations with his wife. If four months pass, it is considered to be a divorce.
imālah: a vowel shift in Arabic where an open vowel rises, ā towards ī, and short a towards i.
imām: Muslim religious or political leader; leader of Muslim congregational worship.
īmān: belief, faith.
'īnah: a transaction in which the price in paid in advance based on the description of the goods purchased.

'Īsā: the Prophet Jesus.
'Ishā': the obligatory evening prayer.
Is-ḥāq: the Prophet Isaac.
Ismā'īl: the Prophet Ishmael.
isnād: a hadith's chain of transmission from individual to individual.
Jāhiliyyah: the Time of Ignorance before the coming of Islam.
Jalūlā': a major battle between the Sassanids and the Muslims soon after the conquest of Ctesiphon which was an overwhelming victory for the Muslim forces.
Jibrīl: the angel Gabriel.
jihad: struggle, particularly fighting in the way of Allah to establish Islam.
jinn: inhabitants of the heavens and the earth made of smokeless fire who are usually invisible.
jizyah: a protection tax payable by non-Muslims living under Muslim rule as a tribute to the Muslim ruler.
Jumāda-l-Ākhir: the sixth month of the Muslim calendar.
Jumāda-l-Ulā: the fifth month of the Muslim calendar.
Jumu'ah: the day of gathering, Friday, and particularly the Jumu'ah prayer which is performed instead of Ẓuhr by those who attend it.
ju'rūr: a bad kind of date, also called 'rat's dung', very small and with a bad smell.
Ka'bah: the cube-shaped building at the centre of the Ḥaram in Makkah, originally built by the Prophet Ibrāhīm ﷺ. Also known as the House of Allah.
kaffārah: atonement, prescribed way of making amends for wrong actions, especially intentionally missed obligatory actions.
kalām: 'theology' and dogmatics. *Kalām* starts with the revealed tradition and employs rationalistic methods in order to understand it and resolve contradictions.
Kalb: an Arab Bedouin tribe in northwestern Arabia, Syria and Mesopotamia.
kasrah: the Arabic vowel i.
Khalīl: "Friend", a title of the Prophet Ibrāhīm ﷺ.
Khārijites: the earliest sect, who separated themselves from the body of the Muslims and declared war on all those who disagreed with them, stating that a wrong action turns a Muslim into an unbeliever.
Khaybar: Jewish colony to the north of Madinah which was laid siege to and captured by the Muslims in the seventh year after the Hijrah because of the Jews' continual treachery.

al-Khiḍr: or al-Khāḍir, "the green one." whose journey with Mūsā is mentioned in the Qur'an 18:65. He may or may not be a Prophet, and often appears to people.
Khorasan: Persian province southeast of the Caspian Sea; a centre of many dissident movements in early Islamic history.
kufr: disbelief, to cover up the truth, to reject Allah and refuse to believe that Muhammad ﷺ is His Messenger.
kunyah: a respectful but intimate way of addressing people as "the father of so-and-so" or "the mother of so-and-so."
Lā ilāha illā-llāh: 'There is no god but Allah.'
li'ān: mutual cursing, a form of divorce in which the husband and wife take oaths when he accuses her of adultery and she denies it.
Lūṭ: the Prophet Lot.
maddah: prolongation. There are three letters which are subject to prolongation in recitation of the Qur'an: alif, wāw and yā'.
Maghrib: the sunset prayer; also the western part of Muslim lands. Today it means Morocco.
maḥram: a male relative with whom marriage is forbidden.
marfū': 'elevated' , a narration from the Prophet ﷺ mentioned by a Companion, e.g. "The Messenger of Allah ﷺ said..."
Maryam: Mary, the mother of 'Īsā.
Masjid al-Ḥarām: the great mosque in Makkah where the Ka'bah is situated.
mawqūf: 'stopped', a narration from a Companion without mentioning the Prophet ﷺ.
Mi'rāj: the ascension of the Prophet Muḥammad ﷺ from Jerusalem through the seven heavens.
mithqāl: pl. *mathāqīl*, 'miskal', the weight of one dinar, the equivalent of 72 grains of barley (equals 4.4 grams).
mu'ḍal: 'perplexing', in hadith, one missing one or two links in the **isnād**.
mudd: a measure of volume. approximately a double-handed scoop.
muftī: someone qualified to give a legal opinion or *fatwā*.
Muhājirūn: Companions of the Messenger of Allah ﷺ who accepted Islam in Makkah and made hijrah to Madīnah.
muḥāqalah: a forbidden sale in which, for instance, unharvested wheat is bartered for harvested wheat, or land is rented for wheat, or wheat for seeds.
Muḥarram: the first month of the Muslim lunar year.
muḥkam: perspicuous, a word or text conveying a firm and unequivocal meaning.

mujmal: ambivalent, requires details and explanation, ambiguous, referring to a category of unclear words.
mukhābarah: see *muzāra'ah.*
mursal: a hadith where a man in the generation after the Companions quotes directly from the Prophet ﷺ without mentioning the Companion from whom he got it.
Mūsā: the Prophet Moses.
mutakallimūn: those who study the science of *kalām*, the science of investigating theological doctrine.
mutashābih: intricate, unintelligible, referring to a word or text whose meaning is not totally clear.
Mu'tazilite: someone who adheres to the school of the Mu'tazilah which is rationalist in its approach to existence. Originally they held that anyone who commits a sin is neither a believer nor an unbeliever. They also held the Qur'an to be created.
muzābanah: a forbidden sale in which something whose number, weight, or measure is known is sold for something whose number, weight or measure is not known.
muzāra'ah: farming partnership, in which someone allows his land to be cultivated in exchange for a portion of the produce.
An-Naḍīr: a Jewish tribe in Madīnah.
nāfilah: (plural nawāfil): supererogatory act of worship.
Najd: the region around Riyadh in Saudi Arabia.
Najrān: a region in the southern Arabian peninsula which borders Yemen.
Nūḥ: the Prophet Noah.
People of the Book: principally the Jews and Christians whose religions are based on the Divine Books revealed to Mūsā and 'Īsā; a term also used to refer to any other group who claim to be following a Book revealed prior to the Qur'an.
People of Hadith: 'the adherents of Hadith', the movement who considered only the Qur'an and hadith to be valid sources of fiqh.
People of Opinion (ra'y): a term used to describe those who use personal opinion to deduce judgement. It was a term used particularly to describe the early Ḥanafīs.
qāḍī: a judge, qualified to judge all matters in accordance with the Sharī'ah and to dispense and enforce legal punishments.
Qaynuqā': one of the Jewish tribes of Madīnah.
qiblah: the direction faced in the prayer which is towards the Ka'bah in Makkah.

qinṭār: pl. *qanāṭīr*, a relatively large measure for food grains, approx., 45 kgs.
qīrāṭ: pl. *qarārīṭ*, a measure of weight with various meanings, either a twelfth of a dirham or a huge weight like that of Mount Uḥud.
Quraysh: one of the great tribes of Arabia. The Prophet Muḥammad ﷺ belonged to this tribe, which had great powers spiritually and financially both before and after Islam came. Someone from this tribe is called Qurashī.
Qurayẓah: one of the Jewish tribes of Madīnah.
Rabīʿ al-Awwal: the third month of the Muslim calendar.
Rabīʿ al-Ākhir: the fourth month of the Muslim calendar.
Rajab: the seventh month of the Muslim calendar.
Rafidites: the *Rawāfiḍ*, a group of the Shiʿah known for rejecting Abū Bakr and ʿUmar as well as ʿUthmān. It is a nickname, meaning "deserters".
rakʿah: a unit of the prayer consisting of a series of standings, bowing, prostrations and sittings.
Ramadan: the month of fasting, the ninth month in the Muslim lunar calendar.
ar-Rawḥā': a place 14 km from Madīnah.
ribā: usury.
Riddah: the defection of various Arab tribes after the death of the Prophet ﷺ which brought about the Riddah War.
rukūʿ: the bowing position in the prayer.
ṣāʿ: a measure of volume equal to four *mudd*s.
Sacred Months: the months of Rajab, Dhu-l-Qaʿdah, Dhu-l-Ḥijjah and Muḥarram in which fighting was forbidden.
ṣadaqah: charitable giving in the Cause of Allah.
sadd adh-dharā'iʿ: the blocking of a means which might lead to undesired consequences.
Ṣafā and Marwah: two hills close to the Kaʿbah.
Ṣafar: the second month of the Muslim lunar calendar.
ṣaḥīḥ: healthy and sound with no defects, used to describe an authentic hadith.
Ṣaḥīḥ: "the Sound", the title of the hadith collections of al-Bukhārī and Muslim.
Salaf: the early generations of the Muslims.
salaf: loan, advance payment.
salām: the expression, *'as-salāmu ʿalaykum,'* or 'Peace be upon you,' used as a greeting and to end the prayer.
salam: a sale in which the price is paid at once for goods to be delivered

later; ownership in the goods passes at the time the contract is made.
Sha'bān: the eighth month in the Muslim calendar
shahādah: bearing witness, particularly bearing witness that there is no god but Allah and that Muhammad is the Messenger of Allah. It is one of the pillars of Islam. It is also used to describe legal testimony in a court of law.
Sharī'ah: The legal modality of a people based on the revelation of their Prophet. The final Sharī'ah is that of Islam.
Shawwāl: the tenth month of the Muslim calendar.
Shayṭān: devil, particularly Iblīs, one of the jinn.
shirk: the unforgivable wrong action of worshipping something or someone other than Allah or associating something or someone as a partner with Him.
Sīrah: biography, particularly biography of the Prophet ﷺ.
Ṣubḥ: dawn prayer
Ṣuffah: a verandah attached to the Prophet's Mosque where the poor Muslims used to sleep.
Sulaymān: the Prophet Solomon.
sunan: plural of sunnah.
Sunnah: the customary practice of a person or group of people. It has come to refer almost exclusively to the practice of the Messenger of Allah ﷺ.
sūrah: a chapter of the Qur'an.
Tābi'ūn: the second generation of the early Muslims who did not meet the Prophet Muhammad ﷺ but learned the dīn of Islam from his Companions.
Tabūk: a town in northern Arabia close to Jordan.
tafsīr: commentary or explanation of the meanings of the Qur'an.
tahajjud: voluntary prayers performed at night after 'Ishā'.
Ṭā'if: a walled town south of Makkah known for its fertility. It was the home of the tribe of Thaqīf.
talbiyah: saying '*Labbayk*' ('At Your service') during the hajj.
Tamīm: one of the largest of the Arab tribes, located in Najd.
tanwīn: nunation.
taqiyyah: concealment of one's views to escape persecution.
taqwā: awe or fear of Allah, which inspires a person to be on guard against wrong action and eager for actions which please Him.
taṣawwuf: Sufism.
tashbīh: comparing or connecting Allah to created things, or making Allah resemble created things.

tawḥīd: the doctrine of Divine Unity.
ta'wīl: allegorical interpretation.
Thaqīf: a tribe based in the town of Ta'if, a branch of the tribe of Hawāzin.
Tihāmah: the Red Sea coastal plain of Arabia.
Uḥud: a mountain just outside of Madīnah where five years after the Hijrah, the Muslims lost a battle against the Makkan idolaters. Many great Companions, and in particular Ḥamzah, the uncle of the Prophet, were killed in this battle.
Umm al-Mu'minīn: literally 'Mother of the Believers', an honorary title given to the wives of the Prophet.
Umm al-Qur'ān: literally 'the Mother of the Qur'an', the opening sūrah of the Qur'an, al-Fātiḥah.
umm walad: a slavegirl who has had a child by her master.
Ummah: the body of Muslims as one distinct Community.
'umrah: the lesser pilgrimage to the Ka'bah in Makkah performed at any time of the year.
ūqiyyah: unit of measurement equal to 40 dirhams in weight or 118.80 gs.
Verandah: *as-Saqīfah*, a roofed porch where the Muslims in Madīnah met after the death of the Prophet ﷺ to choose the first caliph.
walī: pl. *awliyā'*, someone who is a 'friend' of Allah, thus possessing the quality of *wilāyah*. Also a relative who acts as a guardian.
wasq: a measure of volume equal to sixty *ṣā'*s.
Yaḥyā: the Prophet John the Baptist, the son of Zakariyyā.
Ya'jūj and Ma'jūj: the people of Gog and Magog who are to burst forth at the end of time.
Ya'qūb: the Prophet Jacob, also called Isrā'īl (Israel).
Yūnus: the Prophet Jonah.
Yūsuf: the Prophet Joseph.
Zakariyyā: the Prophet Zachariah, the father of Yaḥyā, John the Baptist, and guardian of Maryam.
zakat: a wealth tax, one of the five pillars of Islam.
zakat al-fiṭr: a small obligatory head-tax imposed on every Muslim who has the means for himself and his dependants. It is paid at the end of Ramadan.
zindīq: a term used to describe a heretic whose teaching is a danger to the community or state.
Ẓuhr: the midday prayer.